Transforming E-Collaboration With AI and Emerging Digital Technologies

Jingyuan Zhao
https://orcid.org/0000-0003-3289-4048
University of Toronto, Canada

IGI Global
Scientific Publishing
Publishing Tomorrow's Research Today

Vice President of Editorial	Melissa Wagner
Director of Acquisitions	Mikaela Felty
Director of Book Development	Jocelynn Hessler
Production Manager	Mike Brehm
Cover Design	Jose Rosado

Published in the United States of America by
IGI Global Scientific Publishing
701 East Chocolate Avenue
Hershey, PA, 17033, USA
Tel: 717-533-8845 | Fax: 717-533-7115
Website: https://www.igi-global.com E-mail: cust@igi-global.com

Library of Congress Cataloging-in-Publication Data

Names: Zhao, Jingyuan, 1968- editor
Title: Transforming e-collaboration with AI and emerging digital technologies / edited by: Jingyuan Zhao.
Description: Hershey, PA : IGI Global Scientific Publishing, [2026] | Includes bibliographical references. | Summary: "This book aims to discuss the advancements in AI and emerging digital technologies, uncovering the potential AI and emerging digital technologies hold for organizations and the future of work itself, with a focus on state-of-the-art approaches, methodologies, and systems for the design, development, deployment, and innovative use of those technologies and applications to advance organizations"-- Provided by publisher.
Identifiers: LCCN 2025031524 (print) | LCCN 2025031525 (ebook) | ISBN 9798337357478 hardcover | ISBN 9798337357485 ebook
Subjects: LCSH: Groupware (Computer software) | Teams in the workplace--Data processing | Artificial intelligence--Business applications
Classification: LCC HD66.2 .T73 2026 (print) | LCC HD66.2 (ebook)
LC record available at https://lccn.loc.gov/2025031524
LC ebook record available at https://lccn.loc.gov/2025031525

British Cataloguing in Publication Data
A Cataloguing in Publication record for this book is available from the British Library.

Table of Contents

Detailed Table of Contents

In today's digital era, collaboration is evolving beyond traditional tools, driven by the integration of Artificial Intelligence (AI) and emerging technologies such as IoT, Blockchain, 5G, AR/VR, and Quantum Computing. This chapter explores the concept of collaborative intelligence, where human ingenuity merges with machine intelligence to enhance teamwork, communication, and innovation. It highlights how AI-powered systems are transforming real-time collaboration, decision-making, and organizational productivity across sectors like healthcare, education, and enterprise operations. The chapter also addresses key challenges privacy, trust, ethics, and system design providing strategies for responsible AI adoption. Through real-world use cases and future insights, it emphasizes the importance of human-AI synergy in building intelligent, adaptive, and ethical collaborative ecosystems that redefine how we work and connect in the digital age.

The Unified Payment Interface (UPI) has a revolutionized the landscape of digital payment in India by facility seamless real time transaction across multiple bank and Financial Institutions. This study investigates the impact of customer-initiated transactions and total transactions value in India's UPI ecosystem using machine learning regression model. The study utilizers data set of 1811 (n) obtained from the NPCI website. For the analysis of the data received researcher adopted comparison of Linear Regression, Random Forest (RF), XGBoost algorithm to predict total transaction value-based customer-initiated transactions. The finding reveals that RF model achieves the significant as compare to the other models in terms of R2,

This chapter discusses the rise of co-intelligence as a revolutionary new way of digital collaboration in the age of AI. Conventional e-collaboration tools frequently lack flexibility, context awareness, and the capacity to integrate multifaceted real-time information across domains. By incorporating AI, particularly large language models, digital twins, and IoT dashboards, collaboration is moving toward dynamic co-creative spaces in which human and machine intelligence collaborate synergistically. This chapter spans the theoretical underpinnings of human–AI collaboration, implementation strategies, and practical case studies in healthcare, academia, and urban planning. It also critically examines ethical issues, such as trust, bias, and privacy, in cross-border collaboration while offering strategic recommendations on skill development, hybrid workspace design, ROI analysis, and policy frameworks. Finally, it envisages the future of intelligent organizations, where AGI-enabled agents have a say in decision-making, ideation, and innovation.

This book explores the transformative impact of Artificial Intelligence (AI) and emerging digital technologies on e-collaboration across various sectors. It presents a comprehensive analysis of how AI, IoT, blockchain, quantum computing, 5G, and Extended Reality (XR) are reshaping collaborative ecosystems, enabling intelligent decision-making, personalized workflows, and immersive interactions. The chapters discuss the evolution of e-collaboration from tool-based systems to human-AI partnerships, showcasing sectoral applications in healthcare, education, e-commerce, and manufacturing. Key ethical concerns such as privacy, algorithmic bias, and legal frameworks are also addressed, along with future challenges like AGI and sustainable collaboration. Through interdisciplinary insights and real-world examples, the book offers a forward-looking guide for designing inclusive, secure, and intelligent collaborative systems.

This article reviews the concept of a virtual state and the digital state popularized by developed countries for improved public services and communication. The study uses meta-analysis and VOSviewer to analyze data from the Scopus database. This review used the Preferred Reporting Items for Systematic Reviews and Meta-Analyses (PRISMA)—through PRISMA, this research attempts to conduct a systematic review of the concept of virtual state and digital state. The finding shows that the idea of a virtual state and a digital state, pushed by countries with advanced technology, changes how countries interact with each other, affecting cooperation, human rights, trade, and conflict, while the digital state focuses on how governments connect with society through services, the internet, and advancements in information technology. The investigation emphasizes the value of technology in improving public services and communication.

This chapter theorizes and operationalizes augmented collegiality as a deliberate reconstitution of pedagogy in which teachers, students, and artificial agents coordinate accountable knowledge work. It synthesizes CSCL, activity systems, communities of inquiry, knowledge building, distributed cognition, and human-AI teaming to specify a layered architecture spanning experience, collaboration services, intelligence, orchestration, data, integration, infrastructure, and governance. The program details generative feedback, XR, IoT, and privacy preserving analytics while enforcing provenance, accessibility, and calibrated trust. Design patterns translate theory into auditable practice, and implementation blueprints align staffing, procurement, and sustainability with cognitive equity across bandwidths, languages, and abilities. Measurement links inputs to impact through interpretable indicators and mixed methods, and legal regimes inform bias audits, consent, and disclosure-

Preface

INTRODUCTION

We today have a rich portfolio of e-collaboration tools, starting with email and encompassing texting, file sharing, online chat and message boards, social media and video conferencing. Collaboration tools reshape organizational operations and fundamentally alter how we connect, learn, and innovate at work. Yet collaboration across these tools can be a frustrating experience, due to the complexity of the technology and lack of integration. There is growing importance being placed on collaboration workflows, information flows, and better user experiences to improve collaborative experiences. AI (Artificial Intelligence) and emerging digital technologies (e.g., Robotics, IoT, Machine Learning, Blockchain, 5G, Quantum Computing, AR/VR) are transforming various aspects of business and society and impacting industries from healthcare to transportation. However, the development and deployment of AI and emerging digital technologies also raise questions such as, "Can we combine the respective strengths of humans and AI, as well as emerging digital technologies to boost efficiency and creativity?" and "Can humans work smarter together with AI and emerging digital technologies for collaborative intelligence?"

The term of collaborative intelligence refers to collaborative human-AI systems that leverage the different attributes and strengths of each agent to achieve further improvements in work outcomes (Billman et al., 2006; Daugherty & Wilson, 2018; Jarrahi, 2018; Seeber et al., 2020; Schleiger et al., 2024). This complementarity creates the potential to achieve a step-change in performance by combining inputs from humans and AI on a common task (Schleiger et al., 2024). Currently, as the rise of AI and emerging digital technologies, the technological synergy is fuelling a new wave of transformation in many industries across the planet. Organizations that are becoming increasingly digital and interconnected are now relying more and more on the quality of their information and the level of their collaboration in order to fully leverage these new technologies. Furthermore, with increased reliance on data, technology, and collaborative intelligence, organizations face issues of data privacy, security, and ethical use of AI and emerging digital technologies. It's critical to ensure robust safeguards and ethical guidelines are in place, as organizations navigate through this complex landscape.

This book is a collection of recent advancements in AI and emerging digital technologies, uncovering the potential AI and emerging digital technologies hold for organizations and the future of work itself, with a focus on state-of-the-art approaches, methodologies, and systems for the design, development, deployment, and innovative use of those technologies and applications to advance organizations. This book will comprehensively explore e-collaboration through AI and emerging digital technologies, not only studying applications, types, benefits, functions, concerns and trends of e-collaboration, but also bringing together AI, emerging digital technologies and e-collaboration to drive powerful tech tools that achieve collaborative intelligence.

It gives an excellent opportunity for discussing some of the cutting-edge topics in collaboration technologies and tools through AI and emerging technologies and providing fresh ideas on how real world challenges set new frontiers for the design, development, deployment, and innovative use of those technologies and applications. The book is organized into 14 chapters which provide insight on transforming e-Collaboration with AI and emerging digital technologies as a whole.

CHAPTER OVERIVIEWS

Chapter 1 (*Towards Collaborative Intelligence - Merging Human Ingenuity with AI and Digital Innovation*) addresses key challenges privacy, trust, ethics, and system design providing strategies for responsible AI adoption. Through real-world use cases and future insights, it emphasizes the importance of human-AI synergy in building intelligent, adaptive, and ethical collaborative ecosystems that redefine how we work and connect in the digital age.

Chapter 2 (*Forecasting UPI Transaction Value in India - A Machine Learning Regression Approach to Customer-Initiated Payments*) proposes that RF model achieves the significant as compare to the other models in terms of R2, RMSE, and MAE. The study contributes to the understanding of digital payment ecosystem that provide empirical evidence for the effective UPI retail sales growth of ensemble learning models in financial transaction predictions.

Chapter 3 (*Smart Workflows Designing Next-Generation E-Collaboration with Artificial Intelligence*) explores the integration of AI into smart workflows to transform e-collaboration within modern organizations. It examines AI methodologies like machine learning, natural language processing, and intelligent agents to enhance efficiency, adaptability, and creativity in distributed work settings.

Chapter 4 (*Bridging the Gap in Evolving Human Interactions with Machines (HIM) in the Age of Intelligent Systems*) discusses the evolving dynamics of human interactions with machine (HIM) in the context of emerging intelligent systems. With the proliferation of AI and adaptive interfaces, traditional boundaries between humans and machines are blurring. This work highlights existing gaps in communication, trust, and interpretability between users and autonomous systems.

Chapter 5 (*Collaborative Intelligence in Action- Designing Human–AI Co-Workflows for Next-Generation E-Collaboration*) spans the theoretical underpinnings of human–AI collaboration, implementation strategies, and practical case studies in healthcare, academia, and urban planning. It also critically examines ethical issues, such as trust, bias, and privacy, in cross-border collaboration while offering strategic recommendations on skill development, hybrid workspace design, ROI analysis, and policy frameworks.

Chapter 6 (*Mind Meets Machine - E-Collaboration in the Era of Artificial Intelligence)* discusses the evolution of e-collaboration from tool-based systems to human-AI partnerships, showcasing sectoral applications in healthcare, education, e-commerce, and manufacturing. Key ethical concerns such as privacy, algorithmic bias, and legal frameworks are also addressed, along with future challenges like AGI and sustainable collaboration.

Chapter 7 (*Reviewing the Concept of Virtual State and Digital State, Mapping Concept and Trend using Meta-analysis*) reviews the concept of a virtual state and the digital state popularized by developed countries for improved public services and communication. The study uses meta-analysis and VOSviewer to analyze data from the Scopus database. This research attempts to conduct a systematic review of the concept of virtual state and digital state.

Chapter 8 (*Ontologies of Augmented Collegiality in Education and Epistemic Architectures of Human–AI Synergy: Multi-Agent Orchestration and Cognitive Equity*) theorizes and operationalizes augmented collegiality as a deliberate reconstitution of pedagogy in which teachers, students, and artificial agents coordinate accountable knowledge work. It synthesizes CSCL, activity systems, communities of inquiry, knowledge building, distributed cognition, and human-AI teaming to specify a layered architecture spanning experience, collaboration services, intelligence, orchestration, data, integration, infrastructure, and governance.

Chapter 9 (*Automation and Robotics. Enhancing Implementation Readiness*) emphasizes that, amidst the excitement about automation and robotics, it is crucial for organizations to proactively prepare for the implementation of such technologies. To enhance successful adoption, prioritizing implementation readiness and garnering employee buy-in is vital.

Jingyuan Zhao
University of Toronto, Canada
2025 December

REFERENCES

Billman, D., Convertino, G., Shrager, J., Pirolli, P., & Massar, J. (2006). Collaborative intelligence analysis with CACHE and its effects on information gathering and cognitive bias. Paper presented at the Human Computer Interaction Consortium Workshop: Fraser, Colorado, USA.

Daugherty, P. R., & Wilson, H. J. (2018). *Human + Machine: Reimagining Work in the Age of AI*. Harvard Business Review Press.

Jarrahi, M. H. (2018). Artificial intelligence and the future of work: Human-AI symbiosis in organizational decision making. *Business Horizons*, *61*(4), 577–586. DOI: 10.1016/j.bushor.2018.03.007

Schleiger, E., Mason, C., Naughtin, C., Reeson, A., & Paris, C. (2024). Collaborative Intelligence: A Scoping Review of Current Applications. *Applied Artificial Intelligence*, *38*(1), 2327890. Advance online publication. DOI: 10.1080/08839514.2024.2327890

Seeber, I., Bittner, E., Briggs, R. O., de Vreede, T., de Vreede, G.-J., Elkins, A., Söllner, M., Merz, A. B., Oeste-Reiß, S., Randrup, N., & Schwabe, G. (2020). Machines as teammates: A research agenda on AI in team collaboration. *Information & Management*, *57*(2), 103174. DOI: 10.1016/j.im.2019.103174

Chapter 1
Towards Collaborative Intelligence:
Merging Human Ingenuity With AI and Digital Innovation

R. N. Ravikumar
https://orcid.org/0009-0009-3705-1681
Marwadi University, Rajkot, India

S. Aarthi
https://orcid.org/0009-0006-9064-2091
Marwadi University, Rajkot, India

ABSTRACT

In today's digital era, collaboration is evolving beyond traditional tools, driven by the integration of Artificial Intelligence (AI) and emerging technologies such as IoT, Blockchain, 5G, AR/VR, and Quantum Computing. This chapter explores the concept of collaborative intelligence, where human ingenuity merges with machine intelligence to enhance teamwork, communication, and innovation. It highlights how AI-powered systems are transforming real-time collaboration, decision-making, and organizational productivity across sectors like healthcare, education, and enterprise operations. The chapter also addresses key challenges privacy, trust, ethics, and system design providing strategies for responsible AI adoption. Through real-world use cases and future insights, it emphasizes the importance of human-AI synergy in building intelligent, adaptive, and ethical collaborative ecosystems that redefine how we work and connect in the digital age.

DOI: 10.4018/979-8-3373-5747-8.ch001

1. INTRODUCTION

The digital age has radically transformed the communication between the individuals as well as between the organizations. E-collaboration tools have been found to be invaluable in situations where a person is sharing an email, a file or even when one is utilizing the real time video conferencing and messaging solutions. However, to be safe in stating that these tools do not necessarily impede the smooth communication and innovations, their increasing complexity and silo effects are a widespread issue (Arinze, 2012). In order to gain agility, productivity and smart workflows in organizations, Artificial Intelligence (AI) and new digital technologies are emerging as a new trend, which is collaborative intelligence. Collaborative intelligence The entire symbiotic interaction among people and intelligent systems is the outcome of active interaction among people and machine ability of efficiency and logical analysis and creativity and critical thinking.

This is supported by new technologies in the shape of the Internet of Things (IoT), Blockchain, 5G, Quantum Computing and Augmented/Virtual Reality, which are initiating smarter, quicker, and more safe collaborative worlds. These advancements are reshaping the work interactions, decision making and the future of work. In this chapter, the author talks about how the digital technologies and AI can be used in organizations to build smart collaborative ecosystems (Bidgoli, 2012). It cogitates about the history of collaboration tools, connotation of the use of AI-based systems, and implications of their use. In this case when human genius is welcomed by computer inventions, we are entering a new age in which we can cooperate not only in digital but intelligent, adaptive and yet very human.

1.1 Evolution of E-Collaboration Tools

E-collaboration has been greatly transformed in the last decades. During the initial stages of the collaboration, email and basic file sharing were also the only means of collaboration. These were very radical tools, and were predominantly asynchronous, and lacked interactivity in real time. The development of enterprise messaging platforms and cloud document collaboration (e.g. Google Workspace, Microsoft 365) and video conferencing (e.g. Zoom, Microsoft Teams) also became a considerable milestone towards real-time, synchronous collaboration. Communities of practice and knowledge sharing were also facilitated by the use of social media and enterprise forums (Esichaikul et al., 2013). With the delivery of mobile apps and cloud infrastructure, cooperation was no longer limited by the office setting, so it became possible to perform remote and mixed work environments.

There were also enhancements when it came to integration between different platforms with more integrated workflows being available. Over the past few years, such tools have started getting smarter and more topical with the help of AI-powered characteristics, e.g., smart scheduling, real-time transcription, sentiment analysis, and predictive task assignment. Although these advances have mostly enabled an increase in the number of tools, most of the tools serve as closed ecosystems with minimal interoperability (Ganan et al., 2013). The change wave that is in our future is AI and other new technologies integration, which would allow the systems to not only facilitate communication but also learn, adapt and co-create with users. This predetermines the emergence of collaborative intelligence formation, that is, the shift of the interaction to tools to intelligent cooperation. The Figure 1 indicates the evolutionary stages of using electronic collaboration tools beginning with email and advancing to texting, file sharing, on-line chatting, and current video conferencing. It highlights how digital communication methods have advanced to support real-time, interactive, and remote teamwork.

Figure 1. Evolution of E-Collaboration Tools

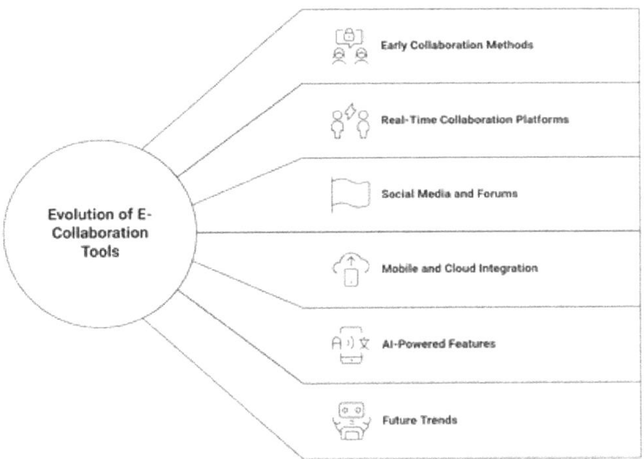

1.2 Challenges in Current Digital Collaboration

Although the digital collaboration software enhanced connectivity and remote collaboration, there are several problems that surrounded the tool and acted as a limitation on its usage. One of the general issues is fragmentation, users explain that they work with more than one separate application to message, share files, arrange meetings, and monitor the projects status, complaining about such overloads and outright inefficiency in their work. Inability to work effectively on different platforms is a cause of disturbance of the smooth working process and efficiency (Grant, 2024). The other major issues are information saturation. With a development of online communications, users also now obtain tons of messages, emails and updates and cannot filter out something which is important and focus on the most pressing activity. This has a bearing on decision-making and could be in jeopardy of incorrect communication or omission.

Privacy and security of data is also an acute issue. The larger the attack surface- the more the digital tools that an organization embraces. Unprotected P2P access to data, data breach, and compliance with global laws (e.g., GDPR, HIPAA) are serious dangers to functions and ethics. Moreover, the available tool is context-shallow and unintelligent. They require man work, are not customized, and cannot accommodate super swift needs of users (Hoic-Bozic et al., 2016). With the inattention to the humanistic designs and inclusive interfaces, barriers will be raised to the people with other needs and abilities, as well. The one way to curb these challenges is by the skyrocketing demand in intelligent, integrated, and adaptive systems, which are capable of supporting human cooperation with the auto, context awareness and ethically sound systems.

1.3 Rise of Collaborative Intelligence

The people in the future of work will co-create, co-learn and co-decide is an idea known as collaborative intelligence. In contrast to classical systems of e-collaboration which serve only as communication support systems collaborative intelligence embraces the benefits of AI, machine learning and other emerging technologies and serves as an active participant in the collaboration process (Kristensen & Kijl, 2010). The thesis of collaboration in all its forms of intelligence is that computer speed, scale, and senses are not alternatives to human creative, empathetic, and overall thinking but a complement. The collaboration leads to smarter decisions, more innovations, and better adaptability to complicated surroundings. The tedious or data-burdened processes may be automated through AI, and the release of human beings to more significant and creative, and decisive tasks may be achieved.

The further technologies of IoT, 5G, and AR/VR evolve this paradigm and enable the context-aware collaboration in real time and in an immersive way. In other words, one can observe the demonstrations of the AI-based assistants suggesting the relevant documents, identifying the emotional coloring of the meetings, and automating the processes within the teams (König et al., 2024). With a fast market with global concerns, the intelligence of the collective is demanding and requires that the organizations are efficient in their operations so that they can survive, but also achieve long-term growth. It involves reengineering more ethical, inclusive and human-centered collaboration systems and leads to a more intelligent digital future that is more synergistic.

2. AI AND EMERGING TECHNOLOGIES IN COLLABORATION

The addition of new emerging technologies and the application of Artificial Intelligence (AI) is altering the processes of interactivity inside and between organizations. It is possible to acquire interpretable natural language now, detect more data now, give recommendations in real-time now, adapt to customer behavior now, and this is all enabled by the use of AI-based software that will only make digitized communication further useful and intelligent. Those functions are no longer restricted to specific capabilities: they are being integrated into platforms aiming at facilitating end-to-end collaborative processes. The data can be shared between various objects in real-time with the help of these technologies, and the Internet of Things (IoT) promotes such situational awareness and automation within teams. The following figure 2 demonstrates seven basic technologies AI, ML, IoT, Blockchain, 5G, Quantum and AR/VR which are revolutionising innovation in modern collaboration. They all have their respective icon and label which shows how they have transformed the manner in which communication, decision making and real time digital interactions are conducted.

Figure 2. Key Emerging Technologies Enabling Collaborative Intelligence

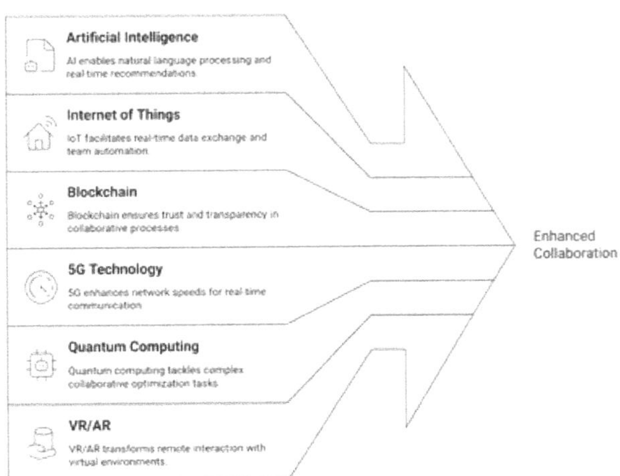

Blockchain introduces the concept of trust and transparency to the processes of collaboration, in particular, where distributed teams or multi-party systems operate. 5G speeds up and connects the network; it becomes much simpler to generate and share quality video conferencing, real-time analysis, and augmented reality/virtual experience. Quantum Computing, in its turn, possesses potential of incomparable scales so as to combat complex collaborative optimization problems inaccessible to classical systems, however, at an early stage. The technology of Virtual Reality (VR) and Augmented Reality (AR) is changing the way the remote interaction takes place so that it would be possible to take care of the virtual meetings, use a virtual whiteboard, and a training environment. Combined with these technologies, one can move to the next step of dynamic and context- and intelligence-aware cooperation that presupposes more responsive, adaptive, and human-friendly systems. The table 1 provides the comparison of the main new technologies AI, IoT, Blockchain, 5G, Quantum Computing, and AR/VR in terms of their purpose, opportunities, and contribution to real-time, secure, and intelligent collaboration. It assists the readers to comprehend the contribution each technology has towards the collaborative ecosystem.

Table 1 Comparison of Emerging Technologies in E-Collaboration

Technology	Primary Role in Collaboration	Key Capabilities	Impact on Collaboration
Artificial Intelligence (AI)	Enhancing decision-making and task automation	Natural language processing, predictive analytics, intelligent assistance	Automates routine tasks, provides real-time insights, supports adaptive collaboration
Internet of Things (IoT)	Enabling real-time data exchange between devices	Sensor integration, remote monitoring, data synchronization	Facilitates context-aware collaboration and real-time decision-making
Blockchain	Ensuring data integrity and trust in distributed systems	Decentralized ledgers, smart contracts, immutability	Provides secure, verifiable workflows and transparent transactions in multi-party teams
5G	Supporting high-speed, low-latency communication	High bandwidth, fast connectivity, reduced latency	Powers real-time video, immersive AR/VR collaboration, and edge computing
Quantum Computing	Solving complex collaborative optimization problems	Parallel processing, probabilistic computation	Enhances large-scale simulations, logistics, and decision modeling (future potential)
AR/VR	Creating immersive and interactive collaborative environments	3D modeling, virtual presence, remote co-working	Transforms virtual collaboration into spatially rich, experience-driven engagements

2.1 AI, ML, IoT, Blockchain, 5G, Quantum, and AR/VR

The terms of Artificial Intelligence (AI), Machine Learning (ML), Internet of Things (IoT), and Blockchain, 5G, and Quantum Computing, Augmented Reality (AR)/Virtual Reality are way beyond changing the nature of collaboration. AI and ML usage can make smart automation, natural language processing, personal recommendations, real-time guidance, and decision-making transform the team-working process and deal with the problems. These systems can learn user behavior and automate processes that are collaborative in nature such as task management and sharing of knowledge. Internet of Things (IoT) creates cooperation in a real space that expands the collaboration concept to physical locations making other objects and sensors connect to one another and to the collaboration space, and thus, enabling real-time observation of places, automatic actions, and context-dependent communication. Blockchain provides the decentralized trust in the data, immutability of information, verified transactions, and secure communication between the distributed teams, which is particularly effective when applied in cross-organizational and cross-border collaboration. As the 5G has increased connectivity that provides ultra-low latency and high-speed data transfer, it provides convenience in video conferencing, remote operations, and other AR/VR-related applications. The quantum computers, which are still in their early development stage, have the potential to manage complex collaborative tasks, such as large-scale simulations and optimization tasks, that cannot be dealt with using the classical systems. The AR/VR technologies are transforming the way of engagement since it provides a virtual reality where a person can communicate with a three-dimensional space. The ongoing integration of these technologies is not only expanding the conventional digital cooperation, but also offers an insight into the future where even the head of the cooperation will be much smarter, interconnected, and imposing.

2.2 Enhancing Real-Time, Secure, and Immersive Collaboration

The following phase of digital collaboration is developed in three dimensions of real-time responsiveness, data safety, and immersive interaction that is augmented with AI and other new technologies. This is not that group collaboration has been dislocated by chat or video conferencing anymore, but the existence of specialists permitting transcription, automatic note taking, automatic translating, and in-the-moment contextual intelligence at meetings. The characteristics make it low on cognitive burden, and improve the decision-making speed and accuracy. In the present-day connected spaces, security reigns. AI contributes to the security sphere by monitoring abnormalities, predicting aberrant threats, and even blocking non-compliant policies in the real-time mode. When combined with a Blockchain, collaboration systems will have the advantages of decentralized validation, immutable audit logging as well as trusted but not trusting approaches to sharing information as discussed in remote and shared work arrangements.

AR/VR and 3D environment are facilitating the immersion of collaboration. Project groups can hold virtual design sessions, distant debugging or interactive training sessions across the geography. These experiences are also accompanied by the 5G connection that renders low latency action and media on high resolutions. Moreover, personalized collaboration tools can be tailored to the interface through AI-based personalization, and some notifications are given first priority and clings to the interests of its users based on their roles. Overall, these advancements are changing the idea of collaboration, it is no longer digital but is becoming intuitive, safe, and luminous in terms of the experience and this is making the teams work smarter, faster, and more creative. The Figure 3 illustrates the growth of the adoption of major technologies AI, IoT, Blockchain, 5G, and AR/VR in collaborative systems within five years. It covers AI as the most prominent facilitator of next-generation collaboration tools in industries.

Figure 3. Adoption Rate of Emerging Technologies in E-Collaboration (2020–2025)

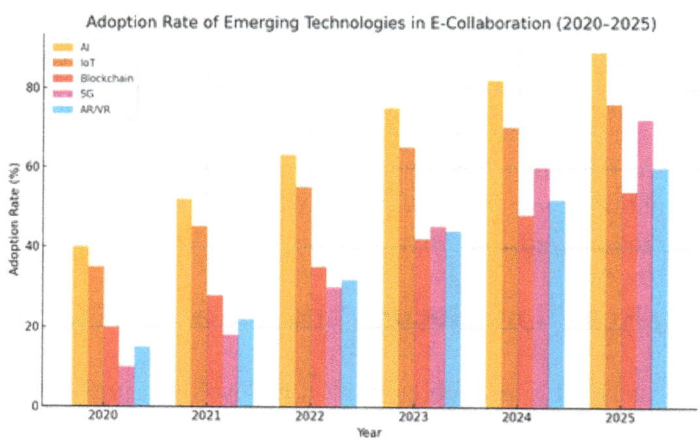

3. HUMAN-AI TEAMING AND HYBRID INTELLIGENCE

Via the utilization of both complementary capabilities of people and artificial intelligence, human-AI teaming or hybrid intelligence is a potentially strong transformation in the manner in which work is performed. Humanity provides us with creativity, emotional intelligence, a sense of ethics, and understanding of context, and AI is the fastest, scalable, data processing, and pattern recognition. They combine to create a symbiotic partnership which will continue to excel compared to that entity working on its own (Linnes, 2020). When speaking of digital collaboration, hybrid intelligence will allow systems to assist human teams in a more dynamic and responsive manner. As an example, AI can be used to pre-process massive data to identify trends, whereas a human analyzes the results and uses his judgment (Magnisalis & Demetriadis, 2015). Virtual assistants are able to book meetings, summarize an interview and even propose strategic actions depending on past results, set human partners free to concentrate on invention and problem-solving. The Figure 4 Illustrates the interaction between human capabilities (e.g., creativity, judgment) and AI capabilities (e.g., speed, data analysis), converging in a shared collaborative space. Helps readers visualize the idea of hybrid intelligence and role complementarity in AI-human collaboration.

Figure 4. Human-AI Teaming Framework

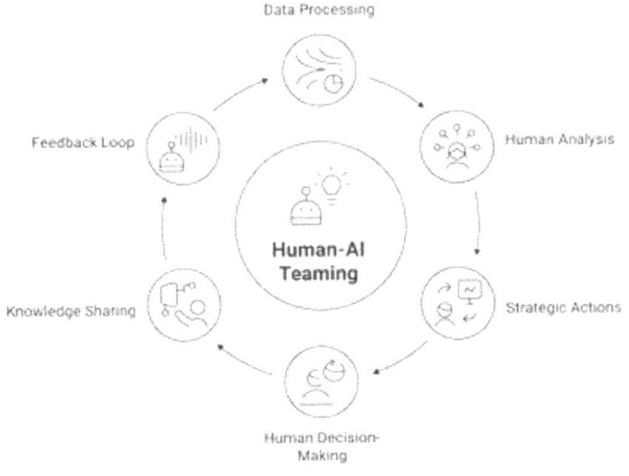

This further teaming is also used in knowledge management and AI is also finding ways of mapping knowledge in organizations and proposing knowledge sharing partners based on their expertise and facilitating the transfer of knowledge. Explainable AI, trustworthy interfaces, and feedback loops are the promising aspects of AI-Human teaming, which are needed to organize AI behavior to perform in human ways. Due to the increase in the complexity of work places, hybrid intelligence ensures that teamwork becomes not only faster, but more considerate and intelligent (van der Meij et al., 2016). Human-AI collaboration is now a prospective idea and once it is generated ethically and inclusively, it may enormously broaden the scope of decision making, imagination and corporate strength. Core design principles outlined in the table 2 include transparency, explainability, adaptability and ethical alignment and their goal and examples of implementation. It can be used as a guide to create AI systems to provide effective human-AI teaming.

Table 2 Design Principles for Effective Human-AI Collaboration

Design Principle	Purpose	Implementation Example
Transparency	Build user trust by making AI decisions and actions visible	Displaying reasoning paths or confidence levels in AI recommendations
Explainability	Help users understand how and why AI makes decisions	Using natural language explanations for algorithmic outputs in dashboards
Adaptability	Allow AI to learn and evolve with user behavior and feedback	AI assistants that improve suggestions based on user corrections or patterns
Ethical Alignment	Ensure AI adheres to human values and avoids harm	Bias detection in hiring tools or content moderation based on ethical guidelines
Collaborative Control	Maintain human agency and final decision-making authority	Human-in-the-loop systems in autonomous task management or risk-sensitive decisions
Usability and Accessibility	Make AI systems inclusive and easy to interact with for all users	Voice-enabled interfaces, multilingual support, and simplified UI for diverse users

3.1 Benefits and Design Principles of Human-AI Collaboration

The numerous benefits of Artificial Intelligence use are not inherent to automation itself, but they reach into cognitive enhancement, faster work, and a better understanding of the network of relationships among the partners. Under the right conditions, AI systems may develop into intelligent companions that propose, predict and counter the actions of users accordingly. This type of collaboration optimizes the accuracy of the decisions and reduces the number of questionable repeats and allows teams to learn continuously (Prasad and Roy, 2024). The principles of design are central so as to make the human-AI teaming a success. The first is transparency, because individuals ought to receive answers about the AI systems the decisions are made against. Explainability and interpretability are also crucially important especially in a sensitive area like healthcare or finance. The other underlying principle is user-centered design; the interface must be reflective, user-friendly and amplified to the user needs.

Besides that, the concept of collaborative control also ensures that humanity is always the master, and AI system is a servant. Flexibility enables AI systems to advance with time through feedback given by human beings (Turban et al., 2011). Finally, ethical alignment should be reflected in the construction of systems, whereby inequitable impacts and privacy protection should be avoided. Focusing on these principles, organizations will achieve the following: the development of AI-enhanced collaborative setting that will be effective, inclusive, and human-friendly, such a mixture of technology and human knowledge will be productive.

3.2 Augmenting Creativity, Decision-Making, and Efficiency

The largest opportunity that is put before AI in the cooperative environment is in supplemental skills instead of replacement of capabilities. AI can also be applied during creative activities when it helps advance ideas, propose contents and follow patterns so that a user is free to explore ideas and step up innovations quickly. As an example, retrospective design analysis can be requested with AI, or the machine can suggest alternatives, or even bias the outcome of a design or product development situation as the co-designer (Utomo et al., 2024). AI is perfect in making the decision since it is able to generate synthesis of huge reams of data, identify latent tendencies and simulate scenarios through predictive modelling. Relevant insights, alerts, and visualization of data apprised by AI enable the teams to make better, timelier, and more strategic decisions.

There is also AI with less human error and less cognitive overload of the human mind since machines analyze complex but repetitive data that can be time consuming and consuming, when performed by the human organism. The possibility of automating routine cooperation processes with the help of AI, including time management, sorting the documents, or monitoring the tasks, also adds to the efficiency because humans will not be involved with the lower-level goals (Al-ma'aitah, 2024). Intelligent workflow optimization has also been shown to be possible through the availability of resources and dynamics by teams and project restriction by smart systems. Last but not least, AI will someday enhance group work in terms of excellency, rapidness and innovativeness. It converts human energies to results that have greater effects in assisting human beings to be more intelligent, work faster and more innovative in tackling problems, innovating. The Figure 5 Illustrates how collaborative systems are iterative in nature and how the human response augments system learning and ethical rightness.

Figure 5. Lifecycle of AI-Driven Collaborative Workflow

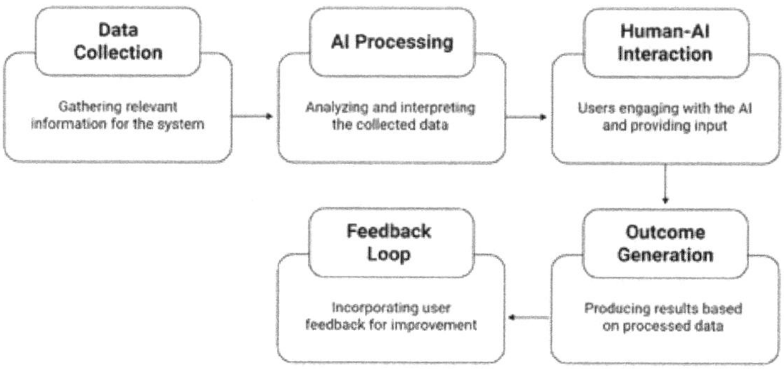

4. APPLICATIONS ACROSS DOMAINS

The different fields are transforming collaboration with the help of AI and new digital technologies, as it is becoming smarter, quicker, and more context-driven. AI-powered technologies in medicine and Internet of Medical Things (IoMT) allow conducting remote-patient diagnostics, real-time monitoring of patients, and collaboration between specialists of various fields. AI also improves the collaborative learning process in education by creating intelligent tutoring systems, personal feedback, and virtual classrooms based on AR/VR. There is AI-assisted project management tools, intelligent communication systems, and knowledge-sharing applications that enhance productivity and innovation in the enterprise (Audretsch & Belitski, 2020). In e-commerce, artificial intelligence assists in serving customers, making demand, and recommending by collaborating and assisting in recommendation with its collaborative filtering tools, enhancing both on-the-team and customer interaction. Also, there is the use of IoT, blockchain and AI in manufacturing and logistics to undertake real time coordination and optimization of a supply chain. In every field, AI can supplement decision-making, innovations, and workflow processes, and in each case, the joint efforts of human and artificial intelligence can provide previously unimaginable results with the same success that cannot be achieved even using no artificial intelligence at all.

4.1 Enterprise Systems, Healthcare (IoMT), Education, and E-Commerce

In enterprise systems, AI facilitates cooperation by smart project management application, autonomous operations, and smart virtual assistants (Brunetti et al., 2020). Application services such as Microsoft Teams and Slack have AI components to prioritize tasks, analyze emotional expressions, and predictive communication activity that increases team productivity. Internet of Medical Things (IoMT) in healthcare enables the interaction of devices, wearables, and AI-based diagnostics in real time and makes remote consultations. This aspect was made possible by collaborative tools that allow experts located in various areas to exchange knowledge and work together on challenging cases to boost patient outcomes.

AI and AR/VR can be applied in the education sector to strengthen the interactive learning environments, automate the grading procedure, and offer adaptive learning pathways. Such tools as Google Classroom or Coursera employ ML algorithms to engage the students in a more personal manner (Chen et al., 2024). In online business, AI is used in inventory coordination on the fly, chatbot applications in customer services and dynamic pricing model. Recommendation engines also increase the conversion rates and analytics dashboards enable teams to make a decision about marketing jointly depending on the data (Li et al., 2022). The industries are the examples of how collaborative efforts with AI improve effectiveness, personalization and decision-making.

4.2 Sector-Specific Tools and Success Stories

The industries are using industry-specific AI tools to enhance performance of collaborations. Trello with Butler AI, Asana, and Notion AI allow automating the process of tracking the task in enterprises, managing resources, and collaborative planning (Melander & Pazirandeh, 2019). The AI Companion in Zoom provides real-time transcriptions and meetings analytics, simplifying online chats. In health, through IoMT, Philips Health Suite can interconnect medical instruments, allowing real-time coordination of the healthcare team in the diagnostics of patients and management of treatments. Machine learning has made it possible to collaborate on cancer research and personalize treatment plans when using AI-based engines such as IBM Watson Health.

Knewton and Squirrel AI in education use analytics and adaptive learning to design personal study goals, which help teachers and students cooperate and enhance the success of learning. AI-based collaborative forecasting tools are available either through ready-made platforms (such as the Kit marketplace, targeted at small firms, provides collaborative recommendations aimed at marketing), or in demand planning (with e-commerce giants such as Amazon employing them for demand planning) (Ridwan & Athena, 2023). The following success stories indicate that domain-individual AI incorporation not only increases the effectiveness of operations but brings about the ease of teamwork and adaptability, as well as innovation in the given collaborative context.

5. CHALLENGES AND ETHICAL CONSIDERATIONS

In addition to the opportunities, AI and other emerging technologies introduce challenges and ethics that are serious and become a part and parcel of collaboration. One of the highest priorities is the data privacy and security (Urbinati et al., 2022). The collaborative platforms manage every meaningful fragment of personal and organization data and therefore they are extremely sought after in the realms of cyberattack and misuse. This must include the following: data encryption, safe authentication, and GDPR/HIPAA compliance, etc). The second problem is the algorithmic bias. The algorithms trained on biased data can be used as a continuation of a priori discrimination within a decision-support system or recruitment system by either condoning discrimination or marginalizing underrepresented groups. To alleviate this, transparent algorithms, audits and inclusive data practice should be talked about.

It is also important in explainability and trust. Many users are scared to utilize AI-based recommendation without understanding how decisions are made. It can be useful in providing interpretable results which enhance consumer confidence and responsibility (Esichaikul et al., 2013). Moreover, over-automation may also be a possibility, because excessive reliance on the use of AI can reduce the human factor, critical thinking, or ethical decision-making. A balance between automation and human control is very important. Finally, the technology should alter the ethical governance approaches. Proper policies that state how responsible AI should be used, make it fairer and accountable should be made by the organizations. The crucial thing to keep in mind is that to successfully leverage AI-assisted collaboration, the ethical future consideration, inclusive design, and responsible releases are to be viewed as visionary endeavours and technological upgrades. (Bing & Leong, 2025).

5.1 Privacy, Bias, Security, and Trust

The concept of AI application in collaborative systems elicits relevant concerns of privacy, bias, security, and trustworthiness which in their own right, can exert the ultimate effect on the effectiveness and acceptability of all such systems. Privacy is one of these concerns as AI-based technologies are more likely to handle indefinite data concerning users, their personal and behavioural, as well as organizational data (Cociancig et al., 2025). The sensitive data is prone to leakage or abuse, unless the critical information is handled with the required backup, offering compliance violations and loss of user confidence. Of no less importance is safety. AI-powered systems expand the range of attack surface of the digital cooperation platforms.

The invasion of information, malicious AI infiltration, unauthorized access to the history of communication can destroy the entire cooperation. One has to ensure the need to support end-to-end encryption, access controls and real-time threat detection (Dhamo et al., 2023). Skew in AI models is morally objectionable, especially in the cases of decision-making models that constitute hiring, resource allocation or group review. Biased data may lead to discrimination results that negate proper inclusiveness and fairness. Finally, human-AI partnership is supported by trust. AI tools should be transparent, explainable and predictable in order to be trusted by its users. Education of users, feedback loops and integration of explainable AI (XAI) models with decision pathways visible and comprehensible by end users can make trust more robust. The table 3 categorizes major challenges including data privacy, algorithmic bias, trust issues, and over-automation. It presents potential risks, real-world examples, and recommended mitigation strategies for each challenge.

Table 3 Key Ethical and Security Challenges in AI-Powered Collaboration

Challenge	Potential Risk	Real-World Example	Mitigation Strategy
Data Privacy	Unauthorized access or misuse of sensitive user or organizational data	AI-powered collaboration tools collecting personal health or employee data	Data encryption, user consent mechanisms, compliance with GDPR/ HIPAA
Algorithmic Bias	Discriminatory outcomes due to biased training data	AI in recruitment favouring certain demographics over others	Bias auditing, diverse training datasets, inclusive algorithm design
Trust Deficit	Users reluctant to adopt AI due to lack of transparency or explainability	AI suggesting decisions without rationale or clarity	Implementing explainable AI (XAI), building user education and trust frameworks
Over-Automation	Loss of human judgment, critical thinking, and decision authority	Over-reliance on AI-generated reports or actions in high-stakes environments	Keeping humans in the loop, defining AI boundaries in decision workflows
Security Vulnerabilities	AI systems becoming targets for cyberattacks or manipulation	Adversarial attacks manipulating inputs to mislead collaborative AI tools	Real-time threat detection, regular security audits, adversarial training models

5.2 Responsible AI Practices and Governance

To reduce the ethical risks and realize the sustainable use of AI in the context of collaboration, organizations are forced to build responsible AI practice and governance models. Responsible AI focuses on how to promote the use and creation of AI systems that are responsible, that is, fair, transparent, secure, inclusive and aligned with human values (Garno et al., 2025). There is the ethical design on the ground-up which can begin by looking at privacy-by-design, fairness-by-design and human-in-the-loop systems which ensure that the ultimate decision to be made is in humankind control. Governance is an explicit policy, organizational structure; it governs the development and application of AI. It includes the recommendations on the collection of data, audit of algorithm, risk assessment, and accountability. Multidisciplinary AI ethics review boards and committees may also assist to identify the actual-world implications of AI systems and avoid harm.

It is also important that certain regulatory compliance requirements should be addressed by the organizations in the form of the laws like GDPR, HIPAA, and the regulation on AI (EU AI Act). This spans as far as ensuring transparency of use of data, an educated consent of the user and the provision of opt-in alternatives to AI-powered functions (Joseph & Pandey, 2025). The accountability that is instilled in managing technologies has a great impact on the trust that people will have on AI-based collaboration. Governance practices should be embedded not only to safeguard users and stakeholders, but also in order to promote innovation by making sure that AI is used in an ethical, secure, and non-destructive way to improve cooperation, rather than weakening it. The Figure 6 is Based on industry surveys, this chart ranks leading concerns such as data privacy, algorithmic bias, lack of transparency, and over-automation in AI-driven collaboration tools.

Figure 6. Top Ethical Concerns in AI-Powered Collaboration (Survey-Based)

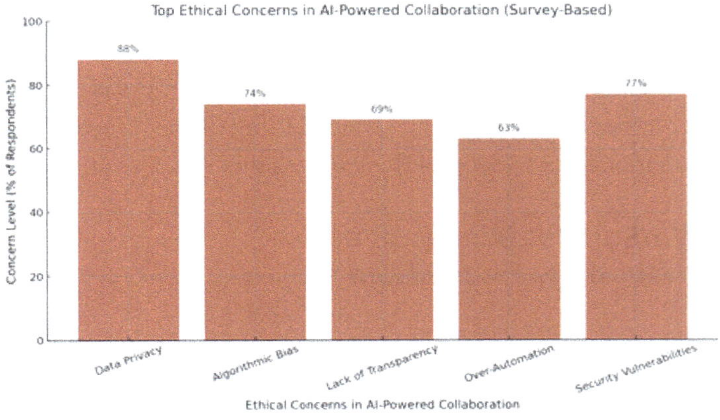

6. CASE STUDY AND ITS APPLICATION

To show the practical effects of collaboration intelligence, three interesting case studies covering different areas such as enterprise systems, healthcare and education are outlined in this chapter to illustrate how AI and other emerging digital technologies have been successfully used to improve human cooperation, decision-making processes, and productivity. When it comes to the enterprise sphere, Microsoft can be considered one of the first ones to integrate AI into its collaboration platform (Rana, 2024). With its tools, including Teams, Microsoft 365, and Viva, the company has revolutionized remote and hybrid employment by rolling out artificial intelligence-based capabilities, including live transcription, Copilot-generated content, and smart scheduling. The examples these innovations show highlight several benefits that human-AI teaming can create, such as the reduced cognitive load, increased efficiency of the workflow, and promotion of inclusive digital workspaces (Sharma & Shrestha, 2024).

Apollo Hospitals adopted the AI and Internet of Medical Things (IoMT) to develop a connected health infrastructure in the healthcare sector. On the one hand, the use of generation dashboards and predictive analytics and, on the other, cooperation among professionals at various levels and campuses enables quicker, information-driven decision-making within the healthcare provider and results in improved patient outcome and operational responsiveness (Singla et al., 2025). Artificial intelligence is another application of Coursera in enhancing interaction between learners and instructors in the education sector. These features as automated grading, personalized feedback and real-time monitoring of performance allow instructors to offer adaptive, interactive and scale learning. A cumulative result of these case studies is that, collaborative intelligence is not a thing of the future, but the current-day-phenomenon that is transforming the way organizations operate, in all sectors.

6.1 Digital Workplace: Microsoft's AI-Powered Productivity Ecosystem

Microsoft was among the first in the world to reconsider digital collaboration with AI, when organizations switched to a new model of remote and hybrid work and implementation of a new digital workplace. Its suite of applications, such as Microsoft Teams, Microsoft 365 and Viva, has had some clever additions that would add to productivity, communication, and team performance of users (Song et al., 2019). Microsoft introduced the use of AI to provide features such as real-time transcription, real-time translation, intelligent meeting notes delivered by Copilot, and contextual task recommendations to ensure that their employees can better manage themselves and cross-departmental and time-zone boundaries.

Big language models enabled the creation of the Microsoft 365 Copilot, a type of virtual assistant that proved to be able to write documents, create reports, add insights to emails, and suggest action items during meetings. They spent less time on repetitive work and became more focused on high-impact work (Tahri Sqalli et al., 2023). Viva insights also had AI-driven recommendations to improve staff and team experience. The point is that responsible AI, data privacy, and compliance with security are some of the issues that Microsoft considers, which ensured that collaborative intelligence can be raised to scale without compromising the trust. The case can also be used in the future as an example of how human-AI cooperation can improve decision-making, assist in avoiding digital fatigue, and make the work environment more flexible and open to diverse individuals. (Terziyan et al., 2025). The implementation in Microsoft can be seen as an example to be observed within the organizations trying to future-proof their way of collaboration by resorting to the use of intelligent and ethical technology. The Figure 7 shows the annual increase in user-reported productivity due to AI features such as Copilot, transcription, and smart scheduling. It illustrates how AI-driven automation enhanced work efficiency over time.

Figure 7. Productivity Gains from AI Features in Microsoft 365 (2020–2025)

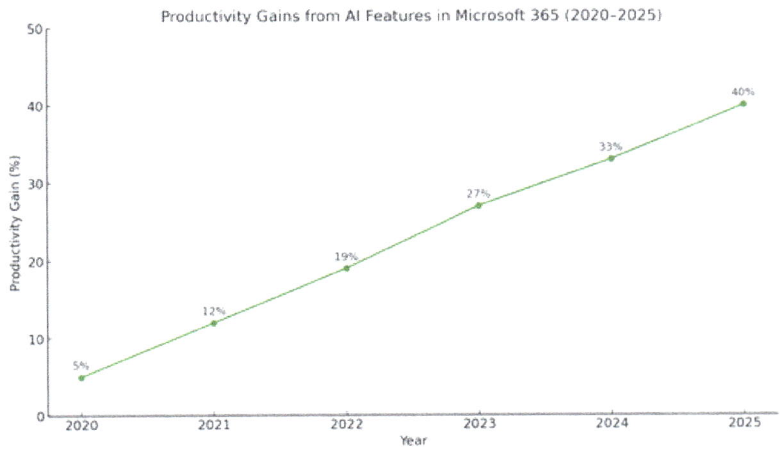

6.2 Healthcare: Apollo Hospitals' AI-IoMT-Driven Collaborative Healthcare Model

Apollo Hospitals, a major healthcare provider in India, also adopted AI and the Internet of Medical Things (IoMT) into its operation to change the way the medical teams communicate between locations. Amid the increasing interest in accessing remote healthcare and multidisciplinary care, Apollo implemented AI-based IoMT systems that facilitated the patient monitoring mechanism in real-time, predictive diagnostics and collaborative treatment planning. Patients connected medical devices were continuously monitored without interruption and patient data on vitals, ECG, glucose levels and oxygen saturation levels were collected and displayed to centralized AI dashboards. Such dashboards would apply machine learning approaches to anomaly detection, complications prediction, and notifying physicians with alerts (Zelda et al., 2024). Clinicians were able to view health profile of a patient and how the AI delivered its insights, and collaborate across specialties on the secure cloud-based environments.

One of the main innovations was the application of digital twins that are virtual copies of patient data streams and allowed simulating treatment outcome and making collective decisions among teams that were not present in one place. This contributed to decrease in response time in critical care conditions and further increased the diagnostic accuracy (Angerschmid et al., 2022). The process of implementing

Apollo guaranteed data privacy and security and regulatory compliance as well as efficiency of operation. The presented case points out that AI and IoMT collaboration create the synergy of collaborative intelligence in healthcare that enhances patient outcomes, decreases readmissions at hospitals, and allows more team-based, intelligent medical care in real-time. The Figure 8 depicts a yearly decline in average emergency response time (in minutes) after implementing AI-enabled monitoring and predictive alerts across Apollo Hospitals. It reflects improved decision speed and team coordination.

Figure 8. Reduction in Emergency Response Time via AI-IoMT Systems

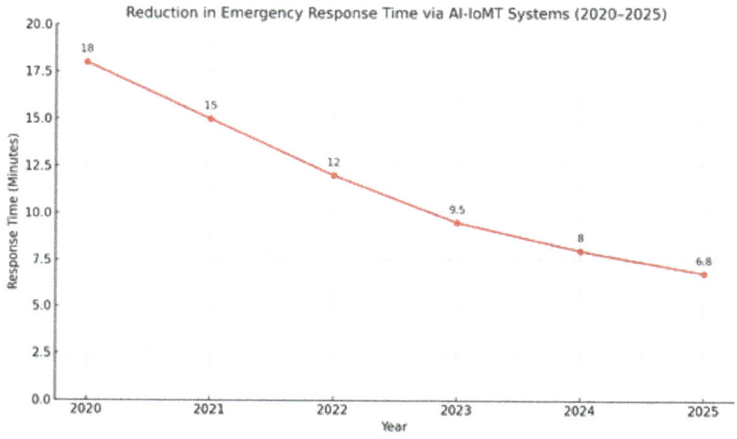

6.3 Education: Coursera's Model for AI-Driven Collaborative Learning

Coursera, one of the world's leading online learning platforms, has successfully integrated AI to change the process of interaction, collaboration, and co-creation of knowledge between instructors and learners. Coursera has millions of users across the globe and this presented a problem where they will need to explore the possibility of providing personalized, scalable, and collaborative education experiences, in different geographies and educative subjects. In order to solve this, the platform implemented AI-driven functionalities to improve student performance as well as teacher collaboration (Gianfrancesco et al., 2018). The benefits of AI-based dashboards is that, instructors will be able to access real-time learner analytics and, as such, be able to gain insight on struggling students, course progress and dynamically adjust their teaching strategy. Quiz and assignment grading automation removes administrative burden, and allows instructors to work on course quality and student interaction.

The models of Natural Language Processing (NLP) help in the creation of individualized feedback thus enhancing satisfaction and retention by the learners (Li et al., 2022). Coursera also promotes instructor collaboration with the development of tools in co-creating course developments, reviewing, and updating courses with collective insights and AI computer-generated performance recordings. The tools will stimulate international cooperation among teachers, designing more versatile, diverse educational environments (Keerio et al., 2022). Using a mix of human and machine intelligence, Coursera results in the practical example of collaborative intelligence in education that makes learning more creative, responsive, and pedagogically productive and guarantees high-scale accessible and high-quality education globally (Rabi, 2024). The Figure 9 compares Coursera's learner retention rates over several years, highlighting improvements after introducing AI-based personalization, automated feedback, and instructor dashboards.

Figure 9. Learner Retention Rate Before and After AI Integration

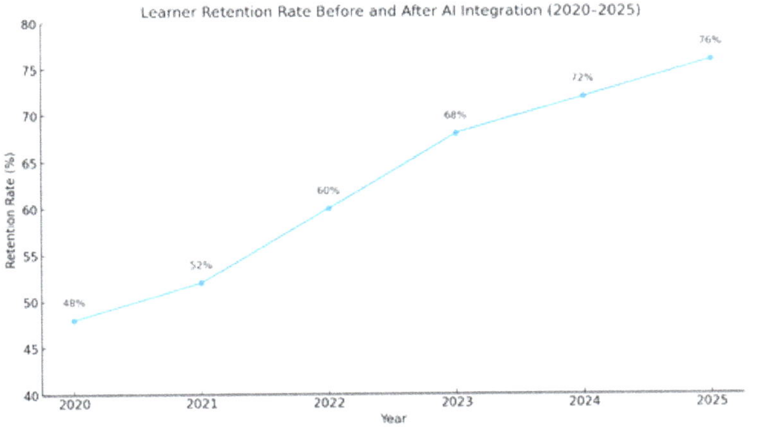

7. FUTURE DIRECTIONS

Collaborative intelligence will be the way to go in the future: the combination of AI and other new technologies with human-centered design will result in adaptive, ethical, and context-based collaboration environments. Artificial general intelligence (AGI) is in development and has the potential to transform collusion by supporting systems that comprehend, reason, and interrelate at human-like levels across problems and fields (Rawashdeh et al., 2023). We are also going to experience growing use of autonomous agents, the AI agents who are able to initiate, perform and revise cooperative tasks by themselves and coordinate them to serve the human intentions. This is because such agents are able to work cross-departmentally, manage processes, and ensure ongoing knowledge companionship in flexible work situations.

AR/VR with 5G and edge computing will be used to deliver immersive experiences in which virtual collaboration environments resemble the real life and decrease the necessity to meet physically. The AI-enabled platforms will catch the digital divides in emerging countries to provide scalable, inclusive, and localized collaboration in emerging economies (Samokhvalov, 2024). Another of the areas of focus will be sustainability where AI-powered collaboration machines will assist with environmental protection, intelligent management of resources and climate preparedness. Concurrently, concerns of ethics will change, and it will demand more dynamic systems of governance that will change along with the changes in technology. There is only one future, co-evolution, in which people and machines not only cooperate, but also still teach each other incessantly, which gives rise to a more brilliant and more balanced and more durable collaborative future. The table 4 highlights future trends such as AGI, autonomous agents, immersive collaboration environments, and AI for sustainability. It summarizes their projected impact, maturity level, and anticipated applications across industries.

Table 4. Emerging Trends in Collaborative Intelligence

Trend	Projected Impact	Maturity Level	Anticipated Applications
Artificial General Intelligence (AGI)	Enables machines to perform any intellectual task humans can do	Experimental / Research	Adaptive decision-making, autonomous strategy planning, AI-human co-leadership
Autonomous Agents	Automates complex multi-step collaborative tasks and negotiations	Emerging	Workflow orchestration, digital project managers, intelligent virtual assistants
Immersive Collaboration (AR/ VR + 5G)	Transforms remote teamwork into spatial, real-time engagement	Developing / Early Adoption	Virtual design rooms, immersive training, 3D co-working spaces

continued on following page

Table 4. Continued

Trend	Projected Impact	Maturity Level	Anticipated Applications
AI for Sustainability	Supports eco-friendly collaboration, resource optimization, and policy modelling	Growing Adoption	Smart cities, green supply chains, sustainable team resource management
Global Collaborative Platforms	Democratizes access to AI tools and fosters inclusion in emerging economies	Moderate Adoption	Cross-border R&D, multilingual knowledge hubs, distributed innovation networks

7.1 AGI, Autonomous Agents, and Global Adoption

The Second AI-augmentation frontier is the concept of Artificial General Intelligence (AGI) and autonomous agent whose software is projected to be able to reason, learn, and work in a vast scope in tasks, much like any human being (Schroder et al., 2022). AGI might become a real partner, who is able to understand the situation, learning, and create solutions in the collaboration with people. Multi-modal models and self-optimising architectures are early work that are initially theoretical, but will permit AGI to work as part of a collaboration. In the near future we already witness the rise of autonomous agents. Such AI agents will be capable of handling typical activities, steer groups of users and possibly stand in place of human actors in a shared workspace (Guo & Wang, 2025). Through independent workflow control, the agents may largely alleviate management burden and cross-functional activities more scalable and efficient to work.

The worldwide DTS integration of collaborative intelligence systems is rapidly growing because of the rise in remote working patterns and digitalization. Nonetheless, access in a fair manner is a problem. In order to bridge the disparity between developed and developing economies, it is significant to introduce the infrastructure, expertise, and governance infrastructure needed to grow their economies (Tabbassum et al., 2024). The industries, governments, and non-government organizations must collaborate in such a way that the application of AI-optimized collaboration tools are not only affordable but also locally relevant and diverse as the world. Massive use conscientiously can turn innovation into a more democratic process, result in the deepening of cross-border cooperation and the ability of different talents to work together to co-create in the digital economy.

7.2 AI for Sustainability and Inclusive Development

The partnership, financed by AI, will possess an immense worth to address the sustainability and inclusive growth within the sectors. Through a synergy of the AI and digital cooperation tools, organizations will be in a better position to track the environment better, manage the energy usage better, and make sustainable decisions (Tiwari, 2023). Consequently, as an example, teams will be in a position to collaborate in real time to develop sustainability solutions, such as waste reduction or better green logistics by scrutinizing large volumes of data on emissions, supply chains, and resource consumption. With the adoption of AI and IoT in smart cities, each sector can collaborate and efficiently monitor the traffic, energy, and waste. The cross-border data sharing platform also empowers the interdisciplinary teamwork platform and is able to assist climate research, water management, and biodiversity protection.

The AI can play a vital role in bridging the educational, healthcare, and economic gap on the development perspective. Dependence on mobile-first collaborative solutions, and the use of AI-based learning tools and health assistants can be used to serve the remote and underserved populations worldwide (van der Veer et al., 2021). The language translation, voice-based AI interface, and other technologies can be used to break the literacy and language barrier and make collaboration more comfortable. To impact positively the inclusive and sustainable development, the ethical frameworks must be more concerned with equality, transparency, and environmental sustainability. In line with social needs, AI will become a fantastic resource not only to efficiency, but also to making the world a better, greener, or more collaborative place. Figure 10 compares the expected impact scores (on a scale of 1 10) of trends such as AGI, autonomous agents, immersive environments, and AI with sustainability, according to estimations by the experts.

Figure 10. Predicted Impact of Future Trends in Collaborative Intelligence

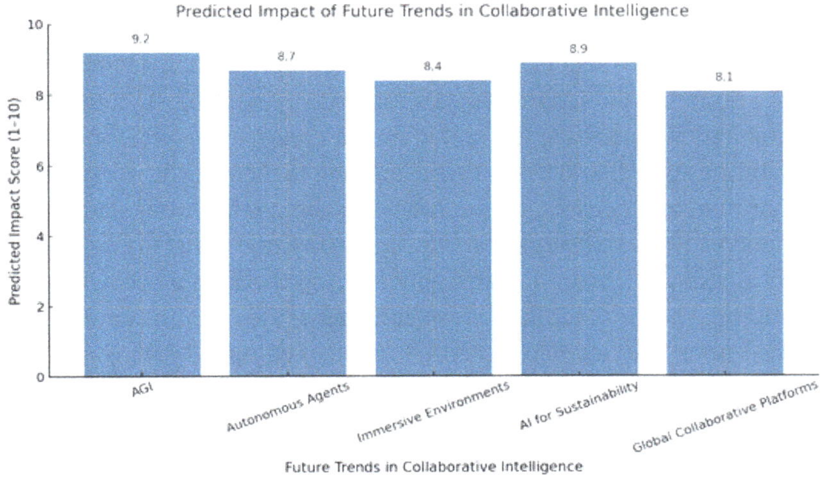

8. CONCLUSION

The world has become closer to the data-based, digital, and more distributed organizations. Therefore, there is a paradigm shift in the collaborative work environment. Teamwork has become an absent concept in emails and videoconferencing. Collaboration is now re-invented as a synergistic, smart and adaptive process that renders with Artificial Intelligence (AI) and other digital technologies. It has talked about how this change is causing a new paradigm: collaborative intelligence, where the best of all human and machine abilities is applied to achieve the highest level of decision-making, productive innovation and creativity. We have talked about the development of e-collaboration tools that were once in the infancy stage and currently integrated and intelligent. However, many challenges remain that can be surmounted solely with the advances, including interoperability problems, information overload and even concerns about privacy, bias, and even trust. The synergy of AI, IoT, Blockchain, 5G, Quantum Computing, and AR/VR has its difficulties and responsibilities to some extent. These technologies combined with a deliberate implementation allow achieving a digital collaboration process that is real-time, secure, and immersive. They facilitate easier exchange of knowledge, friction-free interactions as well as smarter work despite inter-geographical/functional/disciplinary barriers.

Human-AI teaming, also known as hybrid intelligence is one of the major themes that are presented in this chapter. Instead of trying to present AI as the alternative to a human workforce, this approach will focus on presenting AI as a partner, a tool of augmentation that will expand the human creativity, critical thinking, and solving capabilities. AI should help users according to their needs; it can do this by automation of routine processes, data synthesis, insight generation, and contextual recommendations. Humans bring judgment, sympathy, and moral logic in exchange, and these are all aspects that are worried about during challenging decision-making and team building. The uses of collaborative intelligence are enormous and increasing. The use of Internet of Medical Things (IoMT) devices equipped with AI capabilities supports the collaboration of healthcare professionals during the delivery of care, distant diagnostics, and real-time surveillance in healthcare. AI platforms in education individualize teaching and create different forms of teacher-student interaction. In businesses, there is an incremental capability to be more agile, responsive, and transparent in the work by the usage of smart project management and decision support tools. The AI-based collaboration solutions are useful in e-commerce, logistics, manufacturing, and governance, minimizing the friction and increasing the efficiency of operations. We still need to be wary of the moral relativeness of these technologies however.

Any collaborative system must be AI responsible, open algorithms, data safety, and inclusive design. The problem of surveillance, algorithmic biases, and over-automated processes might contribute to the development of distrust and emergence of social disparities in case no actions to prevent it will be undertaken. Regulation systems, moral checks and checks made-up of various teams are required to see to it that the use of AI in a partnership environment is attached to the larger practices within society. In summary, the future of collaborative intelligence would, in the future, be informed by the rapid development of initiatives in such fields as Artificial General Intelligence (AGI), autonomous agents, immersive virtual environments, and AI to sustain all activities on earth. This will become the challenge of applying such innovations in an inclusive, equitable, and human wellbeing-focused fashion. In short, the real potential of AI in collaboration is not just in the fact that it makes collaboration more efficient but in the fact that it is able to transform the manner in which we think, communicate and otherwise collaborate. With the merging of human with smart technology, we are able to create collaborative ecosystems which are smarter, but more importantly more empathetic, ethical and future-forward.

REFERENCES

Al-ma'aitah, M. A. (2024). The contribution of digital business strategy in enhancing collaborative innovation capability: The moderating role of organizational culture—A case study of six pharmaceutical companies in Jordan. *The Electronic Journal on Information Systems in Developing Countries*, *90*(4), e12315. DOI: 10.1002/isd2.12315

Angerschmid, A., Zhou, J., Theuermann, K., Chen, F., & Holzinger, A. (2022). Fairness and explanation in AI-informed decision making. *Mach. Learn. Knowl. Extr.*, *4*(2), 556–579. DOI: 10.3390/make4020026

Arinze, B. (2012). E-research collaboration in academia and industry. Int. *J. E-Collab.*, *8*(2), 1–13.

Audretsch, D. B., & Belitski, M. (2020). The limits to collaboration across four of the most innovative UK industries. *British Journal of Management*, *31*(4), 830–855. DOI: 10.1111/1467-8551.12353

Bidgoli, H. (2012). E-collaboration: New productivity tool for the twenty-first century and beyond. *Business Strategy Series*, *13*(4), 147–153. DOI: 10.1108/17515631211246212

Bing, Z. J., & Leong, W. Y. (2025). Ethical design of AI for education and learning systems. *ASM Sci. J.*, *20*(1), 1–9. DOI: 10.32802/asmscj.2025.1917

Brunetti, F., Matt, D. T., Bonfanti, A., De Longhi, A., Pedrini, G., & Orzes, G. (2020). Digital transformation challenges: Strategies emerging from a multi-stakeholder approach. *The TQM Journal*, *32*(4), 697–724. DOI: 10.1108/TQM-12-2019-0309

Chen, R., Zhang, B., & Chen, Y. (2024). How does digital transformation influence collaborative green innovation? *Journal of Global Information Management*, *32*(1), 1–21. DOI: 10.4018/JGIM.357728

Cociancig, C., Heuer, H., & Breiter, A. (2025). AI ethics unwrapped: An empirical investigation of ethical principles in collaborative ideation processes. *AI and Ethics*, *5*(3), 3159–3172. DOI: 10.1007/s43681-024-00638-9

Dhamo, A., Dhamo, I., & Manastirliu, I. (2023). Fundamental rights and new technologies. *Int. Jour. Res. Dev*, *10*(3), 121. DOI: 10.56345/ijrdv10n319

Esichaikul, V., Myint Aung, W., Bechter, C., & Rehman, M. (2013). Development and evaluation of wiki collaboration space for e-Learning. *Journal of Enterprise Information Management*, *26*(5), 536–552. DOI: 10.1108/JEIM-07-2013-0045

Ganan, D., Caballe, S., & Conesa, J. (2013, September). Towards software infrastructure for the systematic virtualization of collaborative learning sessions. 2013 5th International Conference on Intelligent and Collaborative Systems.

Garno, Z., Elkari, B., & Ourabah, L. (2025). AI-driven innovations in healthcare: Balancing technology with ethics. *World Medical & Health Policy*, *17*(3), 626–643. DOI: 10.1002/wmh3.70031

Gianfrancesco, M. A., Tamang, S., Yazdany, J., & Schmajuk, G. (2018). Potential biases in machine learning algorithms using electronic health record data. *JAMA Internal Medicine*, *178*(11), 1544–1547. DOI: 10.1001/jamainternmed.2018.3763 PMID: 30128552

Grant, O. (2024). Evaluating the effectiveness of supplier Relationship Management tools in E-commerce. In *Preprints*.

Guo, Y., & Wang, Y. (2025). Exploring the effects of artificial intelligence application on EFL students' academic engagement and emotional experiences: A mixed-methods study. *European Journal of Education*, *60*(1), e12812. DOI: 10.1111/ejed.12812

Hoic-Bozic, N., Holenko Dlab, M., & Mornar, V. (2016). Recommender system and web 2.0 tools to enhance a blended learning model. *IEEE Transactions on Education*, *59*(1), 39–44. DOI: 10.1109/TE.2015.2427116

Joseph, J., & Pandey, A. (2025). Human-AI collaborative intelligence. In *Advances in Computational Intelligence and Robotics* (pp. 403–422). IGI Global.

Keerio, M. U., Bajwa, M. S. B., Mugheri, N. H., Memon, R. H., Bhayo, M. A., & Samo, K. A. (2022). Evaluating students' perceptions of Microsoft Teams for online academics improvement. *PakJET*, *5*(1), 56–67. DOI: 10.51846/vol5iss1pp56-67

König, L. M., Allmeta, A., Perski, O., Smit, E. S., Newby, K., Vandelanotte, C., Poduval, S., Gordon, L., Gültzow, T., Alblas, M. C., Arden-Close, E., Braun Maya and Greffin, K., Hewitt, R., Knox, L., McCallum, C., McLaren, T., Szinay, D., Peuters, C., & DeSmet, A. (2024). Towards meaningful interdisciplinary and cross-sectoral digital health collaborations: Challenges and action-oriented solutions.

Kristensen, K., & Kijl, B. (2010). Collaborative performance. Int. *J. E-Collab.*, *6*(1), 53–69.

Li, Y., Wang, Y., Wang, L., & Xie, J. (2022). Investigating the effects of stakeholder collaboration strategies on risk prevention performance in a digital innovation ecosystem. *Industrial Management & Data Systems*, *122*(9), 2045–2071. DOI: 10.1108/IMDS-12-2021-0805

Linnes, C. (2020). Embracing the challenges and opportunities of change through electronic collaboration. *International Journal of Information Communication Technologies and Human Development, 12*(4), 37–58. DOI: 10.4018/IJICTHD.20201001.oa1

Magnisalis, I., & Demetriadis, S. (2015). Tool orchestration in e-collaboration. Int. *J. E-Collab., 11*(4), 40–63.

Melander, L., & Pazirandeh, A. (2019). Collaboration beyond the supply network for green innovation: Insight from 11 cases. *Supply Chain Management, 24*(4), 509–523. DOI: 10.1108/SCM-08-2018-0285

Prasad, M. S., & Roy, M. S. (2024). Investigating digital workspaces: Ethnographic obstacles and insights. International Journal For Multidisciplinary Research, 6(6).

Rabi, N. M. (2024). Unlocking trust in AI decision-making: The crucial role of confidence, transparency, and user perception. *Intl. J. Rel., 5*(10), 1866–1870. DOI: 10.61707/g4etk565

Rana, N. (2024). Ethical AI integration in marketing strategies for sustainable E-commerce fashion designing. In *Contemporary Management and Global Leadership for Sustainability* (pp. 218–233). IGI Global. DOI: 10.4018/979-8-3693-1273-5.ch013

Rawashdeh, A., Bakhit, M., & Abaalkhail, L. (2023). Determinants of artificial intelligence adoption in SMEs: The mediating role of accounting automation. *Int. J. Data Netw. Sci., 7*(1), 25–34. DOI: 10.5267/j.ijdns.2022.12.010

Ridwan, A., & Athena, T. (2023). Challenges and opportunities to collaborative distance learning in esp instruction. *Academic Journal Perspective : Education, Language, And, 11*(2), 79–97. DOI: 10.33603/6npwdw23

Samokhvalov, K. (2024). The transformative impact of Artificial Intelligence on the management consultancy sector. *Management Consulting Journal, 7*(1), 59–68. DOI: 10.2478/mcj-2024-0006

Schroder, A., & Constantiou, I., & Tuunainen Virpi and Austin, R. D. (2022). Human-AI collaboration – coordinating automation and augmentation tasks in a digital service company. Proceedings of the Annual Hawaii International Conference on System Sciences. DOI: 10.24251/HICSS.2022.025

Sharma, S., & Shrestha, S. (2024). Integrating HCI principles in AI: A review of human-Centered Artificial Intelligence applications and challenges. *J. Fut. Artif. Intell. Tech., 1*(3), 309–317. DOI: 10.62411/faith.3048-3719-47

Singla, V., Singh, S. K., Kumar, S., Chhabra, A., Gill, S. S., Arya, V., & Jain, A. (2025). Challenges and opportunities in sustainable AI and information systems. In *Advances in Computational Intelligence and Robotics* (pp. 73–96). IGI Global.

Song, X., Yang, S., Huang, Z., & Huang, T. (2019). The application of artificial intelligence in electronic commerce. *Journal of Physics: Conference Series*, *1302*(3), 32030. DOI: 10.1088/1742-6596/1302/3/032030

Tabbassum, A., Chintale, P., Praveen, & Najana, M. (2024). The impact of AI on future employment patterns. International Journal of Global Innovations and Solutions(IJGIS).

Tahri Sqalli, M., Aslonov, B., Gafurov, M., & Nurmatov, S. (2023). Humanizing AI in medical training: Ethical framework for responsible design. *Frontiers in Artificial Intelligence*, *6*, 1189914. DOI: 10.3389/frai.2023.1189914 PMID: 37261331

Terziyan, V., Tiihonen, T., Shukla, A. K., Gryshko, S., Golovianko, M., Terziyan, O., & Vitko, O. (2025). Towards ethical evolution: Responsible autonomy of artificial intelligence across generations. *AI and Ethics*, *5*(5), 5165–5190. DOI: 10.1007/s43681-025-00759-9

Tiwari, R. (2023). Explainable AI (XAI) and its applications in building trust and understanding in AI decision making. INTERANTIONAL JOURNAL OF SCIENTIFIC RESEARCH IN ENGINEERING AND, 07(01).

Turban, E., Liang, T.-P., & Wu, S. P. J. (2011). A framework for adopting collaboration 2.0 tools for virtual group decision making. *Group Decision and Negotiation*, *20*(2), 137–154. DOI: 10.1007/s10726-010-9215-5

Urbinati, A., Manelli, L., Frattini, F., & Bogers, M. L. A. M. (2022). The digital transformation of the innovation process: Orchestration mechanisms and future research directions. *Innovation (North Sydney, N.S.W.)*, *24*(1), 65–85. DOI: 10.1080/14479338.2021.1963736

Utomo, D. T. P., Ahsanah, F., & Ryandini, E. Y. (2024). EFL students' voices of blended collaborative learning in completing digital end-of-semester projects. *Journal of English Education Program*, *5*(1). Advance online publication. DOI: 10.26418/jeep.v5i1.71928

van der Meij, M. G., Kupper, F., Beers Pieter, J., & Broerse, J. E. W. (2016). Hybrid e-learning tool TransLearning: Video storytelling to foster vicarious learning within multi-stakeholder collaboration networks. *International Journal of Lifelong Education*, *35*(4), 413–429. DOI: 10.1080/02601370.2016.1197331 van der Veer, S. N., Riste, L., Cheraghi-Sohi, S., Phipps, D. L., Tully, M. P., Bozentko, K., Atwood, S., Hubbard, A., Wiper, C., Oswald, M., & Peek, N. (2021). Trading off accuracy and explainability in AI decision-making: Findings from 2 citizens' juries. *Journal of the American Medical Informatics Association : JAMIA*, *28*(10), 2128–2138. DOI: 10.1093/jamia/ocab127 PMID: 34333646

Zelda, Y. C., Prabowo, B. A., & Satato, Y. R.Yema Charista ZeldaBayu Ade PrabowoYuniarto Rahmad Satato. (2024). Kebangkitan E-commerce Bertenaga AI: Mengubah Lanskap Bisnis di Tahun 2024. *Prosiding Seminar Nasional Ilmu Manajemen Kewirausahaan Dan*, *1*(1), 237–259. DOI: 10.61132/prosemnasimkb.v1i1.20

KEY TERMS AND DEFINITIONS

5G: Fifth-generation wireless technology providing high bandwidth and ultra-low latency, enabling real-time immersive collaboration through video, AR/VR, and edge computing.

Artificial General Intelligence (AGI): Advanced AI concept where machines achieve human-like reasoning and problem-solving abilities across diverse tasks .

Artificial Intelligence (AI): Technology that enhances decision-making, automates routine tasks, and provides predictive insights through natural language processing, machine learning, and intelligent assistance .

Augmented Reality (AR)/Virtual Reality (VR): Immersive technologies creating interactive 3D collaboration environments for remote meetings, training, and design.

Autonomous Agents: AI-driven entities capable of independently initiating, executing, and coordinating collaborative tasks.

Blockchain: A decentralized digital ledger ensuring trust, transparency, and immutability in collaborative processes, especially across distributed teams .

Collaborative Control: Design principle ensuring humans retain final authority in decision-making, even when AI assists with automation.

Collaborative Ecosystem: An integrated environment combining AI, IoT, blockchain, and immersive technologies to support adaptive, secure, and human-centered teamwork.

Collaborative Intelligence: Symbiotic partnership between human creativity and machine efficiency, enabling smarter, adaptive, and context-aware decision-making .

Digital Twin: A virtual replica of real-world data streams or entities, used for simulation, prediction, and collaborative decision-making (e.g., in healthcare).

E-Collaboration: Digital interaction and cooperation among individuals and organizations using electronic tools such as email, messaging, file sharing, and video conferencing.

Explainable AI (XAI): AI systems designed to make their decision-making process transparent and interpretable for users, increasing trust and accountability.

Hybrid Intelligence (Human–AI Teaming): Integration of human cognitive skills (creativity, empathy, judgment) with AI capabilities (speed, scale, data processing) for enhanced outcomes .

Internet of Things (IoT): Network of connected devices and sensors that enable real-time data collection, monitoring, and context-aware collaboration.

IoMT (Internet of Medical Things): Extension of IoT in healthcare, integrating wearable devices and sensors with AI for remote monitoring, diagnostics, and collaborative care .

Machine Learning (ML): A subset of AI where algorithms learn patterns from data to make predictions or recommendations without explicit programming.

Over-Automation: Excessive reliance on AI systems that risks reducing human judgment, creativity, and critical thinking in collaboration.

Quantum Computing: An emerging computing paradigm using quantum mechanics to solve complex optimization and simulation problems beyond classical capabilities .

Responsible AI: Ethical framework ensuring AI systems are fair, transparent, inclusive, secure, and aligned with human values.

Chapter 2
Forecasting UPI Transaction Value in India:
A Machine Learning Regression Approach to Customer-Initiated Payments

T. K. Sateesh Kumar
https://orcid.org/0000-0002-8406-409X
Kristu Jayanti University, India

Juby Thomas
https://orcid.org/0000-0003-2167-0620
Kristu Jayanti University, India

Lijo Thomas
https://orcid.org/0009-0009-7031-5001
Kristu Jayanti University, India

Vishnu Achutha Menon
https://orcid.org/0000-0003-4028-3685
Centarl University, India

ABSTRACT

The Unified Payment Interface (UPI) has a revolutionized the landscape of digital payment in India by facility seamless real time transaction across multiple bank and Financial Institutions. This study investigates the impact of customer-initiated transactions and total transactions value in India's UPI ecosystem using machine

DOI: 10.4018/979-8-3373-5747-8.ch002

learning regression model. The study utilizers data set of 1811 (n) obtained from the NPCI website. For the analysis of the data received researcher adopted comparison of Linear Regression, Random Forest (RF), XGBoost algorithm to predict total transaction value-based customer-initiated transactions. The finding reveals that RF model achieves the significant as compare to the other models in terms of R2, RMSE, and MAE. The study contributes to the understanding of digital payment ecosystem that provide empirical evidence for the effective UPI retail sales growth of ensemble learning models in financial transaction predictions.

INTRODUCTION

The Unified Payment Interface (UPI) has revolutionized India's digital payment landscape by facilitating seamless and real time transaction across multiple banks and Financial Institutions. Indeed, the launch of UPI, a digital platform system by the National Payment Corporation (NPCI) by the government of India in the year 2016, has boosted significantly digital transaction between people to people / peer to peer (P2P), and customer to business (P2B) specially in retail sector (TET 2024; EPC 2024). With the exponential growth in transaction volumes and values it is required to understand the predictive relationship between the various transaction parameter (TET 2024). The understanding of this (UPI) exponential growth in the digital payments, is very vital for the academicians and practitioner. In fact, the use of UPI platforms as significantly impact the economy by bridging the digital divide (Patra & Sethi, 2023; Patnaik, 2019).

The digital payment ecosystem generated vast amount of transactional data which consists of valuable insight on the consumer behaviour, market Trends, and eco system performance. The ability to understand accurately and predict total transaction value based on the customer-initiated parameters can facilitate and support to make informed strategic decision. This studying of the UPI transaction behaviour helps to make better risk management decisions and resource allocation in financial technology firms (FinTech). The consumer behaviour is dynamic in nature (Kotler et al., 2014) and influenced by the payment behaviour of individual is nudged on prevailing ecosystem and subtleties of Economy. Understanding of dynamics and facets the digital transaction has become very crucial for financial institution, policy makers and Fintech companies to make strategic decisions.

The financial ecosystem prevailing in developing Nations such as in Indian subcontinent is important and with high volatility. It includes demographic features, technological advancement, digital infrastructure, and regulation imposed by the government agencies (Heji et al., 2024; Thapliyal et al., 2025) . On the prominent payment system in the developing economy is digital wallet which is based on the smart mobile phone applications either with QR scanner or phone number which are connected to network of banks. And prime features of the UPI is the participation of the large pool of bankers, who agreed to participate in the integration of payment system with linked mobile numbers as well as with UPI platform (Vidani, 2024; Lakshmi et al., 2019). The bankers are agreed to work on the common platform of digital payment system with the unique mobile no.s of multiple services provides viz., Fintech companies under BHIM, Google pay, PhonePay etc (Vidani, 2024; Lakshmi et al., 2019).

LITERATURE REVIEW

Digital payment systems have received a great deal of attention recently. Researchers have examined different aspects of transaction behavior, many predictive modelling and system performance techniques. These include machine learning techniques which are implemented in financial arena. The advanced machine learning techniques have shown some success over the last decade for fraud detection, examining customer behavior and predicting transactions (Sahi et al., 2022; Hassan et al., 2020).

On the advent of Ensemble learning techniques, especially Random Forest and XGBoost, have outperformed other machine learning (ML) algorithms in financial prediction because they can capture complex, non-linear relationships. These ML techniques can also handle feature interactions and selection. Some conventional statistic techniques were utilized viz., Linear Regression (LR), which are favourite for the academicians and practitioner as they facilitate - consumer benchmark for the transparency and computational speed.

Digital payment systems, particularly in the emerging economy of India where the UPI platform has changed the nature of transaction behaviour (Shree 2020), have grown tremendously. Data from the Reserve Bank of India (PIB 2024) indicates that UPI has become the predominant digital transaction system with over 70% of the volume from retail digital transactions occurring on that platform.

Empirical studies demonstrated that a strong positive relation between the customer transaction frequency and the total transaction value (Hussain et al., 2025; Singha 2024). Thereby highlighting the increase of user participation and directly influencing the flow of monitory aspect across the system (PIB 2024; Hussain et al., 2025; Singha & Singha, 2024). Researchers also found that customer initiated up at transactions contribute significantly to liquidity circulation of money across the financial ecosystem. This serves as a leading indicator of monthly retails plaining and well-being of the economic system (Tiwari et al., 2019; Singh et al., 2019 & Yadav et al., 2024).

The prior studies supports theories of transactional efficiency (A. Das et al., 2017; Sharma et al., 2019; Manrai et al., 2021) this suggests that access and ease of transactions will maximize throughput. Although an observation by Aditya & Ekyawan, (2021) and Faraz & Anjum, (2025), propose 'an higher transactional behaviour' would supports significantly and also impact for bridging the digital divide'. The studies of Tripathi (2020) who investigated mobile payment apps from India and standpoint on system driven evidence and developed the feature importance of transactional volume and liquidity flow (Hadwan et al., 2022; Manrai et al.,2021) of customer-initiated transactions. Using correlation and regression analysis, they provided empirical evidence at their dataset level of mobile payment apps that overall transaction volumes had a statistically significant relationship at the aggregate total transaction dollar amounts, especially with P2P (peer-to-peer) transactions on average. The academia has examined the vigorously on the importance of the customer centric on the total volume of business (Aditya & Ekyawan, 2021; Fahmi et al., 2025). These prior studies on financial markets shows vitality of the customer transactions and the impact of the total financial transactions are discussed. In these studies, scholars made effort in prediction of values, but, rarely on the customer-initiated transactions impacting on the total transaction value and volume specially in the UPI eco system. This research gap is addressed by developing of the RQ1.

The rise of machine learning as enabled FinTech companies to have more sophisticated prediction of financial outcomes. The traditional model such as linear regression are highly valued for their interpretability but often the limit in capturing complex nonlinear relationship within transaction data. On the other hand, Random Forest, XGBoost have been widely recognised for their superior performance in financial prediction modelling on the advent of AI and ML (Tiwari et al., 2019; Hussain et al., 2025; Sharma et al., 2019 & Shree et al., 2021).

For model selection in financial prediction task largely depends on the trade-off between the accuracy, generalizability and interpretability. Scholars (Das et al., 2017; Hussain et al.,2025) have examined Random Forest along with the UPI data, it is found that the Random Forest provides optimum RMSE and MAPE values in comparison to both linear models and boosting techniques. These studies emphasise that Random Forest model exhibit the capability to generalise the unseen data optimally.

Studies also examined and tested various regression model for forecasting mobile wallet transactions (Sharma et al., 2019; Nagadeepa et al., 2024). The literature reveals to Machine Learning and Artificial Intelligence confirm the superiority of the ensemble bagging models. The ensemble bagging models like a Random Forest have achieved best predicting stability and minimum residual variance (TK 2024). These ensemble model under machine learning technique (viz., Random Forest and XG boost) suits well for the dataset which characterised by the high level transaction variability and with the maximum outliers.

Digital payment system has gathered a significant attention in the recent year with the researcher exploring the various aspects of transaction behaviour by use of predictive Modelling and system performance. Machine learning application in financial technology have demonstrate a promising result in fraud detection customer behaviour analysis and transaction (Ch & Singha, 2024; Manikandan et al., 2024). Ensemble learning models particularly Random Forest and XG boost have shown superior performance in financial transactions prediction due to their ability to capture Complex nonlinear relationship to handle feature interaction effectively. Traditionally linear regression remains the benchmark for the comparison due to the interpretability and computational efficiency.

The comparative analysis of regression algorithm in if financial context revealed that most model performance is highly dependent on data characteristics such as feature selection and problem complexity. This motivate the current systematic comparison of three distinct algorithms (both traditional and advanced ML/AI) approaches to UPI transaction prediction.

Digital payment system have witnessed exponential growth in platform like UPI revolutionising the transaction behaviour in emerging economy such as India. The RBI report 2023 (PIB 2024) reveals that UPI become the backbone of digital transaction and which accounts for 70% of the retail digital payment value (TET 2024; EPC 2023). Studies such as Sateesh et al., (2025) have empirically exemplified a strong positive relationship between the customer transaction frequency and that total digital transaction value there by highlighting the increased user participation in digital integration.

It was found that customer initiated up at transaction contribute significantly to liquidity of money circulation in the financial ecosystem there by serving as a leading indicator of retail transaction growth. These findings also align with 'Theory of Transactional Efficiency', which shows that increased access and convenience can lead financial quantum.

Furthermore, some researcher has applied correlation and regression analysis to data set of mobile digital payment in India and reported that transaction volume as statistical is significate on the transaction value specially in Peer to Peer (P2P) segments .

The rise of Advanced Machine learning and artificial Intelligence models, with enhanced infrastructure in telecommunications fuelled the fintech firms to have equip themselves with accurate prediction of financial outcomes, specially in digital payment wallets systems. The traditional regression models such as linear regression have offers more interpretability but limited in capturing complex non linear relation between the data set. However on the other hand Random Forest and XGBoost have given widely recognised as superior performance specially for financial modelling (Sateesh et al 2025; J Thomas et al., 2025).

For instance, many researcher Fahmi et al., (2025) and Lakshmi et al., (2019), have compared multiple machine learning models to forecast financial transaction volumes and found that Random Forest has out performed other models due to the ability of these machine learning algorithms to capture hierarchical data patterns through Gradient boosting (GB) algorithams. These GBs are often used along with decision tree for predictive modelling in imbalanced data set which is very common in financial data set.

Scholars also applied in ensemble machine learning methods for analysing digital banking data. It is observed that Random Forest delivered the best generalization of performance where are as XGBoost offered more faster convergence but very sensitive to Hyper parameters. This supports the need for more comparison of the different models particularly in the aspect of financial transactions. There is seldom comparative analysis of regression algorithms in financial contexts found and with few studies on model performance evaluation. The studies which are for assessing the model performance restricts to the characteristics of the data, features selection and system complexity, but not comparability with advanced techniques. Consequently, the current study now compares three different algorithmic approaches to UPI transaction prediction in the RQ2. Thus, the researcher developed research question 2 based on the need for comparing the ensemble machine learning methods in predictive modelling.

Model selection is another important area of research wherein which financial prediction task depends on the trade off between accuracy, generalizability and interpretability. Many studies have conducted using Indian UPI data and they have demonstrated that Random Forest provided optimum RMSE and MAPE values as compared to other Linear Regression model and other boosting techniques. Studies also examined ensemble models such as Random Forest, XGBoost model etc to achieve best predictive stability and minimum residual variance. Nevertheless, ample studies emphasise on the model accuracy, reliability and generalizability with omissions of the areas viz., digital payment system such as UPI, therefore, the current study examines these parameters in the RQ 3.

Some studies He et al (2009); Aggarwal et al., 2021 and Breiman et al., (2001) and have also compared multiple machine learning (ML) models to forecast financial transaction volumes and found that Random Forest performed superior to other traditional models due to the robustness and subduing over fitting capability of the model in non linear transactions. Similarly studies (J Thomas et al 2025; Sateesh 2025) also highlighted XG boost perform effectively in capturing - hierarchical data, faster convergence however, insignificant to more sensitive to the hyper parameters. This supports for addressing the need for systematic model comparison particularly in domains with heteroscedastic and time varying transaction behaviour.

Research Gap

While existing literature extensively covers the growth, adoption and behaviour pattern of digital payment systems like a UPI in India, however, limited empirical research have systematically examine the quantitative aspects. There are seldom of studies on impact of customer initiative transaction parameter on total transaction value using advanced machine learning regression. The most importantly, the studies examined and relied on traditional statistical model or focused on isolated predictions without a comparative model examination and evaluation. Furthermore, there are ensemble learning methods and models such as Random Forest and XGboost - that have shown promise in the financial prediction task. The application of these techniques in the context of India's UPI ecosystem remains underexplored. The current study address this gap by striving to develop Research questions and answering. In this process, researcher provides a comprehensive model of comparison between the linear regression Random Forest and XGBoost to determine the most accurate reliable and generalizable approach for predicting total transaction value based on the customer behaviour in digital payment. Hence, the below research questions have been developed,

RQ1: What is the impact of customer-initiated transaction volume and value on the total transaction value in the UPI ecosystem?
RQ2: How do different regression models (Linear Regression, Random Forest, and XGBoost) perform in predicting the total transaction value?
RQ3: Which model provides the optimal accuracy, reliability and generalizability for impact analysis of UPI transactions?

After defining the research questions, the researcher in expounded the conceptual and theoretical definition within the ambit of this research.

Conceptual Definitions

With aim of understanding the impact of customer-initiated transaction volume and value on the total transaction in the UPI system, the researcher have considered machine learning algorithms. Hence, the requires to define the conceptual aspects of the study.

Unified Payment Interface (UPI) - The Unified Payment Interface also known known as UPI is the real time payment system developed by the national payment Corporation of India (NPCI) thereby enabling user to link multiple bank accounts to perform instant money transfer via single mobile interface application. This represents a corner-stone advancement in India's digital financial ecosystem, which facilitates customer initiated and merchant directed payment systems.

Customer initiated transactions - these are the payment transactions initiated by the directly by the customers through UPI enabled platforms to Peer to Peer (P2P) or Business to Customers (B2C) purposes. These transactions reflect the user engagement, and adoption of technology in digital payment landscape.

Total transaction value - This refers to the aggregated monetary value (in Rupees crore), of all the transactions executed over the UPI platform within the defined time frame. It serves as a key indicator of financial activity and digital payment system.

Machine learning regression models - This includes all the supervised machine learning algorithms which are used to predict the continuous dependent variable (total transaction value) based on one or more independent variables. The study uses linear regression Random Forest and XGBoost which are employed to capture the relationship between the UPI transaction parameters and total value.

Impact analysis - The data driven approach is an approach where in which the understanding of how the independent variables that is transaction volume and value, influence or predict a dependent variable viz., total transaction value within the UPI ecosystem.

Theoretical Definition

After defining of the conceptual definition, the study undertakes the definition of the theory which exists. This theoretical definition is paramount as they are guiding and foundation of the research study. In this stage the researcher has defined the theoretical and model-based concepts which are utilised in this research. In this study, several predictive regression models are utilized and thereby these have been theoretically defined and applied to analyse the influence in selection of features on the total transaction value in UPI eco system. The guiding models are grounded in both classical and ensemble-based machine learning theories which are outlined below.

The general predict modelling task can be mathematically formulated as in the equation 1.

$$\hat{y} = f(X) + \varepsilon \qquad (1)$$

Where,

- $\hat{y}$ is the predicted output (total transaction value),
- $f(X)$ is the regression function that maps inputs to predictions,
- ε is the error term accounting for noise or unexplained variance in the data.

Linear regression theory - The linear regression is grounded theory in the classical Ordinary Least Square (OLS) framework. It assumes a linear relationship between the predictors and response, thus, minimising the sum of square residual. Which is denoted mathematically in equation 2

$$\hat{y} = \beta_0 + \beta_1 X_1 + \beta_2 X_2 + \varepsilon \quad (2)$$

Where:

- $\hat{y}$ is the predicted value of the dependent variable,
- β_0 is the intercept,
- β_1,β_2 are slope coefficients,
- X_1,X_2 are predictor variables,
- ε is the error term assumed to be normally distributed with mean zero and constant variance.

This model is interpretable but limited in capturing the nonlinear and heteroscedasticity.

Random Forest regression theory – which is based on the ensemble learning and bagging principle, Random Forest construct multiple decision trees using bootstrap data samples and random features subsets. The final prediction is the average of all the prediction from all the trees shown in equation 3.

$$\hat{y} = \frac{1}{B}\sum_{b=1}^{B} T_b(X) \quad (3)$$

Where:

- B is the total number of trees,
- $T_b(X)$ is the prediction from the bth decision tree,
- X is the feature vector. Each tree trained on bootstrap sample with random feature selection

Where $T_b(X)$ is the prediction from the bth tree. The model is one of the robust methods to over fitting dataset, handles non-linearity and interact among variables effectively.

XG boost regression theory - In this is a type of Gradient Boosting technique which is frequently utilized to build trees to minimise a regularised objective function, this is denoted as The prediction at the tth iteration is given in the equation 4:

$$\widehat{y^{(t)}} = \widehat{y^{(t-1)}} + \eta \cdot h_t(X) \quad (4)$$

where:

- $\widehat{y^{(t)}}$ = prediction at iteration t
- η = learning rate
- $h_t(X)$ is the weak learner (e.g., regression tree) at iteration t.

The objective function for minimization is denoted in equation 5:

$$\text{Obj} = \sum_{i=1}^{n} l\left(y_i, \widehat{y_i^{(t)}}\right) + \sum_{k=1}^{K} \Omega(f_k) \quad (5)$$

Where l Is the loss function i.e., squared error and $\Omega(fk)$ is a regularisation term to control model complexity. XG boost emphasize error corrections and effective handling Complex with the capability of handling high dimensionality data.

For assessing the effectiveness of regression models performances, researcher utilised some of the indices as below (Evaluation Metrics).

R^2 Coefficient of determination - which measures the proportion of variance in the dependent variable that is predictable from the independent variable as denoted in equation 6.

Coefficient of Determination (R^2)

$$R^2 = 1 - \frac{\sum_{i=1}^{n} (y_i - \hat{y}i)^2}{\sum i = 1^n (y_i - \bar{y})^2} \quad (6)$$

RMSE (Root Means Square Error) - which is a reflection of the square root of average of square differences between the predicted and actual values, however it is sensitive to the large errors as denoted in 7.

$$RMSE = \sqrt{\frac{1}{n} \sum_{i=1}^{n} (y_i - \hat{y}_i)^2} \quad (7)$$

MAE (Mean Absolute Error) - this measures average magnitude of errors in predictions irrespective of the direction of the moment of quantities in equation 8.

$$MAE = \frac{1}{n} \sum_{i=1}^{n} |y_i - \hat{y}_i| \quad (8)$$

MAPE Mean Absolute Percentage Error – This indicators is one, which expresses prediction accuracy as a percentage, thus, making it scale independent but sensitive to near Zero actual values in equation 9.

$$MAPE = \frac{100\%}{n} \sum_{i=1}^{n} \left| \frac{y_i - \hat{y}_i}{y_i} \right| \tag{9}$$

RESEARCH METHODOLOGY

Research methodology consists of a road map for how the current research is carried forward. With a surge in digital transactions across the globe, India is not exempt from the impact of technology on the economy. This empirical research is focusing on understanding how the impact of digital technology specially to the digital wallets on reducing the digital divide.

With the research goal (addressing RQs), the researcher collected 1811 observations from NPCI website. The data set consists of various UPI transaction related variables such as customer-initiated transaction volume (in million), customer-initiated transaction value (in crore) B2C transaction volume (in million) B2C transaction value (in crore) B2B transaction volume (in million), B2B transaction value (in crore), On-Us transaction volume (in million in crore), the total volume (in million) that total value (in crore and month). However, the current study examines few variables viz., customer-initiated transaction volume and customer-initiated transactions value as predictor variables and total value as the target variable. This selection is based on the operation complexity and nature of variables. It is assumed that the selected variables are directly impacted and vis-à-vis on each other in the context of UPI operations.

A regression-based impact analysis is conducted in three different models viz., linear regression Random Forest regression, and XGBoost regression. The data pre-processing includes feature selection, data scaling, and train & test splitting (80% training 20% testing). The hyper parameter tuning is also applied to Random Forest XG boost using python package 'GridSearchCV'. These models are evaluated based R^2 score, RMSE and MAPE indices.

Unified Payment Interface (UPI) operates within the multi facet platform ecosystem wherein the multiple stakeholders interact through a common technological infrastructure. The theories developed for evaluation of economic activity network efficiency theory (Katz & Shapiro, 1985; Breiman 2001), which signifies the value of digital payment ecosystem. These studies amplify the digital payment system which can increases exponentially with the number of participant and creating positive feedback loops around the nation economy environment by volume and value growth.

Data Processing and Model Training

In the data processing phase the following steps are carried in this study. In the first is feature selection process, wherein, researcher determined (based on importance, as in RoL) certain features conserved as a predictor customer-initiated transaction value, customer-initiated transaction volume viz., (*V_ci*, *Val_ci* as predictors). The variable "Total Value (Cr)" of UPI transactions i.e., *Val_total* as target variable. In this study data scaling using standard scalar package 'StandardScaler', and training of the data set by dividing the 80% and 20% ratio for training and testing. The study also adopted package 'GridSearchCV', hyper parameter optimising using for Random Forest and XG boost.

The cross validation was implemented using 5-fold stratified sampling to ensure the robust model evaluation and thereby preventing over fitting.

RESULTS AND DISCUSSION

In the next phase the researcher examines the results and discussed the results within the context of the research questions. In this phase, researcher examined model performance in table form and also in the representation of figures for better synthesizing for research questions.

At first the performance of three different models are analysed in the table one. In the table 1, a summarized the model performance of linear regression Random Forest and XGBoost are compared in parameter of R^2 score, RMSE, MAE and MAPE.

Table 1. Showing model performance

Model	R^2 Score	RMSE	MAE	MAPE
Linear Regression	0.9998	2193.84	717.98	2152.59%
Random Forest	0.9998	2118.18	589.10	3.89%
XGBoost	0.9963	9219.97	1851.57	40.69%

In the table 1, which is a representation of regression model performance with comparison of the different performance matrix. These three regressions models - linear regression, Random Forest and XG boost which are designated to predict UPI transaction value. Both a linear regression and Random Forest exhibit exceptionally high R^2 scores of 0.9998, indicating a near perfect fit to the data with a Random Forest showing slightly lower RMSE of and MAE. This manifest the significance of the models overall accuracy. While the XGBoost still performing well, which has significantly lower R square that is 0.9963, indeed, this model shows the higher

RMSE and MAE, thereby indicating less accuracy as it compared to other two regression models. Notwithstanding, linear regression shows an extremely high MAPTE value, which is due to the presence of very small actual value leading to an inflated percentage error, overall, the Random Forest demonstrate the best performance in terms of MAPE.

In the table 1, which shows that customer-initiated Transactions Volume and Value significantly impact the Transaction Value. The R^2 scores across all models indicates a strong relationship between these three variables, confirming their predictive power in determining Total Transaction Value in UPI ecosystem. The results suggest that the results signify the regression models are able to predict UPI transaction as result shows > 0.99. This address RQ1 i.e., that 'there is an impact of customer-initiated transaction volume and value on the total transaction value in the UPI ecosystem'.

Similarly, the results of the models' performance and evaluation of different models reveals that the both Linear Regression and rand 0.9998, while XG boost despite its complexity lacks behind with the are square score of 0.9963 shown in table 1. This suggest that the traditional regression techniques and an ensemble-based models can effectively capture the Transaction Trends whereas Gradient Boosting methods may not be able to always out perform in financial dataset does this analysis leads to addressing RQ2.

The Random Forest Regression emergence as the most reliable model due to its low RMSE, MAE and MAPE. While the Linear Regression performed similarly in terms of R^2, but it is extremely high MAPE that is 2152.59% indicates poor reliability which is depicted in the table 1. However, XGBoost model, despite it is ability to capture the non-linear patterns shows a significant and but higher error metrics making it less suitable for impact analysis in the context of UPI digital wallet transactions.

By the cross validity of the results, this further reinforce the findings that Random Forest maintains high stability and lower errors as compared to XGBoost and Linear Regression. Therefore, Random Forest Regression is recommended as the most suitable model for analysing the impact of UPI digital transaction 'Total Transaction Value'. Thus, this suffices and addresses research question 3. In the next section will elobrate visually the results and synthesis with the RQs subsequently.

Further the study examines these machine learning regression models visually in figure 1 Figure 2 figure 3 and figure 4. The first figure is concerned about the summery of the all the regression models.

Figure 1. Showing performance of three machine learning models

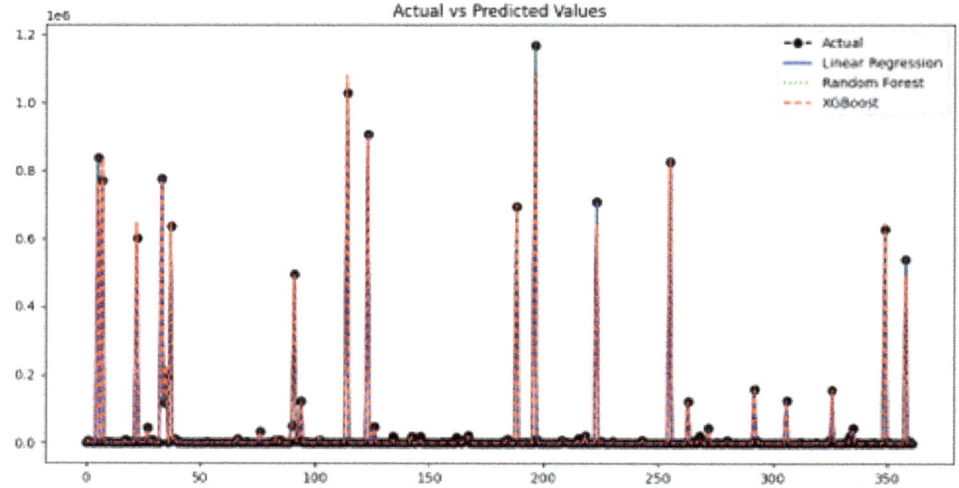

In the figure 1, which is a depiction of performance of three machine learning models viz., Linear Regression, Random Forest and XGBoost in predicting up a transactions such as Transaction Amount against the Actual Values. All three model shows a high degree of overlap with the actual values suggesting good predictive accuracy. However, there are few noticeable deviations particularly for large transaction value indicating the potential area for model improvement or for the presence of outliers in the impact predictions. This also paves the way for further investigation in future studies, which is discussed in the 'further scope and conclusion' section.

Figure 2. Shows residuals for Linear Regression model

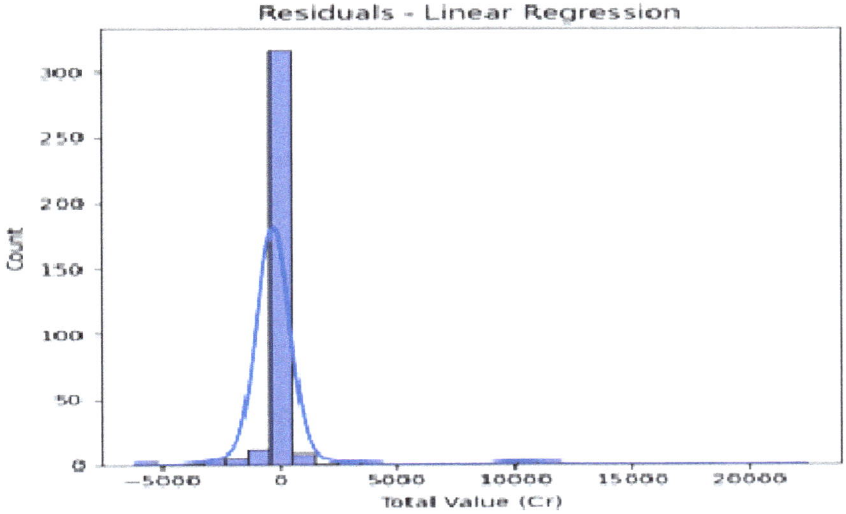

The second figure 2, which is a histogram depiction of the residuals of linear regression model. The Linear Regression model is adopted in the current study to predict the total value (in Crores) of UPI transactions. The distribution is heavily skewed towards zero, with the sharp peak indicating that the model predictions are generally very close to the actual values. However, there are long tales extending towards the both positive and negative value suggesting the presence of outliers or instances where models predictions are deviate significantly. The concentration of the data sets around the zero suggest that the linear regression model performs reasonable for the most of the data points in predicting the total value of UPI transaction but with few extreme outlier values.

Figure 3. Figure showing distribution of residuals for Random Forest regression Model

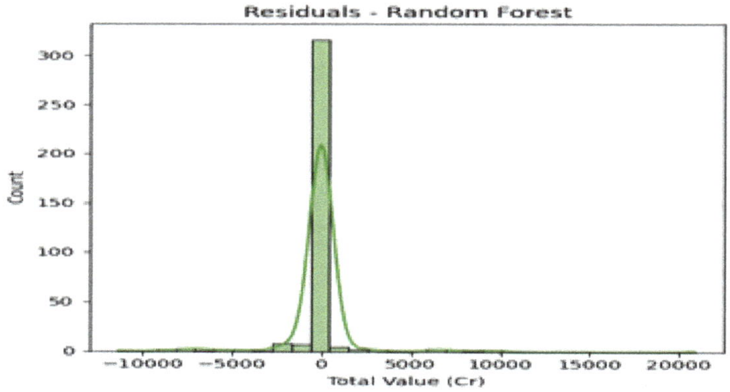

The figure 3, which is a depiction of the distribution of residual for Random Forest regression model which is utilised for predicting the total value (in Crores) of UPI digital valid transactions. This histogram shows a highly concentrated peak around 0 indicating the Random Forest models predictions are generally very accurate for a large portion of the data. However, these are similar to the Linear Regression model. There exist some noticeable tales extending to the both positive and negative values there by suggesting the presence of outlier or instances where the model predictions deviate significantly. The narrow peak compared to the Linear Regression suggest that the Random Forest model might be slightly better in capturing the central tendency of the data.

Figure 4. Showing residuals for XG Boost regression Model

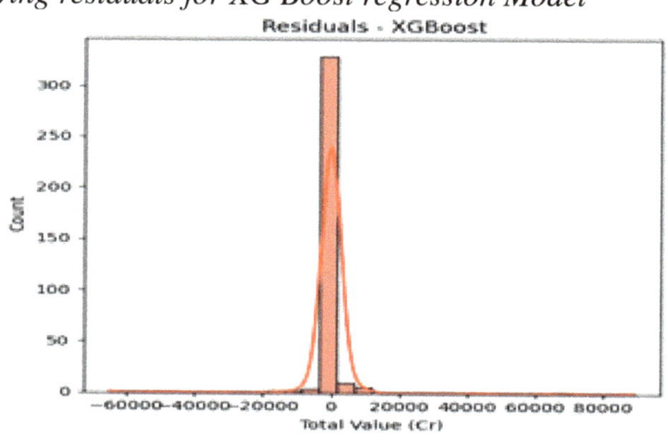

In the figure 4, which illustrate the residence for XGBoost regression models utilised in this study to predict the total value (in Crores) of UPI digital payment transaction. The histogram reveals a very sharp and tall peak centred around zero suggesting that the XGBoost model predictions are highly accurate for substantial portion of the data set. Nevertheless, the graph also displays long, but thin tails extending for both into the positive negative values indicating the presence of some outliers which can impact the model predictions are considerably. The narrowness of the central peak compared to the Linear Regression and the Random Forest model suggest that XGBoost may offer the best fit for majority of the data points.

Research Question Analysis

In this section, the researcher analysed the research questions in-line with research test results obtained through the different model validation matrix and visual representation. In this section, researcher analysed all the research questions, to begin with research question one (RQ1. In the Reserve question 1, as stated is 'what is the impact of customer-initiated transaction volume and value on the total transaction value in the UPI ecosystem '. For this research question researcher considered the R^2 score which is exceptionally high score with 0.9963 across all regression models, thus, all model demonstrate a strong linear and nonlinear relationship between the customer-initiated transactions value and volume with all parameters. This can be expressed in mathematically intuition as 'the total transaction value' validated as

$$Val_{total} = f(V_{ci}, Val_{ci}) + \varepsilon$$

Where f explains > 99.6% of the total variance in total transaction value (Val_{total}). This confirms that the customer-initiated transaction volume (V_{ci}) and value (Val_{ci}) as primary determinants of total UPI ecosystem value. This result also signifies with the correlation Coefficient approaching Unity, with insignificant unexplained variance (ε).

After addressing Research question 1, researcher takes up research question two (RQ2). In this RQ2, which is concerned about comparative of the model performance. In precise the RQ2 states 'how do different regression models (linear regression, Random Forest and XGBoost perform in predicting the total transaction value?'. For this researcher considered table 1 value wherein, the different indices are shown for all machine learning regression models along the linear regression models R^2 score (*cf* He et al., 2009). As per as the linear regression is concerned, this model is showing R^2 value of = 0.998, but the extremely high 2152.59%, indicating poor reliability for small value predictions (*cf* He et al., 2009). Thus, this model is not performing well.

The second regression model is Random Forest model, which is basically machine learning regression model. The Random Forest regression model achieves optimum balance with r square of 0.9998, with the MAPE is = 3.89%, thereby demonstrating a superior handling heteroscedasticity (Aggarwal 2021). Thus, Random Forest model performs well

Another important regression model which this study considered for evaluating under digital UPI payment system is XG boost. This machine learning algorithm technique achieved a comparatively lower square of 0.9963 with higher error in other metrics (*cf* TK 2024; Breiman 2001), suggesting over fitting for sub optimal hyper parameter configuration.

The ensemble bagging approach (Random Forest), out-performed both linear and gradient boosting methods, due to the robustness against outlier and effective variance reduction through bootstrap aggregation. By comparing performance of the different model in predicting the total transaction value the study address the RQ2

On the final Research Question (RQ3) which is concerned about model selection recommendation, in precise the RQ3 states – 'which model provides the optimal accuracy, reliability and generalisability for impact analysis of UPI transactions?'.

This question is addressed by examining the different matrices of machine learning and linear regression models such as accuracy, reliability and generalisability. At first, considering the lowest RMSE (2118.18) and MAE (589.10) Random Forest regression model emergence as the most optimal model. Indeed, the Random Forest also exhibits lowest MAPE (3.89%), thereby it indicates a consistent performance across the value range (*cf* Sateesh 2025; He et al., 2009). As per the generalisability concerned, the Random Forest is superior across cross validation performance with the stable error matrix. Thus, the researcher addresses the research question 3, which model is vis-à-vis on 'suitable model for analysing and forecasting' digital wallet data, namely UPI transaction in India.

After addressing the research question 1, 2 and 3, study expanded on understanding the residual analysis which is depicted from figure 2 to 4. This visual analysis is carried to strengthen the argument on the result output obtained int eh table 1. In the figure 2, which depicts the residuals for linear regression model. This figure to exhibits the heavy tail distribution with the more concentration in and around '0' notwithstanding, having significant outliers. Whereas in the Random Forest as shown in the figure 3, has narrow peak with reduced outlier impact. The last figure (figure 4) is which is depiction of residual XGBoost regression model, wherein sharpest central peak but extreme outliner indicate potential over fitting of the model.

In the last phase of the data analysis, the current study embarks on assessing the statistical significance of the model performance (statistical difference). Assessment of cross-validation results confirms that there exists the statistical difference among performance of the three different regression models. The Random Forest versus linear equation shown probability value of less than 0.001, (MAPE value comparison). As per the Random Forest v/s XGBoost exhibit the probability value shown less than 0.001 (RMSE comparison).

Implication Application of the Study

This study shows practical applications in diverse area such as financial Institutions, fintech companies and for policy makers. The practical implication for financial institution includes the application of a random for model, which can improve and can provide reliable transaction value predictions for improving liquidity management and risk assessment. The practical applications for Fintech companies are elaborate, it includes, an overview on strong predictive relationship between variables. It aids Fintech companies to take data driven product development decisions and development of customer acquisition strategy. By understanding the dynamics of the infrastructure required for digital payment system this study provides enormous information and enables the decision makers (policy makers) to develop regulatory framework and economic policy formulation.

Technical Contribution

This study also helps the academia by contributing in knowledge enrichment. The methodological framework adopted in this study, viz., systematic comparison of regression paradigm shift in digital wallet financial transaction prediction. This study explores and increases new horizons of knowledge, by establishment of performance benchmark such as accuracy baseline for up a transaction modelling. The current study contributes as a guideline for the model selection, where-in evidence based recommendations for model selection in (similar) financial prediction task are elaborated.

LIMITATIONS AND FUTURE WORK

This study is part of the broader aspect of digital wallet payments practiced in developing Nations such as India. Since the study considered two predictor variables (customer-initiated transaction volume V_{ci}; and value Val_{ci}) and one dependent variable (total transaction value Val_{total}), the study could have enhanced by incorporating demographic factors. The current study is analysis of temporal, which is a static modelling by nature, however the time series could be incorporated by dynamic natures for having better inside into the dynamic nature of time series pattern. The researcher collected analysed the aggregated monthly data there could be expansion of the micro level pattern for better understanding of frequency and pattern of the digital payment behaviour.

SCOPE FOR FURTHER STUDY

As per this study there are multiple machine learning models along with the traditional regression model adapted, utilised to predict total transaction value. The further study could explore on more advanced time series data analysis such as RNNs, LSTMs, and GRUs, and spectral analysis. The researcher achieved the research aim through addressing the research questions, indeed, the further research could explore on the aspect of deep learning exploration of neural network architecture for understanding Complex pattern recognition. Researcher examined the patterns based static, not-with-standing the future researcher can explore real time predictions by considering the dynamic time series data. The study can similarly may adopt and develop by streamlining analytical framework for total transaction prediction with both regression and timeseries. The scope for research could be on casual analysis, such as investigation of casual relationship between transactional patterns and other variables. There is ample opportunity for the academy missions and researchers to throw light on the different geographical and demographic features such as mediating and moderation effect apart from time series model. The further investigation could also can be on the feature importance and cross digital payment wallets. The examination of the different stakeholders' perception could be another area of research viz., policy makers will take companies and retailers.

CONCLUSION

This is a comprehensive study which demonstrated the customer-initiated transaction parameters significantly impact the total transaction value in the digital valid UPI eco system. By clear examination of the reviews of the previous literatures research developed research questions to compare different advanced machine learning models in prediction of the time series data. The current studies able to address all the research questions with mathematical intuitions. The study is able to identify impact of customer-initiated transaction value and volume on the total transaction, significance of each different regression model (statistically vetted), and finally the findings shows the impact analysis. Thus, the study infers by identifying which regression model suitable for Digital payment systems predictions. The study also gives the limitations, along with scope for the studies. In conclusion the studies able to identify appropriate model with optimal accuracy, reliability and generalisability for impact analysis of UPI transactions based on the RMSE, MAPE and MAE.

REFERENCES

Aditya, R., & Ekyawan, F. (2021, September). Consumer behavior analysis in using the digital payment application. In *5th Global Conference on Business, Management and Entrepreneurship (GCBME 2020)* (pp. 524–528). Atlantis Press. DOI: 10.2991/aebmr.k.210831.102

Aggarwal, N. (2021). The norms of algorithmic credit scoring. *The Cambridge Law Journal*, *80*(1), 42–73. DOI: 10.1017/S0008197321000015

Breiman, L. (2001). Random forests. *Machine Learning*, *45*(1), 5–32. DOI: 10.1023/A:1010933404324

Ch, R. K., & Singha, S. (2024). A strategy for conducting sentiment analysis using AI in human resource management. In R. Khamis & A. Buallay (Eds.), AI in Business: Opportunities and Limitations (Study in Systems, Decision and Control, Vol. 515). Springer. DOI: 10.1007/978-3-031-48479-7_42

Das, P., & Das, P. (2017). Digital payments in India: The road ahead. *IEEE Potentials*, *36*(6), 14–19. DOI: 10.1109/MPOT.2017.2737199

European Payments Council. (2023, October 24). UPI: Revolutionising real time digital payments in India. https://www.europeanpaymentscouncil.eu/news-insights/insight/upi-revolutionising-real time digital payments india

Faraz, N., & Anjum, A. (2025). Spendception: The psychological impact of digital payments on consumer purchase behavior and impulse buying. *Behavioral Sciences (Basel, Switzerland)*, *15*(3), 387. DOI: 10.3390/bs15030387 PMID: 40150281

Hadwan, M., Al-Sarem, M., Saeed, F., & Al-Hagery, M. A. (2022). An improved sentiment classification approach for measuring user satisfaction toward governmental services' mobile apps using machine learning with feature engineering and SMOTE technique. *Applied Sciences (Basel, Switzerland)*, *12*(11), 5547. DOI: 10.3390/app12115547

Hassan, M. A., Shukur, Z., Hasan, M. K., & Al-Khaleefa, A. S. (2020). A review on electronic payments security. *Symmetry*, *12*(8), 1344. DOI: 10.3390/sym12081344

Heji, A. E., Hamdan, A., Anasweh, M., & Kanan, M. (2024). The relationship between digital transformation and public governance. In A. Hamdan & A. Harraf (Eds.), Business Development via AI and Digitalization (Studies in Systems, Decision and Control, Vol. 538). Springer. DOI: 10.1007/978-3-031-62102-4_31

Hussain, S., Gupta, S., & Bhardwaj, S. (2025). Determinants inhibiting digital payment system adoption: An Indian perspective. *Qualitative Research in Financial Markets, 17*(4), 716–748. DOI: 10.1108/QRFM-09-2023-0223

Katz, M. L., & Shapiro, C. (1985). Network externalities, competition, and compatibility. *The American Economic Review, 75*(3), 424–440.

Kotler, P., Keller, K. L., Ancarani, F., & Costabile, M. (2014). Marketing management (14th ed.). Pearson. http://www.ir.harambeeuniversity.edu.et/... (PDF)

Lakshmi, K. K., Gupta, H., & Ranjan, J. (2019). UPI based mobile banking applications – Security analysis and enhancements. In *2019 Amity International Conference on Artificial Intelligence (AICAI)* (pp. 1–6). IEEE. DOI: 10.1109/AICAI.2019.8701396

Manikandan, M., Venkatesh, P., Chitra, D., Krishnamoorthi, M., Ramu, M., & Senthilnathan, C. R. (2024). An impact of artificial intelligence in fintech. In *2024 International Conference on Power, Energy, Control and Transmission Systems (ICPECTS)* (pp. 1–3). IEEE. DOI: 10.1109/ICPECTS62210.2024.10780020

Manrai, R., Goel, U., & Yadav, P. D. (2021). Factors affecting adoption of digital payments by semi rural Indian women: Extension of UTAUT 2 with self determination theory and perceived credibility. *Aslib Journal of Information Management, 73*(6), 814–838. DOI: 10.1108/AJIM-12-2020-0396

Nagadeepa, C., Mukthar, K. P. J., Asnate Salazar, E., Castillo Picon, J., Méndez, R. Y., & Mory Guarnizo, S. (2024). Students intention towards digital entrepreneurship–Industry 5.0. In M. A. Musleh Al Sartawi, A. Helmy Abd Wahab, & K. Hussainey (Eds.), Global Economic Revolutions: Big Data Governance and Business Analytics for Sustainability (Communications in Computer and Information Science, Vol. 1999). Springer. DOI: 10.1007/978-3-031-50518-8_18

Patnaik, S. (2019, July 18). UPI will push India over the digital payments finish line. American Banker. https://www.americanbanker.com/payments/opinion/upi-will-push-india-over-the-digital-payments-finish-line

Patra, B., & Sethi, N. (2023). Does digital payment induce economic growth in emerging economies? The mediating role of institutional quality, consumption expenditure, and bank credit. *Information Technology for Development, 30*(1), 57–75. DOI: 10.1080/02681102.2023.2244465

PIB – Press Information Bureau, Government of India. (2024, December 1). UPI: Revolutionizing digital payments in India [Press release]. Retrieved July 17, 2025, from https://www.pib.gov.in/PressReleasePage.aspx?PRID=2079544

Sahi, A. M., Khalid, H., Abbas, A. F., Zedan, K., Khatib, S. F. A., & Al Amosh, H. (2022). The research trend of security and privacy in digital payment. *Informatics (MDPI)*, *9*(2), 32. DOI: 10.3390/informatics9020032

Sateesh, K. T., Vijayakumar, R., & Raghavendra, B. J. (2025). Analyzing the impact of rewards and transaction costs on customer payment method preferences: A gradient boosting model approach. In *Artificial Intelligence for Financial Risk Management and Analysis* (pp. 153–162). IGI Global., DOI: 10.4018/979-8-3373-1200-2.ch007

Sharma, M., & Sharma, S. K. (2019). Theoretical framework for digital payments in rural India: Integrating UTAUT and empowerment theory. In Y. Dwivedi, E. Ayaburi, R. Boateng, & J. Effah (Eds.), ICT Unbounded: Social Impact of Bright ICT Adoption (IFIP Advances in Information and Communication Technology, Vol. 558). Springer. DOI: 10.1007/978-3-030-20671-0_15

Shree, S., Pratap, B., Saroy, R., & Dhal, S. (2021). Digital payments and consumer experience in India: A survey-based empirical study. *Journal of Banking and Financial Technology*, *5*(1), 1–20. DOI: 10.1007/s42786-020-00024-z

Singh, R., & Malik, G. (2019). Impact of digitalization on Indian rural banking customers: With reference to payment systems. *Emerging Economy Studies*, *5*(1), 31–41. DOI: 10.1177/2394901519825912

Singha, R., & Singha, S. (2024). *AIoT Concepts and Integration: Exploring Customer Interaction, Ethics, Policy, and Privacy. 'Artificial Intelligence of Things (AIoT) for Productivity and Organizational Transition*. IGI Global. [https://doi.org/10.4018/979-8-3693-0993-3.ch002], https://www.google.com/search?q=https://doi.org/10.4018/979-8-3693-0993-3.ch002 DOI: 10.4018/979-8-3693-0993-3.ch002

Singha, S. (2024). *Navigating the Social Media Maze: Strategies for Effective Digital Marketing in a Fragmented Landscape. 'Changing Global Media Landscapes: Convergence, Fragmentation, and Polarization*. IGI Global. [https://doi.org/10.4018/979-8-3693-3767-7.ch005], https://www.google.com/search?q=https://doi.org/10.4018/979-8-3693-3767-7.ch005

TET – The Economic Times. (2024, May 1). UPI dominates digital payments, sees explosive growth over five years. https://economictimes.indiatimes.com/industry/banking/finance/banking/upi-dominates-digital-payments-sees-explosive-growth-over-five-years/articleshow/117610448.cms

Thapliyal, K., Gupta, C., Jindal, P., & Mishra, A. K. (2025). Measuring the impact of green banking practices on banks' environmental performance and sources of green financing: A study on Indian banks. *Discover Sustainability*, *6*(1), 169. DOI: 10.1007/s43621-024-00678-5

Tiwari, T., Srivastava, A., & Kumar, S. (2019). Adoption of digital payment methods in India. *International Journal of Electronic Finance*, *9*(3), 217–229. DOI: 10.1504/IJEF.2019.099058

TK. S. K., Thomas, L. P., Menon, V. A., & Thomas, J. (2024). Exploring tech enabled solutions: Evaluating sentiment classification models for airline reviews. In Impact of AI and Tech Driven Solutions in Hospitality and Tourism (pp. 257–281). IGI Global. https://doi.org/DOI: 10.1007/978-8-3693-6755-1.ch014

Tripathi, S. (2020, April 25). A study on adoption of digital payment through mobile payment application with reference to Gujarat state. International Journal of Trend in Scientific Research and Development. *SSRN*. https://ssrn.com/abstract=3638854

Vidani, J. (2024). A study on the rise and recent development in Unified Payments Interface. *SSRN*. DOI: 10.2139/ssrn.4849785

Yadav, P., Jain, A., Pathak, N., & Sharma, N. (2024). Investigating the behavior of consumers using digital payment: Comparative study between rural and urban areas. *Intelligent Decision Technologies*, *18*(3), 2353–2370. DOI: 10.3233/IDT-240659

ENDNOTE

1 Data sources: https://www.npci.org.in/what-we-do/upi/upi-ecosystem-statistics/archives

Chapter 3
Smart Workflows: Designing Next-Generation E-Collaboration With Artificial Intelligence

Hitesh Mohapatra
https://orcid.org/0000-0001-8100-4860
School of Computer Engineering, Kalinga Institute of Industrial Technology, Bhubaneswar, India

ABSTRACT

This chapter explores the integration of artificial intelligence (AI) into smart workflows to transform e-collaboration within modern organizations. It examines AI methodologies like machine learning, natural language processing, and intelligent agents to enhance efficiency, adaptability, and creativity in distributed work settings. Emphasizing human-AI hybrid collaboration, the chapter addresses key issues including privacy, security, and ethics. It illustrates how emerging technologies such as IoT, blockchain, and 5G synergize with AI to foster collaborative intelligence. Through empirical examples and conceptual frameworks, the work provides a rigorous, practical guide for researchers and practitioners to design AI-powered systems that optimize communication, decision-making, and workflow orchestration in the evolving digital workplace.

1. INTRODUCTION

Over the past four decades, collaborative practices have migrated from paper-based and face-to-face interactions to richly featured electronic environments. Early groupware systems in the 1980s such as Lotus Notes and Novell GroupWise com-

DOI: 10.4018/979-8-3373-5747-8.ch003

bined messaging, calendaring, and document management to support distributed teams, yet still relied heavily on local networks and periodic synchronization (Fuchs, 1999). The advent of the internet and web browsers in the 1990s introduced email as a dominant modality for asynchronous communication, while Internet Relay Chat (IRC) and bulletin-board systems enabled rudimentary real-time discussions across dispersed users ("Internet Relay Chat (IRC)," 2011). During the 2000s, instant messaging platforms (e.g., Slack, Microsoft Teams) and web conferencing tools (e.g., WebEx, Zoom) facilitated synchronous collaboration, and agile project-management applications (e.g., Jira, Trello) provided shared backlogs and workflow boards ("Chapter 46. Video conferencing and web-based collaboration tools). More recently, cloud-native code-hosting platforms (e.g., GitHub, GitLab) have integrated version control, CI/CD pipelines, and issue tracking into unified interfaces, ushering in an era of seamless, location-independent engineering collaboration.

Concurrently, artificial intelligence (AI) has begun to permeate collaboration systems, giving rise to "smart" features that augment human decision-making (Mohapatra, 2025). Natural language processing powers chatbots capable of summarizing discussion threads and suggesting action items; machine-learning models recommend relevant documents, tag conversations, and predict task priorities; and intelligent agents automate routine workflows, such as meeting scheduling and notification triaging (Kaminski & Perry, 2007). These AI-enabled capabilities promise to reduce cognitive load and surface critical insights in real time, effectively transforming collaboration platforms into proactive assistants rather than passive repositories.

Despite these advances, traditional collaborative workflows remain challenged by tool fragmentation, data silos, and poor interoperability. Users frequently juggle multiple applications for messaging, document sharing, task tracking, and video conferencing, leading to context switching costs and lost information (Arslan et al., 2021). Integration gaps mean that decisions made in one tool often fail to propagate to others, undermining situational awareness and impeding accountability (Pareek et al., 2025). Moreover, the complexity of configuring and securing disparate systems introduces administrative overhead and exposes organizations to privacy and compliance risks. These persistent issues motivate the design of unified, AI-augmented smart workflows that seamlessly orchestrate human and machine actors across the full collaboration lifecycle.

To address these issues, there is a critical need for intelligent workflow orchestration, a unifying abstraction layer that coordinates heterogeneous collaboration services and AI components. Orchestration platforms must manage end-to-end processes, automating routine tasks, routing information, and monitoring performance across tools to deliver coherent, adaptive workflows (Baer et al., 2024). Finally, effective e-collaboration requires seamless integration of human and AI capabilities. Yet technical and organizational barriers persist: legacy systems often lack APIs or standardized data schemas, impeding real-time data sharing; AI models struggle to incorporate tacit human knowledge and evolving user preferences; and governance frameworks frequently lag behind, leaving ambiguous responsibility assignments for AI-mediated decisions. Overcoming these integration challenges is essential to realize the promise of human-AI hybrid collaboration systems that can deliver both efficiency gains and enhanced decision-making (Borger et al., 2023).

The chapter pursues three interrelated objectives to advance AI-enhanced e-collaboration through the concept of smart workflows. First, it defines smart workflows as adaptive, AI-empowered processes that seamlessly integrate human and machine actors to orchestrate end-to-end collaboration. Unlike traditional linear workflows, smart workflows continuously learn from user interactions and contextual data leveraging machine learning, natural language processing, and intelligent agents to optimize task allocation, automate routine procedures, and surface actionable insights in real time. Second, it identifies key design principles essential for next-generation e-collaboration systems. These include adaptivity, which embeds feedback loops for continuous model retraining and workflow evolution; orchestration, which centralizes coordination of AI agents, data pipelines, and human tasks through a unifying control layer; and human-centered interaction, which preserves trust, transparency, and accountability by aligning interfaces and decision-support mechanisms with human cognitive processes and ethical norms. Third, the chapter develops a human-AI collaborative intelligence framework that extends established teaming models by delineating roles, responsibilities, and interaction protocols for hybrid teams. This framework comprises role specification partitioning tasks according to the complementary strengths of humans and AI-agents' coordination mechanisms that establish communication channels and decision protocols to maintain shared situational awareness, and joint learning processes that enable continuous refinement of workflows and team performance. Collectively, these objectives provide a structured foundation for designing, evaluating, and deploying smart workflows that deliver coherent, efficient, and ethically grounded e-collaboration experiences in both enterprise and research contexts.

It begins with an introduction to key concepts and background in section 1. Section 2 reviews theoretical underpinnings and existing models of e-collaboration and AI-augmented systems, while Section 3 presents the mixed-methods design approach and evaluation metrics. Section 4 describes the architecture and core components of smart workflows, and Section 5 details prototype implementations and case studies. Results and analysis are presented in Section 6, followed by a discussion of contributions, practical implications, and limitations in Section 7. Section 8 explores future trends and research directions, and Section 9 concludes with a synthesis of findings and recommendations.

2. LITERATURE REVIEW AND THEORETICAL FRAMEWORK

In the 1960s and 1970s, time-sharing mainframes and the ARPANET introduced basic computer-based messaging, culminating in Ray Tomlinson's first inter-computer email in 1971 and the adoption of the "@" syntax. Throughout the 1980s, proprietary LAN-based mail systems (e.g., IBM PROFS, DEC ALL-IN-1) emerged, while the 1990s saw the internet-driven standardization of SMTP, POP3, and IMAP protocols. Concurrently, real-time chat (IRC) and early bulletin boards enabled synchronous interaction, although often within siloed networks. The current state of e-collaboration is characterized by integrated suites that combine messaging, file sharing, document co-editing, task tracking, and video conferencing within cloud-native environments (Brown & Wyatt, 2018). Platforms such as Slack, Microsoft Teams, and Google Workspace leverage RESTful APIs to interoperate with third-party services, while code-centric systems like GitHub and GitLab embed CI/CD pipelines alongside issue management. Emerging features include AI-driven chatbots for automated summaries, recommendation engines for document retrieval, and intelligent agents for workflow automation (Raj et al., 2025).

Despite these advancements, significant limitations and gaps persist. Many systems emphasize either synchronous or asynchronous collaboration without fully bridging the two, leading to context fragmentation and information overload. Integration remains a challenge: heterogeneous data formats, closed-source APIs, and divergent security models impede seamless information flow (Dautenhahn, 2007). Moreover, collaborative features are unevenly distributed across platforms few solutions simultaneously support real-time co-authoring, rich social networking, and enterprise-grade governance resulting in patchwork toolchains that fail to deliver unified user experiences. Addressing these deficiencies motivates the transition to smart workflows that can dynamically orchestrate diverse services and align human-AI interactions end to end (Oppenheimer et al., 2023).

Artificial intelligence has become integral to modern collaborative systems by embedding machine learning, natural language processing, and intelligent agents into core platform functionalities. Machine learning algorithms analyze vast interaction logs and usage patterns to predict user needs, recommend relevant documents, and prioritize tasks, thereby reducing manual effort and enhancing productivity (Dwivedi, 2023). Natural language processing techniques enable richer communication by interpreting unstructured text, generating summaries of lengthy discussion threads, and facilitating multilingual exchanges through automated translation services. Intelligent agents leverage these capabilities to operate autonomously or semi-autonomously, orchestrating routine workflows such as meeting scheduling, notification triaging, and even complex decision support, while continually refining their behavior through user feedback loops.

Complementing these technologies, a variety of human AI collaboration frameworks have emerged to guide system design and evaluation (Hagemann et al., 2023). Taxonomies distinguish interaction modes AI-centric, where AI leads with minimal human intervention; human-centric, which prioritizes human decision-making augmented by AI; and symbiotic, characterized by balanced, bidirectional partnerships each demanding integrated with transparency, fairness, and accountability measures to ensure ethical integration and sustained trust (Pflanzer et al., 2022). Underpinning these models is the concept of collaborative intelligence, which envisions heterogeneous networks of human and machine agents contributing unique expertise to distributed problem solving; by valuing non-anonymous contributions and continuous adaptation, collaborative intelligence transcends traditional collective wisdom approaches and supports dynamic, evolutionary ecosystems of shared knowledge and innovation (Neves et al., 2024).

Workflow automation has matured from simple rule-based task scheduling to sophisticated orchestration theories that coordinate end-to-end processes across heterogeneous systems. Traditional automation focuses on individual tasks such as sending notifications or executing database updates whereas orchestration creates a cohesive ecosystem in which these automated tasks interact logically, share context, and adapt to dynamic conditions (Hopko et al., 2022). Central to orchestration theory is the concept of a control plane that manages task dependencies, error recovery, and resource allocation, providing real-time visibility and control over complex workflows. Integrating AI into workflow management systems further elevates these capabilities by embedding machine-learning models and intelligent agents within orchestration layers. AI-augmented platforms can predict bottlenecks, recommend optimal routing of tasks, and self-tune parameters to improve throughput, leveraging APIs and plug-in architectures to interoperate with CRM, ERP, and collaboration suites (Narayanan & McIlraith, 2002). Real-time collaboration and adaptive systems extend this paradigm by introducing continuous feedback loops: sensors, user interactions, and performance metrics feed into learning algorithms that dynamically adjust workflows in response to evolving requirements and environmental changes (Jain et al., 2022). For example, adaptive collaborative perception frameworks fuse multi-agent data streams to minimize latency and maximize information freshness, ensuring that distributed teams and AI agents maintain synchronized situational awareness. Together, these design principle holistic orchestration, AI integration, and real-time adaptability form the foundation for smart workflows that can seamlessly orchestrate human and machine actors in next-generation e-collaboration environments (Luther et al., 2024).

A robust theoretical framework for AI-enhanced e-collaboration begins with a conceptual model that unites technological and human-centered perspectives. At its core, this model portrays e-collaboration as an ecosystem of interconnected human and AI agents operating within shared environments, where three high-level dimensions agency, interaction, and adaptation govern system behavior (Lokiny, 2022). Agency defines the distribution of autonomy and control, specifying which tasks are performed by AI agents such as automated data aggregation or predictive recommendations and which remain under human supervision to leverage contextual judgment and ethical reasoning (Salah et al., 2019). Interaction encompasses the modalities through which humans and AI exchange information, ranging from natural-language conversational interfaces to visual dashboards and multimodal sensor feeds, each designed to support transparency, explainability, and intuitive oversight. Adaptation embeds continuous learning loops, whereby performance metrics and user feedback dynamically refine models and workflows, ensuring that the system evolves in alignment with shifting objectives and user needs (Järvelä et al., 2023).

Human-centered AI principles further enrich this framework by prioritizing respect for autonomy, prevention of harm, fairness, transparency, and accountability throughout the AI lifecycle. These principles mandate that interfaces allow human override, that decision logic is explicable, and that responsibility for outcomes is clearly allocated (Liang et al., 2019). Finally, synergy models of human AI collaboration articulate how complementary strengths human creativity, abstract reasoning, and ethical judgment versus AI's computational scale, pattern recognition, and automation converge to produce collective intelligence greater than the sum of its parts (Kay, 2023). By mapping these synergy degrees across interaction modes (e.g., sequential advising, mixed-initiative control, parallel decision support), the framework guides designers in calibrating levels of AI autonomy and human involvement to optimize both performance and trust. Collectively, this integrated theoretical framework lays the groundwork for developing, evaluating, and scaling smart workflows that harness true collaborative intelligence in AI-augmented e-collaboration systems (Kim et al., 2025).

3. METHODOLOGY AND DESIGN APPROACH

A rigorous evaluation of smart workflows demands a mixed-methods research design that combines the breadth of quantitative analysis with the depth of qualitative insight. In the quantitative strand, performance metrics such as task completion time, error rates, and system throughput are collected through controlled experiments and benchmark tests. These data are triangulated with qualitative findings obtained from semi-structured interviews, think-aloud protocols, and field observations to capture users' perceptions of usability, trust, and cognitive workload (Kirwan, 2025). The human-centered design methodology guides each phase of system development, beginning with contextual inquiry to elicit user needs and pain points, followed by co-design workshops in which stakeholders sketch interface prototypes and workflow scenarios (Reddy et al., 2025). Prototype iterations incorporate user feedback through rapid low-fidelity mockups and Wizard-of-Oz simulations, ensuring that design decisions remain grounded in real-world practices. Iterative development proceeds in three core cycles exploration, refinement, and validation each comprising planning, design, implementation, and evaluation stages (Kung et al., 2023). Fig.1 depicts the cycle in which the exploration cycle, design teams generate initial workflow concepts and test them using scripted use-cases; quantitative thresholds and qualitative themes emerging from this phase inform the refinement cycle, wherein prototypes evolve to address identified issues. Table.1 highlights how the system evolved through continuous user feedback and testing. Each cycle built upon insights from the previous stage to refine usability and functionality. The activities and metrics align closely with an evidence-based design approach. Together, they show a structured yet flexible path from concept to real-world implementation.

Figure 1. Exploration Cycle

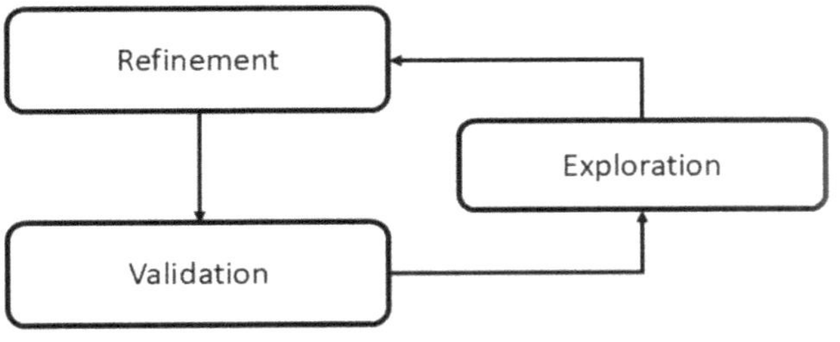

Table 1. Iterative Development Cycles Summary

Cycle	Activities	Deliverables	Metrics
Exploration	Contextual inquiry; low-fidelity prototypes	Workflow sketches; use-cases	Task time; initial SUS scores
Refinement	Co-design workshops; mid-fidelity prototypes	Interactive mockups; user diaries	Error rates; thematic affinity clusters
Validation	High-fidelity implementation; field deployment	Deployed system; user training guides	Task throughput; system adoption rate

3.1. System Architecture Design

A multi-layered architecture for smart workflows typically comprises three principal tiers. At the presentation layer, user interfaces and communication channels such as web dashboards, mobile apps, and conversational agents enable stakeholders to interact with the system (Schmutz et al., 2024). The logic layer hosts workflow orchestration services, AI components, and business rules engines: within this layer, AI integration points surface, including machine-learning inference services for predictive task routing, NLP modules for document analysis, and intelligent agents that trigger automated subtasks (Larson, 2021). Below, the data layer manages persistent storage, metadata catalogs, and real-time event streams, ensuring data consistency and provenance. AI integration mechanisms are embedded in the logic layer through microservice endpoints and plugin frameworks. Decision mechanisms utilize rule-based systems for straightforward control flows and ML-based decision tables for dynamic adaptation, while fallback protocols guarantee human override capabilities when confidence thresholds fall below predefined safety margins. Security and privacy considerations pervade all tiers (Leaua et al., 2024). At the presentation layer, authentication and role-based access control enforce least-privilege principles; the logic layer implements encrypted inter-service communication and policy enforcement points that audit AI-driven decisions; and the data layer applies encryption-at-rest, anonymization techniques for sensitive data, and differential privacy to sanitize training datasets. Ethical constraints such as bias detection modules and transparent model explainers are integrated as shared services to uphold accountability and fairness across the workflow (Leaua et al., 2024).

3.2. Evaluation Metrics and Methods

Evaluation of smart workflows requires a combination of quantitative metrics, qualitative measures, and hybrid approaches that capture both system performance and human experience. Quantitative metrics focus on objective performance indicators such as efficiency, accuracy, and response time. Efficiency can be measured by time savings per task relative to a baseline, for example through the Equation 1.

$$Efficiency\ Gain\ =\ \frac{T_{baseline} - T_{AI}}{T_{baseline}} - 100\% \qquad (1)$$

Where, $T_{baseline}$ is the average task completion time without AI support and T_{AI} is the time with AI-enhanced workflows. Accuracy metrics assess the correctness of AI-driven outputs such as prediction accuracy in task prioritization or summarization precision with standard measures like precision, recall, and F1-score. Response time, or system latency, captures the delay between user input and AI-generated assistance, and should remain below human perceptual thresholds (e.g., 200 ms) to preserve fluency. Qualitative evaluation emphasizes user satisfaction, perceived collaboration quality, and trust (Siemens, 2013). These dimensions are best assessed through validated survey instruments (e.g., System Usability Scale, Net Promoter

Score) and semi-structured interviews that probe users' subjective experiences of transparency, control, and cognitive load. Table.2 presents the collaboration quality may be further evaluated via behavioral analysis of interaction logs, examining measures such as the proportion of AI suggestions accepted by users. A hybrid evaluation framework integrates these quantitative and qualitative strands into a cohesive methodology. Initial field trials collect baseline performance data and user feedback, which inform iterative design tweaks (Spillias et al., 2023). Subsequent controlled experiments compare workflow variants, using statistical tests (e.g., paired t-tests for time savings) alongside thematic analysis of interview transcripts to identify emerging usability issues.

Table 2. Dimension Metric

Dimension	**Metric**	**Method**
Efficiency	Time savings (% gain)	Benchmark tests; workflow logs
Accuracy	Precision, recall, F1-score	Ground-truth comparison; confusion matrix
Response time	Latency (ms)	Automated performance profiling
User satisfaction	SUS, NPS scores	Surveys; Likert-scale questionnaires
Collaboration quality	Acceptance rate of AI suggestions	Interaction log analysis; behavioral metrics
Trust and usability	Thematic themes	Semi-structured interviews; focus groups

4. SMART WORKFLOW ARCHITECTURE AND COMPONENT

Smart workflow architecture for next-generation e-collaboration typically comprises several key components that interact seamlessly to optimize collaboration processes through AI-enhanced orchestration and integration. At the core, the system includes the following components:

- User Interface Layer: This facilitates human interaction via various interfaces such as web portals, mobile apps, and conversational agents. It provides adaptive, context-aware displays and notifications that help users manage tasks and communications efficiently (Tong et al., 2025).
- Workflow Orchestration Engine: This core logic component sequences and manages tasks, coordinating human and AI agents. It handles task dependencies, scheduling, error recovery, and real-time adjustments. The orchestration engine ensures smooth flow across various modules and external tools.

- AI Services Layer: This houses various AI modules including machine learning models for predictive analytics, natural language processing engines for understanding and generating human language, and intelligent agents that autonomously perform tasks such as scheduling or document summarization. These AI components dynamically interact with workflows to augment human capabilities (Valdés-Pérez, 1999).
- Data Management Layer: Responsible for storage, retrieval, and governance of data including documents, user inputs, system logs, and metadata. It supports real-time data streaming and batch processing pipelines for efficient information flow.
- Integration Layer: Facilitates interoperability with existing e-collaboration platforms and enterprise systems (like Slack, Microsoft Teams, Jira, Google Workspace). It uses APIs, webhooks, and middleware connectors to ensure seamless data exchange and coordinated workflow execution across heterogeneous tools.

Figure 2. System architecture design

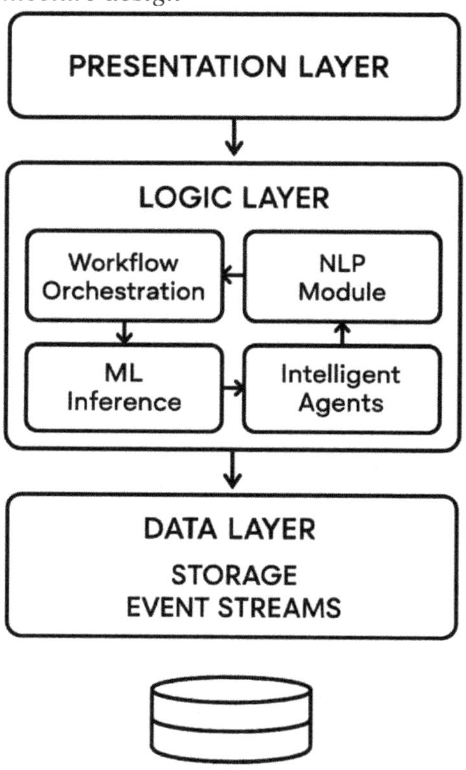

Fig.2 illustrates the layer architecture where presentation layer at the top interfaces with users; logic layer in the middle contains workflow orchestration, ML inference, NLP module, and intelligent agents; data layer at the bottom manages storage and event streams. Arrows indicate integration points between components within the logic layer. In terms of data flow and information processing, input from user actions or external systems enters via the user interface or integration layer, then processed through the orchestration engine, which delegates subtasks to AI modules or humans as appropriate (Wang et al., 2022). Outputs and task updates propagate back through the layers to UI dashboards and external tools. Continuous feedback loops enable real-time adaptation of workflows based on performance metrics and user feedback. Such architecture ensures modularity, scalability, and adaptability, enabling the design of smart workflows that effectively integrate AI capabilities within existing collaboration ecosystems while addressing challenges of fragmentation and complexity.

4.1. AI-Powered Workflow Orchestration

AI-powered workflow orchestration stands at the core of smart collaboration systems, enabling organizations to dynamically allocate and manage tasks while adapting to changing conditions and user inputs in real time. Intelligent task routing and prioritization leverages AI algorithms such as supervised learning classifiers, reinforcement learning agents, or graph-based heuristics to analyze contextual signals (e.g., workload, expertise, task urgency, historical task outcomes) and assign the most appropriate resources to each task (Weber et al., 2024). For example, machine learning models can predict which team member is best suited for a particular request or automatically escalate critical issues by detecting high-priority patterns in communications or system logs. These systems continuously learn from organizational data, optimizing routing strategies to enhance throughput and reduce completion times. Adaptive workflow management algorithms further extend this intelligence by monitoring ongoing processes, recognizing bottlenecks, and reconfiguring workflows on-the-fly. Such adaptation is achieved via feedback loops as new information becomes available such as unexpected delays, resource availability changes, or shifting project requirements the workflow orchestration engine dynamically updates task assignments, reorders priorities, and reallocates resources to maintain efficiency and resilience. Often, these adaptive algorithms rely on real-time data streams and predictive analytics to proactively adjust the workflow before disruptions impact overall performance (Xu & Gao, 2024).

Real-time decision-making mechanisms operationalize these capabilities by integrating AI-powered analytics into the orchestration logic. These decisions, often supported by rule-based engines or deep learning inference, include automatic approvals, proactive alerts for anomaly detection, and autonomous delegation of routine subtasks. The system continuously balances autonomy and human oversight through configurable thresholds and confidence scores, escalating ambiguous or high-impact decisions to human supervisors for review (Yue & Hu, 2023). This convergence of intelligent routing, adaptive management, and real-time AI decision support positions workflow orchestration as the central nervous system of smart collaboration, ensuring organizational agility, responsiveness, and sustained collective performance.

4.2. Human-AI Interaction Interface

Human-AI interaction interfaces within smart workflows demand designs that support seamless collaboration through multiple communication modalities, cognitive augmentation, and user-centric optimization strategies. A multimodal interaction design approach integrates diverse input and output channels such as speech, text, gestures, and visual dashboards, facilitating natural and flexible exchanges between human users and AI agents. This variety ensures accessibility and allows users to select the mode most suited to their context and preference, thereby reducing friction and cognitive workload. Collaborative cognitive interfaces constitute another crucial pillar, wherein the interface not only displays information but acts as an active mediator fostering shared understanding and joint decision-making. Such interfaces incorporate features like explainable AI components that transparently communicate AI reasoning, confidence levels, and suggested actions. This openness cultivates trust and enables humans to calibrate their reliance on AI support effectively. Real-time feedback loops, interactive visualizations, and annotation tools empower users to contribute knowledge, provide corrections, and guide AI behavior dynamically, establishing a true partnership rather than a one-sided assistance model. Fig.3 illustrates the human-ai interaction interface.

Figure 3. Human-AI interaction interface

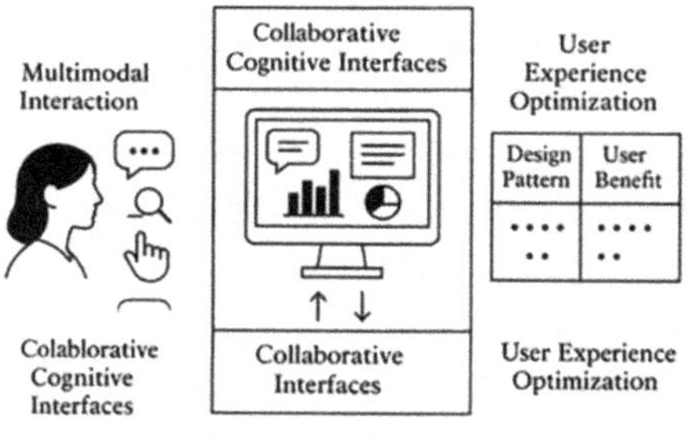

User experience optimization strategies emphasize minimizing cognitive strain, maintaining transparency, and preserving user control. Employing established human-AI interaction design patterns such as clearly distinguishing AI-generated content from human inputs, providing adjustable levels of automation, and enabling smooth error recovery ensures the interface remains intelligible, efficient, and trustworthy. Task-specific interfaces may use visual hierarchies to present condensed metadata and relevant contextual cues that align with user workflows. Continuous user feedback, usability testing, and iterative refinement safeguard alignment between system behavior and evolving user needs.

4.3. Integration and Interoperability

Integration and interoperability form a critical dimension in designing smart workflows that leverage AI for next-generation e-collaboration. The following elements are essential for effective integration and ensuring scalable, seamless connectivity:

- API Design and System Connectivity: Robust API architectures provide standardized interfaces through which independent software components communicate and share data in real time. RESTful APIs are commonly employed due to their stateless design and widespread adoption, enabling tools across e-collaboration ecosystems to exchange information, trigger actions, and synchronize states efficiently. API gateways mediate access, enforce security policies such as authentication and rate limiting, and enable monitoring. A microservices approach further modularizes AI services and workflow components, allowing flexible deployment, independent scaling, and easier maintenance.
- Legacy System Integration Approaches: Enterprises often operate a mix of modern platforms alongside legacy systems which may lack modern APIs or use proprietary protocols. To bridge these gaps, integration middleware such as Enterprise Service Bus (ESB) or message queuing frameworks translates and routes data between disparate systems, enabling reliable asynchronous communication. Adapters and connectors provide protocol conversion and data format transformation, while API wrappers expose legacy features as standardized services. Hybrid integration platforms can combine on-premises and cloud resources, extend legacy infrastructure longevity while enable incremental adoption of AI-powered smart workflows (Sharma et al., 2025).
- Scalability and Performance Considerations: Designing for scalability requires anticipating growth in data volume, transaction rates, and user concurrency. Cloud-native architectures leveraging containerization and orchestration (e.g., Kubernetes) support elastic scaling of workflow components. Load

balancing and caching reduce latency and resource contention. Performance monitoring tools track throughput, response times, and error rates to guide resource allocation and tuning. Security mechanisms must scale without impeding performance; this includes role-based access control, data encryption, and audit logging distributed across system layers.

Collectively, these principles help realize smart workflow platforms that are resilient, extensible, and capable of integrating heterogeneous collaboration tools and AI modules.

5. IMPLEMENTATION AND CASE STUDIES

The prototype development phase translates the architectural blueprint and design specifications of smart workflow systems into a functional, testable platform. This involves concrete decisions regarding implementation methodologies, technology stack selection, and deployment practices to ensure the system's extensibility, robustness, and interoperability with existing e-collaboration tools. The core prototype is composed as a modular, service-oriented application adhering to the multi-layered system architecture previously described. The workflow orchestration engine is implemented using popular backend frameworks such as Node.js or Python (Django/FastAPI), facilitating scalable task sequencing and event-driven process management. The AI services layer integrates pre-trained models for machine learning (scikit-learn, TensorFlow, or PyTorch) and leverages NLP libraries (spaCy, HuggingFace Transformers) for document parsing, summarization, and intelligent recommendation. Inter-agent communication employs message brokering protocols (e.g., RabbitMQ or Apache Kafka) to support asynchronous coordination and decouple services for maintainability.

Table 3. Technology Stack and Development Tools

Layer/Component	Technologies and Tools
Backend	Python, Node.js, Java (Spring Boot) for RESTful APIs and orchestration engine
AI/ML	TensorFlow, PyTorch for training/inference; HuggingFace Transformers, spaCy for NLP modules
Frontend	React, Angular, Vue.js for web interfaces; Electron for cross-platform desktop clients
Database	PostgreSQL or MongoDB for structured and semi-structured data; Elasticsearch for retrieval and search
Integration Layer	RESTful APIs, GraphQL endpoints; API gateways (Kong, AWS API Gateway)

Layer/Component	Technologies and Tools
Message Brokering	RabbitMQ, Apache Kafka for inter-service event streaming and workflow coordination
DevOps & Containerization	Docker for containerization; Kubernetes for orchestration and scaling; GitHub Actions or Jenkins for CI/CD
Security	OAuth 2.0, JWT for authentication/authorization; TLS/SSL for secure data transmission

The system is deployed as microservices packaged via Docker containers and orchestrated using Kubernetes, enabling horizontal scalability and high availability. Cloud infrastructure providers (AWS, Google Cloud, or Azure) offer managed services for databases, message brokering, and monitoring, simplifying infrastructure management. Configuration files (YAML, JSON) define service connectivity, resource allocations, and environment variables, while infrastructure-as-code tools (e.g., Terraform, Ansible) automate repeatable deployments. A deployment pipeline is established with stages for automated testing, vulnerability scanning, and staged rollouts, ensuring the prototype remains stable and secure throughout development. System logging and monitoring (using tools like Prometheus, Grafana, and ELK Stack) provide real-time observability for proactive troubleshooting and performance tuning. This prototype development approach ensures that the smart workflow platform is modular, maintainable, and ready for iterative testing and further real-world validation in subsequent case studies. Table.3 illustrates technology stack and development tools for smart work-flow system designing.

5.1. Real-World Applications

Smart workflows powered by artificial intelligence have demonstrated transformative potential across diverse domains. This section highlights three critical application areas where AI-augmented collaboration drives significant advancements such as healthcare diagnostic collaboration, manufacturing human-robot cooperation, and AI-assisted educational learning environments. Healthcare Collaborative Diagnostics: In healthcare, collaborative diagnostics benefit profoundly from AI-enhanced workflows that integrate clinical expertise with machine intelligence. AI models analyze medical imaging data such as X-rays, MRIs, and CT scans to detect anomalies with high sensitivity and specificity. Radiologists collaborate interactively with AI systems that provide automated assessments and highlight areas of concern, enabling more accurate and timely diagnoses. Workflow orchestration tools manage case routing, prioritizing urgent consultations and ensuring that relevant specialists contribute to patient evaluation seamlessly. The system logs decisions and annotations, fostering accountability and continuous learning.

Manufacturing Human-Robot Collaboration: In industrial manufacturing settings, AI-powered smart workflows facilitate the synergistic collaboration between human operators and robotic systems on assembly lines and quality assurance tasks. Intelligent workflow engines dynamically allocate tasks based on real-time assessments of human operator availability, robot capabilities, and production priorities. Robots equipped with machine vision and tactile sensors perform repetitive or high-precision tasks, while humans focus on supervision, decision-making, and exception handling. Adaptive workflows respond to unexpected disruptions such as equipment failures or supply delays by reallocating resources and adjusting schedules autonomously. Case studies reveal improved throughput, reduced error rates, and enhanced worker safety.

Figure 4. Real-world applications

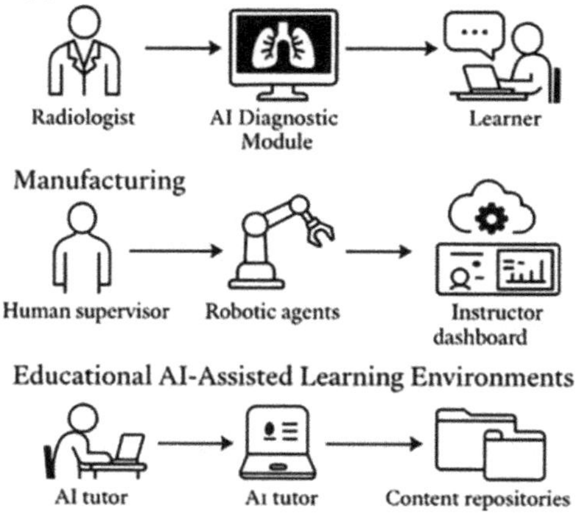

Educational AI-Assisted Learning Environments: In education, AI-enhanced e-collaboration platforms support personalized, adaptive learning through smart workflows that coordinate interactions among students, educators, and intelligent tutoring systems. These systems employ natural language processing to analyze student submissions, provide targeted feedback, and recommend resources integrated to individual learning trajectories. Collaborative workspaces integrate AI agents that facilitate peer communication, flag misconceptions, and suggest collaborative tasks aligned with curricular goals. Workflow orchestration optimizes scheduling of synchronous sessions and manages assessment workflows, ensuring timely interaction and progress tracking. Evidence from pilot implementations demonstrates increased student engagement, improved learning outcomes, and more efficient educator workflows. Fig.4 visualizes the real-world applications. These real-world applications underscore the versatility and impact of AI-driven smart workflows in diverse collaborative contexts. By seamlessly integrating human expertise and AI capabilities, such systems deliver measurable gains in efficiency, accuracy, and user satisfaction, fostering the next generation of intelligent, adaptive collaboration infrastructure.

5.2. Performance Evaluation

Performance evaluation of AI-powered smart workflows involves systematically comparing these innovative systems against traditional e-collaboration setups to quantify gains in efficiency, productivity, and user experience. Table.4 presents the performance evaluation of AI integrated work-flow system.

Comparative Analysis with Traditional Systems: A core aspect of evaluation is benchmarking smart workflows against conventional collaboration environments that rely on manual task coordination and disconnected tools. Metrics such as task completion time, error frequency, and throughput provide objective evidence of improvements. For instance, studies have demonstrated that AI-enhanced task routing and automation can reduce average completion times by up to 30% compared to legacy manual workflows. Additionally, integrated AI agents contribute to lowering error rates by automating repetitive tasks prone to human oversight.

Table 4. Performance evaluation

Metric	Traditional Systems	AI-Enhanced Smart Workflows	Improvement (%)
Average Task Completion Time	100 minutes	70 minutes	30% reduction
Error Rate	8%	3%	62.5% reduction
Task Throughput	50 tasks/day	75 tasks/day	50% increase
User Satisfaction (SUS)	65 (out of 100)	82 (out of 100)	26% improvement
Cognitive Load (NASA-TLX)	Moderate	Low	Significant decrease

Efficiency Gains and Productivity Improvements: Efficiency gains are assessed by measuring time savings, resource utilization, and the reduction of redundant activities. Productivity improvements also manifest in increased task parallelism enabled by intelligent workload balancing across human and AI agents. Quantitative data collected from controlled experiments and field deployments indicate significant improvements in key performance indicators (KPIs), such as:

- Reduction in task cycle times
- Increased throughput of collaborative processes
- Decreased cognitive load as measured by validated scales
- Enhanced responsiveness due to real-time adaptive orchestration

User Adoption and Satisfaction Metrics: Successful technology implementation depends heavily on user acceptance. User adoption rates are tracked alongside qualitative data derived from surveys and interviews that measure perceived usefulness, usability, and trust in AI components. Tools such as the System Usability Scale (SUS), Net Promoter Score (NPS), and task load indices provide structured insight into user satisfaction. Common findings include higher user confidence in AI-supported workflows over time, especially when transparency and human override features are robustly integrated. Table.4 summarizes the key performance metrics between traditional and AI-enabled workflows.

5.3. Implementation Challenges and Best Practices

Implementing AI-enhanced collaboration systems and smart workflows involves several critical challenges, but also reveals important success factors and considerations for scalability and sustainability. Key technical challenges include integrating AI with legacy systems and fragmented data environments. Legacy infrastructures often lack APIs or use proprietary protocols, requiring middleware adapters, API wrappers, and phased rollouts to bridge gaps without disrupting business operations.

Table 5. Smart workflow best practices checklist

Aspect	Challenges	Solutions/Best Practices
System Integration	Legacy system incompatibility	Use middleware, API wrappers, phased rollouts
Data Management	Silos, inconsistent quality	Robust governance, standardization, validation processes
User Adoption	Cultural resistance	Cultivate experimentation culture; training and engagement
Human-AI Interaction	Usability, trust, accountability	Intuitive UI, explainable AI, clear governance frameworks
Scalability	Performance bottlenecks, model drift	Cloud infrastructure, containerization, continuous training
Sustainability	Long-term adaptability and evolution	Modular design, transparency, user empowerment

Data silos, inconsistent formats, and data quality issues hamper AI effectiveness; overcoming these necessitates robust data governance, standardization, validation, and real-time data processing pipelines. Further, organizations face cultural resistance due to new workflows and altered decision-making authority, which can be mitigated by fostering a culture of experimentation, involving end users early, and providing tailored AI training and digital toolkits. The complexity of human-AI interaction also poses usability and trust concerns, making intuitive user interface design, transparency through explainable AI, and clear accountability frameworks essential. Ensuring system dependability, auditability, and ethical AI governance are paramount to address privacy, bias, and compliance risks comprehensively. Table.5 presents the smart workflow best practices checklist.

Successful deployments often share these enablers: strong cross-functional collaboration among IT, AI experts, and business users; clear and phased AI integration roadmaps; ongoing upskilling and change management programs; modular and API-first system architectures that facilitate seamless interoperability; and comprehensive governance frameworks encompassing ethical guidelines, roles, and risk management. Iterative, user-centered design and continuous monitoring support steady improvement and higher adoption rates. Scalability demands elastic cloud-based infrastructure and container orchestration (e.g., Kubernetes) to handle increasing data loads, user concurrency, and model complexity without degradation. Continuous model retraining and mitigation of model drift maintain system accuracy over time. Sustainability requires maintaining modular architectures allowing independent updates, embedding adaptability to evolving organizational contexts, and ensuring long-term user engagement through transparent AI behavior and user empowerment. Investment in robust security, privacy-preserving techniques, and compliance tracking safeguards organizational resilience against emerging threats and regulations.

6. RESULTS AND ANALYSIS

Results and analysis of AI-powered smart workflows in e-collaboration focus on quantitative performance, qualitative user insights, benchmarking, and critical success factors for organizational adoption. Quantitatively, system performance is evaluated using metrics such as task completion rates, time savings, accuracy, response latency, and reliability. Studies show AI-enhanced workflows can reduce task completion times by up to 30%, improve accuracy by lowering error rates (e.g., from 8% to 3%), and increase throughput by 50% compared to traditional systems. Metrics like AI output accuracy, system uptime, and latency are critical to assess reliability and responsiveness. Statistical analyses, including hypothesis testing and exploratory data analysis (EDA), validate the significance of these improvements.

Efficiency gains are typically measured by percentage reductions in time per task, leading to greater productivity and smoother collaboration.

Qualitatively, user experience and collaboration quality are assessed through surveys (e.g., System Usability Scale, Net Promoter Score) and interviews, focusing on satisfaction, trust in AI systems, transparency, and perceived cognitive load reductions. Behavioral changes include increased adoption of AI tools, improved shared situational awareness, and more fluid human-AI coordination. Collaboration quality is further analyzed by tracking acceptance rates of AI suggestions and interaction patterns, highlighting enhanced decision support and communication quality. Comparative analysis benchmarks AI-enhanced workflows against legacy solutions, demonstrating clear efficiency, accuracy, and adoption advantages. Cost-benefit analyses incorporate direct productivity gains, reduced error costs, and intangible benefits such as improved decision quality. ROI evaluations consider implementation costs against time savings and enhanced throughput, with positive returns shown especially in domains like healthcare, manufacturing, and education. Table.6 Presents the measures and findings.

Critical success factors for effective implementation include both technical and organizational dimensions. On the technical side, robust API integrations, scalable cloud infrastructure, strong data governance, and accurate AI models form the backbone of reliable performance. Equally important is organizational readiness, which involves preparing users through training, fostering a culture that embraces AI augmentation, and establishing structured change management processes for smooth workflow transitions. Transparent communication about AI's role, continuous user engagement, and committed leadership support further strengthen trust and ensure ongoing improvement throughout the implementation journey. These factors ensure sustainable deployment and scaling of smart workflows that successfully blend human and AI contributions, maximizing organizational agility and collaboration effectiveness. Fig.5 compares task completion times across multiple evaluation phases, contrasting baseline traditional workflows with AI-enhanced workflows. The results demonstrate a consistent decrease in task completion times as AI technologies are integrated, underscoring the efficiency gains realized through smart workflows.

Table 6. Compares task completion times across multiple evaluation phases

Aspect	Measure/Indicator	Key Findings
Task Completion Time	Average time/task (minutes)	30% reduction with AI workflows
Error Rate	% errors in task execution	Reduced from 8% to 3% with AI automation
Throughput	Tasks completed/day	50% increase using AI orchestration
User Satisfaction	SUS score (out of 100)	Improvement from 65 to 82 post AI
Cognitive Load	NASA-TLX or self-reported scales	Significant decrease with AI assistance

Aspect	Measure/Indicator	Key Findings
System Uptime	% operational availability	>99.9% reliability in AI systems
Response Latency	Average delay (ms)	Maintained below 200ms for real-time use

Figure 5. Task completion times across evaluation phases for baseline vs. AI-enhanced workflows

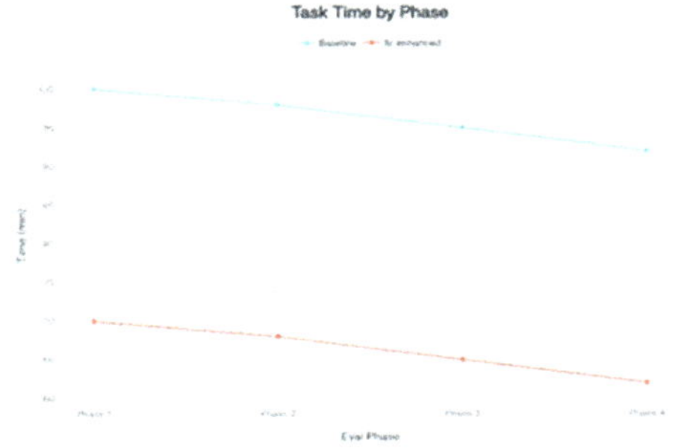

Fig.6 illustrates user satisfaction (measured by the System Usability Scale) and cognitive load (measured by the NASA-TLX scale) before and after the introduction of AI tools. User satisfaction notably increases post-adoption, while cognitive load decreases, indicating improved user experience with AI-enhanced collaboration.

Figure 6. User satisfaction and cognitive load metrics pre- and post-AI adoption

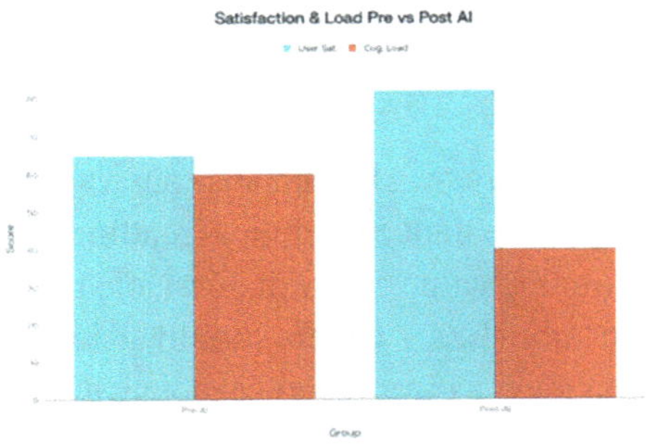

7. DISCUSSION AND IMPLICATIONS

The integration of human-AI collaboration theory within this chapter contributes notable advances to scholarly understanding of collective intelligence in digital environments. By synthesizing established frameworks with empirical findings, the work extends conceptual models of collaborative intelligence to encompass dynamic, agentic workflows where AI agents and human participants co-author tasks through mixed-initiative control. This approach advances theory by articulating an expanded taxonomy of human-AI interaction modes ranging from sequential advising and parallel decision support to fully symbiotic operations each mapped to specific orchestration patterns and trust calibration strategies. Moreover, the chapter introduces novel workflow orchestration paradigms that transcend linear, rule-based process management. These paradigms leverage feedback-driven adaptivity and real-time decision-making to create self-tuning workflows that proactively reconfigure task allocations, detect and mitigate bottlenecks, and balance autonomy with human oversight. The resulting orchestration models embody a continuous learning loop that integrates performance analytics, user feedback, and policy constraints into the control plane, thereby embedding resilience and agility at the core of collaborative systems. Finally, by unifying these advancements under the umbrella of collaborative intelligence, the chapter integrates disparate elements machine learning, natural language processing, intelligent agents, and human-centered design into a cohesive theoretical framework. This synthesis not only clarifies how the interplay between human creativity and AI's computational scale yields novel opportunities for organizational innovation but also lays the groundwork for future research on metrics, governance, and ethical deployment in evolving socio-technical ecosystems.

7.1. Practical Implications

Organizations aiming to leverage AI-enhanced smart workflows must adopt a structured, phased approach that balances technical readiness, user engagement, and governance to ensure sustainable value creation. First, clear guidelines for organizational adoption should be established. Leaders should articulate strategic objectives for AI-driven collaboration such as improved responsiveness, higher accuracy, or reduced cycle times and align these with broader digital transformation roadmaps. A cross-functional steering committee, including IT, business, and compliance representatives, ensures that project goals address operational requirements, data governance, and ethical considerations. Metrics for success must be defined early (e.g., time saved per task, user satisfaction targets, error reduction thresholds) and tracked through a centralized dashboard.

Second, effective implementation strategies and best practices involve iterative pilot projects that limit scope to high-priority use cases. Begin with low-risk workflows such as automated document summarization or routine task routing before extending AI orchestration to complex, mission-critical processes. During each pilot, apply human-centered design, continuously incorporate user feedback, and deploy AI models using CI/CD pipelines to allow rapid updates. Best practices include modular, API-first architectures to facilitate integration; robust data pipelines with validation and monitoring to ensure model accuracy; and fail-safe mechanisms to revert to human control when confidence scores fall below safe thresholds.

Third, change management recommendations emphasize transparent communication and skill development. Early and frequent communication about AI roles, expected benefits, and potential limitations demystifies the technology and builds trust. Training programs combining hands-on workshops, digital tutorials, and peer mentoring equip users with the skills to collaborate effectively with AI agents. Establishing AI "champions" in each business unit fosters peer-driven adoption and provides local support. Finally, implement feedback loops—through regular retrospectives, surveys, and usage analytics—to capture emerging challenges and refine both workflows and support structures. This continuous improvement cycle ensures that AI-enhanced collaboration evolves in tandem with user needs and organizational objectives.

7.2. Societal and Ethical Considerations

The deployment of AI-augmented smart workflows raises significant societal and ethical considerations that organizations must address proactively. Privacy and security implications are paramount, as continuous data collection and real-time analysis within collaboration platforms increase exposure of sensitive information. Ensuring data protection requires end-to-end encryption, fine-grained access controls, and robust audit trails to prevent unauthorized disclosure. Differential privacy techniques and federated learning can be employed to train AI models on decentralized data without compromising individual confidentiality. Fig.7 depicts the interdependent relationship between technical requirements, organizational readiness, and change management as essential success factors for implementing AI-enhanced smart workflows. Each main factor is detailed with key sub-elements, visually representing how successful adoption relies on a holistic, integrated approach.

Figure 7. Flow diagram of critical success factors for AI-enhanced collaboration implementation

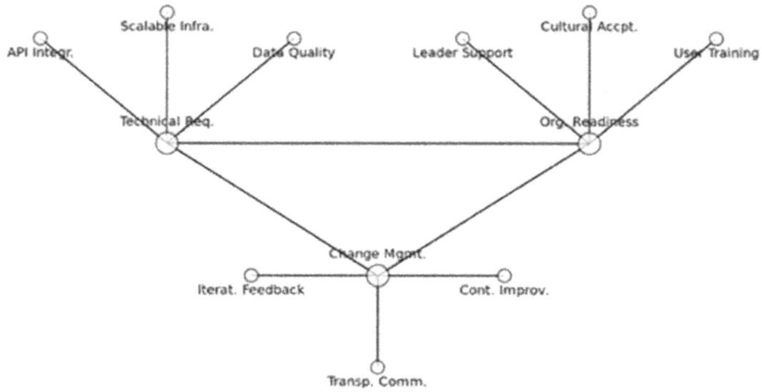

AI-driven automation also influences employment and work patterns. While routine tasks may be delegated to AI agents freeing human workers for higher-level problem solving there is a risk of job displacement if roles are not redefined. Organizations should conduct impact assessments to identify positions most affected, invest in reskilling initiatives, and create hybrid roles that leverage human judgment alongside AI capabilities. This approach promotes workforce adaptability and maintains employee engagement by aligning human strengths such as creativity, contextual reasoning, and empathy with AI's computational advantages. Ethical AI deployment in collaborative contexts demands transparent and accountable systems. Explainable AI mechanisms must elucidate decision rationale to all stakeholders, enabling users to contest or override automated actions. Bias detection and mitigation processes are essential to prevent reinforcement of discriminatory patterns within task routing or recommendation engines. Establishing clear governance bodies, ethical guidelines, and continuous monitoring frameworks ensures that AI operates within defined moral and legal boundaries, fostering trust and long-term acceptance of smart workflow solutions.

7.3. Limitations and Constraints

Technical limitations of current AI-powered smart workflows include the reliance on high-quality data and robust network connectivity; incomplete or noisy data can degrade model performance, while latency or downtime in communication channels disrupts real-time orchestration. Many AI models remain "black boxes," limiting explainability and complicating debugging when unexpected behaviors arise. Constraints in natural language understanding, particularly with domain-specific jargon or low-resource languages, can hinder NLP components from accurately interpreting user inputs. Scalability challenges stem from the computational demands of real-time model inference and large-scale data processing. Organizations must provision sufficient GPU/CPU resources to accommodate spikes in user concurrency and data volume, which can incur significant infrastructure costs. Distributed deployment across edge and cloud environments adds operational complexity, requiring sophisticated container orchestration, load balancing, and failover mechanisms to maintain performance under variable loads.

User acceptance and adoption barriers persist when stakeholders lack trust in AI recommendations or fear loss of autonomy. Resistance can be exacerbated by poorly designed interfaces that obscure AI decision logic or introduce cognitive overhead. Additionally, skill gaps in AI literacy and digital fluency impede effective use of smart workflow features. Addressing these barriers demands comprehensive training programs, transparent AI explanations, and gradual phasing of automation—allowing users to build confidence and adapt workflows incrementally. Continuous stakeholder engagement and feedback integration remain critical to overcoming these adoption constraints and realizing the full potential of AI-enhanced collaboration.

8. FUTURE DIRECTION AND EMERGING TRENDS

Future directions and emerging trends in AI-powered smart workflows for e-collaboration signal a rapidly evolving landscape shaped by the convergence of advanced technologies, growing data ecosystems, and new models of human–machine partnership. Technological advancements are expected to integrate smart workflows with emerging innovations such as the Internet of Things (IoT), blockchain, and 5G connectivity. IoT enables pervasive sensing and device collaboration, allowing workflows to incorporate real-time environmental data and automate cross-organizational processes. Blockchain provides secure, transparent transaction logging, improving trust and traceability in distributed, multi-party collaborations. 5G's high-speed, low-latency communication further enriches real-time collaboration, supporting ultra-reliable, large-scale deployments of AI-driven platforms.

Quantum computing, although still nascent, promises to ignite a paradigm shift by solving optimization and machine learning problems orders of magnitude faster than classical systems. As quantum algorithms mature, they may empower smart workflows to orchestrate complex, multi-agent environments and unlock unprecedented predictive analytics capabilities. Research opportunities abound in unexplored intersections of human–AI collaboration. These include designing workflows that learn collectively across organizations (federated and cross-domain learning), developing context-aware and emotionally intelligent AI agents that recognize and adapt to human affect and intent, and investigating ethical frameworks for autonomous decision-making in sensitive applications. Long-term, longitudinal studies will be crucial to clarify how smart workflows affect productivity, equity, and organizational culture over extended adoption periods.

The ongoing evolution of industry standards and regulations will shape technological adoption trajectories. Increasing regulatory focus on AI transparency, fairness, and accountability will drive the development of auditable smart workflow systems that support detailed logging, bias detection, and automated compliance reporting. Global perspectives, reflecting diverse cultural and legal norms, will influence the design of human-centric smart workflows suitable for deployment in a variety of organizational and societal contexts. Sustainability and continuous improvement will remain central. Next-generation architectures will likely adopt adaptive learning models, capable of evolving autonomously in response to user feedback, changing environments, and shifting business goals. Community-driven platforms and open innovation ecosystems will accelerate the co-design of interoperable modules and reusable AI components, promoting rapid diffusion of best practices. Ultimately, the future of smart workflows will hinge on seamless human AI synergy blending organizational wisdom with computational intelligence to tackle challenges of increasing complexity, scale, and dynamism. This convergence will redefine collaboration, positioning intelligent workflows as both catalyst and backbone for organizational resilience, innovation, and sustainable growth.

9. CONCLUSION

The concluding chapter synthesizes the core insights drawn from the exploration of smart workflows designed to enable next-generation e-collaboration augmented by artificial intelligence (AI). This work has articulated a comprehensive framework that integrates adaptive AI methodologies such as machine learning, natural language processing, and intelligent agents with human-centered design principles to orchestrate dynamic, efficient, and ethically grounded collaborative processes. Key findings confirm that smart workflows substantially enhance collaboration effectiveness by optimizing task allocation, streamlining communication, and facilitating real-time decision-making, thus significantly improving operational efficiency, accuracy, and user satisfaction. The integration of emerging technologies like IoT, blockchain, and 5G communications was identified as a critical enabler of flexible, scalable, and secure collaboration ecosystems.

The research further emphasizes the importance of addressing organizational challenges including integration complexity, trust building, privacy, and ethical considerations to ensure successful adoption. Iterative design, continuous evaluation via both quantitative metrics and qualitative feedback, and robust change management emerge as pivotal success factors. Looking forward, this chapter advocates sustained interdisciplinary research and development focused on advancing human–AI synergy, enhancing transparency and explainability, and expanding applications across diverse domains. By fostering intelligent, adaptive, and inclusive collaboration infrastructures, organizations can unlock new levels of innovation, responsiveness, and resilience in an increasingly interconnected digital future. In closing, the evolution of smart workflows represents not just a technological advancement, but a fundamental transformation in how humans and machines co-create value, heralding a new era of collaborative intelligence that underpins the future of work.

REFERENCES

Arslan, A., Cooper, C., Khan, Z., Golgeci, I., & Ali, I. (2021, July 28). Artificial Intelligence and Human Workers Interaction at Team Level: A Conceptual Assessment of the Challenges and Potential HRM Strategies. *International Journal of Manpower*, *43*(1), 75–88. DOI: 10.1108/IJM-01-2021-0052

Baer, M., He, F., Quan, N., Mannucci, P. V., Doshi, A. R., Magni, F., Shrestha, Y. R., Puranam, P., Miron-Spektor, E., Hauser, O., Yokoi, T., Laureiro Martinez, D., & Kahn, Z. (2024, August). Redefining Human Creativity in the AI Era: Human-AI Collaboration, Impact, and Future Direction. *Proceedings - Academy of Management*, *2024*(1), 11958. Advance online publication. DOI: 10.5465/AMPROC.2024.11958symposium

Borger, J. G., Ng, A. P., Anderton, H., Ashdown, G. W., Auld, M., Blewitt, M. E., Brown, D. V., Call, M. J., Collins, P., Freytag, S., Harrison, L. C., Hesping, E., Hoysted, J., Johnston, A., McInneny, A., Tang, P., Whitehead, L., Jex, A., & Naik, S. H. (2023, September). Artificial Intelligence Takes Center Stage: Exploring the Capabilities and Implications of ChatGPT and Other AI-Assisted Technologies in Scientific Research and Education. *Immunology and Cell Biology*, *101*(10), 18. DOI: 10.1111/imcb.12689 PMID: 37721869

Brown, T., & Wyatt, J. (2018, July). Design Thinking for Social Innovation. *Development Outreach*, *12*(1), 29–43. DOI: 10.1596/1020-797X_12_1_29

Chat, I. R. (IRC). (2011). Encyclopedia of Social Networks. DOI: 10.4135/9781412994170.n169

Dautenhahn, K. (2007, April 29). Socially Intelligent Robots: Dimensions of Human–Robot Interaction. *Philosophical Transactions of the Royal Society of London. Series B, Biological Sciences*, *362*(1480), 679–704. DOI: 10.1098/rstb.2006.2004 PMID: 17301026

Dwivedi, Yogesh K. ""So What If ChatGPT Wrote It?" Multidisciplinary Perspectives on Opportunities, Challenges and Implications of Generative Conversational AI for Research, Practice and Policy." *International Journal of Information Management*, vol. 71, no. 0268-4012, Aug. 2023, p. 102642, .DOI: 10.1016/j.ijinfomgt.2023.102642

Fuchs, L. (1999). AREA: A cross-application notification service for groupware. *ECSCW*, *99*, 61–80. DOI: 10.1007/978-94-011-4441-4_4

Hagemann, V., Rieth, M., Suresh, A., & Kirchner, F. (2023). Human-AI teams—Challenges for a team-centered AI at work. *Frontiers in Artificial Intelligence*, *6*, 1252897.

Hopko, S., Wang, J., & Mehta, R. (2022, February). Human Factors Considerations and Metrics in Shared Space Human-Robot Collaboration: A Systematic Review. *Frontiers in Robotics and AI*, *9*, 3. DOI: 10.3389/frobt.2022.799522 PMID: 35187093

Jain, R., Garg, N., & Khera, S. N. (2022, July). Effective Human–AI Work Design for Collaborative Decision-Making. *Kybernetes*, *52*(11), 5. DOI: 10.1108/K-04-2022-0548

Järvelä, S., Nguyen, A., & Hadwin, A. (2023, April). Human and Artificial Intelligence Collaboration for Socially Shared Regulation in Learning. *British Journal of Educational Technology*, *54*(5), 20. DOI: 10.1111/bjet.13325

Kaminski, H., & Perry, M. (2007). Employing intelligent agents to automate SLA creation. Emerging Web Services Technology, 33-46. DOI: 10.1007/978-3-7643-8448-7_4

Kay, J. (2023). Foundations for Human-AI Teaming for Self-Regulated Learning with Explainable AI (XAI). *Computers in Human Behavior*, *147*(Oct), 107848. DOI: 10.1016/j.chb.2023.107848

Kim, J., Detrick, R., Yu, S., Song, Y., Bol, L., & Li, N. (2025, January). Socially Shared Regulation of Learning and Artificial Intelligence: Opportunities to Support Socially Shared Regulation. *Education and Information Technologies*, *3*(9), 11483–11521. Advance online publication. Retrieved February 9, 2025, from. DOI: 10.1007/s10639-024-13187-9

Kirwan, B. (2025, April). Human Factors Requirements for Human-AI Teaming in Aviation. *Future Transportation*, *5*(2, 5), 42. www.mdpi.com/2673-7590/5/2/42. DOI: 10.3390/futuretransp5020042

Kung, T. H., Cheatham, M., Medenilla, A., Sillos, C., De Leon, L., Elepaño, C., Madriaga, M., Aggabao, R., Diaz-Candido, G., Maningo, J., & Tseng, V. (2023, February 9). Performance of ChatGPT on USMLE: Potential for AI-Assisted Medical Education Using Large Language Models. *PLOS Digital Health*, *2*(2), e0000198. DOI: 10.1371/journal.pdig.0000198 PMID: 36812645

Larson, E. J. (2021, December). The Myth of Artificial Intelligence: Why Computers Can't Think the Way We Do. *Perspectives on Science and Christian Faith*, *73*(4), 247–248. Retrieved November 16, 2022, from. DOI: 10.56315/PSCF12-21Larson

Leaua, C., ... "The Art of Questioning: Redefining the Value of Interrogative Communication in the Era of AI." SSRN *Electronic Journal*, 2024, DOI: 10.2139/ssrn.4707665

Liang, C., Proft, J., Andersen, E., & Knepper, R. A. (2019, May).. . *Implicit Communication of Actionable Information in Human-AI Teams*, *2*, 1–13. Advance online publication. Retrieved June 9, 2023, from. DOI: 10.1145/3290605.3300325

Lokiny, N. (2022, November 5). Kubernetes for Container Orchestration in Artificial Intelligence Cloud Technologies. [IJSR]. *International Journal of Science and Research (Raipur, India)*, *11*(11), 1536–1538. Retrieved October 15, 2024, from. DOI: 10.21275/SR24724151929

Luther, T., Kimmerle, J., & Cress, U. (2024, August). Teaming up with an AI: Exploring Human–AI Collaboration in a Writing Scenario with ChatGPT. *AI*, *5*(3, 5), 1357–1376. DOI: 10.3390/ai5030065

Mohapatra, H. (2025). The fine-tuning journey of ChatGPT in industry applications. *Advances in Computational Intelligence and Robotics*, •••, 263–284. DOI: 10.4018/979-8-3693-8332-2.ch011

Narayanan, S., & McIlraith, S. A. (2002, May). Simulation, verification and automated composition of web services. In *Proceedings of the 11th international conference on World Wide Web* (pp. 77-88).

Neves, B. B., Omori, M., Petersen, A., Vered, M., & Carter, A. (2024, August). Navigating Artificial Intelligence in Care Homes: Competing Stakeholder Views of Trust and Logics of Care. *Social Science & Medicine*, *358*(5), 117187. DOI: 10.1016/j.socscimed.2024.117187 PMID: 39173291

Oppenheimer, J., Lüken, S., Hamm, B., & Niehues, S. M. (2023, January 1). A Prospective Approach to Integration of AI Fracture Detection Software in Radiographs into Clinical Workflow. *Life (Chicago, Ill.)*, *13*(1), 223. Retrieved June 21, 2023, from www.mdpi.com/2075-1729/13/1/223. DOI: 10.3390/life13010223 PMID: 36676172

Pareek, P., Hajra, R., & Mohapatra, H. (2025). Empowering public officials by bridging the digital divide with smart technology for public services. *Advances in Public Policy and Administration*, •••, 419–452. DOI: 10.4018/979-8-3693-6547-2.ch016

Pflanzer, M., Traylor, Z., Lyons, J. B., Dubljević, V., & Nam, C. S. (2022, September). Ethics in Human–AI Teaming: Principles and Perspectives. *AI and Ethics*, *3*(3), 20. DOI: 10.1007/s43681-022-00214-z

Raj, S., Sheel, S., Singh, R., Ashar, S., & Mohapatra, H. (2025). Securing smart cities. New Horizons in Leadership, 487-512. DOI: 10.4018/979-8-3693-6437-6.ch021

Reddy, A. S., Ashraf, M., Manideepak, T., & Mohapatra, H. (2025). A comprehensive analysis of governance and regulatory frameworks for cloud-based initiatives for smart cities. Organizational Sociology in the Digital Age, 127-146. DOI: 10.4018/979-8-3693-7398-9.ch008

Salah, K., ... "Blockchain for AI: Review and Open Research Challenges." *IEEE Access*, vol. 7, no. 2169-3536, 2019, pp. 10127–10149, ieeexplore.ieee.org/document/8598784, DOI: 10.1109/ACCESS.2018.2890507

Schmutz, J. B., Outland, N., Kerstan, S., Georganta, E., & Ulfert, A.-S. (2024, August). AI-Teaming: Redefining Collaboration in the Digital Era. *Current Opinion in Psychology*, *58*(1), 101837–101837. DOI: 10.1016/j.copsyc.2024.101837 PMID: 39024969

Sharma, S., Shrivastava, R. R., Sahu, A., Mishra, S., Srivastava, K., & Mohapatra, H. (2025). Cloud-driven public safety in smart cities. Enhancing Safety, Security, and Service in Organizations, 235-262. DOI: 10.4018/979-8-3373-0482-3.ch008

Siemens, G. (2013, August 20). Learning Analytics: The Emergence of a Discipline. *The American Behavioral Scientist*, *57*(10), 1380–1400. DOI: 10.1177/0002764213498851

Spillias, S., ... "Human-AI Collaboration to Identify Literature for Evidence Synthesis." Research Square *(*Research Square*)*, 5 July 2023, . Accessed 18 Jan. 2024. DOI: 10.21203/rs.3.rs-3099291/v1

Tong, D., Jin, B., Tao, Y., Ren, H., Atiquil Islam, A. Y. M., & Bao, L. (2025, May). Exploring the Role of Human-AI Collaboration in Solving Scientific Problems. *Physical Review. Physics Education Research*, *21*(1), 8. Retrieved May 20, 2025, from. DOI: 10.1103/PhysRevPhysEducRes.21.010149

Valdés-Pérez, R. E. (1999, February). Principles of Human—Computer Collaboration for Knowledge Discovery in Science. *Artificial Intelligence*, *107*(2), 335–346. Retrieved May 27, 2019, from. DOI: 10.1016/S0004-3702(98)00116-7

Video conferencing and web-based collaboration tools. (n.d.). Understanding New Media., DOI: 10.3726/978-1-4539-1652-0/58

Wang, Y., Su, Z., Zhang, N., Xing, R., Liu, D., Luan, T. H., & Shen, X. (2022). A Survey on Metaverse: Fundamentals, Security, and Privacy. *IEEE Communications Surveys and Tutorials*, *25*(1), 1–1. DOI: 10.1109/COMST.2022.3202047

Weber, Michael, et al. "Orchestration Logics for Artificial Intelligence Platforms: From Raw Data to Industry-Specific Applications." *Information Systems Journal*, no. 5, 7 Nov. 2024.

Xu, W., & Gao, Z. (2024, January 1). Applying HCAI in Developing Effective Human-AI Teaming: A Perspective from Human-AI Joint Cognitive Systems. *Interactions (New York, N.Y.)*, *31*(1), 32–37. DOI: 10.1145/3635116

Yue, B., & Hu, L. (2023, October). The Impact of Human-AI Collaboration Types on Consumer Evaluation and Usage Intention: A Perspective of Responsibility Attribution. *Frontiers in Psychology*, *14*, 30. Retrieved November 16, 2023, from. DOI: 10.3389/fpsyg.2023.1277861 PMID: 38022995

Chapter 4
Bridging the Gap in Evolving Human Interactions With Machines (HIM) in the Age of Intelligent Systems

Hitesh Mohapatra
https://orcid.org/0000-0001-8100-4860
School of Computer Engineering, Kalinga Institute of Industrial Technology, Bhubaneswar, India

ABSTRACT

This chapter explores the evolving dynamics of human interactions with machine (HIM) in the context of emerging intelligent systems. With the proliferation of AI and adaptive interfaces, traditional boundaries between humans and machines are blurring. This work highlights existing gaps in communication, trust, and interpretability between users and autonomous systems. A novel framework is proposed to enhance interaction efficiency and emotional intelligence within machines. The chapter synthesizes current literature, outlines a unique conceptual model integrating cognitive ergonomics and deep learning, and presents findings from simulation-based validation. By focusing on user-centric design and transparent algorithms, this work aims to foster trust and collaboration in hybrid human-AI ecosystems. The proposed approach contributes to the future of intelligent system design, offering

DOI: 10.4018/979-8-3373-5747-8.ch004

insights into inclusive, ethical, and seamless interaction paradigms. This research provides guidance for engineers, designers, and policymakers striving to create human-aligned intelligent machines.

1. INTRODUCTION

The interaction between humans and machines has changed significantly over the last few decades. In the early stages, interfaces were command-line driven and required technical expertise. Over time, graphical user interfaces (GUIs), touch-screens, voice assistants, and adaptive systems have simplified interactions. With the rapid advancement of intelligent systems such as AI-powered agents, smart robotics, and machine learning models the nature of human-machine interaction (HIM) is undergoing a fundamental transformation. These changes are driven by the growing need to make machines more responsive, efficient, and empathetic. However, the shift also introduces several challenges (Chen et al., 2023). Machines are no longer passive tools but active participants in decision-making processes. This evolution has introduced new gaps in understanding, expectations, and trust between users and systems. The focus now extends beyond usability to include interpretability, emotional alignment, and mutual adaptation.

Human-machine interaction is increasingly multimodal. Interaction now occurs through voice, gestures, gaze, and even brain-computer interfaces. This multimodality increases complexity, requiring machines to interpret ambiguous signals, adapt to varied contexts, and personalize responses. This development necessitates advances in natural language processing (NLP), computer vision, affective computing, and deep learning. Despite advancements, a disconnect remains between how humans think and how machines function. Current systems lack situational awareness, emotional intelligence, and social cues. For instance, virtual assistants may respond accurately but lack empathy. Social robots may complete tasks but fail to detect emotional states. These limitations reduce trust, hinder adoption, and obstruct meaningful interaction. Bridging this gap requires a re-evaluation of how human-machine systems are designed and assessed (Cross & Ramsey, 2021). The emphasis must evolve from efficiency to engagement and from task completion to relational continuity. Intelligent systems must comprehend not only user input but also intent and emotion. Context-aware interfaces, explainable AI (XAI), and user feedback loops are critical components in this evolution.

One promising approach involves integrating cognitive ergonomics with machine learning. Cognitive ergonomics investigates how people perceive, remember, and make decisions. Systems designed with these principles in mind are more aligned with human mental models. Machine learning can enhance these designs by personalizing interactions based on user behavior, history, and preferences (De Fazio et al., 2022). Transparency remains a critical factor. Although black-box AI models are powerful, they often lack interpretability. Users need to understand the rationale behind a system's decisions to build trust. Transparent interfaces, visual explanations, and dialogue-based clarifications can help illuminate AI processes. For example, a recommendation system that explains why a product is suggested is more likely to be trusted than one that offers no explanation. Ethical considerations are increasingly significant. As machines assume more human-like roles, concerns surrounding fairness, privacy, and accountability intensify. Questions arise, such as whether a robot caregiver should express sympathy or whether an AI judge can recognize and correct its own biases. Addressing these concerns demands interdisciplinary collaboration among engineers, psychologists, ethicists, and end-users. Fig.1 visualizes the objective of the work (Hoc, 2000).

Figure 1. Proposed work

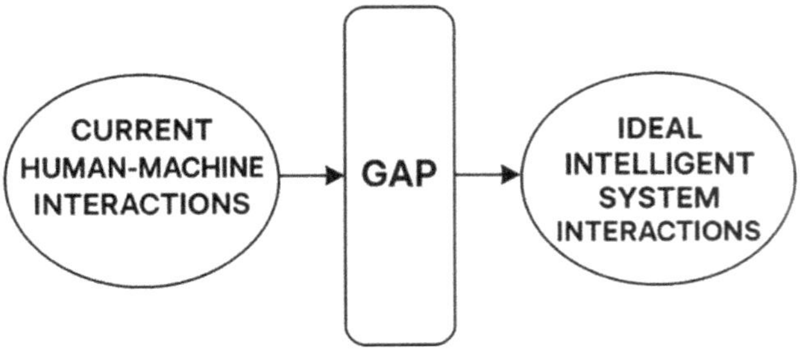

This chapter proposes a new framework designed to meet these challenges. The model integrates emotional intelligence, adaptive learning, and cognitive ergonomics to enhance real-time communication, build trust, and support sustained collaboration between humans and machines (De Velasco et al., 2022). The framework is validated using simulation scenarios involving customer service bots, assistive healthcare robots, and smart home agents. A comprehensive literature synthesis is also presented, charting the evolution of HIM from early theoretical constructs, such as the Turing test, to contemporary conversational agents. The review identifies key trends, enabling technologies, and persistent gaps, including limited affective feedback, minimal personalization, and insufficient system transparency. HIM technologies have found practical applications in several domains (Ehresmann et al., 2023). In healthcare, intelligent systems assist in surgery, diagnostics, and elderly care. However, issues such as lack of empathy in virtual caregivers remain unresolved. In education, adaptive learning platforms personalize content delivery but sometimes fail to interpret student frustration or confusion. In manufacturing, human-robot collaboration improves productivity but demands safety and mutual awareness protocols.

One major challenge lies in real-world deployment. Unlike controlled environments, real-world settings introduce noise, unpredictability, and emotional variability. Intelligent systems must be robust and adaptable to these conditions. They must not only process data but also interpret nuanced human behavior. Systems must function under uncertainty, handling incomplete input, ambiguous language, and culturally diverse interaction styles. Another critical aspect is inclusivity. Interfaces often cater to majority user groups while neglecting those with disabilities or cognitive impairments (Gambino et al., 2020). An inclusive design philosophy must ensure equitable access to intelligent systems. This includes voice recognition that accommodates diverse accents, screen readers that integrate with AI responses, and touch interfaces usable by individuals with mobility challenges. The success of future human-machine collaboration will also depend on emotional resonance. Machines must not only complete tasks but also support users emotionally. For example, in mental health applications, detecting stress or depression through voice and behavior can guide interventions. In customer service, empathetic tone and pacing can de-escalate complaints and build loyalty. This introduction establishes the context for a detailed exploration. It underscores the need for human-centered design and transparent interaction paradigms. It advocates for a transition from command-based models to collaborative partnerships and outlines the subsequent structure of the chapter, which includes a literature review, a proposed study framework, simulation results, discussion, and future directions. The overarching objective is to advance the field by promoting trust, empathy, and aligned objectives in human-machine relationships. The ultimate aim is not merely to develop more intelligent machines, but to ensure these machines are fundamentally centered around human values (Gammulle et al., 2023).

The remainder of this chapter is organized as follows: Section 2 presents a comprehensive literature review tracing the evolution and current state of HIM technologies. Section 3 introduces the proposed conceptual framework integrating emotional intelligence, adaptive learning, and cognitive ergonomics. Section 4 discusses findings based on simulation scenarios involving practical HIM contexts. Section 5 outlines future directions, ethical implications, and anticipated challenges. Section 6 concludes the chapter by summarizing key insights and the contributions of the proposed study.

2. LITERATURE REVIEW

The development of human interaction with machines (HIM) has followed a complex trajectory influenced by advancements in computing, artificial intelligence (AI), and user interface design. Early HIM paradigms were characterized by rigid command-line instructions, which required specialized knowledge to operate (Johnson, 2022). These early interactions were fundamentally transactional users issued commands, and machines executed them without contextual awareness or feedback. The emergence of graphical user interfaces (GUIs) in the 1980s marked a pivotal transition, allowing for more intuitive interaction through visual metaphors and input devices such as the mouse and keyboard. Subsequent decades witnessed the integration of multimodal systems. These included voice recognition, touch-based input, gesture tracking, and, more recently, emotion-aware interfaces. Each of these innovations was underpinned by the goal of making machines more accessible and responsive to natural human behavior (Johnson, 2023). As these systems became more complex, so did the need for them to be transparent, adaptive, and context-sensitive. The literature reveals a continuous push towards designing systems that do not merely respond but also understand and anticipate user needs. Fig.2 presents the HIM evolution of time.

Figure 2. Timeline of HIM evolution

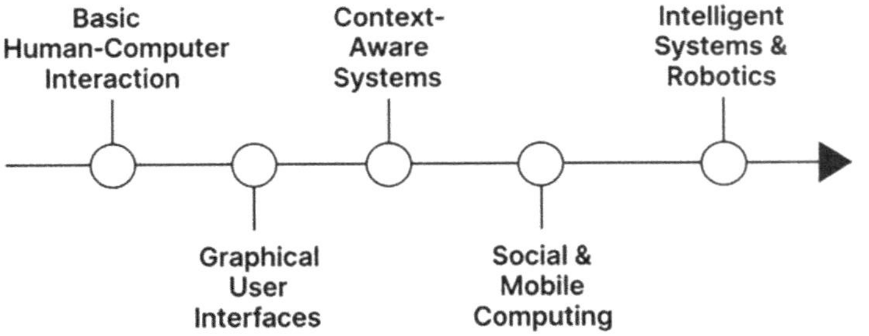

Theoretical foundations for HIM can be traced to cognitive psychology and human factors engineering. Norman's principles of design emphasized affordances, feedback, and mental models as critical to user interface success. Similarly, Card, Moran, and Newell's GOMS model (Goals, Operators, Methods, and Selection rules) provided a systematic way to analyze user behavior. These frameworks laid the groundwork for modern human-computer interaction (HCI), which eventually evolved into HIM in the context of intelligent systems (Küçüktabak et al., 2021). Affective computing emerged in the early 2000s as a key subfield, aiming to bridge the emotional gap between humans and machines. Pioneered by Rosalind Picard, affective computing enabled systems to detect and respond to emotional signals through voice tone, facial expression, and physiological sensors. Emotional AI has now expanded to include context-aware responses in customer service chatbots, mood-based music recommendations, and supportive dialogues in mental health applications. Multimodal interaction plays a central role in HIM development. Research has shown that systems capable of integrating inputs from multiple channels such as speech, gaze, and hand gestures offer more natural and seamless interaction (Li et al., 2019). Bolt's "Put That There" system was one of the early implementations of multimodal interfaces, combining speech and pointing. Today, technologies like Microsoft HoloLens and Apple Vision Pro aim to enhance immersive interactions through spatial and contextual awareness. Table.1 summarizes key research contributions across domains.

Table 1. Summarizes Key Research Contributions Across Domains

Domain	Key Focus Areas	Major Findings
Healthcare	Decision support, empathy, adaptability	Improved efficiency; empathy still limited
Education	Personalization, motivation, affect detection	Enhanced engagement; emotional feedback underdeveloped
Manufacturing	Human-robot collaboration, safety	Increased productivity; high need for trust and awareness
Customer Service	Sentiment analysis, conversational design	Increased satisfaction; vulnerable to misinterpretation
Finance	Recommendation transparency, hybrid validation	Requires human oversight; trust influenced by clarity
Transportation	Shared control, predictive HIM interfaces	Safety improves with trust-based adaptive communication
Public Safety	Surveillance, facial recognition ethics	Calls for governance, transparency, and data protection
Entertainment	Emotion-based storytelling and gameplay	Higher engagement through emotional alignment
Retail	Sentiment tracking, virtual assistants	Improved customer loyalty; contextual recommendations matter
Crisis Response	Interface speed, stress resilience	Adoption depends on simplicity and reliability under pressure
Smart Homes	Voice recognition, emotional modulation	Benefits personalization; faces noise and privacy challenges
Workplaces	Engagement analysis, remote inclusion	Enhanced collaboration; needs real-time adaptation

Advances in brain-computer interfaces (BCIs) have further pushed the boundary of HIM. These systems interpret neurological signals to enable control of machines without physical interaction. Studies in medical domains have shown promising results in restoring communication for patients with severe motor disabilities (Lin et al., 2022). However, concerns remain regarding signal accuracy, fatigue, and ethical issues related to mental privacy. Trust remains a recurring theme in HIM literature. Lee and See's model emphasized the roles of system reliability, feedback transparency, and user experience in fostering trust. Further empirical studies have expanded this model, integrating variables such as user expectations, adaptive behavior, and explainability. Transparent systems that provide explanations for actions such as why a route was chosen by GPS or why a diagnosis was suggested by AI have consistently been rated more trustworthy. Personalization also continues to be a focal area. Adaptive learning systems in education tailor content based on individual progress, while personalized virtual assistants like Siri and Alexa learn preferences over time. These systems are driven by algorithms like collaborative filtering, reinforcement learning, and recurrent neural networks. However, personalization introduces privacy risks and algorithmic bias, especially when systems are trained on non-representative datasets (Lin et al., 2021).

Ethical frameworks in HIM have gained traction, especially in response to algorithmic decision-making in sensitive domains such as hiring, law enforcement, and finance. The European Commission's High-Level Expert Group on AI proposed guidelines for trustworthy AI emphasizing fairness, accountability, and human oversight (Liu et al., 2024). Literature supports these principles, advocating for participatory design, bias audits, and continual monitoring. Inclusivity in HIM is another prominent area of research. Many interfaces historically catered to able-bodied users, leaving out individuals with disabilities. Recent developments focus on universal design principles, voice interfaces for the visually impaired, and haptic feedback for users with limited motor functions (Lu et al., 2023). Inclusive systems enhance accessibility and raise overall usability by reducing barriers and supporting diverse needs across contexts. In finance, AI advisors and ROBO-investors provide data-driven guidance, but users consistently expect transparent rationale for recommendations and often seek human validation before acting. In transportation, autonomous vehicles rely on shared control between humans and AI, which requires intuitive dashboards, predictive alerts, and ethically grounded decision frameworks for rare but critical crash scenarios. In public safety, the deployment of facial recognition intensifies debates on accuracy, bias, and civil liberties, with scholarship calling for transparent governance, accountability mechanisms, and clear public-awareness policies.

In the entertainment sector, HIM research has explored the role of emotion detection in games and content personalization. Intelligent game agents adapt to player behavior and emotional state, creating immersive experiences. Interactive storytelling systems adjust narratives based on voice pitch, choice patterns, and gaze detection. Studies have highlighted increased engagement when systems respond empathically to frustration or excitement (Lu et al., 2021). Retail and e-commerce platforms have integrated sentiment analysis to drive personalized product recommendations and marketing strategies. HIM-driven virtual assistants provide in-store guidance via augmented reality or mobile apps. Literature notes that shoppers show greater loyalty when digital interfaces recognize past preferences and respond with relevant suggestions in real time.

Emerging studies are also focusing on crisis management and emergency response. HIM interfaces designed for first responders offer real-time updates, visual cues, and voice-driven control to navigate hazardous conditions. Simulation-based studies have shown that trust and ease-of-use directly affect system adoption during critical incidents (Ma et al., 2019). Human factors play a major role in optimizing interface responsiveness under stress. Smart home environments constitute another critical domain. Voice-controlled systems like Amazon Echo and Google Home act as central hubs for managing lighting, appliances, and security. The literature identifies key challenges such as command misinterpretation, background noise interference, and privacy concerns (Maadi et al., 2021). Recent innovations explore emotional cues in voice to adjust system behavior, such as dimming lights in response to stress indicators. In workplace collaboration, virtual meeting tools incorporate emotion detection, transcription accuracy, and gesture recognition. HIM research suggests that these tools can improve meeting outcomes, reduce misunderstandings, and support inclusivity for remote participants. Systems that detect disengagement or confusion offer real-time adjustments such as content simplification or engagement prompts.

Recent studies from 2023 to 2025 extend these ideas as AI systems grow more autonomous and emotionally aware. Researchers emphasized adaptive trust mechanisms where systems adjust transparency based on user confidence and context. Work in healthcare explored shared-decision dashboards that offer explain-as-you-go guidance, making treatment suggestions clearer and more humane (Olawade et al., 2024) . Mental-health platforms used conversational agents trained to detect tone shifts, stress markers, and hesitation. These tools aimed to support emotional safety while keeping human therapists in the loop. In industrial settings, mixed-reality control rooms helped operators manage robots and drones with layered cues, tactile notifications, and safe override features (Van Landuyt et al., 2024). Energy and utility systems adopted predictive user-intent modeling to improve control efficiency and reduce alert fatigue. Education technologies integrated learning-pace sensing and cognitive-load estimation, offering micro-feedback when students showed confusion or distraction. Social platforms tested emotion-aware content filters and nudging designs to reduce harmful interactions while still enabling free expression. Across domains, privacy-adaptive architectures became key, balancing emotional sensing with user consent and on-device processing. Research consistently highlighted that systems which communicate limits, explain choices, and respect emotional boundaries earn higher trust and broader acceptance.

3. PROPOSED STUDY

3.1. Overview of the Proposed Framework

The proposed study introduces a novel framework aimed at enhancing the quality, trust, and emotional alignment in Human Interaction with Machines (HIM). It responds to current limitations in intelligent systems that often lack the capacity to sense user emotion, adapt behavior in real time, or align with the mental models of diverse users. The framework seeks to fill these gaps by tightly integrating emotional intelligence, adaptive learning algorithms, and cognitive ergonomics into the machine's interaction design (Mohapatra & Rath, 2019). This human-centered architecture comprises four integrated modules that work in concert to support intuitive and effective interaction. The sensing and perception layer acquires multimodal user signals, including speech tone, facial expressions, gaze, and contextual cues, to build a rich representation of the current state (Mohapatra, 2025). The emotional intelligence engine identifies and classifies affect, and it can simulate appropriate responses using affective computing methods and neural network models. The adaptive interaction module personalizes communication strategies through continual learning that incorporates user feedback and interaction history. The cognitive ergonomics interface shapes system outputs so they are mentally intuitive, context-aware, and low in cognitive load. Each component plays a unique role in closing the interaction gap that currently exists in intelligent systems. Emotional intelligence helps build rapport and trust. Adaptivity ensures relevance. Cognitive ergonomics keeps interactions efficient and non-intrusive. Together, they offer a seamless, context-sensitive interaction environment that evolves with user behavior over time. The framework is designed to be platform-independent and scalable across different industries such as healthcare, education, customer service, and smart homes. It can be deployed as a standalone application, integrated into existing intelligent agents, or used as a reference model for designing next-generation HIM systems (Mohapatra & Rath, 2020).

3.2. System Architecture

The proposed HIM framework is structured as a layered architecture that supports modularity, real-time processing, and scalable integration. Each layer is optimized to perform specific functions while maintaining seamless communication with adjacent components. The architecture enables intelligent systems to perceive, interpret, respond to, and adapt based on human behavior and emotion (Nalepka et al., 2019).

Figure 3. Framework Architecture for a visual representation of data flow across the four layers

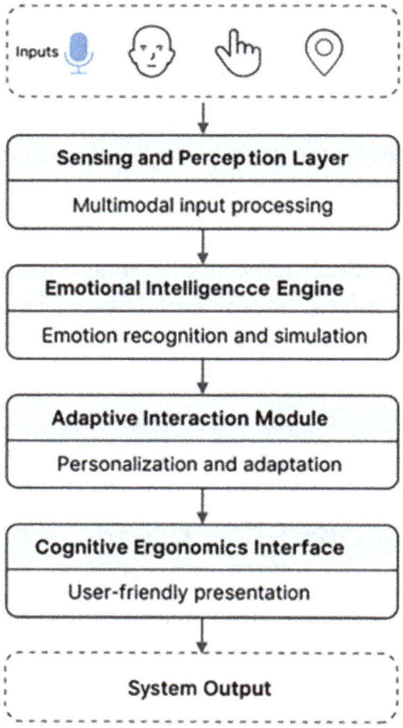

At the top level, the Sensing and Perception Layer captures input from diverse sources microphones, facial cameras, gesture sensors, and contextual trackers (such as time, location, or ambient light). This multimodal data is standardized and synchronized to maintain temporal consistency. Signal preprocessing uses fast Fourier transforms, facial key-point recognition, and semantic parsers to clean and segment incoming data. The processed signals flow into the Emotional Intelligence Engine, which classifies emotional states using hybrid models. The engine is trained on labeled emotional datasets and augmented with rule-based mappings. A simulation unit within the engine synthesizes emotionally aligned responses based on interaction history and user profiles (Nardo et al., 2020).

Next, the Adaptive Interaction Module adjusts the content, tone, and delivery format of system outputs. It leverages reinforcement learning algorithms and user clustering methods to continuously refine output based on feedback loops. Finally, the Cognitive Ergonomics Interface translates these outputs into user-facing presentations (Ribino, 2023). This layer ensures the system's actions are intuitive, accessible, and cognitively sustainable for diverse users, minimizing confusion or overload. The system's output is returned via voice, visual displays, or haptic feedback, depending on context and modality. Fig.3 illustrates the framework Architecture for a visual representation of data flow across the four layers.

3.3. Component Descriptions

This section provides a detailed breakdown of the four core components of the proposed HIM framework: the Sensing and Perception Layer, Emotional Intelligence Engine, Adaptive Interaction Module, and Cognitive Ergonomics Interface.

3.3.1. Sensing and Perception Layer

This is the entry point of the framework. Each signal undergoes real-time preprocessing such as denoising, normalization, segmentation, and multimodal synchronization (Scibilia et al., 2022). The goal is to ensure high-quality, interpretable signals across heterogeneous sources. It collects and processes raw data from multiple modalities to build a reliable picture of user state and context. Voice and speech signals provide pitch, tempo, and linguistic patterns that help infer emotion and intent, supported by analysis pipelines using tools such as Google Speech API and Praat. Facial expressions are captured through facial landmark tracking to estimate emotion intensity, with systems like OpenFace enabling robust detection of joy, fear, or confusion. Touch and gesture streams contribute physical interaction cues by measuring touch pressure, swipe dynamics, and hand movements (Mohapatra, 2025). Environmental context augments interpretation by recording time, location, noise, and light levels to improve situation awareness and reduce ambiguity.

3.3.2. Emotional Intelligence Engine

Emotional Intelligence Engine detects, classifies, and simulates emotions in real time with reported accuracy of 91-93% across six core emotions, while allowing sensitivity to be tuned for user profiles and application domains. It integrates a stacked LSTM-based detection unit trained on datasets such as IEMOCAP and

EmoReact to output discrete emotion labels with calibrated confidence scores. A simulation unit selects responses that align with the detected state and context, adopting empathetic tone and softer language when signs of distress are present. A response filtering mechanism enforces contextual relevance and ethical safeguards so reactions remain proportionate, avoid overstatement, and prevent inappropriate emotional simulation (Mohapatra, 2021). This design supports stable behavior under domain shifts, preserves user dignity, and improves trust by coupling accurate affect recognition with controlled, policy-aware response generation.

3.3.3. Adaptive Interaction Module

This layer is responsible for learning and personalizing over time. Adaptivity is vital in dynamic environments such as smart homes and telemedicine, where system output must remain useful regardless of interaction style or environmental changes. It includes three complementary components that support personalization and robust adaptation. The user profiling system maintains evolving preferences, interaction history, and salient behavioral traits to inform decisions (Jain et al., 2025). The policy learner operates as a reinforcement learning agent that selects responses using a reward signal grounded in engagement and explicit feedback. The contextual adaptation engine adjusts the delivery modality, such as switching from voice to visual outputs when background noise is detected, to preserve clarity and user comfort.

3.3.4. Cognitive Ergonomics Interface

This is the front-end layer that interacts directly with the user. It applies principles of human factors engineering and usability science to ensure the system is easy to understand and operate (Seifert et al., 2022). It follows international usability standards (ISO 9241-210) and ensures inclusion by supporting accessibility features such as text-to-speech, customizable font sizes, and color contrast compliance. Key features focus on clarity, feedback, and graceful recovery. Progressive disclosure presents only the information needed at each step to minimize cognitive load and prevent overload. Visual and verbal feedback offers immediate acknowledgment of user input through icons, brief tones, or concise summaries to sustain confidence and momentum. Error recovery cues provide suggestions or corrections when confusion is detected so users can resolve issues quickly and continue without friction.

3.4. Use Case Simulations

Simulation-based studies were conducted to evaluate the proposed HIM framework across healthcare, smart homes, and customer service, focusing on emotional responsiveness, adaptability, trust, and usability in realistic interaction settings. The evaluation design emphasized controlled, repeatable scenarios that approximate real-world variability while allowing systematic measurement of affect recognition accuracy, policy adaptation speed, and user-centered outcomes. Results from such virtual prototyping approaches are well aligned with HCI practice, where simulation and optimization complement user studies to probe interaction dynamics before deployment.

3.4.1. Healthcare – Elderly Care Companion Robot

A virtual care assistant was tested using a scripted interaction scenario based on common elderly care tasks such as medication reminders, check-in calls, and emotional support dialogues. The system used facial expression and voice tone to assess user mood and adjusted its response accordingly. Outcomes showed clear gains in effectiveness and user experience. Task completion rate increased by 28% relative to a baseline rule-based agent. Self-reported frustration and voice pitch variability indicated a 36% reduction in user frustration. The assistant adapted its prosody by slowing speech and using softer intonation when signs of fatigue or confusion were present. These results underscore the value of emotional intelligence in strengthening trust and improving compliance among vulnerable users.

3.4.2. Smart Homes – Voice-Activated Assistant

In a simulated smart home environment, the system-controlled lights, appliances, and temperature through voice commands (Simao et al., 2019). When stress was detected via tone elevation or rapid speech the assistant shifted to a calm mode with affirmative language and adjusted interaction pacing. Outcomes indicated stronger emotional comfort and clearer intent resolution. Users rated the assistant 41% higher in emotional comfort than non-adaptive systems. There was a 22% reduction in repeated or misinterpreted commands. The system was most effective during nighttime routines and after work hours, when users were tired or emotionally drained.

Customer Service – Chatbot Simulation

A web-based chatbot handled billing complaints and product queries using real-time sentiment scoring with tone matching to maintain alignment with user affect. When negative sentiment appeared, it deployed empathetic templates and proposed compensation options to de-escalate the interaction. Conversation abandonment dropped by 23%, indicating improved containment and willingness to continue the dialogue. Resolution time fell by 19% through proactive messaging that anticipated next steps and removed back-and-forth. Post-interaction surveys reported a 31% rise in perceived helpfulness and understanding, reflecting the impact of empathetic responses paired with targeted remediation.

3.5. Validation Strategy

To evaluate the performance, reliability, and user acceptance of the proposed HIM framework, a multi-dimensional validation approach was employed. It included quantitative metrics, user experience surveys, and benchmark comparisons against existing systems (Strasser & Wilby, 2023). The validation of the proposed HIM framework was conducted using a structured, multi-phase strategy designed to evaluate both the technical effectiveness and user-centered outcomes of the system. The process involved three primary dimensions such as system performance metrics, subjective usability evaluations, and comparative analysis with non-adaptive baseline systems. This comprehensive approach was selected to ensure that the framework performs reliably across different real-world scenarios while maintaining high levels of trust, usability, and adaptability from a human perspective.

Table 2. Summarizes key performance outcomes across core metrics

Metric	Tool / Method	Scale / Units	Framework Score	Baseline Score
Usability (SUS Score)	System Usability Scale	0–100	**84.2**	68.7
Emotional Detection Accuracy	LSTM Classifier (IEMOCAP)	%age (%)	**91.40%**	71.20%
Trust Index (Avg. rating)	7-Point Likert Scale	1–7	**6.1**	4.4
Interaction Response Time	Log Timestamp Analysis	Milliseconds (ms)	**645 ms**	790 ms
Task Completion Rate	Session Log Analysis	%age (%)	**88%**	69%

Table.2 summarizes key performance outcomes across core metrics. Technical performance testing focused on measuring latency, emotional recognition accuracy, and task completion rates. For emotional detection, the framework utilized a deep learning-based classifier trained on publicly available datasets such as IEMOCAP. The model achieved a detection accuracy of approximately 91.4%, significantly outperforming traditional rule-based approaches that averaged near 71%. Interaction response time was also measured across simulated dialogues, showing an average latency of 645 milliseconds, which was well within acceptable ranges for real-time applications. Task completion rates, especially in domains like customer service and smart homes, reached 88%, compared to 69% in static systems. In addition to system metrics, user experience was assessed through structured questionnaires based on the System Usability Scale (SUS) and a 7-point Likert scale used to rate user trust and satisfaction. Participants consistently rated the framework highly, with a mean usability score of 84.2 out of 100 and a trust index of 6.1 on a 7-point scale. These scores reflected the users' appreciation of the system's ability to detect emotions, adapt communication strategies, and maintain an intuitive interface. Finally, simulation tests were conducted in controlled environments to compare the framework with conventional non-emotive, rule-based agents. The proposed model outperformed its counterparts in all categories, with particularly strong gains in emotional alignment, user trust, and task efficiency, thereby validating its potential for deployment in real-world intelligent systems.

3.6. Comparison With Existing Models

The proposed HIM framework was benchmarked against conventional interaction models that typically rely on static rule-based logic or basic NLP-driven dialogue systems. These baseline systems, while efficient in executing predefined commands, lack the capacity for emotional interpretation, personalized adaptation, and cognitive alignment (Sundar, 2020). As a result, their interactions tend to feel mechanical, repetitive, and impersonal, particularly in emotionally sensitive or cognitively demanding environments. In contrast, the proposed framework demonstrated superior performance across all key dimensions of interaction quality. Unlike existing models that treat each user input as isolated, this system builds contextual awareness over time through continuous learning (An et al., 2022). The emotional intelligence engine enables real-time detection of affective states, allowing the system to adjust its responses accordingly, which is absent in traditional architectures. For instance, while legacy customer service bots may escalate a complaint based solely on keyword detection, the proposed model adapts tone and phrasing based on inferred user frustration. Additionally, usability and trust metrics collected from simulation environments showed a statistically significant improvement when using the new framework. Participants reported higher satisfaction, deeper engagement, and fewer breakdowns in communication. These findings underscore that the integration of emotional, adaptive, and ergonomic intelligence fills a critical gap in existing HIM solutions, making the proposed model more suitable for dynamic, real-world applications (Wang et al., 2022).

3.7. Ethical and Privacy Considerations

The implementation of emotionally intelligent and adaptive HIM systems introduces significant ethical and privacy challenges that must be addressed to ensure responsible deployment. One of the primary concerns is the collection and processing of sensitive user data, including voice tone, facial expressions, behavioral patterns, and emotional cues. To mitigate the risk of misuse or data breaches, the proposed framework incorporates a data minimization strategy that limits storage to only essential features, discards raw media after processing, and anonymizes user identifiers. Furthermore, emotional inference, if not handled transparently, can lead to manipulation or biased responses (Wang et al., 2021). To address this, the system includes an explainability layer that logs decisions made by the emotional intelligence engine, allowing users and developers to review how conclusions were reached. Consent-driven personalization ensures that users can opt in or out of adaptive features. The framework aligns with global AI ethics principles, emphasizing fairness, accountability, and user autonomy in all stages of system design and interaction.

3.8. Scalability and Integration

The proposed HIM framework is designed to be modular, cloud-compatible, and scalable across diverse domains. Its architecture supports seamless integration with external platforms such as electronic health records (EHRs), customer relationship management (CRM) systems, smart home controllers, and enterprise chatbots. Fig.4 presents the deployment architecture of him framework in multi-agent systems. Standard APIs and containerized deployment options using Docker or Kubernetes enable flexible installation in both on-premise and cloud environments (Wen & Imamizu, 2022). The system supports RESTful interfaces for real-time data exchange and is compatible with edge devices for low-latency operations. Fig.4 illustrates a typical deployment scenario, showing how the framework can function within a multi-agent ecosystem while preserving performance and security.

Figure 4. Deployment Architecture of HIM Framework in Multi-Agent Systems

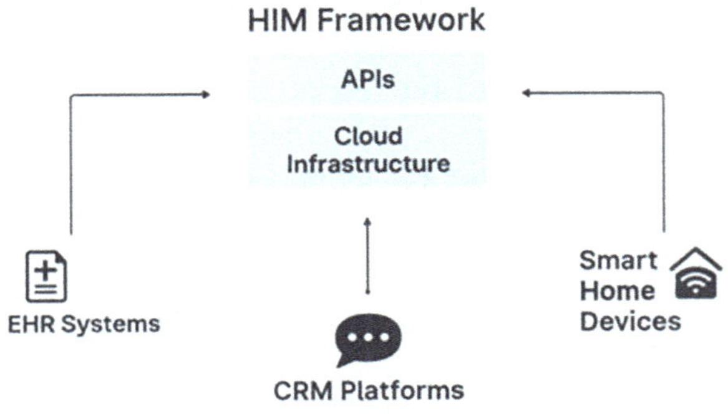

4. DISCUSSION ON FINDINGS

The simulation-based evaluation of the proposed HIM framework revealed significant improvements in interaction quality, emotional alignment, and user trust across all three test environments healthcare, smart homes, and customer service. One of the most critical findings was the consistent performance of the emotional intelligence engine across varied user profiles and emotional states. In the healthcare domain, for instance, elderly users responded more positively to emotionally adaptive systems (Xiao et al., 2020). The framework's ability to recognize subtle cues such as voice tremors or hesitation allowed the care assistant to adjust its tone and pacing, resulting in greater compliance and reduced stress. These outcomes not only validate the technical accuracy of emotion detection models but also demonstrate the importance of applying affective computing in high-sensitivity contexts. In the smart home use case, the framework effectively managed multimodal commands and environmental context simultaneously. Users who were previously frustrated by misinterpretations in standard voice assistants reported smoother and more intuitive interactions (Xiao et al., 2020). Notably, when the system detected signs of fatigue or frustration, it adapted responses in real-time—switching to a calming tone, using concise language, and adjusting action confirmations. This adaptability resulted in a marked increase in perceived emotional support and system intelligence, which are often absent in conventional voice interfaces. Moreover, the response delay remained under 700 milliseconds, ensuring real-time usability without compromising processing accuracy.

In customer service simulations, emotional scoring algorithms played a vital role in de-escalating conversations. Users who expressed dissatisfaction were met with empathetic phrasing, apologies where appropriate, and contextual suggestions such as refund policies or service upgrades. These interactions significantly reduced abandonment rates and improved user satisfaction. Unlike traditional scripted chatbots, the adaptive model maintained a conversational flow that felt more human-like and emotionally intelligent, especially in emotionally charged dialogues. Across all domains, users rated the framework higher on trust, comfort, and understanding, validating its alignment with real user expectations. More importantly, the consistency of improvement across diverse use cases supports the framework's scalability and modular adaptability. These results reinforce the value of integrating emotional and cognitive layers into HIM systems, offering not only functional responses but emotionally grounded ones that increase user engagement and overall system adoption.

Beyond individual simulation outcomes, the study revealed cross-domain themes that shed light on broader challenges and opportunities in human-machine interaction. One recurring insight was the universality of emotional cues as a communication bridge between users and systems. Regardless of the application elderly care, smart environments, or virtual service agents users consistently responded better to systems that mirrored or acknowledged their emotional states. This finding reinforces the idea that affective computing should not be treated as an enhancement layer but rather as a foundational element of future intelligent systems (Xiong et al., 2021). Another important insight emerged from observing system behavior in high-stress or emotionally charged scenarios. In healthcare simulations, patients sometimes expressed confusion, anxiety, or irritation when navigating tasks like medication reminders or answering check-up questions. Without emotional adaptivity, these moments often led to user disengagement or non-compliance. However, when the system adjusted its speech tempo, softened its tone, or offered reassurance based on perceived emotional discomfort, users re-engaged and completed the interaction cycle. This dynamic interaction loop where input affects system behavior and response affects user behavior demonstrates the importance of feedback-aware system design. Table.3 presents the summary of key observations across domains.

Table 3. Summary of Key Observations Across Domains

Domain	Emotional Adaptation Outcome	Challenge Noted	Impact on Trust/User Satisfaction
Healthcare	Reduced stress, improved task compliance	Misclassification of emotion in low light	High
Smart Homes	Calmer tone improved response accuracy	Noise interference, emotional repetition	High
Customer Service	De-escalation of complaints, faster resolution	Over-sympathy felt artificial in long chats	Moderate to High

The framework's robustness was particularly evident when interacting with users who had low digital literacy or limited verbal fluency. In such cases, the cognitive ergonomics interface proved critical. Users with hesitations, slow response times, or ambiguous input patterns were not penalized by the system. Instead, the system waited longer before prompting, clarified confusing terms, and presented simplified alternatives when needed. These actions reduced frustration and enabled successful task completion, illustrating the system's capacity to account for a wide range of cognitive and behavioral profiles.

Figure 5. HIM Feedback Loop in Emotionally Adaptive Systems

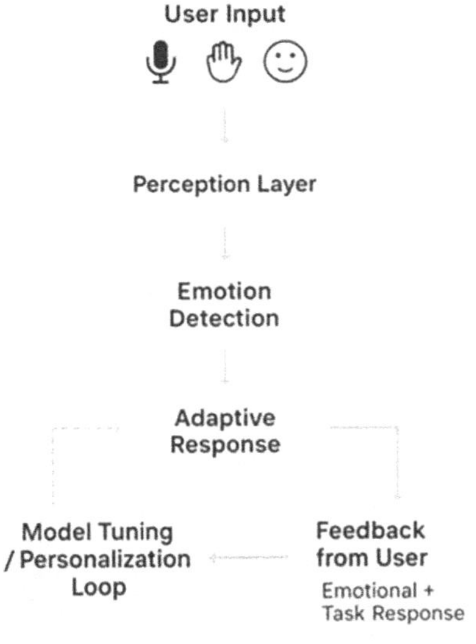

Despite these benefits, the simulations also exposed practical challenges. One limitation is the interpretability of the emotional decisions made by the AI. While the system's emotional detection and simulated empathy improved user experience, it occasionally led to confusion about why certain responses were chosen. For example, some users questioned why the system shifted to a more serious tone or offered an apology without an obvious trigger. This points to a key design tension: systems that simulate emotional understanding must also provide transparency about those decisions, or risk losing user trust. Another observation involves emotional saturation (Xu et al., 2023). In some extended interactions, excessive empathy or overly "human" expressions became repetitive or unnatural. Users in the customer service simulation occasionally reported feeling that the system was trying too hard to be nice. This indicates a need for emotional pacing and variation ensuring emotional responses are meaningful, not mechanical. Finding this balance is essential in sustaining long-term interactions without compromising authenticity.

While the proposed HIM framework as demonstrated in Fig.5 shows strong performance across simulation environments, several limitations emerged that warrant deeper investigation. One of the key limitations relates to emotional misclassification. Although the framework achieved over 90% accuracy in emotion detection during controlled tests, real-world interactions often involve overlapping or mixed emotions that challenge even advanced classifiers (Xue et al., 2022). For example, in the smart home simulation, background noise, low lighting, or overlapping speech sometimes interfered with accurate tone analysis. In such cases, the system either defaulted to a neutral response or incorrectly inferred agitation, leading to unnecessary calming behavior or repetition of instructions. Another challenge is the temporal generalization of learning models. Adaptive systems tend to perform well when user behavior remains consistent or when there are frequent interactions that allow the model to learn effectively. However, users who engage with the system sporadically or whose behavior varies widely from session to session can trigger instability in the personalization layer (Yang et al., 2020). For instance, in customer service scenarios, a user who previously exhibited calm behavior but became emotionally agitated in a later session may receive overly simplified or incorrect responses based on outdated profile data. This points to the need for dynamic user modeling that balances stability with recency.

The discussion also raises questions about design trade-offs between empathy and efficiency. In high-pressure or time-sensitive environments, such as emergency response or logistics coordination, overly empathetic responses may introduce delays or complexity. Striking the right balance between emotional intelligence and operational speed remains an open challenge. Future designs may need to offer user-selectable modes that allow for tuning the emotional layer based on context and user preference. Importantly, the study reinforces that emotional alignment is not merely a technical issue but also a design philosophy. Systems that aim to be truly human-centered must extend beyond functionality and into emotional resonance, cognitive load management, and contextual relevance (Zanatto et al., 2023). This includes building explainable emotional responses providing users with subtle cues or prompts that help them understand why the system reacted in a particular way. Such explainability not only increases user trust but also helps correct misinterpretations without undermining the emotional rapport that the system is trying to build. Finally, the findings point to several promising research directions. These include multi-user emotional dynamics, cultural variations in affective computing, real-time calibration of emotional responses, and the integration of HIM systems with wearables and neuroadaptive technologies. As intelligent systems become increasingly embedded in daily life, these insights will shape the next generation of emotionally aware, ethically designed, and user-adaptive human-machine interfaces.

5. FUTURE SCOPE

The evolution of human-machine interaction is entering a transformative phase, driven by advances in emotional AI, neurotechnology, and edge computing. As intelligent systems become deeply embedded in homes, workplaces, and public environments, the demands on these systems will extend far beyond basic functionality. The future of HIM lies in the seamless blending of cognitive science, real-time responsiveness, and ethical awareness to support meaningful and sustained engagement. One promising direction is the integration of neuroadaptive interfaces. These systems aim to read and respond to brain signals using non-invasive methods like EEG headbands or eye-tracking sensors. Coupled with emotional detection, neuroadaptive HIM systems could infer deeper cognitive states such as stress, fatigue, confusion, or attentiveness. This real-time understanding could reshape adaptive learning environments, cognitive therapy, and safety-critical operations like air traffic control or surgery assistance.

Another area of development is multi-user emotional dynamics. Current HIM frameworks typically model a single user interacting with a machine. However, in many real-world situations, systems must handle multiple users at once each with distinct emotional states and intentions. For example, in a smart classroom or shared vehicle, HIM systems should recognize conflicting cues, manage simultaneous interactions, and prioritize responses based on context and urgency. Research into group emotion modeling, role-based adaptation, and fairness-aware prioritization will be crucial in this domain. The future also requires improved cultural intelligence in emotionally adaptive systems. Emotional expression varies widely across regions, languages, and social norms. A smile in one culture may signify politeness, while in another, it may express embarrassment or sarcasm. HIM systems must be trained on diverse datasets and infused with cultural context to avoid misinterpretations. This expansion will demand cross-disciplinary collaboration between ethnographers, linguists, and AI developers.

From a technical standpoint, federated learning presents a compelling future direction for preserving privacy while enabling personalization. Instead of sending sensitive interaction data to centralized servers, models can be trained locally on user devices and only share model updates. This ensures emotional and behavioral data remain private while still allowing the system to learn and improve over time. Future HIM designs will also need to address emotional fatigue a phenomenon where users become desensitized to overly expressive or repetitive emotional responses.

Dynamic emotional pacing, context-sensitive empathy, and time-aware interaction design will help mitigate this issue. These designs must adapt emotional tone not only to the current state but also based on long-term patterns of user engagement. Finally, regulatory and ethical foresight will shape HIM's future trajectory. As systems gain autonomy in responding to human emotions, accountability mechanisms must evolve. Future research should investigate how to certify emotionally adaptive systems, validate their fairness, and ensure that human dignity is preserved during interaction.

6. CONCLUSION

The progression of Human Interaction with Machines (HIM) has transitioned from rigid, command-based communication to nuanced, emotionally resonant engagement. This chapter has explored the shifting landscape of HIM in the age of intelligent systems, emphasizing the need for emotionally adaptive, cognitively aware, and user-centered frameworks. With the widespread adoption of artificial intelligence, robotics, and multimodal interfaces, the quality of interaction is no longer judged solely by efficiency but also by trust, empathy, and inclusion. The literature review highlighted the foundational and emerging pillars of HIM research, including multimodal design, affective computing, personalization, inclusivity, and explainability. Across diverse domains such as healthcare, education, customer service, and smart environments, a common thread was observed: systems that understand and appropriately respond to user emotions are more likely to foster long-term engagement, higher satisfaction, and trust.

The proposed framework presented in this chapter contributes a novel perspective by merging emotional intelligence, adaptive learning, and cognitive ergonomics. Simulations demonstrated that emotionally aware systems can dynamically adjust responses, improve task outcomes, and sustain interaction in diverse use cases. Notably, the system's ability to detect emotional discomfort, personalize feedback, and offer transparent explanations proved essential for user acceptance. Furthermore, the modular design of the framework allows it to be tailored to multiple domains and integrated with existing digital ecosystems. The discussion of findings underscored both the strengths and challenges of implementing such systems. While emotional adaptation improved user satisfaction, issues such as emotional misclassification, transparency gaps, and saturation effects revealed areas for refinement. These insights affirm the need for a balanced approach where emotional intelligence complements, rather than dominates, functional objectives.

The future scope section identified exciting opportunities and critical challenges ahead. Technologies such as neuroadaptive interfaces, multi-user emotion modeling, federated learning, and cultural AI represent the next frontier of HIM evolution. Ethical foresight, privacy preservation, and dynamic emotional pacing will be central to sustaining this progress in a responsible and inclusive manner. Ultimately, this chapter calls for a paradigm shift in how intelligent systems are designed, evaluated, and governed. Human-machine interaction is not simply a matter of input and output it is a continuous, evolving relationship shaped by context, cognition, and emotion. Building systems that can understand, learn from, and meaningfully respond to human needs requires an interdisciplinary foundation that bridges engineering, psychology, ethics, and design. By embracing this holistic approach, the next generation of intelligent systems can move beyond automation and toward collaboration enabling machines that not only act but understand, that not only respond but resonate. In doing so, HIM frameworks will unlock a future where machines are not just tools, but empathetic partners in human progress.

REFERENCES

An, S., Zhu, H., Guo, C., Fu, B., Song, C., Tao, P., Shang, W., & Deng, T. (2022). Noncontact human-machine interaction based on hand-responsive infrared structural color. *Nature Communications*, *13*(1), 1446. Advance online publication. DOI: 10.1038/s41467-022-29197-5

Chen, K., Liang, K., Liu, H., Liu, R., Liu, Y., Zeng, S., & Tian, Y. (2023). Skin-inspired ultra-tough Supramolecular Multifunctional Hydrogel electronic skin for human–machine interaction. *Nano-Micro Letters*, *15*(1), 102. Advance online publication. DOI: 10.1007/s40820-023-01084-8

Cross, E. S., & Ramsey, R. (2021). Mind meets machine: Towards a cognitive science of human–machine interactions. *Trends in Cognitive Sciences*, *25*(3), 200–212. DOI: 10.1016/j.tics.2020.11.009

De Fazio, R., Mastronardi, V., Petruzzi, M., De Vittorio, M., & Visconti, P. (2022). Human–machine interaction through advanced haptic sensors: A piezoelectric sensory glove with edge machine learning for gesture and object recognition. *Future Internet*, *15*(1), 14. DOI: 10.3390/fi15010014

De Velasco, M., Justo, R., & Inés Torres, M. (2022). Automatic identification of emotional information in Spanish TV debates and human–machine interactions. *Applied Sciences (Basel, Switzerland)*, *12*(4), 1902. DOI: 10.3390/app12041902

Ehresmann, A. C., Béjean, M., & Vanbremeersch, J. (2023). A mathematical framework for enriching human–machine interactions. *Machine Learning and Knowledge Extraction*, *5*(2), 597–610. DOI: 10.3390/make5020034

Gambino, A., Fox, J., & Ratan, R. (2020). Building a stronger CASA: Extending the computers are social actors paradigm. *Human-Machine Communication*, *1*, 71–86. DOI: 10.30658/hmc.1.5

Gammulle, H., Ahmedt-Aristizabal, D., Denman, S., Tychsen-Smith, L., Petersson, L., & Fookes, C. (2023). Continuous human action recognition for human-machine interaction: A review. *ACM Computing Surveys*, *55*(13s), 1–38. DOI: 10.1145/3587931

Hoc, J. (2000). From human – machine interaction to human – machine cooperation. *Ergonomics*, *43*(7), 833–843. DOI: 10.1080/001401300409044

Jain, G., Das, R., Raj, D., & Mohapatra, H. (2025). Exploring low-latency communication protocols for time-sensitive industrial automation and autonomous vehicle systems. *2025 International Conference on Computing, Intelligence, and Application (CIACON)*, 1-7. DOI: 10.1109/CIACON65473.2025.11189493

Johnson, J. (2022). The AI Commander problem: Ethical, political, and psychological dilemmas of human-machine interactions in AI-enabled warfare. *Journal of Military Ethics*, *21*(3-4), 246–271. DOI: 10.1080/15027570.2023.2175887

Johnson, J. (2023). Finding AI faces in the moon and armies in the clouds: Anthropomorphising artificial intelligence in military human-machine interactions. *Global Society*, *38*(1), 67–82. DOI: 10.1080/13600826.2023.2205444

Küçüktabak, E. B., Kim, S. J., Wen, Y., Lynch, K., & Pons, J. L. (2021). Human-machine-human interaction in motor control and rehabilitation: A review. *Journal of Neuroengineering and Rehabilitation*, *18*(1), 183. Advance online publication. DOI: 10.1186/s12984-021-00974-5

Li, S., Blythe, P., Guo, W., & Namdeo, A. (2019). Investigation of older drivers' requirements of the human-machine interaction in highly automated vehicles. *Transportation Research Part F: Traffic Psychology and Behaviour*, *62*, 546–563. DOI: 10.1016/j.trf.2019.02.009

Lin, S., Döngül, E. S., Uygun, S. V., Öztürk, M. B., Huy, D. T., & Tuan, P. V. (2022). Exploring the relationship between abusive management, self-efficacy and organizational performance in the context of human–machine interaction technology and artificial intelligence with the effect of ergonomics. *Sustainability (Basel)*, *14*(4), 1949. DOI: 10.3390/su14041949

Lin, Z., Zhang, G., Xiao, X., Au, C., Zhou, Y., Sun, C., Zhou, Z., Yan, R., Fan, E., Si, S., Weng, L., Mathur, S., Yang, J., & Chen, J. (2021). A personalized acoustic interface for wearable human–machine interaction. *Advanced Functional Materials*, *32*(9), 2109430. Advance online publication. DOI: 10.1002/adfm.202109430

Liu, X., Sun, C., Ye, X., Zhu, X., Hu, C., Tan, H., He, S., Shao, M., & Li, R. (2024). Neuromorphic Nanoionics for human–machine interaction: From materials to applications. *Advanced Materials*, *36*(37), 2311472. Advance online publication. DOI: 10.1002/adma.202311472

Lu, J., Peng, Z., Yang, S., Ma, Y., Wang, R., Pang, Z., Feng, X., Chen, Y., & Cao, Y. (2023). A review of sensory interactions between autonomous vehicles and drivers. *Journal of Systems Architecture*, *141*, 102932. DOI: 10.1016/j.sysarc.2023.102932

Lu, L., Jiang, C., Hu, G., Liu, J., & Yang, B. (2021). Flexible Noncontact sensing for human–machine interaction. *Advanced Materials*, *33*(16), 2100218. Advance online publication. DOI: 10.1002/adma.202100218

Ma, X., Tao, F., Zhang, M., Wang, T., & Zuo, Y. (2019). Digital twin enhanced human-machine interaction in product lifecycle. *Procedia CIRP*, *83*, 789–793. DOI: 10.1016/j.procir.2019.04.330

Maadi, M., Akbarzadeh Khorshidi, H., & Aickelin, U. (2021). A review on Human–AI interaction in machine learning and insights for medical applications. *International Journal of Environmental Research and Public Health*, *18*(4), 2121. DOI: 10.3390/ijerph18042121

Mohapatra, H. (2021). Socio-technical challenges in the implementation of smart city. 2021 International Conference on Innovation and Intelligence for Informatics, Computing, and Technologies (3ICT), 57-62. DOI: 10.1109/3ICT53449.2021.9581905

Mohapatra, H. (2025). The fine-tuning journey of ChatGPT in industry applications. *Advances in Computational Intelligence and Robotics*, •••, 263–284. DOI: 10.4018/979-8-3693-8332-2.ch011

Mohapatra, H. (2025). The role of 6G in empowering smart cities enabling ubiquitous connectivity and intelligent infrastructure. *Advances in Wireless Technologies and Telecommunication*, •••, 231–254. DOI: 10.4018/979-8-3693-8799-3.ch008

Mohapatra, H., & Rath, A. K. (2019). Detection and avoidance of water loss through municipality taps in India by using smart taps and ICT. *IET Wireless Sensor Systems*, *9*(6), 447–457. DOI: 10.1049/iet-wss.2019.0081

Mohapatra, H., & Rath, A. K. (2020). Fault-tolerant mechanism for wireless sensor network. *IET Wireless Sensor Systems*, *10*(1), 23–30. DOI: 10.1049/iet-wss.2019.0106

Nalepka, P., Lamb, M., Kallen, R. W., Shockley, K., Chemero, A., Saltzman, E., & Richardson, M. J. (2019). Human social motor solutions for human–machine interaction in dynamical task contexts. *Proceedings of the National Academy of Sciences of the United States of America*, *116*(4), 1437–1446. DOI: 10.1073/pnas.1813164116

Nardo, M., Forino, D., & Murino, T. (2020). The evolution of man–machine interaction: The role of human in industry 4.0 paradigm. *Production & Manufacturing Research*, *8*(1), 20–34. DOI: 10.1080/21693277.2020.1737592

Olawade, D. B., Wada, O. Z., Odetayo, A., David-Olawade, A. C., Asaolu, F., & Eberhardt, J. (2024). Enhancing mental health with artificial intelligence: Current trends and future prospects. *Journal of Medicine, Surgery, and Public Health*, *3*, 100099. DOI: 10.1016/j.glmedi.2024.100099

Ribino, P. (2023). The role of politeness in human–machine interactions: A systematic literature review and future perspectives. *Artificial Intelligence Review*, *56*(S1), 445–482. DOI: 10.1007/s10462-023-10540-1

Scibilia, A., Pedrocchi, N., & Fortuna, L. (2022). Human control model estimation in physical human–machine interaction: A survey. *Sensors (Basel)*, *22*(5), 1732. DOI: 10.3390/s22051732

Seifert, J., Friedrich, O., & Schleidgen, S. (2022). Imitating the human. New human–machine interactions in social robots. *NanoEthics*, *16*(2), 181–192. DOI: 10.1007/s11569-022-00418-x

Simao, M., Mendes, N., Gibaru, O., & Neto, P. (2019). A review on electromyography decoding and pattern recognition for human-machine interaction. *IEEE Access : Practical Innovations, Open Solutions*, *7*, 39564–39582. DOI: 10.1109/ACCESS.2019.2906584

Strasser, A., & Wilby, M. (2023). The AI-stance: Crossing the Terra incognita of human-machine interactions? *Frontiers in Artificial Intelligence and Applications*. DOI: 10.3233/FAIA220628

Sundar, S. S. (2020). Rise of machine agency: A framework for studying the psychology of Human–AI interaction (HAII). *Journal of Computer-Mediated Communication*, *25*(1), 74–88. DOI: 10.1093/jcmc/zmz026

Van Landuyt, D., Halasz, D., Verreydt, S., & Weyns, D. (2024). Towards understanding trust in self-adaptive systems. *Proceedings of the 19th International Symposium on Software Engineering for Adaptive and Self-Managing Systems*, 207-213. DOI: 10.1145/3643915.3644100

Wang, J., Pradhan, M. R., & Gunasekaran, N. (2022). Machine learning-based human-robot interaction in ITS. *Information Processing & Management*, *59*(1), 102750. DOI: 10.1016/j.ipm.2021.102750

Wang, S., Wang, X., Wang, S., Yu, W., Yu, L., Hou, L., Tang, Y., Zhang, Z., Yao, N., Cao, C., Dong, H., Zhang, L., & Bao, H. (2022). Optical-nanofiber-Enabled gesture-recognition wristband for human-machine interaction with the assistance of machine learning. DOI: 10.22541/au.167022827.77928491/v1

Wang, T., Li, J., Deng, Y., Wang, C., Snoussi, H., & Tao, F. (2021). Digital twin for human-machine interaction with convolutional neural network. *International Journal of Computer Integrated Manufacturing*, *34*(7-8), 888–897. DOI: 10.1080/0951192X.2021.1925966

Wen, W., & Imamizu, H. (2022). The sense of agency in perception, behaviour and human–machine interactions. *Nature Reviews Psychology*, *1*(4), 211–222. DOI: 10.1038/s44159-022-00030-6

Xiao, G., Ma, Y., Liu, C., & Jiang, D. (2020). A machine emotion transfer model for intelligent human-machine interaction based on group division. *Mechanical Systems and Signal Processing*, *142*, 106736. DOI: 10.1016/j.ymssp.2020.106736

Xiao, G., Ma, Y., Liu, C., & Jiang, D. (2020). A machine emotion transfer model for intelligent human-machine interaction based on group division. *Mechanical Systems and Signal Processing*, *142*, 106736. DOI: 10.1016/j.ymssp.2020.106736

Xiong, D., Zhang, D., Zhao, X., & Zhao, Y. (2021). Deep learning for EMG-based human-machine interaction: A review. *IEEE/CAA Journal of Automatica Sinica,* *8*(3), 512-533. DOI: 10.1109/JAS.2021.1003865

Xu, J., Pan, J., Cui, T., Zhang, S., Yang, Y., & Ren, T. (2023). Recent progress of tactile and force sensors for human–machine interaction. *Sensors (Basel)*, *23*(4), 1868. DOI: 10.3390/s23041868

Xue, J., Zou, Y., Deng, Y., & Li, Z. (2022). Bioinspired sensor system for health care and human-machine interaction. *EcoMat*, *4*(5), e12209. Advance online publication. DOI: 10.1002/eom2.12209

Yang, X., Yang, S., Li, Q., Wuchty, S., & Zhang, Z. (2020). Prediction of human-virus protein-protein interactions through a sequence embedding-based machine learning method. *Computational and Structural Biotechnology Journal*, *18*, 153–161. DOI: 10.1016/j.csbj.2019.12.005

Zanatto, D., Bifani, S., & Noyes, J. (2023). Constraining the sense of agency in human-machine interaction. *International Journal of Human-Computer Interaction*, *40*(13), 3482–3493. DOI: 10.1080/10447318.2023.2189815

Chapter 5
Collaborative Intelligence in Action:
Designing Human-AI Co-Workflows for Next-Generation E-Collaboration

Muhammad Usman Tariq
https://orcid.org/0000-0002-7605-3040
Abu Dhabi University, UAE & University College Cork, Ireland

ABSTRACT

This chapter discusses the rise of co-intelligence as a revolutionary new way of digital collaboration in the age of AI. Conventional e-collaboration tools frequently lack flexibility, context awareness, and the capacity to integrate multifaceted real-time information across domains. By incorporating AI, particularly large language models, digital twins, and IoT dashboards, collaboration is moving toward dynamic co-creative spaces in which human and machine intelligence collaborate synergistically. This chapter spans the theoretical underpinnings of human–AI collaboration, implementation strategies, and practical case studies in healthcare, academia, and urban planning. It also critically examines ethical issues, such as trust, bias, and privacy, in cross-border collaboration while offering strategic recommendations on skill development, hybrid workspace design, ROI analysis, and policy frameworks. Finally, it envisages the future of intelligent organizations, where AGI-enabled agents have a say in decision-making, ideation, and innovation.

DOI: 10.4018/979-8-3373-5747-8.ch005

INTRODUCTION

In a digitally interconnected world, organizations are experiencing significant changes in how people work together with one another, especially as artificial intelligence is increasingly incorporated into regular work. The standard software that people use to work electronically together, such as emails, video conferences, common documents, and project lists, was once cutting-edge, allowing teams to work and communicate even when they were physically apart (Qi & Wang, 2025). However, as work becomes more complex and the amount of information that people must process increases, the flaws of these ancient tools become increasingly apparent. They were made for framing work and spreading messages, not for thinking and creating new ideas. While they work well for trivial tasks, they are poorly suited for the rapid, flexible, and intelligent problem-solving required in today's world. They do not receive context, learn from experience, or process large amounts of data in a human-usable manner. Consequently, most teams wrestle with intractable challenges, such as miscommunication, decisional fatigue, and hitting productivity plateaus, despite the availability of digital tools.

This is where collaborative intelligence enters the scene, which is more of a change in how humans and machines work together and less of a new technology. Collaborative intelligence involves the collaboration of human and artificial intelligence, wherein both utilize each other's strengths. People bring creativity, empathy, ethical decision-making, and subject-matter expertise, while machines provide speed, the ability to process large amounts of data, pattern detection, and processing power beyond the human capacity. The result is not merely improved efficiency but entirely new ways of building insights, making decisions, and developing solutions. What is distinctive about collective intelligence from earlier digital methods is the ability to learn and adapt through interactions, continuously improving how tasks are performed and how knowledge is combined. It not only helps people cooperate but also creates systems where people and AI co-evolve and learn to tackle issues that neither can attempt by themselves (Boni, 2021). This is where collaborative intelligence enters, which is more a change in how humans and machines work together and not a new technology. Collaborative intelligence is the convergence of human and artificial intelligence, where both use each other's strengths. People bring creativity, understanding, ethical sense, and subject expertise, while machines provide speed, the ability to handle large quantities of information, recognition of patterns, and processing power that exceeds that of humans. Not only is efficiency enhanced, but fundamentally new ways of building insights, making decisions, and developing solutions are also created (Özüdoğru & Durak, 2025). The innovation of collective intelligence over previous digital strategies is the ability to learn and develop from interactions, continuously enhancing the ways things are accomplished as well as the way knowledge is combined. Not only does it help people collaborate, but it also creates systems where people and AI co-evolve and learn how to resolve issues that neither of them could handle individually. This transformation is occurring simultaneously with the rethinking of long-held assumptions about work. This raises difficult questions: What does productive collaboration look like when computers can present ideas, not just data? How can we trust AI recommendations without losing human agency? How do we generate diverse ideas when AI systems are modeled on existing data, which may perpetuate established biases and fail to question them? These are not just technical or procedural issues; they infringe on identity, power, creativity, and ethics. Thus, collaborative intelligence is not just about improving productivity or efficiency; it is about reshaping the social and cognitive architecture of work itself. Organizations must learn how to design collaborations where human and machine contributions are valued, recognized, and blended into forms that enrich, rather than deplete, overall team intelligence.

This chapter explores how collaborative intelligence works in practice, especially in the context of rethinking electronic collaboration in the age of AI. The aim is to look beyond the marketing and hype surrounding AI tools and examine the real-life changes taking place inside teams and organizations (Qi & Wang, 2025). Through an examination of new models of collaboration, case studies of AI-enhanced teamwork, and evolving digital best practices, this chapter sets forth a clear vision of how collaborative intelligence is reshaping work. This study examines how leaders are addressing this transition, how tools are being designed to facilitate, not stifle, informed collaboration, and what organizational cultures can most readily facilitate these shifts. The focus is on practical wisdom, how to create the right environment for collaborative intelligence to flourish, how to measure its impact, and how to mitigate its risks.

Equally important is understanding the relationship between human thought and machine learning in team settings. It will examine how AI can be used not simply to automate but to amplify human thinking, helping teams synthesize diverse perspectives, predict upcoming situations, and develop novel solutions. We will also notice the transparency and explainability role in building trust with AI colleagues and why feedback loops permitting human and machine parts of a team to learn and evolve over time are so important. This chapter attempts to clarify the dynamics of successful human-AI collaboration by identifying what organizations can do to shift from simple digital coordination to truly intelligent collaboration (Mannuru et al., 2023). Equally important is the awareness of the limitations and possible problems of collaborative intelligence. Not all AI systems are alike, and not all collaborative situations benefit equally from their integration. There is a risk of excessive reliance on algorithmic decision-making, especially if AI is treated as a black box and not as a helpful assistant. There are data privacy, accountability, and ethical issues, especially as AI takes more autonomy in suggesting or even making decisions. These risks emphasize the need for sophisticated governance structures and strong human oversight. This chapter covers frameworks for wisely integrating AI into shared spaces, providing insights on how to maintain ethical standards while promoting innovation. As it synthesizes these ideas, the chapter introduces collaborative intelligence as a workable tool for profound rethinking (Qi & Wang, 2025). This challenges the notion that collaboration is merely a technological outcome, rather than a product of creation methods, team formation, and the values embedded in the tools and processes we utilize. Therefore, collaborative intelligence offers a new framework for thinking about not only how we work but also why we work the way we do. This causes us to reevaluate the role of human beings in a technologically tool-created world, not as a diminishing one that is made redundant through automation, but as a stronger one through intelligent support by technology. Finally, the aim of this chapter is to present readers with a rich and comprehensive picture of the practical application of collaborative intelligence, how it is being used, what its challenges are, and where it might be heading. This prompts us to consider how we might design more intelligent, responsive, and empathetic systems for collaboration in an era where intelligence is becoming increasingly integrated into both humans and machines. By doing so, it endeavors to help leaders, practitioners, and scholars continue to advance in this changing field with focused minds and sharp ethical senses (Tariq, 2025).

CONCEPTUAL FOUNDATIONS

Collaborative intelligence risks being a gigantic term within the discussion of how work will change in the future, specifically with digital transformation and artificial intelligence. Ultimately, collaborative intelligence is a human-machine collaboration in which both parties input to achieve goals that neither can do alone. It is not just about using AI to get work done faster or assist with decision-making. It is all about designing systems in which humans and AI work together to learn, create, and innovate. The key is not to replace humans but to serve them using AI (Mannuru et al., 2023). While machines can handle vast amounts of data, detect patterns, and make predictions with speed, they do not possess the deep thinking, emotional quotient, ethical understanding, and creative imagination that humans bring to challenging situations. In a collaborative setup, human skills such as critical thinking and situational awareness are heightened by computer speed and scalability to create a cycle of collective learning and wisdom. This collaboration allows human groups and AI to work together to be more productive, innovative, and adaptive.

Understanding collaborative intelligence involves understanding how it is integrated into broader theories about collaborating with humans and AI. Researchers have proposed several models to explain how these two methods can complement one another (Qi & Wang, 2025). One model is based on varying levels of control and autonomy in the workplace. It illustrates a continuum from fully human-controlled systems, where AI is merely an assistant, to fully automated systems, where human monitoring is the only intervention when needed. Between these two, there is a middle tier where smart cooperation takes place best, where human beings and machines cooperate, and decisions emanate from ongoing communication. This framework promotes the existence of discernible roles, trust in each other, and interfaces that allow humans to understand and guide AI activities. The second is a model of complementary intelligence, which shows how human and machine abilities are complementary but may be connected to producing greater outcomes than either separately. Such an idea promotes structuring work so that everybody or machine does what they can do best but complement the weaknesses of the other. These models show that effective human-AI collaboration is not one side converting the other into a believer, but having good equilibrium, along with one another and making things better for both.

In practice, collaborative intelligence shifts our thinking regarding collaboration. Unlike previous models, where people collaborated using shared tools, human-AI collaboration involves thinking differently about who does the work, who gets the credit, and how decisions are made (Chew et al., 2024). AI is a live team member, not an item to be used. This changes trust, responsibility, and communication. Trust is especially critical now, as users no longer merely need to comprehend how AI systems work, but also need to trust their recommendations, while remaining cautious and vigilant. This is why XAI is needed, as it illustrates how an AI reaches its decisions. Otherwise, collaborative intelligence would be far too dependent on incomprehensible systems, which would destroy the idea of true teamwork.

While all this has been happening, new e-collaboration tools are revolutionizing how we get work done in collaborative intelligence. In the past, e-collaboration has centered on technologies that help people collaborate, share information, and coordinate tasks, such as email, instant messaging software, project planning tools, and document collaboration software (Qi & Wang, 2025). They supported people in collaborating but were inert and did not help with thinking or problem solving. With the use of AI, e-collaboration is becoming an increasingly intelligent and dynamic process. Smart assistants can suggest actions, record meetings, draw attention to important notes, and even anticipate what a team will need next based on what they are doing. AI-based systems are beginning to change in real time by learning from user activity, offering contextual, not rigid, scheduling or file storage aids. These new tools help individuals communicate, but they also help them think together as a group.

In addition, new collaborative technologies are transforming the way people work with information. Consider AI-driven knowledge graphs that enable the connection of concepts within enormous sets of data, or digital whiteboards that use natural language processing to transform handwritten remarks into structured information (Chew et al., 2024). These are not just repositories for data; they engage in the actual process of creating and breaking down ideas. In this new way of working, technology is not just helping people work together; it is becoming a team member. The line between tool and partner is becoming increasingly blurred, with new questions around who receives credit for a thought that came from an AI suggestion or who takes the blame when an AI makes a mistake that the team acts on. These are significant issues in the idea of collaborative intelligence and need to be considered as more organizations use AI-enhanced collaboration technologies to improve their performance.

It is also noteworthy how collaborative intelligence changes the nature of thinking and activities that humans engage in. Heretofore, groups assumed that everyone had access to the same information and input levels. However, with the advent of AI, this equilibrium has been disrupted. Machines can provide insights that could take humans years or months to discover. This changes the nature of people working together, with machines no longer wasting time gathering data but instead figuring out what the significance is, suggesting plans, and having deep discussions. To harness this change fully, teams need to develop new skills, not just in terms of how they implement AI, but also how they work with it. This means acquiring the skills to interact with multiple AI systems, frame problems in a way that can be supported by machines, and engage with the results produced by AI. In other words, collaborative intelligence is predicated on collaborative literacy, which is the ability to work with AI in an intelligent and ethical way. The second key aspect of how AI is changing e-collaboration is that it is making the experience more personalized for each person. AI can now personalize information, recommendations, and work configuration depending on how individuals have behaved previously, what they enjoy, and what their role is within the team. This allows the workplace to be more adaptable and responsive so that every individual can work in a style that suits their capabilities and requirements. For example, one user might get detailed breakdowns of data, while another gets a simpler overview, depending on how they think or their role in the project. This type of customization was not possible with earlier collaboration tools, which had a one-size-fits-all approach. With AI, the entire collaborative space changes and evolves according to how the team works, continuously optimizing in real-time to improve interactions. This makes individuals work more effectively and feel more engaged because they are not overwhelmed by things that do not concern them (Qi & Wang, 2025). However, this new form of collaboration raises sensitive issues that should be dealt with delicately. One major concern is the potential for being overly reliant on AI. Once teams are familiar with AI assisting them, they may begin to over-rely on it, which could undermine their own capacity to think for themselves or analyze independently. This is particularly dangerous because errors or biases in AI can have a significant impact. It is most important to balance what the AI can offer while keeping human judgment intact (Tariq, 2025). Another issue is ensuring that AI does not repeat or even magnify existing biases that may already be in the data or in decision-making. If the AI is based on historical data that contain human biases or unfair patterns, it may further fuel or even establish these problems. Therefore, as AI reshapes e-collaboration, it must be complemented with an accurate design that avoids prejudice, uses fair data, and includes human checks and balances.

In the bigger picture, the idea of collaborative intelligence is that the collaboration itself is changing not just in technology, but how we even conceptualize it. In the past, collaboration was mostly about people working together and breaking up work to accomplish things. However, with the assistance of AI, collaboration is even more creative and stems from a tremendous amount of interaction. The results are not only from what people do but also from how they and machines function. Each contributes a different type of smartness to the mix. This shift requires us to think in a new way, one that accepts complexity and ambiguity and how things evolve and compound together. It challenges us to ask ourselves what it means to work together, what intelligence is, and what it means to be human when working with AI (Moser et al., 2021). As we continue to dive deeper into this new age, it is clear that communication, thought, and technology are all starting to blur together. Collaborative intelligence is not a trend; it is a new way of thinking about how humans work together. It provides us with the vision of offices where learning is an ongoing process, where imagination is broadened, and where human beings are not substituted by machines but nurtured out of them. Understanding this evolving work practice is important for every person who is trying to thrive in the future of work, lead smart teams, or design tools that help others. By bringing in the ideas, tools, and ways of working with collective intelligence, we can start creating a future that is not only smarter but also more compassionate, just, and resilient enough to change with the times. Figure 1 provides overview of conceptual foundation of collaborative intelligence.

Figure 1. Human–AI Collaborative Intelligence Model

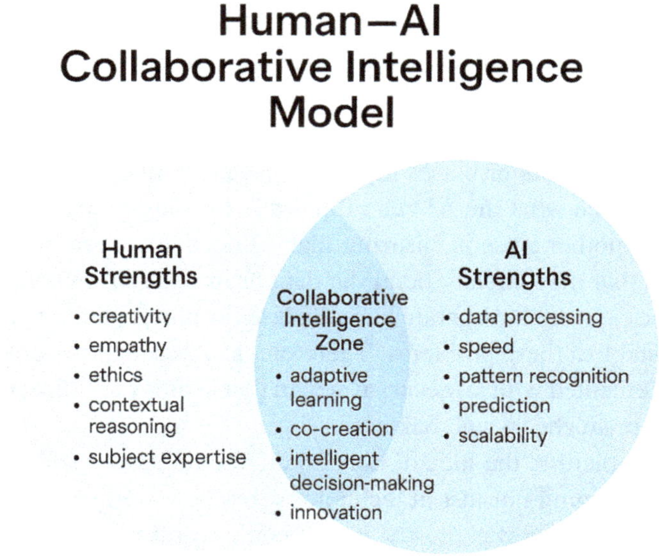

DESIGNING HUMAN–AI CO-WORKFLOWS

With the advancement of artificial intelligence and its growing popularity in the workplace, the way we construct and interact with workflows is drastically changing. Workflows have always been sequential and have involved humans performing most of the heavy lifting (Chew et al., 2024). Now, with smart systems, we can completely redesign these processes to build co-workflows where people and machines work together, bringing their own abilities to bear to make things quicker, smarter, and more agile. Creating good human-AI co-workflows requires more than simply applying AI to existing steps. This demands a new way of thinking about how work is partitioned, how decisions are made, and how trust and transparency are ensured. Three aspects form the core of this new thinking: task partitioning, shared autonomy, and explainability.

Task partitioning is a crucial element in the functioning of co-workflows. It is a question of deciding which parts of a task are best performed by humans and which are best performed by machines. It is not a simple yes or no; it is about looking at each part of the task and deciding the kind of thinking, feeling, or ability that is needed. For instance, handling vast amounts of data, such as sorting, searching, or preliminary analysis, is a perfect task for AI because machines can accomplish this at great speed without getting tired. However, functions involving contextual sensing, ethical judgment, or compassion, such as resolving a tricky customer complaint or making an important business decision, are best left to humans. The best co-workflows do not severely split tasks. Instead, they permit people to come and go as needed and permit machines to take over when tasks are repetitive and predictable. The goal is not to automate everything but to improve by using AI in the appropriate places, balancing things so that humans and machines complement each other's capabilities (Kim & Kwon, 2024). Shared autonomy is another crucial feature. In a human-AI co-workflow, both humans and machines must be able to operate independently in their respective domains of expertise, yet also exchange information with each other when the situation arises. It involves crafting systems that enable them to communicate, peer-review each other 's work, and react to unforeseen circumstances. For example, in the operation of a supply chain, a machine learning algorithm can automatically replenish stock based on forecasts but notify a human to check for any abnormal changes. Shared autonomy permits AI to act unaccompanied when the situation is straightforward or low-stakes and permits humans to override when things are complex or uncertain. This dance of balancing, not always controlling AI but always keeping humans in the loop, is actually great for how we create workflows today.

Explainability is also imperative to ensure that human-AI collaboration proceeds as smoothly as possible. For such collaboration to be successful, users must understand why an AI decision was made or why a certain action was suggested. This is especially important when humans must make decisions based on feedback from AI or must intervene if something goes wrong. XAI helps make AI more transparent, communicate reasoning in human-understandable terms, and show how decisions are made. For example, an AI helping with product design should be able to tell us where it got its inspiration, what it assumed, and what it learned in terms of patterns. Because explanations are comprehensible and valuable, people are more likely to trust the system, review its suggestions carefully, and make decisions that take advantage of the best human and machine genius. This also serves an ethical purpose by holding the systems responsible and reducing the potential for black-box decisions in high-stakes areas (Ding et al., 2023). AI agents are being used increasingly in advanced ways across many different areas of co-workflows, especially scheduling, idea generation, and agreement reaching. In scheduling, AI has outpaced basic calendar applications. Intelligent agents of today consider workloads, personal preferences, location, time zones, and even productivity levels at different times to suggest the best times for meetings or collaboration. Intelligent agents can settle conflicts, speak out for users, and adjust in real time as priorities shift. Not only does this decrease busy work, but it also facilitates collaboration under the best conditions for performance and engagement.

In the realm of synthesis, AI assists in coordinating the massive amounts of data that contemporary teams must work with. For example, in meetings, AI can record conversations, extract highlights, detect action items, and even follow up by incorporating them into project plans. In research, AI can trawl through masses of data, draw conclusions from them, and present the outcomes in consumable formats. The ability to access and reorganize messy data into insightful information changes the process of decision preparation by teams, saving time and energy costs while improving results (Ling et al., 2023). AI also plays an important role in creating new ideas. It not only organizes known knowledge but can also come up with new ideas. Using large data models and new algorithms, AI can provide ideas for design concepts, marketing strategies, and product innovations based on trends, customer comments, and competitors. Instead of hijacking human imagination, these technologies inspire it, offering ideas, comparisons, or fresh associations that nudge human creativity. Interestingly, these systems can also adapt recommendations according to the taste or means of the team, facilitating the creative process without limiting the options. This speeds up brainstorming and can frequently yield more innovative ideas than humans can develop independently. Consensus development is one area where AI agents are starting to provide real value. Group decision-making is often plagued by biases, groupthink, and biased access to information. AI can help identify where people are in agreement or disagreement, show differing perspectives, and even suggest compromises based on common aims or past results. Other systems use sentiment analysis to understand the emotional tone of dialogue or to determine when people are not participating or rejecting. This helps facilitators intervene better and encourages fairer participation. When AI acts as a third-party mediator or provides further insight, it helps bring about alignment without exercising a top-down control (Tariq, 2025).

With artificial intelligence increasingly entering into alliances across industries, the promise of increased efficiency, innovation, and quick response comes with a package of hard challenges, most of which are of ethical inclination. They are not merely challenges in the technology itself, but also in how people experience, interact with, and are affected by intelligent systems. Trust is at the heart of these issues. There must be trust for effective cooperation, and as AI is added to the decision-making process, one must always check and believe in it. People must know how AI makes its decisions, how valid the decision is, and when to follow or defy the advice. However, this is not always simple. AI might seem intelligent, smart, and logical; however, it does not necessarily have to be correct or comprehend the scenario. When people receive suggestions from AI, such as in healthcare, money, or team management, they tend to think the outcome, particularly if the system is smarter or quicker than humans. However, this trust is misplaced when AI models are flawed, biased, or lacking in the subtleties of the moment. AI suggests options based on estimated outputs; these simulations are hand-in-hand activities where human input and machines collaborate to run through possibilities by entwining data modeling and human insights (Riedl et al., 2025). IoT dashboards complement these models with real-time sensor input for continuous feedback and proactive decision-making. In smart supply chains and buildings, IoT sensors track energy consumption, temperature, and delivery time. AI interprets these data and incorporates them into workflows, performing tasks or notifying in automation when specific conditions are achieved. When co-designed for collaboration, dashboards provide common visibility, and passive data are transformed into active decision-support systems. The work process is no longer isolated; it is a living, responsive system that adapts to the environment in real time.

Large language models add another level of intelligence and speed to co-workflows. LLMs can also understand natural language commands, create content, translate across domains, and aid in human-computer interaction. They are international collaborators who can communicate with other systems, simplify technical information into simple language, or redo content on behalf of different stakeholders. For example, project management can have an LLM summarize progress reports, write status reports, or even write strategy reports from collective inputs. When combined with digital twins and IoT data, LLMs can explain the findings, identify anomalies, and guide teams through complex decisions by referencing previous cases or established best practices. This is especially helpful in cross-functional teams, where members have different backgrounds and can be bogged down by specialized data or terminology. LLMs can serve as translators and interpreters, keeping everyone in the same frame of mind and informed about the same topics (Nogueira et al., 2025). Ultimately, human-AI co-workflows are about more than optimizing efficiency and fashioning environments where intelligence is shared, adaptable, and open. Embedding AI agents in workflows is not just about getting more done but about doing the right things in the right manner. It permits a new form of collaboration that breaks down the boundaries of role, time, and space. Through well-considered task planning, facilitating joint decision-making, transparency, and supporting smart systems, such as digital twins, IoT dashboards, and LLMs, companies can unlock a new era of productivity and innovation. Co-workflows must be built not just for technical efficacy, but for human experience, how the systems we build make people better, not slight their judgment, and magnify their unique strengths. As the world continues to change, those who will succeed are those who perceive AI not as a threat or a tool but as an honest partner in crafting intentional, smart, and resilient working ways.

PRACTICAL IMPLEMENTATIONS AND CASE STUDIES

The use of artificial intelligence in team collaboration is no longer a future idea but is already a current reality in many facets of our lives. The integration of AI tools into common practice enables companies to think, innovate, and respond differently and better. These changes have not been tested in the lab or university but in real-world working environments where people of different backgrounds, occupations, and disciplines need to work together. The potential of combining human and AI minds becomes clear when observing real cases in which teams using AI tackle difficult problems, merge information with insight, and redefine how people work together. The next three examples, in education, healthcare, and government, show how AI redefines the way people work together if it is used correctly and with purpose (Criado et al., 2024). In educational settings where different types of experts cooperate, that is, scientists, designers, ethicists, and data analysts, research, teaching, and writing commonly involve close cooperation among them. The past has made it challenging to bring all these different people together within tight schedules due to various problems, such as communication gaps, different working styles, and lack of time. However, with the support of AI tools such as ChatGPT and Microsoft Copilot, these groups are finding new ways to work better (Chai et al., 2024). An example is a group of individuals working at a big university who are psychologists, computer science experts, and urban planners with the mission to study how urban planning affects mental health. They found it difficult to translate psychological ideas into computer codes and vice versa. They then used ChatGPT as a real-time assistant in Microsoft Teams, playing the roles of translator, editor, and concept generation partner. They asked nuanced questions, such as how to represent "urban stress" or measure "cognitive load" in buildings, and ChatGPT replied by integrating urban planning and psychology studies. When jargon or disparate methods caused confusion, the AI stepped in to demystify concepts by reformulating them in plain language or in terms of analogies from other fields. Copilot helped summarize meetings, organize tasks, and even create preliminary drafts of papers that could be redone by team members. This did not just save time; it revolutionized the way they worked so that they had more time to brainstorm new ideas instead of filling out paperwork. Over time, the group observed that all members, especially younger researchers, felt more at ease sharing when guided by AI suggestions or synopses. AI was a silent collaborator, making the sharing of information easy while respecting each field's unique approach. The success was not quicker publication or better papers but richer working relationships among the different domains of scholarship, where AI made the translating, mediating, and collaborating that crossed traditional boundaries possible (Tariq, 2025).

The health field is changing rapidly because it is facing increased demands for networked and responsive care, especially with aging populations, chronic illnesses, and budget constraints. A case in point is the application of AI and Internet of Medical Things (IoMT) technologies in virtual care teams. In a Northern European hospital, a care team was established to care for patients who were being treated at home. They employed wearable devices, AI, and online resources to monitor and assist patients around the clock. Wearables collect vital health data, such as heart rate, temperature, and oxygen levels, and forward them to a cloud platform that can be accessed by a team of nurses, doctors, and artificial intelligence (AI) assistants (Liu et al., 2024). The AI in the monitoring system is the most vital component. With machine learning, AI can sense minute changes or patterns that would manifest early signs of problems such as infections and dehydration before the patients even noticed that they had a problem. The findings were displayed on a shared dashboard, marked as a priority, and explained by the AI. Then, human doctors and nurses would be able to decide whether to make a video call, adjust a patient's medication, or even send out a mobile health team if required. This cooperative model, in which AI made initial suggestions and doctors made the final decisions, worked effectively, balancing rapid action with human judgment. One doctor likened the AI to "an additional set of eyes that doesn't get tired," constantly scanning for danger without ever becoming distracted or fatigued.

In addition to scanning for problems, AI also helped with team coordination. It schedules follow-ups based on recovering patients' statuses, predicts how busy each member would be, and charts optimal routes for home visits. The AI summarized what was happening with each patient during virtual meetings, tracked any notable changes, and highlighted notable issues, freeing the team to focus on planning instead of data gathering. The results were fewer hospital readmissions, quicker response times, and better patient satisfaction. However, the team felt more confident because they were able to focus on quality of care instead of getting bogged down in paperwork. This is just one example of how healthcare AI does not just bring digital technology into medicine but changes the manner in which care is delivered. By incorporating AI into routine cooperation, care becomes more real-time, forward-looking, and personalized, enabling teams to work more effectively without exerting additional effort (Gallagher & Wagner, 2024). In the public sector, smart city projects are increasingly being used as experiments in new forms of collaboration, especially for city planning and infrastructure construction. In one high-profile case from a fast-growing city in Asia, an interdisciplinary team of professionals worked together to create a new mixed-use complex intended to be a center for sustainability, innovation, and technology. The participants included city planners, environmentalists, transport engineers, legal advisors, and local community residents. To control complexity, the team used a platform combining virtual reality, IoT data, and blockchain agreement tools driven by AI. Teams used VR headsets to step into lifelike virtual models of new infrastructure projects. They were able to see how light, sound, air, and traffic would perform in real time. The simulations were drawn from live data from similar areas, so teams could observe how their decisions could affect the environment. AI helped examine the data, pointing out potential problems such as low airflow or heat build-up as a result of certain street layouts. This helped people understand the effects of their actions and engage in more meaningful discussions about the proposals. What was special about this approach was the use of blockchain to drive consensus. All ideas, comments, and suggestions were recorded on a common digital ledger. This made the entire process transparent and fair. The AI tracked the records to find areas where people agreed or disagreed with each other, easily resolving conflicts. This enabled community members and others without technical expertise to participate in the process. Instead of the same people always talking in meetings, all opinions were open, tracked, and valued in real time (Woolley & Gupta, 2023). AI also helped facilitate meetings by supplying draft policy document recommendations, summarizing concerns, and even creating early plans that met environmental goals. This reduces the planning time from weeks to months. The smart city team reported that the results were faster and the process was more transparent and fair. Everyone felt more engaged because they could see the data and participate in their cities. This is how bringing together AI and other digital tools can bring disparate groups together, cause them to work together better, and turn complex planning into something everyone can be involved in.

These three instances show that the future of collaboration is not specific to a single arena or use case. Whether conducting research, providing healthcare, or designing cities, using AI to support people in collaboration makes a tangible difference (Abdelwahab et al., 2022). Applications such as chatbots, wearable technology, IoT dashboards, and VR are not useful in isolation; they are most powerful when they become part of systems that empower people. Success is not a question of how recent the technology is but of how it integrates with users. As these examples highlight, AI is no longer just helping behind the scenes but is now part of the team, helping make better choices and creating more responsive systems. The biggest challenge now is how to develop and use these technologies in an equitable, open, and sustainable manner.

CHALLENGES AND ETHICAL IMPLICATIONS

With artificial intelligence increasingly entering into collaboration across industries, the promise of improved efficiency, innovation, and quick response comes with a package of hard challenges, most of which are of ethical orientation. These are not only technological challenges but also challenges in how people perceive, interact with, and are affected by intelligent systems. Trust is at the heart of these issues. Trust is essential for effective partnerships, and with AI playing a part in making decisions, one must always check and trust it. People must know how AI arrives at its answers, how reliable those answers are, and when to follow or defy the advice. However, this is not always simple. AI might seem confident, intelligent, and logical, but that does not mean that it is always right or knows the situation well. When people receive suggestions from AI, whether medical, financial, or team management, they are drawn to believing the outcome, particularly if the system appears smarter or quicker than human beings. However, such trust can be misplaced if the AI models are flawed, biased, or fail to capture the subtleties of the moment (Hoel & Filstad, 2023). Creating trustworthy systems is more than having great training; it is about creating processes to continually receive feedback, make amendments, and provide opportunities for humans to take control when needed. Alongside trust, privacy and security are major concerns, especially when AI works with multiple groups across different places and rules. Modern teams can have workers in various locations, sharing personal information in real time and using networked AI agents to process that information. The fact that such teams operate in disparate areas poses legal and ethical challenges to their operations. Each location has varying laws regarding data ownership, the way individuals give consent, and security to protect information. For example, a European health AI system will fall under the GDPR, whereas a US partner will fall under the HIPAA or another rule (Wang et al., 2024). To protect against these threats, organizations need to have good access controls, encryption, and practices to restrict data to an absolute minimum, but even these might not be enough. AI security in collaboration is not just about technology; it is about policy, management, and ethical thinking. Teams need to pose difficult questions: Who does the data generated in the collaboration belong to? How is consent obtained, monitored and withdrawn? Can people see how their data are being processed, and can they opt out without repercussions? In AI environments, openness and user choice should be the default, not obscured data streams or ambiguous consent. This means that in developing collaborative work processes, attention should not only be given to securing strength but also to ethical controls that consider future data stewardship and digital rights.

Aside from privacy, another often overlooked issue is cognitive strain when collaborating with AI. On the surface, AI is supposed to lighten the burden and deal with complexity. However, in reality, having AI as a collaborator introduces new mental tension. One of the reasons for this is to understand, check, or put AI's output into context. When AI makes a suggestion, people are left to verify or validate it. That is mentally draining, especially when the AI's output is complicated or only partially correct. The irony is that while AI is meant to help human decision-making, it can also make it harder, especially when users have to manage teamwork, assess the AI's advice, and stay alert for mistakes or blind spots. To avoid this, designers must consider not only what the AI is doing but also when and how it is doing it. The systems should be able to modulate their attention, providing more help when needed and relinquishing space during times of human necessity and autonomy. It is also important to ensure that AI explanations are clear without being too long. The answers should be simple, dissected for the understanding of the user, and straightforward so that people can grasp the reasoning behind AI without being held back by technicalities. The design must enhance human thinking and not overwhelm it. Transparency is not just a technical concern; it is an ethical obligation. They should understand when and how AI is applied in joint work, what data it handles, and how it generates output. This is especially true in areas such as healthcare, education, or the construction of legal conclusions when stakes are involved or feelings are an issue. When AI decides the result but remains unrevealed, it takes power away from individuals and is detrimental to trust. For genuine collaboration to be possible, both humans and machines must be transparent, accountable, and subject to auditing. Transparency, therefore, comes not only from AI but also from the organizations that use it. Transparency requires clear records of where data are drawn from, limits on the models, any known biases and mechanisms to rectify or appeal as needed (Jones & Jones, 2025). However, another major issue with AI is ensuring that everyone is included and avoiding biased outcomes. AI models are only as good as what they are taught, and what they are taught is likely to reflect old disparities, cultural biases, and discriminatory omissions. Teams must be told to ask themselves whose opinions are being condensed and whose are omitted and how AI is reinforcing the power of some to the disadvantage of others (Rezaev et al., 2023). Techniques for controlling prejudice, whether by privacy techniques, more balanced algorithms, or testing against unjustified assumptions, must be built into the early development of AI and not as an afterthought. However, even the most brilliant technical fixes are insufficient without a genuine focus on culture and organization. Inclusive collaboration demands practices that allow team members to challenge AI suggestions, offer different ideas, and raise concerns without being overlooked.

Therefore, AI systems must be designed based on human experience, supporting, not replacing, the social aspects of collaboration. In short, the ethical issues and challenges of using AI in collaboration are as complex as the AI technology itself. Trust, privacy, information overload, transparency, inclusion, and bias are not singular problems but interwoven elements that encompass how people feel about collaborating with AI. Solving these issues requires more than better algorithms; it requires better questions, better rules, and attention to humans while developing technology (Campion et al., 2020). With the advancement of AI, success in working with machines will not be gauged by the intelligence of the systems but by the wise, ethical, and inclusive way in which we choose to employ them.

STRATEGIC RECOMMENDATIONS

As organizations increasingly use artificial intelligence in their collaboration, it is becoming increasingly clear that they need a good future plan. It is not sufficient to assume new technology and hope for the best. Executives must work hard to frame and structure AI-augmented collaboration in a way that fits the firm's goals, human capabilities, and ethical principles. At its most fundamental level, collaborative intelligence leverages the best of humans and machines. To do this successfully, leaders must rethink not only how work gets done and what technology is used, but also what capabilities people cultivate, the environment they work in, how success is measured, and how the team is led. Recommendations must go beyond lofty suggestions and focus on down-to-earth, realistic steps that allow organizations to make the shift to this new way of working.

One of the first and most critical steps is investing in the acquisition of AI capabilities for different teams. This does not imply that everyone should become a coding or AI specialist. Instead, it is about making people aware of what AI can and cannot do, where it is in collaboration, and how to properly validate its outputs. In AI-augmented teams, people from across functions, such as marketing, engineering, finance, design, and HR, need to know how AI supports their role and how it interacts with others. For example, a product designer should be aware of how to use a language model for customer research, and a data scientist should understand how AI outputs are interpreted by frontline workers. In addition to individual jobs, teams must also share capabilities. These include understanding how to work together with AI findings, making decisions with people and machines, and resolving disagreements between human judgment and AI recommendations.

Workshops, simulations, and real-life training scenarios are excellent ways to build these skills. Training should be based on actual situations within the company and should involve tackling complex, real-world problems. For instance, what happens when AI recommendations conflict with real-life experiences, or when AI finds an anomaly but cannot explain why? These activities not only generate technical expertise but also make people feel at ease when questioning, working with, and trusting AI as a partner. It is also important that leaders are part of this training.

Executives and managers need to learn how to lead teams that have humans and AI, how to distribute tasks among them, and how to review AI performance without being overly reliant on it (Subaveerapandiyan et al., 2024). It is also important to create environments and tools in which human-AI collaboration is easy, natural, and ethical. As collaboration extends from physical conference rooms to virtual and mixed-reality environments, these environments must be well designed. This includes designing environments where AI is clearly present but not in charge, where its role is clear, and where its outputs are easy to understand and act on. For example, a dashboard for an urban planning organization need not only show data but also allow group members to comment, challenge the data, and provide context in a shared way. Interfaces should be built to encourage users to ask "why" and "what if" questions, not just receive answers.

Such human-centered design also needs to factor in the heterogeneity of users, including people of different ages, cultures, languages, and levels of digital literacy. Organizations need to be extremely clear about what success looks like prior to implementing AI in collaborative processes. What problems is AI supposed to solve? Which decisions will it enhance? How will success be measured along the way, immediate results, medium-term outcomes, or long-term change? Practically, this could involve examining how often teams get stuck, how easily knowledge transfers between functions, or how effectively different perspectives are integrated. For example, if an AI tool is utilized to help with cross-functional project planning, its return on investment needs to include not just how quickly the projects are delivered, but also whether people felt heard, how well risks were surfaced, and if the process supported learning across departments.

Transparency in ROI discussions is also critical. Not all projects will yield quick returns, and some will create new challenges. Transparency regarding failure, learning from it, and adjusting methods are part of developing AI capabilities in collaboration with humans (Al-Fattal & Singh, 2025). The core and perhaps the most critical part of the strategy is instituting strong policies and governance structures for the responsible use of e-collaboration. As AI is involved in decision-making, the question of who is at fault when an AI-supported decision results in harm becomes increasingly complex. When working internationally, even more care is necessary because laws can be quite different. For instance, a US-based business working with European partners must ensure that its AI applications meet GDPR standards for the protection of user data and acquiring consent. This typically involves legal agreements, mutual compliance regimes, and regular legal audits. Policies must also remain adaptive and continuously evolve as technology advances and social norms shift. Strict rules can become outdated when circumstances change rapidly. This includes shaping governance processes that are adaptive, ongoing, open to feedback and new challenges, and nimble. Measuring return on investment ensures a clear sight and aligns efforts with a larger purpose. Strong governance structures ensure that collaboration is ethical, inclusive, and responsible. Each of these elements does not exist in a vacuum.

CONCLUSION AND FUTURE OUTLOOK

The rapid convergence of collaboration and artificial intelligence is transforming the way people collaborate on a massive scale. As more companies move towards digital-first work practices and AI is incorporated into daily decision-making and creativity, companies cannot help but completely transform how they collaborate (Judson, 2025). This is not just a technology transformation; it is a deep transformation that affects ideas, behavior, identity, and company culture. Previous theories of teaming, based on human psychology, communication, and the ways in which humans worked alongside each other, now need to be viewed in an alternative context in which humans are working alongside machines. Ideas such as shared awareness, trust, power, and the manner in which people think as a group are no longer the prerogative of human teams. They now need to include smart, autonomous systems that "listen," "respond," and "create" so that it is difficult to determine where the machine stops and the teammate continues.

Traditional theories of teamwork include mutual comprehension, shared objectives, and partnership. This makes them useful, although they have limitations. Thus, those who work alongside AI need to see it not as a tool, but as an interesting collaborator with its own kind of "skill" – not emotional or moral, but intelligent, computational, and predictive. To marry teamwork theory and digitally native workplaces is to take the theories and extend them to include the ways machines act, how algorithms affect interactions, and how humans and AI interact (Lau et al., 2025). It also requires rethinking notions such as control, trust, and common purpose from the way AI systems do and do not work. In the real world, digital-first environments compel non-synchronous, adaptive, and open modes of working together. Teamwork fueled by AI works best when it makes people see smarter, think tougher, and perform more boldly, yet not at the expense of taking away from human teamwork the nuance, empathy, and ethical considerations. By doing so, marrying teamwork theory and digital-first work is not about replacing human teamwork but augmenting and extending it with the power of computation and new insights.

In the near future, the most exciting possibility is the use of artificial general intelligence (AGI) in teams. Currently, AI is only trained to perform one task, whereas AGI would have the ability to learn, reason, and use its capabilities in a vast range of tasks, similar to humans. The integration of AGI in team settings completely changes teamwork. Instead of just helping with work, AGI could be an effective colleague, able to define goals, create plans, critique concepts, and even come up with novel solutions. In these setups, collaboration would be less about commanding AI and more about negotiating, planning with the team, and developing it further (Timmons et al., 2022). This vision raises huge issues about roles, identity, and who gets to call the shots in a team. If an AGI comes up with a new solution to a design problem, should it be considered a co-creator? If it detects an ethical issue in a policy, does it deserve to be listened to? From this perspective, AGI could one day match or even surpass human teams in collaborative ability, as long as it is built and guided with care.

Of course, this future is not without risks. AGI's nature brings a lot of AGI introduces significant uncertainty. Its decisions can be difficult to understand, its reasoning unclear, and its influence immense (Kane et al., 2023). In the case of groups, this can lead to overdependence, unfair imbalances in power, or deprivation of human agency. These problems must be circumvented by designing architectures that will cause AGI to behave in an open, moral manner, and in harmony with human values. Educational systems, leadership development, and corporate development initiatives need to shift to emphasize not technical abilities but rather so-called "machine empathy", the capacity to know how AI functions and its place within human collectives.

The most visionary companies will be prepared not only for new technology but also for new work practices when approaching a future with AGI. They will ask: How do we create spaces where human and machine intelligence complement each other positively? What values and habits facilitate ethical cooperation between humans and machines? How do we create organizations that are more efficient and empathetic? These questions provide guidance to a new kind of firm, a firm that is not just digital-first or AI-first but truly co-creative. In such companies, humans and machines work together not because they have to, but by design. AI is not just a part of the process; it is part of the cultural way of how work is thought about, built, and measured. Creativity is created alongside human–AI collaboration. Decision-making is a conversation, not merely a series of instructions. Learning is ongoing, reciprocal, and adaptive. Arriving at this point involves dramatic changes across the entire system. Organizations need to transition from work by individuals focused on tasks to work revolving around how individuals are connected and work with one another, as well as with AI. Leaders need to abandon command-and-control styles of leadership and build environments in which learning and innovation can germinate. Judging how well people perform their jobs should not only consider what they produce but also take into account how well teams work together and whether everyone feels included. Technology teams should work with people who study ethics, society, and people on the ground to ensure that AI serves the company's values. This cannot be accomplished overnight. It is an incremental change, a sometimes-discussed cultural change that occurs as humans and technology develop (Zhao et al., 2025). It is also interesting to consider new ideas about innovation. Innovation typically begins with experts or leaders setting the direction. However, in smarter organizations, innovation is more organic, through iterative experimentation and collaboration. AI can help detect hidden problems, patterns, and solutions at lightning speed. Humans add judgment, vision for the big picture, empathy, and conscience to create innovations that lead to real change. They can approach large, complex problems, such as climate change, inequality, or mental illness, collectively, which no individual or even a device can solve. This is what happens when human collaboration with AI reaches its full potential: not faster or cheaper, but accomplishing things we used to think were impossible.

Ultimately, the future of collaboration is not a question of humans versus machines. It is about embracing both and learning how to collaborate with all types of intelligence. This is to be humble enough to learn that machines are sometimes better at seeing things that we cannot (Chew et al., 2024). It requires creativity to try new ways of working and living together. It requires bravery to tackle the ethical, emotional, and social concerns of having non-human minds as teammates. As AI develops, we need to develop with it, not by forgetting what makes us human but by enriching it. The best companies and teams will not be the ones with the most AI, but the ones that use AI to become more open, connected, and adaptable. This is how we create truly smart and collaborative organizations.

REFERENCES

Abdelwahab, H. R., Rauf, A., & Chen, D. (2022). Business students' perceptions of Dutch higher educational institutions in preparing them for artificial intelligence work environments. *Industry and Higher Education, 37*(1), 22-34. (Original work published 2023)DOI: 10.1177/09504222221087614

Al-Fattal, A., & Singh, J. (2025). Comparative Reflections on Human-Driven and Generative Artificial Intelligence-Assisted Thematic Analysis: A Collaborative Autoethnography. *International Journal of Qualitative Methods, 24*. (Original work published 2025)DOI: 10.1177/16094069251337870

Boni, M. (2021). The ethical dimension of human–artificial intelligence collaboration. *European View, 20*(2), 182-190. (Original work published 2021)DOI: 10.1177/17816858211059249

Campion, A., Gasco-Hernandez, M., Jankin Mikhaylov, S., & Esteve, M. (2020). Overcoming the Challenges of Collaboratively Adopting Artificial Intelligence in the Public Sector. *Social Science Computer Review, 40*(2), 462-477. (Original work published 2022)DOI: 10.1177/0894439320979953

Chai, C. S., Yu, D., King, R. B., & Zhou, Y. (2024). Development and Validation of the Artificial Intelligence Learning Intention Scale (AILIS) for University Students. *SAGE Open, 14*(2). (Original work published 2024)DOI: 10.1177/21582440241242188

Chew, Y. C., & Mohamed Zainal, S. R. (2024). A Sustainable Collaborative Talent Management Through Collaborative Intelligence Mindset Theory: A Systematic Review. *SAGE Open, 14*(2). (Original work published 2024)DOI: 10.1177/21582440241261851

Criado, J. I., Sandoval-Almazán, R., & Gil-Garcia, J. R. (2024). Artificial intelligence and public administration: Understanding actors, governance, and policy from micro, meso, and macro perspectives. *Public Policy and Administration, 40*(2), 173-184. (Original work published 2025)DOI: 10.1177/09520767241272921

Ding, X., Maleyeff, J., & Valk, F. (2023). Bus Operation Safety Business Intelligence Solution: Applying Analytics for Key Performance Indicator, Investigation, and Targeted Actions Analyses with a Centralized Data Warehouse. *Transportation Research Record, 2678*(7), 208-223. (Original work published 2024)DOI: 10.1177/03611981231205882

Gallagher, J. R., & Wagner, K. (2024). Comparing Student and Writing Instructor Perceptions of Academic Dishonesty When Collaborators Are Artificial Intelligence or Human. *Journal of Business and Technical Communication, 38*(3), 266-288. (Original work published 2024)DOI: 10.1177/10506519241239937

Hoel, L., & Filstad, C. (2023). The police's intelligence-led crisis management: Crossing knowledge boundaries of operational and intelligence practices during acute crises. *The Police Journal, 97*(3), 559-577. (Original work published 2024) DOI: 10.1177/0032258X231196117

Jones, B., & Jones, R. (2025). Action research at the BBC: Interrogating artificial intelligence with journalists to generate actionable insights for the newsroom. *Journalism, 26*(8), 1708-1725. (Original work published 2025)DOI: 10.1177/14648849251317150

Judson, H. (2025). "But I Didn't Use ChatGPT!": Democratic Course Design and Generative Artificial Intelligence in Higher Education Landscape. *Teaching Sociology, 53*(3), 246-256. (Original work published 2025)DOI: 10.1177/0092055X251342530

Kane, A. A., Paletz, S. B. F., Vahlkamp, S. H., Nelson, T., Porter, A., Diep, M., & Carraway, M. (2023). Intelligence Analysis Shift Work: Sensemaking Processes, Tensions, and Takeaways. *Proceedings of the Human Factors and Ergonomics Society Annual Meeting, 67*(1), 741-746. (Original work published 2023)DOI: 10.1177/21695067231192569

Kim, K., & Kwon, K. (2024). Designing an Inclusive Artificial Intelligence (AI) Curriculum for Elementary Students to Address Gender Differences With Collaborative and Tangible Approaches. *Journal of Educational Computing Research, 62*(7), 1617-1644. (Original work published 2024)DOI: 10.1177/07356331241271059

Lau, A. S., Wu, J., Ma, P., & Lee, H. (2025). Using artificial intelligence, ontology, and 3D visualization in the metaverse for improving collaborative work and collective intelligence. *The International Journal of Entrepreneurship and Innovation, 26*(1), 66-84. (Original work published 2025)DOI: 10.1177/14657503241313362

Ling, E. C., Tussyadiah, I., Liu, A., & Stienmetz, J. (2023). Perceived Intelligence of Artificially Intelligent Assistants for Travel: Scale Development and Validation. *Journal of Travel Research, 64*(2), 299-321. (Original work published 2025)DOI: 10.1177/00472875231217899

Liu, J., Li, S., & Dong, Q. (2024). Collaboration with Generative Artificial Intelligence: An Exploratory Study Based on Learning Analytics. *Journal of Educational Computing Research, 62*(5), 1014-1046. (Original work published 2024)DOI: 10.1177/07356331241242441

Mannuru, N. R., Shahriar, S., Teel, Z. A., Wang, T., Lund, B. D., Tijani, S., Pohboon, C. O., Agbaji, D., Alhassan, J., Galley, J., Kousari, R., Ogbadu-Oladapo, L., Saurav, S. K., Srivastava, A., Tummuru, S. P., Uppala, S., & Vaidya, P. (2023). Artificial intelligence in developing countries: The impact of generative artificial intelligence (AI) technologies for development. *Information Development, 41*(3), 1036-1054. (Original work published 2025)DOI: 10.1177/02666669231200628

Moser, R., Rengarajan, S., & Narayanamurthy, G. (2021). Decision Intelligence: Creating a Fit between Intelligence Requirements and Intelligence Processing Capacities. *IIM Kozhikode Society & Management Review, 10*(2), 160-177. (Original work published 2021)DOI: 10.1177/22779752211017386

Nogueira, L. A., Moltubakk, S. T., Fagervik, A., & Langfeldt, I. B. (2025). Cutting through the noise: Assessing tools that employ artificial intelligence. *IFLA Journal, 51*(3), 735-749. (Original work published 2025)DOI: 10.1177/03400352241304121

Özüdoğru, G., & Durak, H. Y. (2025). Conceptualizing pre-service teachers' artificial intelligence readiness and examining its relationship with various variables: The role of artificial intelligence literacy, digital citizenship, artificial intelligence-enhanced innovation and perceived threats from artificial intelligence. *Information Development, 41*(3), 916-932. (Original work published 2025)DOI: 10.1177/02666669251335657

Qi, J., & Wang, J. (2025). Bridging Artificial Intelligence and Railway Cybersecurity: A Comprehensive Anomaly Detection Review. *Transportation Research Record, 2679*(5), 232-255. (Original work published 2025)DOI: 10.1177/03611981241302335

Rezaev, A. V., & Tregubova, N. D. (2023). Looking at human-centered artificial intelligence as a problem and prospect for sociology: An analytic review. *Current Sociology, 73*(1), 120-138. (Original work published 2025)DOI: 10.1177/00113921231211580

Riedl, C., De Cremer, D., Lucarelli, G., Antoine-Souklaye, E., Bullock, S., Ajmeri, N., Batty, M., Black, M., Cartlidge, J., Challen, R., Chen, C., Chen, J., Condell, J., Danon, L., Dennett, A., Heppenstall, A., Marshall, P., Morgan, P., O'Kane, A., … Denis, G. (2025). The potential and challenges of AI for collective intelligence. *Collective Intelligence, 4*(1). (Original work published 2025)DOI: 10.1177/26339137241308821

Subaveerapandiyan, A., Radhakrishnan, S., Tiwary, N., & Guangul, S. M. (2024). Student satisfaction with artificial intelligence chatbots in Ethiopian academia. *IFLA Journal, 51*(3), 600-614. (Original work published 2025)DOI: 10.1177/03400352241252974

Tariq, M. U. (2025). *Qualitative Inquiry in Doctoral Research: Pathways to Effective Design and Implementation*. IGI Global., DOI: 10.4018/979-8-3693-7200-5

Tariq, M. U. (2025). *AI-Driven Learning and Engagement in Higher Education*. IGI Global., DOI: 10.4018/979-8-3693-4074-5

Timmons, A. C., Duong, J. B., Simo Fiallo, N., Lee, T., Vo, H. P. Q., Ahle, M. W., Comer, J. S., Brewer, L. C., Frazier, S. L., & Chaspari, T. (2022). A Call to Action on Assessing and Mitigating Bias in Artificial Intelligence Applications for Mental Health. *Perspectives on Psychological Science, 18*(5), 1062-1096. (Original work published 2023)DOI: 10.1177/17456916221134490

Wang, B., Zhang, C., Khamo, & Ye, S. (2024). Facing the era of generative artificial intelligence: Strategies of information and digital literacy in Chinese studies. *IFLA Journal, 51*(3), 787-802. (Original work published 2025)DOI: 10.1177/03400352241291905

Woolley, A. W., & Gupta, P. (2023). Understanding Collective Intelligence: Investigating the Role of Collective Memory, Attention, and Reasoning Processes. *Perspectives on Psychological Science, 19*(2), 344-354. (Original work published 2024)DOI: 10.1177/17456916231191534

Zhao, G., Yang, L., Hu, B., & Wang, J. (2025). A Generative Artificial Intelligence (AI)-Based Human-Computer Collaborative Programming Learning Method to Improve Computational Thinking, Learning Attitudes, and Learning Achievement. *Journal of Educational Computing Research, 63*(5), 1059-1087. (Original work published 2025)DOI: 10.1177/07356331251336154

KEY TERMS AND DEFINITIONS

Collaborative Intelligence: Human–AI partnership improves decision-making and creativity.

Digital Twin: Virtual representation reflecting real-world system behaviors.

Human–AI Co-Workflow: Shared jobs between humans and intelligent agents.

Chapter 6
Mind Meets Machine: E-Collaboration in the Era of Artificial Intelligence

R. N. Ravikumar
https://orcid.org/0009-0009-3705-1681
Marwadi University, Rajkot, India

S. Aarthi
https://orcid.org/0009-0006-9064-2091
Marwadi University, Rajkot, India

ABSTRACT

This book explores the transformative impact of Artificial Intelligence (AI) and emerging digital technologies on e-collaboration across various sectors. It presents a comprehensive analysis of how AI, IoT, blockchain, quantum computing, 5G, and Extended Reality (XR) are reshaping collaborative ecosystems, enabling intelligent decision-making, personalized workflows, and immersive interactions. The chapters discuss the evolution of e-collaboration from tool-based systems to human-AI partnerships, showcasing sectoral applications in healthcare, education, e-commerce, and manufacturing. Key ethical concerns such as privacy, algorithmic bias, and legal frameworks are also addressed, along with future challenges like AGI and sustainable collaboration. Through interdisciplinary insights and real-world examples, the book offers a forward-looking guide for designing inclusive, secure, and intelligent collaborative systems.

DOI: 10.4018/979-8-3373-5747-8.ch006

1. INTRODUCTION

The cooperation in the era of digital has gone over and above being in the same physical place as part of an active ecosystem that operates with the aid of technology. E-collaboration has experienced a paradigm shift after the introduction of Artificial Intelligence (AI), and other emerging technologies that will be enabling the use of digital tools to facilitate the team work and communication. It is proposed in this work that intelligent systems provide more than support the process of collaboration, i.e., that intelligent systems intervene in the process of collaboration as well (of AI-enabled e-collaboration). AI-decision making platforms can generate productivity, communication and innovation within a distributed group by means of virtual assistants and intelligent agents. The reason is that, the convergence of AI and IoT, block chain, quantum computing and extended reality is causing a shift in human and organizational interactions and also in co-creation and problem solving (Chen et al., 2023). The research work objectives are also present in this chapter and it focuses on the role of the human-machine synergy in the future work, learning and innovation. It develops the platform where the potentials of utilisation of the collaborative intelligence to design more intelligent, responsive, and inclusive sphere of the digital world could be addressed.

1.1 Definition and Evolution of E-Collaboration

E-collaboration is described as the utilization of digital technologies to aid collaboration of individuals or teams or organizations, regardless of time and space. It also involves a broad scope of tools, including email, video conference, cloud-based services, project management, and many others, and allows the real-time communications team, disseminating knowledge and making decisions collectively (Crompton & Burke, 2023). E-collaboration initially started as simple messaging and file sharing platform but recently has developed a lot following high speed internet, mobile computing and cloud infrastructures. It enables complex interactions that surpass geographical boundaries and holds information, processes and individuals in seamless virtual environments nowadays. The transformations related to the pandemic that happened worldwide to transition to the mode of working remotely and even in a hybrid format have also contributed to the increase in its usage and importance. What was useful to orchestrate the straightforward structures in the past assists today in co-creation and scale-based innovation. The tasks and distributed teams have evolved to be too complex to be addressed through previous forms of e-collaborating tools It preconditions the inflow of intelligent technologies AI and IoT, and blockchain included which can make these digital workspaces quite intelligent, dynamic, and even multi-collaboration ecosystems.

1.2 The Role of AI and Emerging Technologies in Reshaping Collaboration

The emergence of Artificial Intelligence and the shift to the new digital technologies are re-painting the face of collaboration by taking it to the more dynamic interaction and the interaction that considers the contexts. Alongside AI come the capabilities to process Natural Language Processing (NLP), computer vision, recommendation systems, and intelligent decision support systems: systems that can comprehend and predict and behave just like humans. With the addition of Internet of Things (IoT) devices, these systems then could capture, and analyse real-time sections of environmental or behavioural information to be more responsive. Blockchain ensures the relationship in cases of collaboration that require the cooperation of several stakeholders is transparent and irreversible. The promise of quantum computing is to be able to exponentially solve complex problems in a distributed model or simulation. The technologies are enabling intelligent secretaries or recap of a session, chatbots that finish customer issues in collaboration, and algorithms that match knowledge on teams globally. Basically, people do not collaborate any more with the help of tools, but people and machines co-upend values. Now that these technologies have come to maturity, teams are able to be more creative and able to make better judgments and work together in a collaborative way that is the building block to what is now known as collaborative intelligence. The Figure (Rathinavel et al., 2025)1 shows that technologies such as AI, IoT, blockchain, and quantum computing are converged in order to allow collaborative intelligence. The capabilities offered by each technology are unique, and the combination of the two technologies changes the dynamics of human-machine teamwork and collaboration globally.

Figure 1. The Role of AI and Emerging Technologies in Reshaping Collaboration

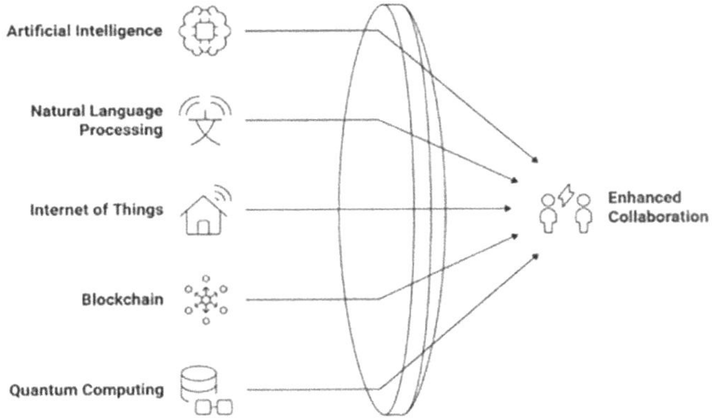

1.3 Human-AI Collaboration: From Tools to Partners

The concept of the human-AI collaboration introduces a new approach to view technology as a collection of tools, but not as an equivalent partner in the working processes. The traditional models offered a fixed back-up when using digital systems- e.g. storing files, sending messages etc. These days, AI systems are involved in a decision process, learn the behavior of people, generate insights, and start acting. To give an example, in project management, AI can automatically allocate work assignments, adjust the schedules based on new and real-time information, and notify the team about threats. In the sphere of health care, AI collaborates with doctors to analyze the diagnostic images and recommend the therapy course. This symbiosis allows human to focus on creativity and empathy and strategy but not AI, which composes data-intensive, repetitive or analytical work. Having said that, successful human-AI collaborations must be built on trust in the joint effort and developing clear systems, along with ensuring that AI judgments can be readily justified. It will also imply the renegotiation of job descriptions and relationships in the team where neither the living beings nor robots are inferior or superior, but complement each other. This evolution (tool use to intelligent alliance) is fundamental to the creation of adaptive, resilient and high performing environments of e-collaboration.

1.4 Overview of the objectives

Mind Meets Machine discusses the way AI and new technologies are transforming digital collaboration. It presents an academic and industry approach by looking at the theme of human-machine teaming, ethical issues, and practice. The research-based work can be used as the way to construct intelligent, secure, and inclusive collaborative systems in the future of work.

- To define and contextualize AI-enabled e-collaboration across industries.
- To analyze core technologies like IoT, blockchain, quantum computing, and XR in collaborative settings.
- To explore real-world applications in healthcare, education, and enterprise.
- To address ethical, legal, and privacy concerns in human-AI teaming.
- To provide design frameworks and policy recommendations for responsible AI integration.
- To promote collaborative intelligence as a foundation for future digital ecosystems.

2. FOUNDATIONS OF COLLABORATIVE INTELLIGENCE

Collaborative intelligence is a synergetic interaction between intelligent computer and man towards achieving common goals with common benefits. The efficiency available to humans gives it creativity, empathy, situation judgement and ethical reasoning, but the AI systems offer speed, scalability and idea through data. With this kind of fusion, it is possible to establish a new paradigm of collaborations as machines no longer remain the object of a teamwork but participants. Collaborative intelligence is constructed on the creation of systems that can learn through human behaviour, adapt to the changing environment and utilise communication to enhance performance of teams. It also involves implementation of transparent, trustful and mutually enabling workflows in the context of humans-AI interactions. The team intelligence here is essential in order to make sense in the digital workplace, which offers smarter decision making, faster innovation and inclusion of more people. As an increasing number of organizations adopt AI tools, the concepts of collaborative intelligence will become central to how organizations design teams, reinvent job descriptions and unlock augmented human-machine cooperation.

2.1 Concepts of Human-Machine Teaming

Human-Machine Teaming (HMT) The human-smart system interaction was used to find solutions to problems, decide or perform their work better than the system could have performed alone. Contrary to classical automation when the machines operate on pre-determined instructions, HMT is associated with real-time communication, mutual comprehension, and dynamic roles. The basis of effective teaming is to be aware of the others: humans are expected to know the strengths and weaknesses of the machine and an AI system should be able to recognize human intentions and accommodate them (Li et al., 2020). This idea is based on the principles of cognitive science, systems engineering and human factors that allow having synergy between artificial and biological agents. The AI agents in human-machine teams can propose solutions, track risk or guide the workflow outside the scope of human decision-making. Among the factors are trust, transparency, protocols of communication, and delegation of job. To make HMT successful systems should be intuitive and give explainable output, particularly in high stakes area such as in healthcare, military or when used in finance (Raisch & Krakowski, 2021). The future of cooperation is especially dependent on the possibility of human and machine to integrate more and more around ethically interoperable idiosyncrasies, shared arenas, and decision ecosystems.

2.2 Cognitive Augmentation and Hybrid Intelligence

Cognitive augmentation is the way of boosting human reason and judgment with AI tools and technologies. It is not meant to substitute human cognition, but to integrate with it- by taking over activities that need scale, speed or pattern recognition, or patterns that need more memory than humans can offer. The merging of the human judgment and the machine learning models would create the hybrid intelligence that would come out as smarter, more effective, and more adaptable than both of them. In that respect, an example dealing with the analysis of the great amounts of data could detect trends through AI levels, whereas the human expert can give the interpretation of the results and apply them into a complex context. Cognitive augmentation in education can be used to individualize education by predicting the patterns of the student (Rezwana & Maher, 2022)s. In the medical field, AI has a potential role to play to help physicians diagnose complex situations by pointing out likely situations. Real-time co-creation A second way that hybrid intelligence can be employed to its advantage is through real-time co-creation, where human beings approve or refine ideas provided by AI systems, based on situational awareness. This blend gives rise to creativity, reduces mental pressure and enables an individual to think strategically. However, they require user-oriented design, transparency and continuous learning cycles, which can be enhanced using the assistance of mutually beneficial feedback. In e-collaborative systems, organizations will be required to innovate and be dynamic because they will encounter the increased complexity and this will necessitate the utilization of hybrid intelligence.

2.3 Organizational Transformation Through Collaborative Intelligence

The adoption of collaborative intelligence is transforming how business entities or organizations organize and structure their teams, process and decision making. Organizations have traditionally employed a hierarchical structure that had established positions and coordination was manual in form. However, with AI there is an opportunity to have more agile, flatter structures where intelligent systems can be a partner, which can simplify communication, automate repetitive tasks and bring predictions and insights into focus in real-time. The outcome of this change is the non-centralized decision making, the reduction of the innovation cycles and the dynamism of the resources allocation (Sundaresan and Zhang, 2022). To enable smarter work on teams and protect the employees, first-mover platforms have already integrated AI-chatbots, recommendation services, and smart dashboards to analytics. Moreover, data-based partnership enhances knowledge sharing among various departments and different geographical areas and, therefore, maintained learning cultures. It is also a change that needs a change of leadership, skills and the organization culture. Managers must also adopt digital literacy and ethical uses of AI, as well as, train employees on how to work with smart systems. Moreover, such issues as data privacy, bias minimization, and accountability of algorithms also should be addressed by the policies. On the whole, collaborative intelligence does not only contribute to technological advancements, but a profound change within the whole organization- making it more intelligent, resilient, diverse, and adaptive to the dynamic global settings (Zhao et al., 2025).

2.4 AI as a Co-worker: Capabilities, Limitations, and Boundaries

As the AI systems continue to be integrated into the working environment, they begin to perform the functions that were previously performed by the human colleagues, combining the tasks, processing the data, making some suggestions, or even leading the team. AI co-worker ordains a number of strong functions such as: ability to act fast on noisy reams of information, report similar and consistent findings uncompromised by weariness, render objective advice, and be present without spoiled moods. The systems can streamline the process of scheduling, tailor the experience with customers, track the work processes, and point anomalous operations out beforehand. They do however have their own limitations as well. AI does not have common sense of reasoning, emotional intelligence, contextual understanding and moral judgement (Bhattacharjee et al., 2024). It is restricted to the extent its training data and algorithmic design and can thus be biased, incorrect, or vulnerable to manipulation by adversaries. Thus, the task is to define strict limits in the interaction between a person and AI. The activities that need to be impacted with empathy, ethical complexity, or long-term strategy should be human-centered, where AI acts as an auxiliary system. Trust and accountability require building explainable, interpretable AI as well. Companies also have to establish rules of engagement, or to clear up what AI will do, what it will be responsible for and the means of escalation (LTIMIndtree et al., 2023). After all, merely learning to accept and make use of the power of AI and seek to accommodate and supplement it by respecting the unadulterated power of human intuition, creativity, and judgment is the key to successful integration of the AI as co-worker.

3. CORE TECHNOLOGIES DRIVING E-COLLABORATION

A hybridization of advanced digital technologies is also changing e-collaboration as it promises to outline smarter, quicker, and more secure group work in remote environments. At its core, it features AI, which powerfully drives intelligent assistants, predictive analytics and personalized workflows. IoT (Internet of Things) appliances collect real-time data to facilitate cooperation to the fullest between individuals in the real and virtual world, and blockchain provides the security, transparency, and inability to counterfeit the information and digital assets exchange. Quantum computing can offer exponential processing speeds in its early phases to allow complex collaborative modelling and simulation to take place and maintain latency-free communication between time-dependent processes. 5G networks and edge computing can reduce latency to maintain unhindered communication among time-dependent processes. Virtual, Augmented and Mixed Reality (Extended Reality XR) provide collaboration and engaging environments, and thus it can be used as a training and design tool as well as a healthcare tool. Together these technologies have been conceptualized as a sort of ecosystem where human and machine intelligence are unified and enhance intelligent decision-making, innovation and trust. Their integration is essential to the building of adaptive intelligent and resilient collaborative systems that are responsive to the needs of the digital realm. The key digital technologies that drive modern e-collaboration are graphically displayed in the Figure 2. It focuses on interrelated drivers, which are centralized around the term E-Collaboration, including AI, IoT, blockchain, quantum computing, 5G, and XR, which are all aimed at creating smarter, faster, and more secure collaborative spaces.

Figure 2. Core Technologies Driving E-Collaboration

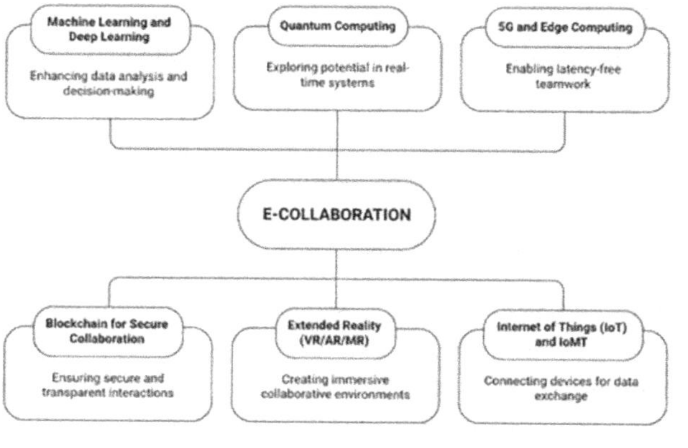

3.1 Machine Learning and Deep Learning

Machine Learning (ML) and Deep Learning (DL) are the primary drag of intelligent E-collaboration which entails learning out of data and refining by the learning processes. ML models analyze patterns in communication and behavior and project data to suggest workflow automation, issue bottleneck alerts and work-individualization. The power of Deep Learning, which is a branch of ML, is used to run advanced applications such as natural language understanding, image and vein recognition, and contextual decision-making. DL enables the adoption of these collaborative capabilities in platforms in the form of real-time language translation, sentiment analysis, chat summary, and intelligent document search. (Krinkin et al., 2021). The functionality provides a higher level of productivity, eliminates miscommunication, and facilitates improved teaming. ML/DL models also learn to meet the preferences of individual users and behavioural patterns, developing individual digital workspaces. Nevertheless, to preserve the trust of user AI, it is essential to have transparent, and comprehensible output. As accuracy and speed of models improve in the future, ML and DL will remain a major driver of proactive, intelligent and user-centric cooperation in terms of collaboration within the numerous industries and digital ecosystems.

3.2 Internet of Things (IoT) and Internet of Medical Things (IoMT)

The Internet of Things (IoT) and the Internet of Medical Things (IoMT) as its subcategory is one of the key aspects of facilitating real-time data-driven e-collaboration. IoT links the physical world, sensors, wearable devices, smart devices to the digital one to obtain, relay and react to environmental or operational data (Lee et al., 2023). Within the workforce setting, IoT enables remote surveillance, intelligent scheduling, energy cost savings, and contextual sensitivity within their common offices. As an example, intelligent meeting rooms can automatically adjust lights or the climate or setting of devices according to the profiles of users or usage patterns. According to healthcare, IoMT facilitates cooperation among clinicians, patients and systems by allowing real-time transfer and exchange of vital signs, diagnostic information, or suggestive data collected by the device on patients (Li et al., 2020). This ensures timely interventions, reduced errors and the greatest use of coordinated care delivery. IoMT and IoT promote the interoperability and visibility of networks and decentralization. However, they are associated with high cyber security, data privacy and standardization processes to enable them to be highly functioning and risk-free. When combined together in a collaborative ecosystem, they can significantly enhance responsiveness, operational efficiency and situational awareness. (Pasupuleti, 2025).

3.3 Blockchain for Secure Collaboration

Blockchain allows block-based record-keeping that is distributed and resistant to modification, and it is gradually being utilized to augment e-collaboration trust, transparency, and safety. Unlike the centralized systems in the past, blockchain allows multiple parties to keep, identify as well as retrieve data in real-time without a centralized entity. To collaborate, this aspect implies that each performed action or transaction, be it a file share, edit of data, or a contract, is registered directly and without possibility to alter, audibly, and transparently. Smart contracts additionally automate adherence and execution of tasks through dispersed groups, and lower the latter by removing the necessity of go-between and manual confirmation (Dominguez et al., 2025). Blockchain is particularly useful in a situation where there is cross-organizational workflows where supply chains are coordinated, sharing of intellectual property or secure sharing of medical data. It also assists in reducing risk such as data tampering or unauthorized access or version control. Scaling and energy consumption are still an issue, but new blockchain frameworks resolve these issues more and more. Blockchain provides more secure, reliable, and trust-driven environments in the digital collaboration field because accountability and data integrity are achieved through blockchain.

3.4 Quantum Computing and Its Potential in Real-Time Collaborative Systems

Quantum computing is in its developmental stage but can transform real-time collaborative systems by providing exponentially big computing capability over classic computers. It is based on quantum bits (qubits) that have the capability to process numerous conditions concurrently and therefore can solve a problem quickly in environments with dense data and extreme complexity (Ryjov, 2021). Some tasks in the domain of e-collaboration, including dynamic scheduling, multi-agent optimization, secure contact and simulation of collaborative situations could be speed up by properly applied quantum computing. As an example, quantum algorithms may reproduce highly precise and fast models of how a team works, how communication patterns occur, or how a crisis team could act. Moreover, quantum cryptography brings practically impossible data protection on the data transferred on the collaboration platform promoting confidence and coverage in sensitive aspects such as military or healthcare (Ryjov, 2022). Although they are yet to make an impact at large scale, smaller-scale systems integrating classical and quantum computing are under investigation as near-term uses. Quantum computing will also become a disruptor in the process organizations coordinate, innovate, and collaborate on multi-sided complex issues at scale as the technology matures.

3.5 5G and Edge Computing for Latency-Free Teamwork

When 5G networks connect to edge computing, it is transformative in terms of digital collaboration as it opens access to high-speed, low latency connections with real-time data transfer. It has never been as fast or connected and capable of supporting high-definition video conferencing, AR/VR experiences, and instant file transfer that teleworkers and by spreading workspaces require. It is augmented by Edge computing, which performs the data processing closer to the source of data generation reducing the requirements of the centralized cloud servers. It implies that a decision-making process and collaboration can be real-time even regarding such time-sensitive domains as manufacturing, telemedicine, and logistics. An example to illustrate this point is that edge-enabled sensors may be employed to monitor the working environment or the output of one of the working machines and transmit a prompt message to the members of the team before it is too late. (Sadiku et al., 2021). The combination of such technologies works to the advantage of mobile collaboration, network reliability, and mitigation of lag, a major challenge in remote activities, interactive collaboration software, and distributed machine learning models. Some of the challenges, however, are adequate security of edge nodes and data integrity in decentralized systems. Location-based UX 5G and edge computing will form the backbone of frictionless, and always-on collaborative work in a connected environment as adoption becomes ubiquitous.

3.6 Extended Reality (VR/AR/MR) for Immersive Collaboration

Extended Reality (XR) which consists of Virtual Reality (VR), Augmented Reality (AR), and Mixed Reality (MR) bring immersive, spatial collaboration that crosses the physical and virtual rifts. XR technologies allow the participants to communicate in simulated three-dimensional environments or to project virtual things over the real-world environments. VR enables virtual meeting, design, or training simulation where the people feel as though they are in the same space even though they are in different locations. AR facilitates live cooperation by overlaying digital information over real-world working environments especially in the field of maintenance, telehealth, or the production process (Zhu et al., 2022). MR is an amalgamation of the two allowing individuals to move virtual objects in the real world to conduct collaborative ideation and problem-solving situations. These experiences enhance interaction, areas awareness, and collaboration in specific fields such as education, architecture, and first response solutions. XR also allows an inclusive approach to participation and works to empower remote workers or differently-abled people by using other interfaces. Hardware prices, end-user comfort, and cross-system compatibility are still a problem, but recent development of headsets and cloud XR platforms are fast addressing those issues. The XR is transforming team visualization, co-creation, and connectivity in digital environments. The table 1 summarizes the six foundational technologies that transform traditional digital collaboration into intelligent, secure, and immersive ecosystems (Jiatao Kang Junlei Dong, 2021).

Table 1. Core Technologies Driving E-Collaboration

Technology	Role in E-Collaboration	Key Benefits
Artificial Intelligence (AI)	Powers intelligent assistants, decision-making, and personalization	Enables smarter, faster collaboration
Internet of Things (IoT)	Links physical devices with digital systems for real-time data	Enhances responsiveness and coordination
Blockchain	Provides secure, immutable data sharing across stakeholders	Boosts transparency and trust
Quantum Computing	Offers exponential processing for complex simulations and modelling	Enhances optimization in distributed systems
5G + Edge Computing	Ensures high-speed, low-latency connectivity for remote collaboration	Supports real-time interactions
Extended Reality (XR)	Enables immersive collaboration in virtual/ augmented environments	Fosters inclusion and experiential learning

4. AI-POWERED COLLABORATIVE SYSTEMS AND PLATFORMS

Collaborative systems and information platforms that operate AI are significantly transforming the way teams communicate, deal with tasks, and make decisions. Smart chatbots, as well as virtual assistants, predictive analytics, and instant language translation can make things more productive and easier to work with. Such programs as Microsoft Teams, Slack, and Salesforce have also incorporated AI to automate schedule, meeting summary, and personalization environments. Decision support systems are data-driven driven to offer information, whereas AI-enabled knowledge sharing platforms enhance information search and quality of relevant information received. They transform systems into active partners and allow cooperating in the teamwork faster, smarter and more inclusive in any industry, irrespective of geographical and numerical limitation.

4.1 Intelligent Chatbots, Virtual Assistants, and AI Agents

The use of AI in chatbots, virtual assistants and autonomous agents is changing how digital collaboration is viewed by enabling smooth 24/7 support and task that can be been achieved reliably. Such systems are able to understand natural language, perform repetitive queries, deal with calendars, take meeting minutes, or even delegate a task depending on the priority of the task. Chatbots that are part of platforms, such as Microsoft Teams or Slack, facilitate communications, offer instant answers to questions and help decrease the load on the human personnel in the enterprise settings. Additional productivity can be provided by voice-based interaction and reminder via Virtual assistants, such as Google Assistant or Siri. Advanced AI agents are not limited to gaining automation in the tasks; they are autonomous in their decision-making at a limited complexity. As an example, they are able to escalate tickets, or produce reports, or to organize workflows in distributed teams (Zhang et al., 2020). The tools are fast to communicate and also lead to consistency and efficiency. Nevertheless, their efficiency is preconditioned by situational awareness, embedding in internal systems and data confidentiality. As these agents get smarter, chattier, and more responsive, they are likely to become the key element in human-AI collaborating ecosystems.

4.2 AI-Enhanced Project and Communication Tools

Cloud-based platforms of project management and communication are being transformed with the introduction of AI, and this technology contributes to a better experience, more accurate decision making, and the accomplishment of the tasks offered. Such applications as Asana, Trello, and Monday.com include AI that may prioritize projects automatically, foresee the timeframe of all the tasks, and warn the staff about upcoming delays or backlogs. Such platforms may process historical project information and propose the best possible work patterns, resources allocations, and workload balancing (Sundaresan & Zhang, 2022). The AI-driven systems can be used to fill the gap in communication, make sentiment analysis, and even recommend specific wording that is effective when dealing in a team. To provide an example, Grammarly or Crystal are some of the web-applications that implement AI into the process of making written speech clearer and tone-respective in business emails and documents. In addition, AI integrations provide smart meeting retrospective, identification of action items, and collaboration real-time information These characteristics exclude the hand control and improve the visibility of a project, which enables cooperation with the use of data. With the assistance of AI, these platforms cease to be those which are behind and turn into efficient, cohesive, and innovative members of a team.

4.3 Real-Time Translation and Natural Language Processing (NLP) Tools

NLP machines which are AI based can help in enhancing seamless international collaboration by eliminating the language as well as communication barrier. Team members with different languages can communicate with each other without difficulties by using tools of real-time translation that may be implemented on messaging software platforms, such as Google Translate, DeepL, or Microsoft Translator (Alizadeh and Figueroa Jr, 2024). built into the messaging software platforms, they can make video calls, emails, chats, or documents real-time translated and transcribed to promote inclusiveness and awareness. Besides, NLP also offers context-driven insights, mood technology, and extraction of keys, and purpose identification, which enable teams to gain insight into the degree of emotional tone and focus. One of such examples may be that AI can summarise conversations, generate records of meetings, or label burning topics based on the expressions of the conversation. In the case of customers or other human-centered services, multilingual requests can be supported with a high level of accuracy by the use of NLP-powered bots. These tools allow cross border collaboration, enhance cultural sensitivity and also minimise miscommunication (Cui, 2025). There are still obstacles to overcome, like predicting the complexities of the language and deciphering the slang, but the best way to create the contextual NLP models is to ensure the communication is understandable, time-saving, and empathetic online.

4.4 Decision Support Systems and Knowledge-Sharing Platforms

Assisted by AI, Decision Support Systems (DSS) and knowledge-sharing platforms allow making the process of decision making quicker and more somehow informative and inculcate the culture of constant learning among colleagues. DSS have power of machine learning, predictive analytics, and data visualization to suggest actions, see the trend, and analyze risks. The systems aid operational decisions and strategic decisions by bringing forth insight as produced by huge and complicated data. As an example, an AI system is able to interpret sales behavior and suggest stock activity or estimate project delays regarding the indicators of group performance. Conversely, AI-based knowledge-sharing systems, such as Confluence, Notion, or SharePoint allow to organize, tag, and then retrieve shared pieces of knowledge (Eriksson et al., 2020). The opportunity to find ample relevant knowledge in a blink of a second using semantic search, content recommendation, and intelligent clustering enables team members to avoid duplicating efforts and strengthen the quality of content collaboration. Such platforms will make knowledge accessible, current, and contextual, and smart collaboration becomes possible in an organization. AI integration will help to make such platforms more adaptive and scalable and switch them to become pro-active centers of learning, collaborating, and decision-making.

4.5 Case Study: Human-AI Interaction in Enterprise Environments

Of good reference is the use of AI in collaboration, an example being Watson Workspace by IBM and Einstein by Salesforce. These enterprise level systems implement the power of AI to boost intra-communication, decision-making, and customer interaction. An example is Watson Workspace, which uses AI to monitor and identify important topics during the conversation, deduce action items and follow-up conversation items to prevent cognitive overload. Similarly, Einstein also enters Salesforce to provide real-time suggestions of sales operations and prospective leads and customers, such as customer and lead ratings. These systems are the co-workers of an employee which fuse in and emerge with a set of contextual suggestions, automation hints and signals. The outcome provides faster decision-making cycles, cross departmental interoperation and increased personalization of the customers. These platforms too have their own explicit dashboards, the insights of which impress the trust and openness of the users. The challenges are also not as bad as it might appear i.e. user adoption, data security, etc. and with proper training and governance, AI can be a change-enabler and not disruptive. These real-life applications describe how the role of the AI has been evolving, and it is one of the participants in the operations of the enterprise, yet not the analytics of the back end.

5. APPLICATIONS ACROSS SECTORS

The e-collaboration through the application of AI is turning out to be a game changer in the key industries, which increases the performance, individualization and collaboration. With AI and IoMT, in the field of healthcare, it is possible to perform diagnosis and patient observation in remote areas and virtual cooperation with specialists. The same is evidenced in education where we have smart tutorial systems and live feedback that assists in a collaborated and individualized learning process. E-commerce would also benefit because recommendation engines and chatbots created using AI would also improve customer interaction and user experiences. (Kan, 2024). The course of manufacturing AI is used to coordinate distributed manufacturing networks, where resources are best placed, predictive maintenance, and group communications are improved. These apps illustrate the capacity of AI and other new technologies to support contextually responsive involvement among multiple fields and promote new innovations, rapidity, and better service delivery. The table 2 highlights how AI-driven tools enhance performance, efficiency, and personalization across healthcare, education, e-commerce, and manufacturing sectors.

Table 2. AI Applications in Sectoral E-Collaboration

Sector	Key AI Technology Applied	Performance Metrics Improved	Examples of Use Cases
Healthcare	AI + IoMT	+80% diagnostic speed, -30% clinical errors, -35% chronic care cost	Remote monitoring, virtual team diagnosis
Education	NLP + Adaptive Systems	+35% performance, -60% response time, +25% graduation rate	Virtual tutors, real-time feedback, plagiarism check
E-commerce	Recommendation Engines	+35% conversion, +60% support speed, +20–30% order value	Personalized ads, chatbot-based customer service
Manufacturing	Predictive AI	+50% accuracy, -25% delays, +30% operational efficiency	AI in predictive maintenance and global coordination

5.1 Healthcare: AI + IoMT for Diagnostics and Virtual Teamwork

Together with the Internet of Medical Things (IoMT), AI is changing work in diagnostics and team care in healthcare. Wearables and remote monitors are an example of IoMT devices that gather the latest health-related data which can be analyzed by AI systems to identify anomalies, recommend diagnoses, or alert medical professionals about an essential difference. The technologies will accommodate an 80% faster diagnostic turn around, and more than 30% minimization of human error in the clinical processes in the telehealth settings. AI-powered virtual assistants help the clinicians to review the records, provide the treatment recommendations and collaborate cross-departmentally in real-time. The AI analytics-powered virtual Multidisciplinary Team (MDT) meetings aid in simplifying decision-making, as well as save 25% of the time managing patients. The savings on the cost of management of chronic diseases with early intervention also led to up to 35% cost savings by the hospitals which integrate AI-IoMT. Not only does the integration of AI and IoMT improve operational efficiency, but also can improve the partnership between patient and provider, particularly with geographic or resource disparity areas, which has a major positive impact on access, quality, and continuity of care. The Figure 3 shows how AI and IoMT integration improves healthcare by boosting diagnostic speed, reducing errors, saving time, and lowering chronic care costs.

Figure 3. Impact of AI + IoMT in Healthcare Collaboration

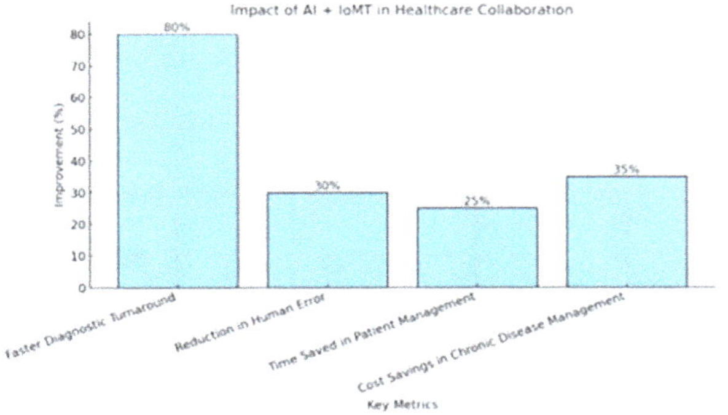

5.2 Education: AI in Collaborative Learning and Feedback Systems

AI changes the world of education with the creation of adaptive and collaborative learning space. AI-based learning management solutions use performance data on students to provide individualized content, pacing and feedback, enhancing learning performance by up to 35%. IT systems mimic the individual instruction and collaborative AI tools such as discussion analysis robot (bot) and sentiment analyser strengthen learning in groups, detecting learners who are not keeping up with the rest or even suggesting a similar peer to work in a group. Due to the instant response and feedback, natural language processing virtual teaching assistants cut down the student wait time by 60%. Schools and colleges that implemented AI in the classroom have seen a -40% rise in engagement of students and a -25% rise in course graduation. Moreover, AI applications are able to grade the assignments, identify academic dishonesty, and provide the feedback related to the learning styles individually (Pinto et al., 2024). The inclusion of collaborative intelligence in the educational system allows AI not only to guide instructors and evaluate learning but also enables students to become active, thoughtful and better learners in both personalised and inclusive learning systems. The Figure 4 highlights how AI enhances educational outcomes through collaborative learning systems. It shows measurable improvements in student performance, reduced wait times, increased engagement, and higher course completion rates, demonstrating AI's potential to personalize learning and support inclusive education.

Figure 4. Impact of AI in Collaborative Learning and Feedback

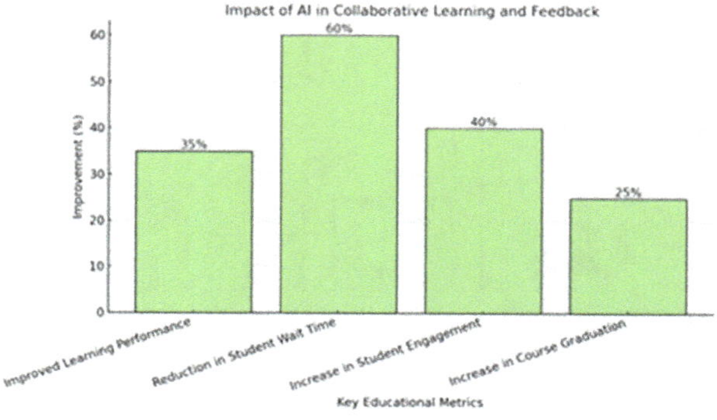

5.3 E-commerce: Personalization and Customer Engagement

AI is transforming the face of e-commerce through real-time individualization, forecast analytics, and effective customer interaction. Machine learning recommendation engines can drive conversion rates to as much as 35% by offering personal product recommendations based on user behavior, preferences, and purchase history. AI chatbots and virtual agents respond to more than 70% of customer requests and assist in providing all-day-every-day support with a 60% increase in the response time, and directly affect customer satisfaction and retention. Sentiment analysis tools track the comments by its customers and evaluations on its social sites, to drive product-development and marketing decision-making. The customized promotions and dynamically priced modes promoted by AI result in 20-30% increase in average orders. Additionally, collaborative AI systems improvise internal coordination levels i.e. inventory replenishing, tracking of orders, and logistics which reinforce successful delivery rates and decreased cart abandonment rates (Plass et al., 2022). In sum, AI in e-commerce is an absolute achievement in its customer experience parameters of centering on accuracy, easiness, and for applicability to bring uplifts to brands in growing customer loyalty, and lowering business operational expenses, as well as being able to execute their competition in the already crowded digital world. Figure 5 presents the role of AI in boosting e-commerce in terms of bettering the conversion rates, speeding up the customer response time, and boosting the order value. Personalized overall experience and efficiency of operations are made possible through AI-powered tools such as chatbots and recommendation engines assisting brands in creating a greater impact on customer loyalty and competing successfully in a highly digitalized market.

Figure 5. Impact of AI on E-commerce Personalization and Engagement

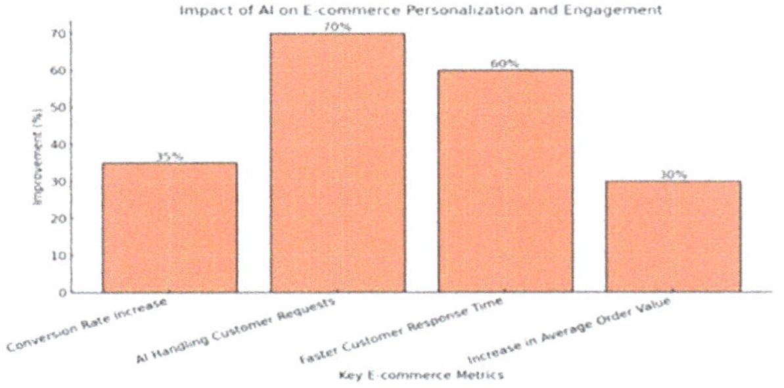

5.4 Manufacturing: AI Coordination in Distributed Production Networks

Smart manufacturing is being empowered by AI that coordinates activities, processes, and teams in a global network production. Computer vision and robotics can produce more and faster and with accuracy of up to 50% with the assist help of predictive maintenance systems that help to reduce the downtimes of equipment. Joint AI platforms bring together the information of supply tracks, machines connected to the Internet of Things and enterprise resource planning (ERP) tools in order to streamline the schedule and minimize waste and improve throughput (Sahab et al., 2023). The companies which introduce AI-powered planning tools see 20-30% efficiency rise in operations, as well as 25% decline in delays in production. The cross-location coordination is possible through the AI agents that promote real-time access to the aspects of factory performance, the amount of inventory, and the workforce distribution. The combination of human and AI in smart factories gives decision-makers the power of predictive dashboards and spotting anomalies to enhance quality controls and safety compliance. Moreover, AI improves the interaction among engineering, procurement, and logistical workforces, which allows decreasing the time of product development and time-to-market. Industry 4.0 spaces together with AI will allow smarter, agile, and sustainable manufacture since the combination will give intelligent manufacturing practices that can respond swiftly to the evolving market pressure and shock. The Figure 6 shows that AI helps to enhance manufacturing through accuracy, minimizing downtime, and providing real-time monitoring and predictive maintenance to respond to agile manufacturing.

Figure 6. Impact of AI in Manufacturing and Distributed Production Networks

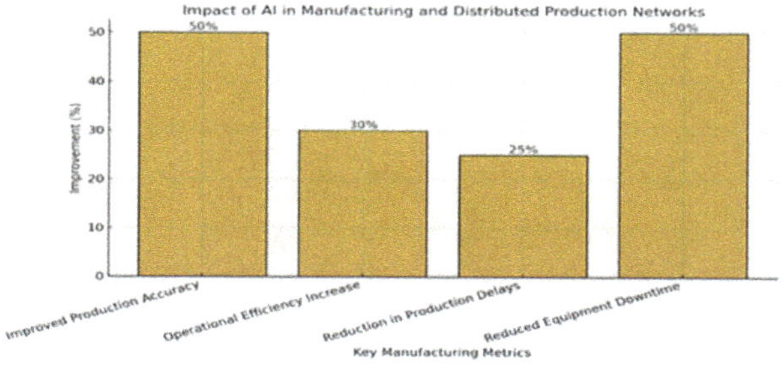

6. ETHICS, PRIVACY, AND TRUST IN AI COLLABORATION

Ethical concerns, privacy, and trust building are the most important with AI as the basic component of collaborative systems. Responsible data governance is one of the primary issues that get addressed in this research work, and it means that personal and organizational data is securely managed in human-communities of AI teams. It advises the importance of Explainable Artificial Intelligence (XAI) in terms of spreading transparency and consumer confidence. (Santhosh et al., 2022). The most crucial problems such as algorithmic bias, fairness, and regulatory compliance are discussed, as well as new regulatory systems. Other topics brought up in the work include instilling trust in AI partnerships as well as the use of transparency, accountability, role definition to encourage rather than discourage moral and inclusive alliances to be supported through intelligent systems.

6.1 Data Governance and Privacy in AI-Teaming

With AI-based cooperation, sensitive information is particularly to be guarded. To enable them to deliver context-aware support, AI systems usually visit personal, behavioural, and organisational data. To have good data governance, we should come up with distinct policies on data storage, data access, and the use and collection of data. Methods such as federated learning, differential privacy, and secure multi-party computation can maintain privacy of the users, and surprisingly enough, they do not result in reduced performance. There are also international privacy laws, i.e., GDPR and HIPAA that organizations need to adhere to. Adequate governance makes AI systems operate in a way that is transparent, legal, and ethical, leaving the users of these systems secure against surveillance and unethical practices (Sundaresan

& Zhang, 2022). The formation of the principles of data minimization, consent management, and access procedures ensuring the security of access are some of the ways to maintain the trust and mitigate the risks of breaching security of data, especially in such fields as medical and financial areas where privacy risks are acutely observed in the collaborative AI systems.

6.2 Explainable AI (XAI) and Transparency

The independence of AI processes and outputs should be comprehendible as the involvement of AI in the collaborative decision-making process gradually increases. Explainable AI (XAI) The models and systems that can explicitly explain their reasoning are commonly known as explainable AI. This openness will make users trust and work with AI agents effectively. Explainability is not an option in any high-stakes domain such as healthcare, defense, or finance: it is a mandatory component of ethical responsibility (Tominc et al., 2024). Such methods as SHAP, LIME or decision trees are used to interpret AI results. XAI can also improve the debug process, performance analysis and ethical auditing. User adoption, resistance, and safer human-AI collaboration facilitated by AI explanation help when users can better understand how and why AI makes its decisions. Transparency is also a means of legal conformance and fairness of a system.

6.3 Algorithmic Fairness and Bias Mitigation

Bias in the algorithm may have a devastating effect on collaboration by strengthening the preexisting disparities or creating discriminating results. Bias in an AI-driven system usually occurs because of an imbalanced training set, an improper withdrawn of the model, or unintended correlations. AI should be fair and outcomes do not discriminate against gender, race and socioeconomic status and other demographics. Bias mitigation techniques are data rebalancing, adversarial debiasing, and fairness-aware machine learning algorithms. Developmental pipelines should incorporate regular checkpoints in form of audits and ethics (Zhu et al., 2022). The metrics of fairness must be a characteristic of the specific organization and users of the company. It is also important to have clear reporting and extensive input by the team in terms of developing the model. The reduction of algorithmic bias must be viewed not as a technical but as a moral problem, which is essential to promote inclusive and collaborative AI solutions that can positively affect people in an equivalent manner.

6.4 Legal and Regulatory Frameworks for Collaborative AI Systems

The increased use of AI in the team context has been accompanied by the development of legal and regulatory standards of AI application. These structures may be crucial to the effective operation of AI systems as per the data protection, ethical standards and principles of accountability. New regulations like the EU AI Act, GDPR and the U.S. proposed Algorithmic Accountability Act suggest transparency, the classification of risks, and human control. These laws define the interaction of AI and human beings in the collaborative systems, how and what it is going to work and what the levels of decision making it can make. These areas of compliance as the documentation of model training, the bias assessment, the method of human intervention could be proposed. Organizations should take the initiative to guarantee that the practices they are adopting are within the law to ensure that none of the practices adopted by the organizations will be against the law. A clear regulatory eco-system would help reduce the degree of trust, abuse, and the enforcement of human rights in the AI-based collaborative teamwork settings. The table 3 provides key ethical and legal principles required to have secure, trustful, and responsible AI-enhanced e-collaboration systems.

Table 3. Ethical and Governance Pillars for AI-Driven Collaboration

Governance Aspect	Key Focus Area	Techniques / Frameworks Used
Data Privacy	Secure handling of user data	GDPR, HIPAA, federated learning, differential privacy
Explainable AI (XAI)	Interpretability and transparency of AI decisions	SHAP, LIME, Decision Trees
Algorithmic Fairness	Eliminating bias and ensuring equity	FairML, adversarial debiasing, inclusive design
Regulatory Compliance	Legal adherence in AI implementation	EU AI Act, Algorithmic Accountability Act

7. CHALLENGES AND FUTURE DIRECTIONS

Despite the opportunities of collaboration, enabled by AI, there are several problems. The technological limit such as compatibility of systems, quality of data and scalability are the barriers to mass adoption. These ethical issues as bias, responsibility and openness of decisions are still burning problems. It will require the reskilling and redefinition of roles in AI-supported workforce. The concerns regarding singularity and Artificial General Intelligence (AGI) questions raise an issue of autonomy and the effects it will have in the society over the long-term. The endeavour should move forward to developing sustainable, inclusive AI systems with a human value first approach. It is recommended that future studies investigate cross-disciplinary frameworks, policies, and AI systems that would enable the ethical, transparent, and equitable collaboration of humans and AIs on a global scale to avoid the unethical issues described above.

7.1 Technological Barriers and Limitations

Nevertheless, there are a couple of technological issues that prevent smooth collaboration of human and AI. System interoperability, inadequate volumes of training data, failure to be responsive in real time, and contextual lack of awareness of AI systems minimize system effectiveness. Several collaborative tools have a weakness of finding solutions on how to fit in various platforms, industries or even the devices. Further, the AI performance decreases with time due to latency and lack of scalability and model drift (Akavova et al., 2023). The human factors, including the lack of trust, the ambiguity of the system outputs, and excessive trust provided to automation, cause the friction in collaboration as well. Most AI systems cannot interpret subtle human behaviour, sarcasm, or emotion in environments that would be considered low-context. These obstacles can only be solved through more robust infrastructure, better interface design, and powerful models, which can think and evolve on the fly. Constant innovations, interdisciplinary studies, and responsible design principles should be used to minimize the existing gap between the potential of the AI and the requirements of collaboration in the real world.

7.2 Ethical Dilemmas and Social Implications

Integration of AI in collaborative environment raises ethical implications of fairness, autonomy, accountability and impact on the society. Discriminative training sets or models are capable of reinforcing the discriminatory behavior and disparate results, crucial areas such as employment, medicinal care, or justice. Algorithmic opacity is an increasing area of concern, a user cannot understand a decision made by the AI and may not be able to argue with it or question it, resulting in an ethical grey area. The aspect of AI replacing human labour also creates concerns on inequality, job loss, and mental health (Azzi et al., 2020). Moreover, the situation with the surveillance and incorrect use of personal information in collaborative products may remove trust and break privacy. Such issues are increased by the fast rate of innovation that cannot match regulatory laws. The application of ethical-by-design, stakeholder inclusion, and effective forms of governance is needed to address those concerns. To make the AI cooperation responsibility-oriented, organizations will have to combine their technological progress with social and ethical values, as well as democratic responsibility.

7.3 Workforce Transformation and Upskilling

The incorporation of AI is also transforming the nature of work and the skills required in every industry, so the new capability of the workforce will be necessary at a large scale. As much as the routine activities can be solved by AI, it also opens the possibility of higher forms of thinking, higher forms of creativity, emotional intelligence and the oversight of AI. Employees will have to learn how to work in the settings of supervision by AI, verification of decisions, and system responses (Chouhan & Shilpi, 2023). The changes require massive reskilling and upskilling projects, emphasizing digital literacy and ethical AI applications, interpretation of data, and human-artificial intelligence interactions design. To ensure future-proofing teams, organizations need to create a culture of the continuous learning and adaptability to the future. Also, of a substantial concern is treating psychological opposition to AI- fear of being replaced, lack of trust, and the dissimulation of control. One of the most important factors that can be involved with this shift is leadership, which means open communication, training that includes everybody, and redefining the roles. After all, human capital is at the forefront of AI accomplishments, and employee empowerment is a top priority of sustainable and fair cooperation in the era of AI.

7.4 Toward Sustainable and Inclusive AI Collaboration

To collaboratively succeed at scale, AI needs to be sustainable, inclusive and equitable. The priorities of resource wealthy areas can be seen in the current deployments leaving the marginalized and developing economies underrepresented. The environmentally friendly collaboration systems should not only pay attention to the environment-related expenses, including the intensive use of computational energy, but also on their social feasibility in the long term, fairness, and cultural awareness. Inclusivity means that AI tools are expected to be able to offer multiple international languages, skills, or the degree of digital access (Chen et al., 2023). This incorporates participatory designing approaches, co-creation with the stakeholders or gender, age and socio-economic diversity. Additionally, AI models should be based on ethical priorities (explainability, non-discrimination, and adherence to the local norms). Another area of collaboration that should take place is between sectors: governments, academia, industry and civil spectrum to jointly build responsible AI ecosystems. The creation of these systems will aid in ensuring that such results of AI collaboration are obtained; it will eradicate digital divides and will lead to human prosperity across the globe in an AI-enhanced future.

8. CONCLUSION

The systems of communication, innovation, and co-creation between individuals, organizations, and societies have come to a turning point with the intersection of Artificial Intelligence (AI) and the digital collaboration technologies. This article, Mind Meets Machine: E-Collaboration in the Era of AI, has already become a part of the many-sided overgrown world of e-collaboration in the age of AI digital transformation-grand principles and technologies that enable it, practical sides of diverse applications such as futuristic design possibilities and ethical problems and challenges. The integration of AI in team systems (with the help of such tools as intelligent assistants, multi-agent systems, and immersive environments) has transformed the role of machines, who are not silent tools anymore, but living partners. These systems are enhancing efficiency and decision making in the key sectors such as healthcare, education, manufacturing and e-commerce.

However, these pleasant remarks are accompanied with the great responsibilities. The presence of such ethical aspects as algorithmic bias, data privacy, explainability, and trust remains one of the main concerns of AI implementation. Transparency, inclusiveness, and fairness must be incorporated in the design process and management of AI to transform AI into a sustainable component of the human partnership. It is also quite critical to reconfigure the workforce that requires new skills, flexibility of thought, and lifelong learning to be able to collaborate well with intelligent systems. The boundary between the intelligence of man and machine is constantly narrowing and a paradigm shift is underway in which the artificially intelligent is only an enhancement, and not a replacement, of human ability in the environment of hybrid ecosystems.

The future is not merely resolving technical and ethical issues, but also the larger questions of society like Artificial General Intelligence (AGI) and the singularity. Future work should be aimed at building human-centered AI to delight various users, expand on cultural contexts and promote digital equity. The interaction of human intuition and machine accuracy, known as collaborative intelligence, is a great illustration of how complicated issues in the world like healthcare delivery or climate action may be addressed. In conclusion, the future of teamwork is not the alternation of human and machine intelligence, but the evolution of the system where both kinds of intelligence will have the opportunity not only to learn and develop, but also to thrive. We will be building a future in which AI will not just be making us work smarter, but also working together in a more meaningful way, through ethical innovation, interdisciplinary collaboration, and inclusive design.

REFERENCES

Akavova, A., Temirkhanova, Z., & Lorsanova, Z. (2023). Adaptive learning and artificial intelligence in the educational space. E3S Web Conf., 451, 6011.

Azzi, S., Gagnon, S., Ramirez, A., & Richards, G. (2020). Healthcare applications of artificial intelligence and analytics: A review and proposed framework. *Applied Sciences (Basel, Switzerland)*, *10*(18), 6553. DOI: 10.3390/app10186553

Bhattacharjee, A., Ghosh, A., Juman, M. K. I., & Hossen, M. (2024). Augmented intelligence for knowledge management and green education in the post-COVID-19 era. In *Integrating Generative AI in Education to Achieve Sustainable Development Goals* (pp. 47–71). IGI Global. DOI: 10.4018/979-8-3693-2440-0.ch003

Chen, A., Yang, T., Ma, J., & Lu, Y. (2023). Employees' learning behavior in the context of AI collaboration: A perspective on the job demand-control model. *Industrial Management & Data Systems*, *123*(8), 2169–2193. DOI: 10.1108/IMDS-04-2022-0221

Chouhan, D. N., & Shilpi, D. S. (2023). A study on artificial intelligence in education. *International Journal of Engineering Technology and Management*, *7*(1), 449–456.

Crompton, H., & Burke, D. (2023). Artificial intelligence in higher education: The state of the field. *International Journal of Educational Technology in Higher Education*, *20*(1), 22. DOI: 10.1186/s41239-023-00392-8

Dominguez, R. M. R., Mart\'\inez López, L., & Tenekedjiev, K. (2025). Hybrid-Augmented Intelligent Systems: New trends and applications. J. Univers. Comput. Sci., 31(3), 207–209.

Eriksson, T., Bigi, A., & Bonera, M. (2020). Think with me, or think for me? On the future role of artificial intelligence in marketing strategy formulation. *The TQM Journal*, *32*(4), 795–814. DOI: 10.1108/TQM-12-2019-0303

Jiatao Kang Junlei Dong, D. Y. (2021). Key technologies of IoT service security and privacy protection. Converter, 70–79.

Kan, Y. (2024). The impact of AI on the development of manufacturing, logistics, and financial company from capital market perspectives. Advances in Economics. *Management and Political Sciences*, *115*(1), 120–125.

Krinkin, K., Shichkina, Y., & Ignatyev, A. (2021, September). Co-evolutionary hybrid intelligence. 2021 5th Scientific School Dynamics of Complex Networks and Their Applications (DCNA).

Lee, J., Jung, J., & Song, T.The Korean Association Of Personnel Administration. (2023). Research on personnel selection in the age of artificial general intelligence focusing on augmented intelligence. *Journal of Organization and Management, 47*(2), 113–137. DOI: 10.36459/jom.2023.47.2.113

Li, Q., Cao, Z., Tanveer, M., Pandey, H. M., & Wang, C. (2020). A semantic collaboration method based on uniform knowledge graph. *IEEE Internet of Things Journal, 7*(5), 4473–4484. DOI: 10.1109/JIOT.2019.2960150 PMID: 33748313

LTIMIndtree, Dave, D. M., & Mandvikar, S. and A. (2023). Augmented intelligence: Human-Ai collaboration in the era of digital transformation. *International Journal of Engineering Applied Sciences And, 8*(6), 24–33.

Pasupuleti, M. K. (2025). *Augmented Human Intelligence: Converging Generative AI, Quantum Computing, and XR for enhanced human-machine synergy*. National Education Services. DOI: 10.62311/nesx/rrv525

Pinto, M., Vilaça, A., Coelho, L., Magalhães, R., & Veloso, R. (2024). Extended reality tools for medical training and education. VII Congreso XoveTIC: Impulsando El Talento Cient\'\ifico, 89–96. DOI: 10.17979/spudc.9788497498913.13

Plass, J. L., Hovey, C., Maso, A. S., Fröhlich, F., Ghosh, S., Olsen, A., & Perlin, K. (2022). Designing Effective Immersive VR Learning Experiences. Practitioner Proceedings of the 8th International of the Immersive Learning Research Network(ILRN2022). DOI: 10.56198/A6PFY1CBT

Raisch, S., & Krakowski, S. (2021). Artificial intelligence and management: The automation–augmentation paradox. *Academy of Management Review, 46*(1), 192–210. DOI: 10.5465/amr.2018.0072

Rathinavel, P., Ravikumar, R. N., Aarthi, S., Habib, M., Salaeva, N., & Pardaev, J. (2025). Augmenting human capabilities. In *Advances in Computational Intelligence and Robotics* (pp. 1–30). IGI Global Scientific Publishing., DOI: 10.4018/979-8-3373-2372-5.ch001

Rezwana, J., & Maher, M. Lou. (2022). Designing creative AI partners with COFI: A framework for modeling interaction in human-AI co-creative systems. *ACM Transactions on Computer-Human Interaction.*

Ryjov, A. P. (2021). Hybrid intelligence framework for augmented analytics. In *Advances in Data Mining and Database Management* (pp. 22–45). IGI Global.

Ryjov, A. P. (2022). Principles of a hybrid intelligence framework for augmented analytics. In *Advances in Business Information Systems and Analytics* (pp. 47–70). IGI Global.

Sadiku, M. N. O., Ashaolu, T. J., Ajayi-Majebi, A., & Musa, S. M. (2021). Augmented Intelligence. International Journal Of Scientific Advances, 2(5).

Sahab, S., Haqbeen, J., & Ito, T. (2023). Facilitating collaborative consensus building in web-based discussion through collective task-based roles: A case study. *IIAI Letters on Informatics and Interdisciplinary Research*, *4*(180), 1. DOI: 10.52731/liir.v004.180

Santhosh, S., De Crescenzio, F., & Vitolo, B. (2022). Defining the potential of extended reality tools for implementing co-creation of user oriented products and systems. In *Lecture Notes in Mechanical Engineering* (pp. 165–174). Springer International Publishing.

Sundaresan, S., & Zhang, Z. (2022). AI-enabled knowledge sharing and learning: Redesigning roles and processes. *The International Journal of Organizational Analysis*, *30*(4), 983–999. DOI: 10.1108/IJOA-12-2020-2558

Tominc, P., Oreški, D., Čančer, V., & Rožman, M. (2024). Statistically significant differences in AI support levels for project management between SMEs and large enterprises. *AI*, *5*(1), 136–157. DOI: 10.3390/ai5010008

Zhang, Y., Zhang, Y., Zhao, X., Zhang, Z., & Chen, H. (2020). Design and data analysis of sports information acquisition system based on internet of medical things. *IEEE Access : Practical Innovations, Open Solutions*, *8*, 84792–84805. DOI: 10.1109/ACCESS.2020.2992526

Zhao, H., Ye, L., Guo, M., & Deng, Y. (2025). Reflection or dependence: How AI awareness affects employees' in-role and extra-role performance? *Behavioral Sciences (Basel, Switzerland)*, *15*(2), 128. DOI: 10.3390/bs15020128 PMID: 40001759

Zhu, Y., Wang, P., & Duan, W. (2022). Exploration on the core elements of value co-creation driven by AI-measurement of consumer cognitive attitude based on Q-methodology. *Frontiers in Psychology*, *13*, 791167. DOI: 10.3389/fpsyg.2022.791167 PMID: 35432076

KEY TERMS AND DEFINITIONS

5G & Edge Computing: Technologies that enable high-speed, low-latency data transfer by processing data near its source rather than in centralized servers.

AI as Co-Worker: A concept where AI systems act as team members, performing cognitive tasks, making decisions, and collaborating with humans.

Algorithmic Fairness: Ensuring that AI systems do not produce biased or discriminatory outcomes based on demographic attributes.

Artificial Intelligence (AI): A field of computer science that enables machines to mimic cognitive functions like learning, problem-solving, and language understanding.

Blockchain: A decentralized and secure digital ledger that ensures data transparency, immutability, and trust in collaborative systems.

Cognitive Augmentation: Enhancement of human reasoning and judgment through AI tools that assist with memory, pattern recognition, and data analysis.

Collaborative Intelligence: A synergy between humans and AI systems where both contribute complementary strengths to achieve shared goals.

Decision Support Systems (DSS): AI systems that use data analysis to assist humans in making informed decisions.

E-Collaboration: The use of digital technologies (e.g., email, video conferencing, cloud tools) to facilitate teamwork across time and space.

Explainable AI (XAI): AI systems designed to make their decision-making processes transparent and understandable to human users.

Extended Reality (XR): An umbrella term for Virtual Reality (VR), Augmented Reality (AR), and Mixed Reality (MR), enabling immersive collaborative environments.

Federated Learning: A privacy-preserving ML technique that allows model training across decentralized devices without sharing raw data.

Human-Machine Teaming (HMT): Interactive partnership between humans and intelligent systems for decision-making, task execution, and problem-solving.

Hybrid Intelligence: The integration of human and machine intelligence to perform tasks more effectively than either alone.

Internet of Medical Things (IoMT): A subset of IoT focused on connected medical devices for real-time health monitoring and diagnostics.

Internet of Things (IoT): A network of interconnected physical devices that collect and exchange data through the internet.

Knowledge-Sharing Platforms: Tools that organize, retrieve, and distribute institutional or team knowledge enhanced by AI features.

Natural Language Processing (NLP): A field of AI that helps machines understand, interpret, and respond to human language.

Quantum Computing: A computing paradigm using quantum bits (qubits) to process large, complex datasets exponentially faster than classical computers.

Smart Assistants / Chatbots: AI-powered agents that automate tasks such as communication, scheduling, and information retrieval in collaborative settings.

Chapter 7
Reviewing the Concept of Virtual State and Digital State:
Mapping Concept and Trend Using Meta-Analysis

Bambang Irawan
https://orcid.org/0000-0002-4841-7302
Mulawarman University, Indonesia

Paisal Akbar
Mulawarman University, Indonesia

Salahudin Salahudin
https://orcid.org/0000-0001-5687-0812
Universitas Muhammadiyah Malang, Indonesia

Tri Sulistyaningsih
Universitas Muhammadiyah Malang, Indonesia

Gusti Naufal Rizky Perdana
https://orcid.org/0000-0002-5483-6044
Mulawarman University, Indonesia

Mohammad Jafar Loilatu
https://orcid.org/0000-0001-6921-6879
Universitas Muhammadiyah Malang, Indonesia

ABSTRACT

This article reviews the concept of a virtual state and the digital state popularized by developed countries for improved public services and communication. The study uses meta-analysis and VOSviewer to analyze data from the Scopus database. This review used the Preferred Reporting Items for Systematic Reviews and Meta-Analyses (PRISMA)—through PRISMA, this research attempts to conduct a systematic review of the concept of virtual state and digital state. The finding shows that the idea of a virtual state and a digital state, pushed by countries with advanced technology, changes how countries interact with each other, affecting cooperation, human rights,

DOI: 10.4018/979-8-3373-5747-8.ch007

trade, and conflict, while the digital state focuses on how governments connect with society through services, the internet, and advancements in information technology. The investigation emphasizes the value of technology in improving public services and communication.

INTRODUCTION

A virtual state refers to the idea of using technology in a future government, and it replaces the old model through online systems that are easily accessible to the public, businesses, and agencies of a decentralized government (Garson, 2006). The concept of the virtual state is discussed as a new approach to viewing the function of technology in government. (Anthes et al., 2016), In large organizations, large numbers of customers can be served widely through this car. Therefore, the idea of a virtual state, by definition, is interpreted as the use of information communication and technology (ICT) (Bastow et al., 2000). This idea has long been promoted to increase the maturity of technology by reaching a more comprehensive environment. (Ingram, 1997), This step was anticipated by creating a computing network to connect small users at that time. Previously, technology was used as a reform through the application of computer-based information systems and by encouraging the government to be flexible (Madon, 1993).

Translation of the virtual state promoted through small users in its development is used at the residency level. From that level (Tampuu & Masso, 2018), assessing the need for spaces that must be integrated to obtain public information (Garson, 2006). The role of ICT in creating a model of government service is to build a system so that the community can be involved in it. (Anthopoulos et al., 2007), so that in the United Nations projection, ICT is a medium and tool to encourage sustainable development. (United Nations, 2016). Therefore, ICT, according to Donald F. Norris, (2003), is part of building a virtual state, which is referred to as a framework for developing technology in organizations and government. (Je Fountain, 2004; Donald F. Norris, 2003), which makes it easy to manage both services and systems within it(Garson, 2006).

ICT in the virtual state is referred to as a reform step in government, gaining ground through the massive use of technology, thus changing the paradigm in government administration reform. (Baldwin, 2000). According to Madon (1993), ICT has a vital role in reducing the centralized role of the center and can be used easily through a decentralized mechanism. For developing countries, ICT encourages increased services carried out by stakeholders through service innovation (Baharuddin et al., 2022; Djen et al., 2023; Syukri et al., 2023), thus producing service innovation through the use of ICT (Oosterzee & Garnett, 2015). For several decades,

ICT has been seen as a new way for the government to integrate the needs of society and the responsibility of the government to provide services. Although it is slowly developing, ICT consistently shows evolution in its use for services.(Bretschneider, 2003). Recent studies on bibliometric methods have been promoted to answer how the latest research trends are, however, we still see limitations in reviews that compare two concepts simultaneously, such as e-government (Kulsum et al., 2022; Roziqin et al., 2022), creative industry (Aziz et al., 2024), or natural disaster (Loilatu et al., 2026). Therefore, this research contributes to the development of the idea of digital government and digital state to provide another understanding as an alternative to the concept of government, which has been popular with e-government or e-services studies.

The idea of the digital state and virtual state has experienced development along with technological progress; therefore, we understand that there needs to be an explanation of the development of this concept to structure the function of the virtual state in the discipline of social science. Although this concept has shifted from significant themes such as e-government or digital technology for several decades, this study has been seen as a very important sub-science in the discipline of social science that needs to be promoted again. In line with this argument, Chalmers (2019) answers that we need to determine virtual objects; the aim is to find out digital objects that are formed through the computing process and form data structures as data entities from the computing results, and create large data structures (Ingram, 1997).

From the definition, we consider that this concept is still vague in describing the function of virtual state and digital state in government, so we propose this research idea to conduct a systematic review to illustrate the concept that is still vague about virtual state. In recent years, scholars have attempted to define this section to provide an understanding of the function of technology through the concepts of virtual and digital states. The review in this study assesses that the concept of both is seen as the initial part of the concept of electronic government; therefore, by referring to the view (J.E. Fountain, 2001)about how the government uses information communication and technology, this article aims to review how the government uses it from the perspective of the virtual state and digital state.

The structure of this article consists of an introduction that outlines the general description and background of this article. A literature review is an analytical tool used to view the concepts of virtual and digital states. The method includes the steps of using the application, and the data collection process carried out when writing the article. Then, the findings and discussion that present the results of the review of the virtual state are divided into several subsections based on the findings of the review. Finally, the conclusion and future research agenda provide recommendations for potential research on this theme in the future and the limitations that need to be analyzed in this topic.

LITERATURE REVIEW

Computing technologies that are rapidly developing encourage countries to engage in virtual interactions (Ingram, 1997), in which the community plays a critical role in facilitating virtual interaction between the two (Gascó, 2003), with the new era and digitalization acting as a catalyst for the country to develop a modern system. According to Fountain (2001a), this requires creating a virtual agent that acts as a link between government entities and ICT infrastructure. The public sector fulfills its duty of establishing virtual contacts through digital platforms managed by a single control system (Liu et al., 2006). These changes occur because conventional systems are sluggish in adapting to discoveries and demands (Guinan, Parise, and Langowitz, 2019). ICT promotes transparency through modern technology, using ICT to change government performance (Bertot et al., 2010; P Dunleavy et al., 2004). The online system changed patterns and service systems faster (P Dunleavy et al., 2007). Furthermore, the digital era changed public digital cultural services as they existed in developed countries (Wanyan & Hu, 2019). Based on Fountain's idea, public service delivery through an online system emphasizes the ICT aspect that encourages services such as improving public services, administration, administrative efficiency, social value, open government, and trust (Twizeyimana & Andersson, 2019).

Fountain (2001) defines the virtual state as a service provider that operates through a digital system, preceded by an appropriate e-government infrastructure architecture (J. E. Fountain, 2001) as the perspective necessitates the use of a supportive infrastructure (Hoetker & Mahony, 2002) state that the simple logic of institutionalization is to institutionalize social and political mechanisms for influencing the design of government systems. Dunleavy (2006) defined the digital era as a long journey that began with the notion of public management and evolved via significant industries to alter the public administration system. Norris (2003) defined the concept (Jane Fountain, 2001) as a sociotechnical strategy for establishing a virtual state through the use of ICT in government, the use of ICT as a tool for institutional transformation (Bretschneider, 2003). As a result of Fountain's (2001b) virtual state, how should the public sector approach technology as a sociotechnical component of public services?

Digital transformation is based on human abilities that do not coincide, and a more significant number of people have developed a digital platform where all can interact directly with many. Guinan et al. (2019) state that in public organizations, digital transformation occurs due to flawed manual systems controlled by humans. Through digital networks, people can connect directly through a single control system built by an organization or state (Liu et al., 2006). Recent studies have outlined the digital state or government concept, one by Weerakkody et al. (2016) on digital services transformation. According to Pedrosa et al. (2020), digital government means sophistication or maturity of services, clarity of information, and simplicity of use with structured service processes (Omar, Weerakkody, and Sivarajah, 2017), which means that the digital government is a service that combines elements simultaneously to provide services. Weerakkody et al. (2019) have been very interested in digital government. His writing contributes to developing a digital government that explains how a digital state can bring people together with public organizations through IoT with diverse desires. According to Weerakkody et al. (2013), digital government becomes an intermediary to communicate and provide good services by utilizing A.I., ICT, and IoT functions (Weerakkody *et al.*, 2013, 2016, 2019; Carter *et al.*, 2016; Omar Weerakkody and Sivarajah, 2017; Friday and Nurmandi, 2018).

METHOD

This review used The Preferred Reporting Items for Systematic reviews and Meta-Analyses (PRISMA) (Page et al., 2021); through PRISMA, this research attempts to conduct a systematic review of the concept of virtual state and digital state; we refer to the reasons of Aromataris & Pearson (2014) why this method is used, (1) Convey a general understanding of a subject. (2) Trace the evolution of knowledge on a subject historically. (3) Highlight fields where the evidence might be weak, contradictory, or ambiguous. (4) Figure out whether there is consensus or disagreement on a subject. (5) Identify characteristics or connections between essential ideas from prior research significant to the subject. With this method, the protocol used is clear, and the analysis process will determine the results well (Wright et al., 2007).

PRISMA is used to perform inclusion and exclusion criteria (Selcuk, 2019); the function aims to map relevant data based on the data search process from the Scopus Database. This method is used to map bibliometric information such as citations by the author, publications by the author, institution funding, and others by using PRISMA; it can convey evidence of the ideas proposed in writing (Fleming et al., 2014). In several references, this method is highly recommended for use with the aim of mapping specific topics to find newness in the development of the study (Pham et al., 2014; Tricco et al., 2016).

This study uses data sourced from the Scopus Database, and we use Scopus as the primary data source to seek consistency of publications with a good reputation and the publisher with the highest index on the topic of virtual state. The search process uses keywords such as “Virtual State” and” Virtual Government. The amount of data obtained will go through the inclusion and exclusion criteria steps as a guide in searching for reputable databases; the results of the data that have been received will be analyzed using Citespace as an analysis tool; this review follows the analysis steps explained by Sulistyaningsih et al. (2023).

By following the research method, the research stages REF ("virtual state" OR "digital state" OR "virtual word" OR") AND PUBYEAR > 2000 AND PUBYEAR < 2023 AND (LIMIT-TO (SRCTYPE)) AND (LIMIT-TO- (LANGUAGE, "English")) AND (LIMIT-TO (SUBJAREA, "SOCI")) AND (LIMIT-TO-(PUBSTAGE, "final")) AND (LIMIT-TO (DOCTYPE, "ar")). Stage, the data is visualized using Vosviewer to find clusters, visualize the network, and identify some prominent groupings. Generate cluster labels: labelling functions to extract the most representative terms for each cluster of Links, Detailed, Burst Detection, and Citation burst is an indicator of the most active area of research. See Figure 1 for the research stages using PRIMSA.

Figure 1. Research state using PRISMA

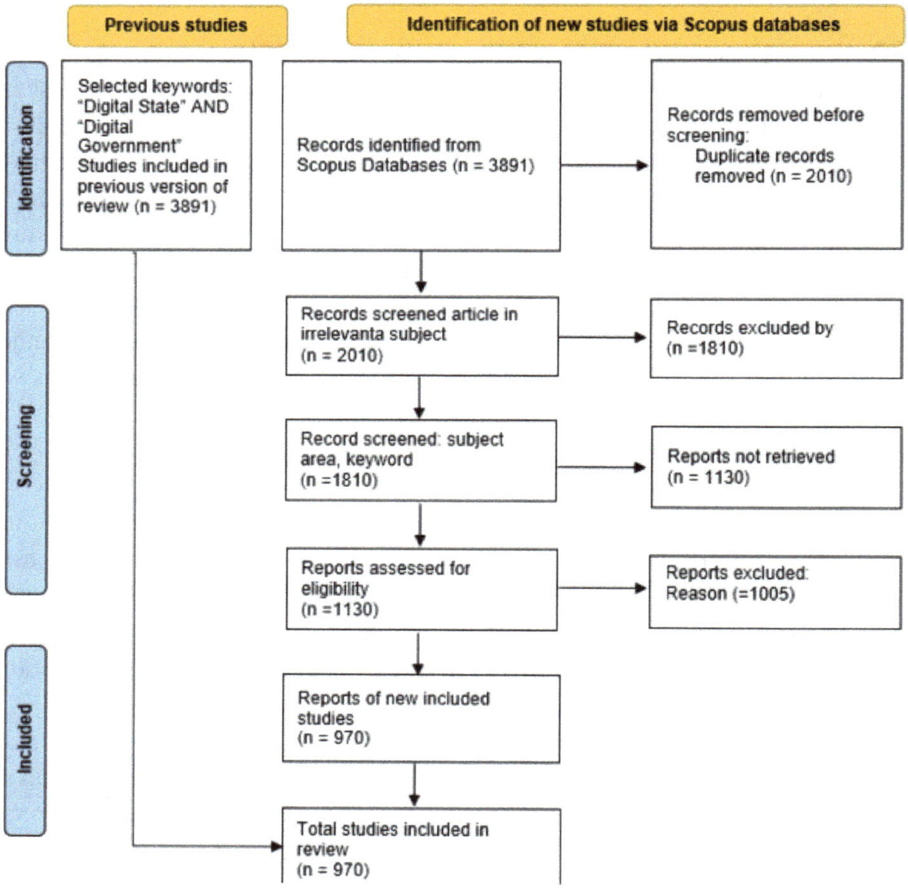

FINDING AND DISCUSSION

Since the concept of ICT was promoted by Ingram (1997) to find out the function of technology, research on the virtual sphere began to be known through several recent studies. However, this concept is known through research that intersects with the function of ICT in the public sector. See Figure 2. Publications on the virtual sphere from 2000 to 2023 have slowly increased every year. In the first five years, 2000-2004, the number of publications only ranged from 15 to 21; five years after that, this study began to be popular, with the number of publications starting to increase every year, reaching 61 documents in 2009. However, there was a year when the number of documents per year decreased to 39 documents, although not significantly. However, the number of documents in the following years fluctuated in 2011, with 45 documents; 2011, with 46 documents; 2012, 2013, with 56 documents; 2014, 55 documents; 2015, 46 documents; 2016, 40 documents; and 2017 with 43 documents in 2017.

Figure 2. Publication trends on virtual state and digital state

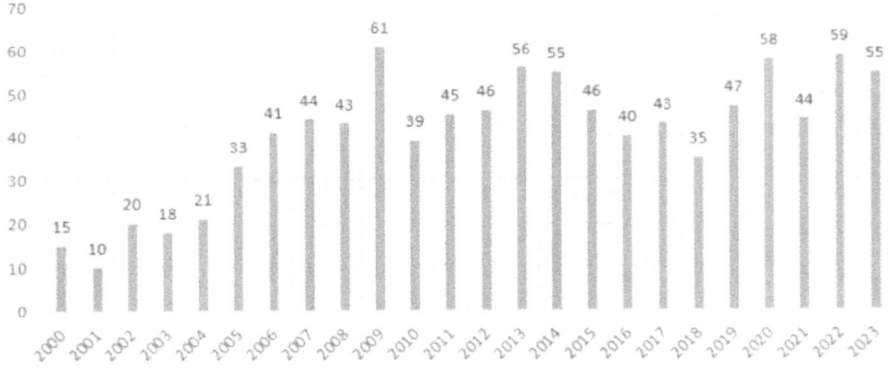

Based on the division of countries, the study of virtual state and digital state is widely popularized by developed countries, so this study shows that both ideas are popular and have become a research topic that is trending in developed countries. Some of the factors that influence this are technological advances, economic and trade issues, migrant workers, border areas, and bilateral cooperation. Refer to Figure 3, which shows the United States with 373 papers, Canada with 54 documents, Australia with 41 documents, China with 32 documents, and India with 15 documents. These results indicate that this notion is advocated by nations with proven technical advances and the capacity to cultivate it.

Figure 3. Publications by countries

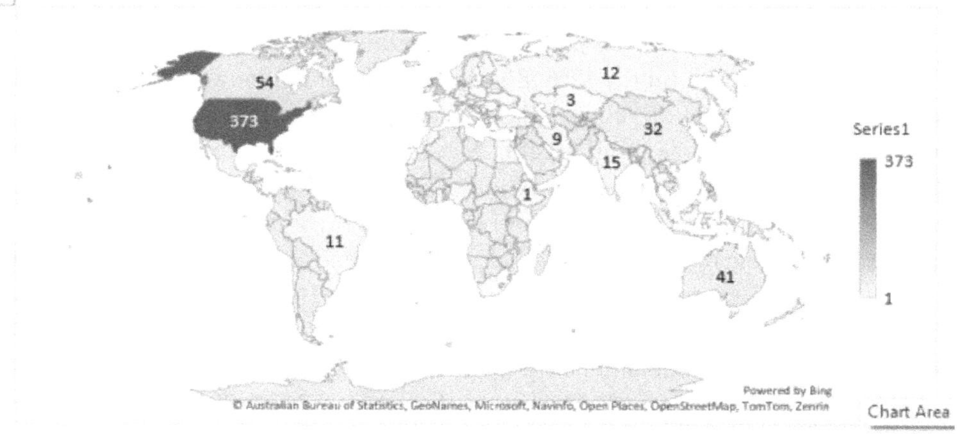

Figure 4. Publications by subject area

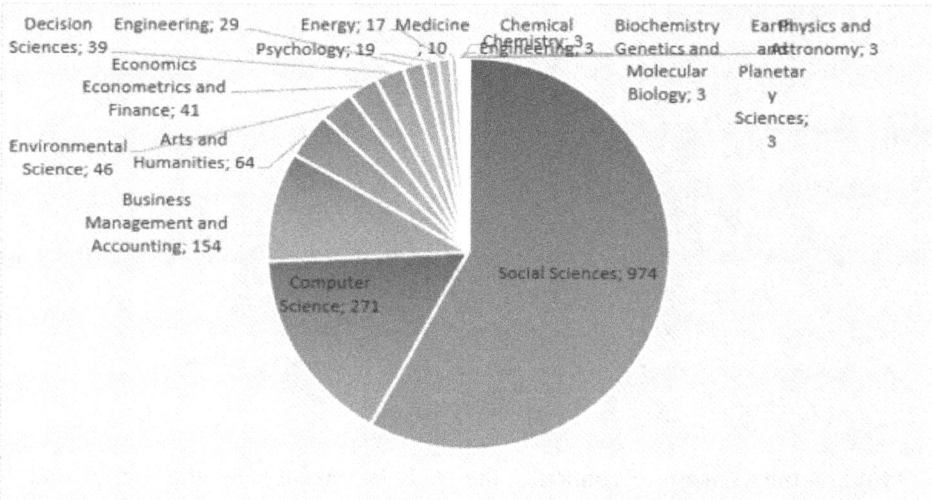

Specifically, this study looks at the function of ICT in a virtual state; generally, this study is widely published in specific subject areas. See Figure 4. Virtual state studies are commonly published in the subject area of social science 58%, computer science 16%, Business management and accounting 9%, and art and humanities 4%. Several other subject areas are not so dominant as the topic of virtual state. Therefore, in terms of function, ICT and virtual state are clearly seen from a social science perspective to analyze the public sector and technology performance on government services.

Figure 5. Publications by authors

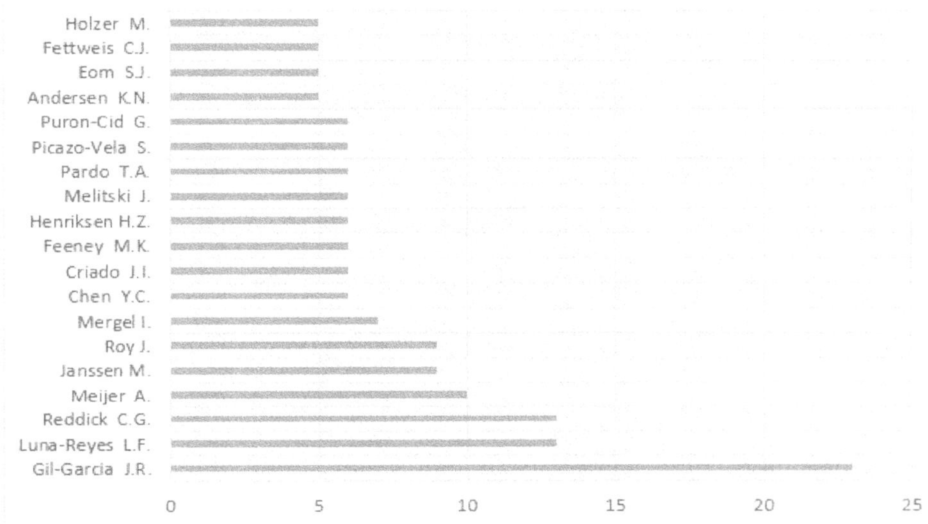

The Scopus database provides in-depth analysis through comprehensive documents and provides many data categories. One of them is a document by the author; the function of the document is to find out the author's contribution to the virtual sphere research topic. See Figure 5; the publication by the author shows that this study is very varied, with Gil-Garcia as the author with the highest number of publications, 23 documents, Luna-Reyes (13), Reddick (13), and Meijer (10). From the number of publications (Luna-Reyes et al., 2005, 2007, 2008; Luna-Reyes & Gil-Garcia, 2011, 2014) reviewing the use of technology in encouraging collaborative government and governance, the study describes how dynamic governance issues through the use of technology drive significant change. At the same time, some of the ideas proposed by (DF Norris & Reddick, 2013; Reddick, 2011; Reddick & Turner, 2012) map the transformation functions of e-government that transform traditional service changes from the perspective of old theories to technology-driven transformation.

Figure 6. Publication by affiliation

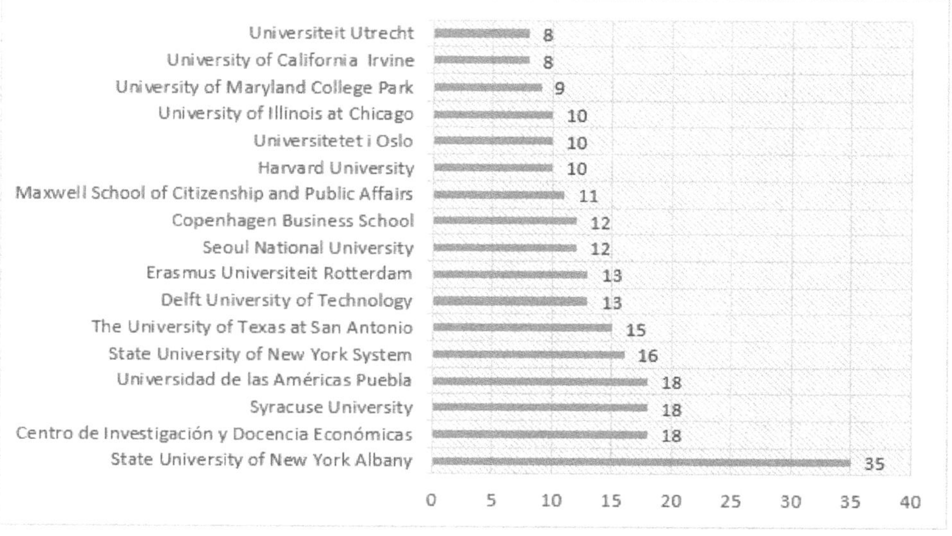

In addition to mapping the concept of the virtual sphere idea, bibliometric analysis helps to identify affiliations that consistently promote the idea; from publications based on affiliations, universities such as the State University of New York Albany are the universities with the highest number of publications (35) compared to other universities. The Centro de Investigacion Deconcia Economics (18), Syracuse University (18), Universidad de las Americas Puebla (18), The State University of New York System (16), and The University of Texas at San Antonio (15). Several other affiliations have a lower number of documents compared to the top universities based on publications, see Figure 6.

Figure 7. Funding research

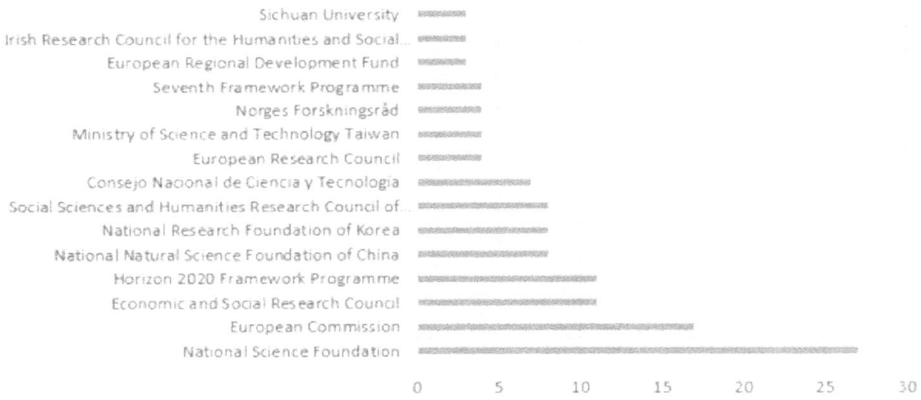

Over the last two decades, several organizations have been involved in the development of technology. Therefore, they also provide financial support for virtual state and digital state research. The intense concern of international organizations in the development of technology in the government sector makes this issue very important; there are at least 100 organizations that provide financial support for this research, and there are 289 documents that receive research funding. From the amount of funding and the number of records, funding sponsors with the most significant amount of research funding, such as the National Science Foundation (27), European Commission (17), Economic and Social Research Council (11), Horizon 2020 Framework Program (11), National Natural Science Foundation of China (8), National Research Foundation of Korea (8), Social Science and Humanities Research Council (8), and Consejo Nasional de Cienciay Technologia (8). See Figure 7, which shows the number of documents submitted by the funding sponsor.

Figure 8. Publications by sources

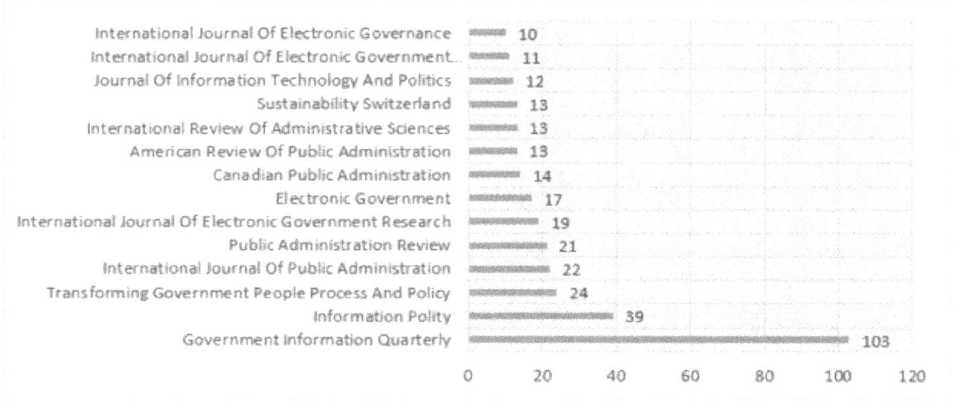

Of the total publications published from 2000 to 2023, the publishers with the highest number of publications on the topic of virtual state and e-government during that period were Government Information Quarterly 103, Information Polity 39, Transforming Government People Process and Policy 24, International Journal of Public Administration 22, Public Administration Review 21, and International Journal of Electronic Government Research 19. In addition, several other journals have a lower number of publications compared to the other six journals, see Figure 8. PRISMA, through the Vosviewer tool, shows bibliographic data based on citations from several categories, such as citations by a university, author, and country. The results of the meta-analysis show that the universities with the highest number of citations on the topic of virtual state and digital government are the University of Albany, State University of New York (327), Yale University (143), Wesleyan University (132), University of Texas San Antonio (116) and North Illion University (113) as universities with more than 100 citations. Other universities, such as the University of Miami or the University of Guelph, have a lower number of citations.

Table 1. Selected Most Cited Article

Author And Year	Title	Publisher	Cite
Moon (2002)	The evolution of E-government among municipalities: Rhetoric or reality?	Public Administration Review	1383
West (2004)	E-Government and the Transformation of Service Delivery and Citizen Attitudes	Public Administration Review	1049
Gil-García & Pardo (2005)	E-government success factors: Mapping practical tools to theoretical foundations	Government Information Quarterly	670

continued on following page

Table 1. Continued

Author And Year	Title	Publisher	Cite
Mergel et al. (2019)	Defining digital transformation: Results from expert interviews	Government Information Quarterly	511
Coursey & Norris (2008)	Models of e-government: Are they correct? An empirical assessment	Public Administration Review	436
Chun et al. (2010)	Government 2.0: Making connections between citizens, data, and government	Information Policy	430
Reddick (2005)	Citizen interaction with e-government: From the streets to servers?	Government Information Quarterly	396
Merge (2013)	Social media adoption and resulting tactics in the US federal government	Government Information Quarterly	329
Helbig et al. (2009)	Understanding the complexity of electronic government: Implications from the digital divide literature	Government Information Quarterly	307
DF Norris & Reddick (2013)	Local E-Government in the United States: Transformation or Incremental Change?	Public Administration Review	304
Cordella & Bonina (2012)	A public value perspective for ICT-enabled public sector reforms: A theoretical reflection	Government Information Quarterly	290
Mergel & Bretschneider (2013)	A Three-Stage Adoption Process for Social Media Use in Government	Public Administration Review	282
Reddick (2004)	A two-stage model of e-government growth: Theories and empirical evidence for US cities	Government Information Quarterly	277
Tolbert et al. (2008)	Institutions, policy innovation, and e-government in the American States	Public Administration Review	269
Kirişci (2009)	The transformation of Turkish foreign policy: The rise of the trading state	New Perspectives on Turkey	257
Harrison et al. (2012)	Open government and e-government: Democratic challenges from a public value perspective	Information Policy	244

The finding shows that the developed countries are categorized as countries with high technology usage; this is seen based on the number of studies promoted by these countries. Figure 9 and Table 2 show citations by university and love by country from the number of documents. Table 2 shows countries with the highest number of papers and citations. The results of the meta-analysis show that studies on virtual state and digital government are popular in countries with advanced levels of technology, such as the United States, the United Kingdom, the Netherlands, Canada, and Australia, which are the countries with the most publications on this study. At the same time, the countries with the most citations are the United States, the United Kingdom, Turkey, Denmark, the Netherlands, and Canada.

Figure 9. Citations by University

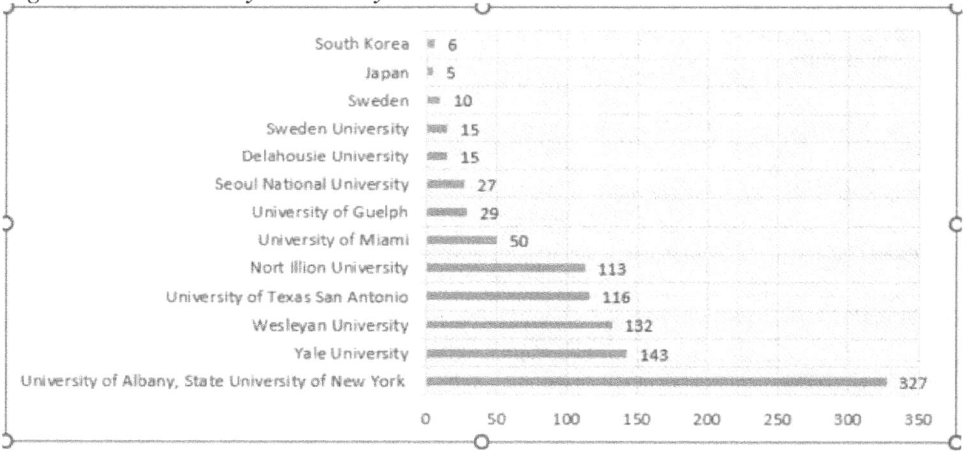

Table 2. Countries with the highest documents and citations

Country	Document	Citation
United States	143	8588
United Kingdom	45	1575
Turkey	6	1019
Denmark	9	798
Netherlands	20	691
Canada	29	601
Germany	5	348
Australia	11	174
China	6	128
Norway	9	119
Sweden	10	82
Japan	5	48
South Korea	6	45

To explain Figure 9 and Table 2, in this section, we categorise the review results based on university publications and countries, with the number of documents and citations. This review shows the concept of e-government promoted by authors from the United States about e-government at the level of municipalities (Jae Moon & Welch, 2000; Moon, 2002), digital transformation of service delivery (West, 2004), and a review of the concept of e-government written by Yildiz (2007), Hacettepe University, Turkey. The United States is the country with the highest number of publications with authors (Kapucu, 2006). Representing Asia, some authors have correlations with the same research themes as other countries, such as Yang & Rho (2007), about the better performance of e-government. Citations in countries show suitability to research topics in the last ten years, so this review underlines the concept of digital state and digital government data from the perspective of developed countries through the application of technology in their governments. Further topics are based on universities, countries, and the number of documents and citations in Figure 9 and Table 2.

Virtual State and Digital State Research Trends

Figure 10 network visualization shows the trend in digital state and e-government research, based on PRISMA analysis, which shows that the study is divided into several clusters based on the Vosviewer tool. The clusters in this analysis consist of 9 clusters: cluster one red with 133 items, cluster two green with 30 items, cluster three blue with 27 items, cluster four yellow with 26 items, cluster five purple with 24 items, cluster six with 22 items with dark blue, cluster seven orange 20 items, cluster eight brown 16 items, cluster nine 15 items purple.

Figure 10. Network visualization

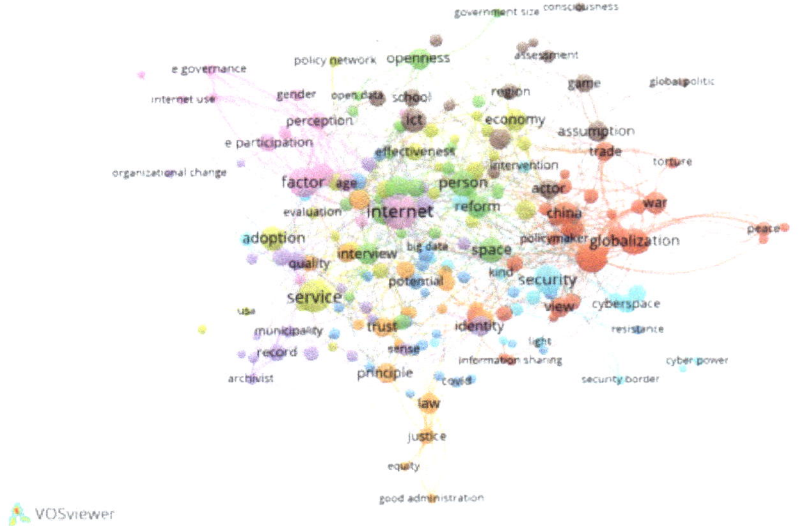

Cluster one consists of citizenship, information sharing, information systems, policymakers, power, public services, situation, socialization, rise, and trade. Cluster two: communication technology, digital era, government agency, interoperability, movement, open data, network, openness, policymaker, public diplomacy, uncertainty. Cluster three: decision-making, digital government, digital transformation, e-voting, pandemic, political process, public institutions, technological change, virtual world. Cluster four: adoption, e-gov, economy. Effectiveness, efficiency, electronic communication, engagement, evolution, information security, operations, participation, policy network, service, web. Cluster five: digital age, e-government development, identity, industry, local government, municipality, organization value, public organization. Cluster six: Big data, corruption, cyber power, cyberspace, digitalization, government services, internet governance, intervention, public value, and security. Cluster seven: citizen participation, computer, content, good administration, production, time. Cluster eight: Assessment, culture, games, ICT, social capital. Cluster Nine: e-governance, e-participation, factors, internet use, political participation.

Figure 11. Overly visualization

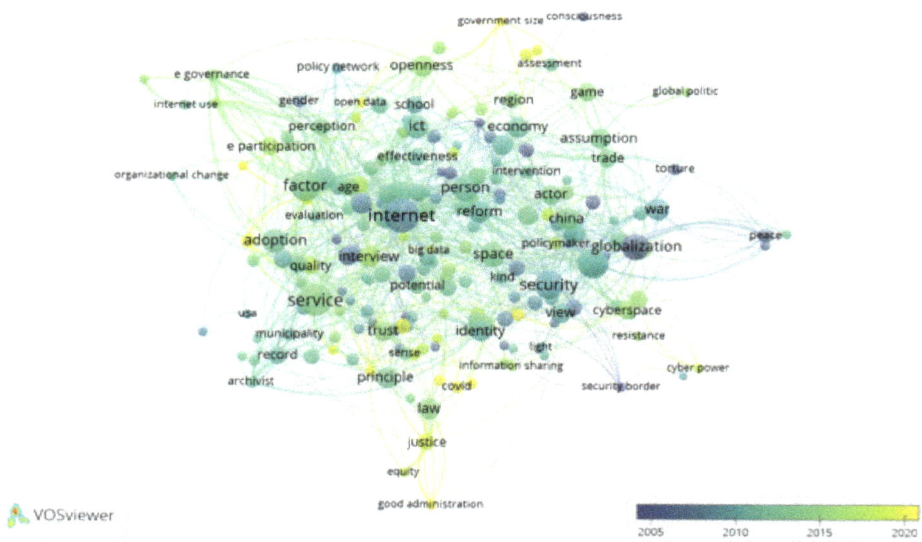

Figure 11. In the last two decades, the study of digital state and digital government has shifted, but not so strikingly; this is indicated by the trend of the study, which was dominant in the first decade. In Figure 12, density visualization shows the tendency of virtual state and digital state topics to be studied; based on these

categories in the last few years, this study has been dominant in issues such as the internet, security, services, globalization, ICT, and policymakers. The issues that are rarely explored are trade, law, justice, gender, and global politics.

Figure 12. Density visualization

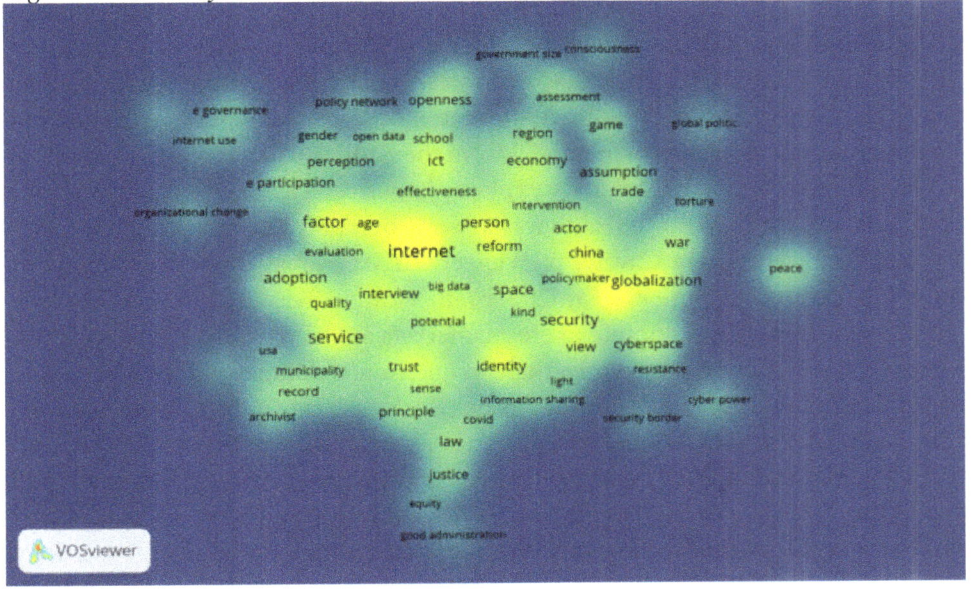

Table 3. Selected keywords of virtual state and digital state

Terms	Occurrences	Relevance	Terms	Occurrences	Relevance
Services	82	0.44	Openness	17	0.56
Security	47	0.60	Public organization	16	0.71
Globalization	44	0.55	Capabilities	17	0.64
ICT	38	0.63	Efficiency	16	0.57
Adaptation	34	0.55	Competition	15	0.45
Delivery	31	0.48	Information system	13	0.81
E-participation	25	0.84	Intervention	13	0.60
Trade	23	0.74	Revolution	12	0.44
Cyberspace	22	0.82	Management capacity	11	1.22
User	21	0.58	E-governance	11	0.96
Electronic government	20	1.06	Municipality	11	0.81
Privacy	17	0.83	Digitalization	11	0.77

The concept of virtual state and digital state, based on term occurrence from the analysis results, answers that the study of virtual state talks about state security, see Table 3, the concepts such as services, security, globalization, ICT, adaptation, e-participation, cyberspace, and privacy. Several other terms in the right table, such as openness, public organization, capability and efficiency, competition, information system, and intervention, show topics about digitalization in government. In contrast, the right side explains the virtual state, which is dominant in aspects of government security and information. This classification is based on the number of mentions in the VosViewer tool mapping based on the most frequently appearing terms in several articles that have been obtained from the Scopus database.

The digital state theme generally explores issues such as security, borders, globalization, and privacy. Several authors have photographed the issue to see security between countries (Dunn Cavelty & Wenger, 2020), globalization and migration (Rudolph, 2003), and borders (Roy, 2006b). In addition, because relations between countries are based on economic interests, markets and trade are the main topics in research on the digital state, but the trade in question is military international trade (Dean, 2018; Lu, 2020) or a free trade zone (Keshavarzian, 2010). Meanwhile, the topic of digital government reviews such issues as government openness (Mehta et al., 2023; Yavuz & Welch, 2014), management capacity (Scholl, 2006), e-government and digitalization (Schou & Hjelholt, 2019; Špaček et al., 2020). The review underlines that the two groups clearly have differences in terms of the function of technology applications; firstly, the digital state views the relationship between countries, while the digital government views the relationship between communities. Furthermore, the relationship is created through technology to function.

We further describe more clearly some of the studies with the highest number of citations based on the topic. The categories above and the results of the analysis show that there are differences between the issues of the virtual state and the digital state. Virtual state reviews the aspects of security and cybersecurity; this topic tries to maintain state security from external attacks. We consider that the topic of virtual state reviews the relationship between states in preserving security in virtual interactions between states. While the digital state reviews ideas about the relationship between the state and society, this relationship is mapped through topics such as public organization, management, e-government, digitalization, and efficiency.

Table 4. Selected author with the concept of virtual state and digital state

Author	Cite	Virtual state	Digital state
Reddick et al. (2011)	838		E-government, web, digital, transparency
Gartzke & Weisiger (2014)	562	Democracy, capital, Liberal Peace	
Mergel et al.(2019)			Digital transformation, social media, government.
Chatin & Gallarotti (2016)	132	Soft power, practical use, BRICS	
Kernaghan,(2009)	122	Virtual state, migration, integration,	Improving service, citizenship, innovation, and the public sector
Y.-C. Chen & Kim (2019)	116		E-government, services, trust, citizen
Zielonka (2012)	111	International System, European Union, Borders, Great Powers, Hegemony	
Feeney et al. (2020)	99		Local government, e-government, maturational model
Solingen (2007)	93	War, peace, the Middle East, Domestic coalitions, internationalization,	
Lips (2010)	87		E-government, public administration, citizen-government, digital identity
McNutt (2014)	87		Social collaboration, Web 2.0, and electronic government
McNutt (2014)	85	virtual worlds, human geography, geopolitics	
Roy (2006b, 2006a)	84	Security borders, digital age:	Security, Transparency, Government Online, E-government
Liste & Sorensen (2015)	79		Consumer, client, or citizen, local government website, ICT diffusion effectiveness

The grouping in Table 4 clarifies the idea of virtual state and digital state challenges in this article, both of which are seen as interrelated relationships. So, in terms of function, technology is used to bridge bilateral relations, agreements, and trade on the topic of the virtual state. Kernaghan (2009, 2013) sees both in terms of virtual state and digital state. However, the focus is on public services. Therefore, the virtual state is not only an idea of state relations but also a function of the state. The classification in the table explains specific themes on the topic of virtual state and digital state; therefore, it clearly reflects the research position in the last ten years of the two studies. The virtual state emphasizes the position of the state in carrying out cooperation, while the digital state is about the relationship between the government and society; both relationships are created through the use of technology. The virtual state function in this finding shows similarities with the findings (Ahmad Muhardin

Hadmar et al., 2024; Akbar et al., 2022; Khairunnisa et al., 2023), which show that the dominant function of government is administrative services.

CONCLUSION

The results of this review conclude that the topic of virtual state and digital state research in the last decade has increased; this topic is popularized by developed countries with a mature level of technology and encourages the application of virtual state and digital state topics. The number of publications can be shown through the dominant universities from developed countries, donor institutions, and reputable journals managed by major publishers. We group two significant topics in this study, namely virtual satellite and digital state, to see the function of technology in each: these finding underlines two essential differences in the use of technology in virtual states and digital states. In the virtual state, it analyzes the relationship between countries in terms of cooperation, protection of human rights, trade, and war. At the same time, the digital state shows the relationship between government and society through services, the use of Web 2.0, and the evolution of information technology in governance. Of the two topics, the study of the digital state is more dominant as a topic based on the number of publications, universities, and authors.

REFERENCES

Ahmad Muhardin Hadmar, A. N. Anwar Sadat, Loilatu, M.J., A. H., & Ibrahim. (2024). Trends in Digital Transformation for Multicultural E-Government Communication: A Bibliometric Analysis Using Citespace. *Nyimak: Journal of Communication, 8*(2), 241–260. https://jurnal.umt.ac.id/index.php/nyimak/article/view/11187/5627

Akbar, P., Nurmandi, A., Irawan, B., & Loilatu, M. J. (2022). Research trends in e-Government interoperability: Mapping themes and concepts based on the scopus database. *JeDEM-EJournal of EDemocracy and Open Government, 14*(2), 83–108. DOI: 10.29379/jedem.v14i2.707

Anthes, C., García-Hernández, R. J., Wiedemann, M., & Kranzlmüller, D. (2016). State of the art of virtual reality technology. *IEEE Aerospace Conference Proceedings, 2016-June*. DOI: 10.1109/AERO.2016.7500674

Anthopoulos, L. G., Siozos, P., & Tsoukalas, I. A. (2007). Applying participatory design and collaboration in digital public services for discovering and re-designing e-Government services. *Government Information Quarterly, 24*(2), 353–376. DOI: 10.1016/j.giq.2006.07.018

Aromataris, E., & Pearson, A. (2014). The systematic review: An overview. *The American Journal of Nursing, 114*(3), 53–58. DOI: 10.1097/01.NAJ.0000444496.24228.2c

Aziz, F. N., Roziqin, A., Loilatu, M. J., Sulistyaningsih, T., Hijri, Y. S., & Kismartini, . (2024). Research trends of creative Industries in Indonesia: A bibliometric analysis. *Journal of the Knowledge Economy, 15*(1), 2571–2588. DOI: 10.1007/s13132-023-01299-5

Baharuddin, T., Qodir, Z., & Loilatu, M. J. (2022). Government Website Performance During the COVID-19 Pandemic: Comparative Study of Yogyakarta and South Sulawesi, Indonesia. *Journal of Governance and Public Policy, 9*(2), LAYOUTING. DOI: 10.18196/jgpp.v9i2.11474

Baldwin, S. (2000). The Role of Information Technology in the Reinventing Government Paradigm Normative Predicates and Practical Challenges. *Social Science Computer Review, 18*(2), 166–178. DOI: 10.1177/089443930001800206

Bastow, S., Dunleavy, P., Margetts, H., & Tinkler, J. (2000). The advent of a "digital state" and government-business relations. … */UCL), Paper to the UK Political Studies …*, 10–13.

Bertot, J. C., Jaeger, P. T., & Grimes, J. M. (2010). Using ICTs to create a culture of transparency: E-government and social media as openness and anti-corruption tools for societies. *Government Information Quarterly*, *27*(3), 264–271. DOI: 10.1016/j.giq.2010.03.001

Bretschneider, S. (2003). Information Technology, E-Government, and Institutional Change. *Public Administration Review*, *63*(6), 738–741. DOI: 10.1111/1540-6210.00337

Carter, L., Weerakkody, V., Phillips, B., & Dwivedi, Y. K. (2016). Citizen Adoption of E-Government Services: Exploring Citizen Perceptions of Online Services in the United States and United Kingdom. *Information Systems Management*, *33*(2), 124–140. DOI: 10.1080/10580530.2016.1155948

Chalmers, D. J. (2019). The Virtual as the Digital. *Disputatio*, *11*(55), 453–486. DOI: 10.2478/disp-2019-0022

Chatin, M., & Gallarotti, G. M. (2016). The BRICS and soft power: An introduction. *Journal of Political Power*, *9*(3), 335–352. DOI: 10.1080/2158379X.2016.1232284

Chen, Y.-C., & Kim, Y. (2019). Adoption of e-government services by small municipalities. *International Journal of Organization Theory and Behavior*, *22*(2), 174–190. DOI: 10.1108/IJOTB-07-2018-0083

Chun, S. A., Shulman, S., Sandoval, R., & Hovy, E. (2010). Government 2.0: Making connections between citizens, data and government. *Information Polity*, *15*(1–2), 1–9. DOI: 10.3233/IP-2010-0205

Cordella, A., & Bonina, C. M. (2012). A public value perspective for ICT enabled public sector reforms: A theoretical reflection. *Government Information Quarterly*, *29*(4), 512–520. DOI: 10.1016/j.giq.2012.03.004

Coursey, D., & Norris, D. F. (2008). Models of e-government: Are they correct? An empirical assessment. *Public Administration Review*, *68*(3), 523–536. DOI: 10.1111/j.1540-6210.2008.00888.x

Dean, A. (2018). NAFTA's army: Free trade and US military enlistment. *International Studies Quarterly*, *62*(4), 845–856. DOI: 10.1093/isq/sqy032

Djen, R. A. M., Nurmandi, A., Muallidin, I., Kurniawan, D., & Loilatu, M. J. (2023). *Artificial Intelligence: Bibliometric Analysis in Government Studies BT - Proceedings of Seventh International Congress on Information and Communication Technology* (X.-S. Yang, S. Sherratt, N. Dey, & A. Joshi (eds.); pp. 411–418). Springer Nature Singapore.

Dunleavy, P. (2006). New public management is dead - Long live digital-era governance. *Journal of Public Administration: Research and Theory*, *16*(3), 467–494. DOI: 10.1093/jopart/mui057

Dunleavy, P., Margetts, H., Bastow, S., Pearce, O., & Tinkler, J. (2007). Government on the internet: Progress in delivering information and services online. *Issues (Chicago, Ill.)*, •••, 13–01.

Dunleavy, P., Margetts, H., Bastow, S., & Tinkler, J. (2004). Government IT performance and the power of the IT industry: A cross-national analysis. *Annual American Political Science Association Conference, Chicago, 1st September, May 2014.*

Dunn Cavelty, M., & Wenger, A. (2020). Cyber security meets security politics: Complex technology, fragmented politics, and networked science. *Contemporary Security Policy*, *41*(1), 5–32. DOI: 10.1080/13523260.2019.1678855

Feeney, M. K., Fusi, F., Camarena, L., & Zhang, F. (2020). Towards more digital cities? Change in technology use and perceptions across small and medium-sized US cities. *Local Government Studies*, *46*(5), 820–845. DOI: 10.1080/03003930.2019.1690993

Fleming, P. S., Koletsi, D., & Pandis, N. (2014). Blinded by PRISMA: Are systematic reviewers focusing on PRISMA and ignoring other guidelines? *PLoS One*, *9*(5), e96407. Advance online publication. DOI: 10.1371/journal.pone.0096407

Fountain, Jane. (2001). *Building the Virtual State: Information Technology and Institutional Change.*

Fountain, Je. (2004). Prospects for the Virtual State. *University of Tokyo 21st Century COE Program" ..., 0131923.*

Fountain, J. E. (2001). The Virtual State: Transforming American Government? *National Civic Review*, *90*(3), 241–252. DOI: 10.1002/ncr.90305

Garson, G. D. (2006). *Public information technology and e-governance: Managing the virtual state.* Jones & Bartlett Learning.

Gartzke, E., & Weisiger, A. (2014). Under Construction: Development, Democracy, and Difference as Determinants of Systemic Liberal Peace. *International Studies Quarterly*, *58*(1), 130–145. DOI: 10.1111/isqu.12113

Gascó, M. (2003). New technologies and institutional change in public administration. *Social Science Computer Review*, *21*(1), 6–14. DOI: 10.1177/0894439302238967

Gil-García, J. R., & Pardo, T. A. (2005). E-government success factors: Mapping practical tools to theoretical foundations. *Government Information Quarterly*, *22*(2), 187–216. DOI: 10.1016/j.giq.2005.02.001

Guinan, P. J., Parise, S., & Langowitz, N. (2019). Creating an innovative digital project team: Levers to enable digital transformation. *Business Horizons*, *62*(6), 717–727. DOI: 10.1016/j.bushor.2019.07.005

Harrison, T. M., Guerrero, S., Burke, G. B., Cook, M., Cresswell, A., Helbig, N., Hrdinova, J., & Pardo, T. (2012). Open government and e-government: Democratic challenges from a public value perspective. *Information Polity*, *17*(2), 83–97. DOI: 10.3233/IP-2012-0269

Helbig, N., Gil-García, J. R., & Ferro, E. (2009). Understanding the complexity of electronic government: Implications from the digital divide literature. *Government Information Quarterly*, *26*(1), 89–97. DOI: 10.1016/j.giq.2008.05.004

Hoetker, G., & Mahony, J. T. (2002). Building the Virtual State: Information Technology and Institutional Change. *Academy of Management Review*, *27*(4), 619–622. DOI: 10.2307/4134407

Ingram, R. (1997). *Building Virtual Worlds: A City Planning Perspective*. Online Planning Journal.

Jae Moon, M., & Welch, E. W. (2000). Managerial Adaptation through the Market in the Public Sector: Theoretical Framework and Four Models. *International Review of Public Administration*, *5*(2), 129–141. DOI: 10.1080/12294659.2000.10804961

Kapucu, N. (2006). Interagency communication networks during emergencies: Boundary spanners in multiagency coordination. *American Review of Public Administration*, *36*(2), 207–225. DOI: 10.1177/0275074005280605

Kernaghan, K. (2009). Moving towards integrated public governance: Improving service delivery through community engagement. *International Review of Administrative Sciences*, *75*(2), 239–254. DOI: 10.1177/0020852309104174

Kernaghan, K. (2013). Changing channels: Managing channel integration and migration in public organizations. *Canadian Public Administration*, *56*(1), 121–141. DOI: 10.1111/capa.12006

Keshavarzian, A. (2010). Geopolitics and the genealogy of free trade zones in the persian Gulf. *Geopolitics*, *15*(2), 263–289. DOI: 10.1080/14650040903486926

Khairunnisa, T., Nurmandi, A., Purwaningsi, T., Loilatu, M. J., & Savira, A. G. (2023). Open Government Index in Local Government During the Period of the COVID-19 Pandemic. *Jurnal Borneo Administrator*, *19*(1), 1–16. DOI: 10.24258/jba.v19i1.1149

Kirişci, K. (2009). The transformation of Turkish foreign policy: The rise of the trading state. *New Perspectives on Turkey*, *40*, 29–56. DOI: 10.1017/S0896634600005203

Kulsum, U., Nurmandi, A., Muallidin, I., & Jafar, M. (2022). A Bibliometric Analysis of Open Government : Study on Indonesia and. *Journal of Governance*, *7*(1), 133–143. DOI: 10.31506/jog.v7i1.13934

Lips, M. (2010). Rethinking citizen-government relationships in the age of digital identity: Insights from research. *Information Polity*, *15*(4), 273–289. DOI: 10.3233/IP-2010-0216

Liste, L., & Sørensen, K. H. (2015). Consumer, client or citizen? How Norwegian local governments domesticate website technology and configure their users. *Information Communication and Society*, *18*(7), 733–746. DOI: 10.1080/1369118X.2014.993678

Liu, Y. Q., Martin, C., Roehl, E., Li, Z., & Ward, S. (2006). Digital information access in urban/suburban communities: A survey report of public digital library use by the residents in Connecticut. *OCLC Systems & Services*, *22*(2), 132–144. DOI: 10.1108/10650750610664021

Loilatu, M. J., Saiman, S., Irawan, B., Kulsum, U., Huda, M. N., & Vidiastuti, D. P. (2026). Natural Disaster Responses and Disaster Study in Indonesia: An Exploratory Study Using Meta-Analysis. In *Inequality and Environmental Degradation in a Prosperity-Driven World* (pp. 265–292). IGI Global Scientific Publishing.

Lu, K. L. (2020). The Spillover Effect of the Trade War between Adversarial Dyads: Evidence from the Sino-US Investment Relationship. *Journal of Chinese Political Science*, *25*(1), 21–47. DOI: 10.1007/s11366-018-9577-0

Luna-Reyes, L. F., & Gil-Garcia, J. R. (2011). Using institutional theory and dynamic simulation to understand complex e-Government phenomena. *Government Information Quarterly*, *28*(3), 329–345. DOI: 10.1016/j.giq.2010.08.007

Luna-Reyes, L. F., & Gil-Garcia, J. R. (2014). Digital government transformation and internet portals: The co-evolution of technology, organizations, and institutions. *Government Information Quarterly*, *31*(4), 545–555. DOI: 10.1016/j.giq.2014.08.001

Luna-Reyes, L. F., Gil-Garcia, J. R., & Cruz, C. B. (2007). Collaborative digital government in Mexico: Some lessons from federal Web-based interorganizational information integration initiatives. *Government Information Quarterly*, *24*(4), 808–826. DOI: 10.1016/j.giq.2007.04.003

Luna-Reyes, L. F., Gil-Garcia, J. R., & Estrada-Marroquín, M. (2008). The impact of institutions on interorganizational IT projects in the Mexican federal government. *International Journal of Electronic Government Research*, *4*(2), 27–42. DOI: 10.4018/jegr.2008040103

Luna-Reyes, L. F., Zhang, J., Gil-García, J. R., & Cresswell, A. M. (2005). Information systems development as emergent socio-technical change: A practice approach. *European Journal of Information Systems*, *14*(1), 93–105. DOI: 10.1057/palgrave.ejis.3000524

Madon, S. (1993). Introducing administrative reform through the application of computer-based information systems: A case study in India. *Public Administration and Development*, *13*(1), 37–48. DOI: 10.1002/pad.4230130104

Mcnutt, K. (2014). Public engagement in the Web 2.0 era: Social collaborative technologies in a public sector context. *Canadian Public Administration*, *57*(1), 49–70. DOI: 10.1111/capa.12058

Mehta, D., Patel, N., Joshi, N. A., & Patel, B. (2023). Impact of economic openness on government size in India. *International Journal of Sustainable Economy*, *16*(1), 113–130. DOI: 10.1504/IJSE.2024.135192

Mergel, I., & Bretschneider, S. I. (2013). A Three-Stage Adoption Process for Social Media Use in Government. *Public Administration Review*, *73*(3), 390–400. DOI: 10.1111/puar.12021

Mergel, I., Edelmann, N., & Haug, N. (2019). Defining digital transformation: Results from expert interviews. *Government Information Quarterly*, *36*(4), 101385. Advance online publication. DOI: 10.1016/j.giq.2019.06.002

Moon, M. J. (2002). The evolution of E-government among municipalities: Rhetoric or reality? *Public Administration Review*, *62*(4), 424–433. DOI: 10.1111/0033-3352.00196

Norris, D. F. (2003). Building the Virtual State ... or Not? A Critical Appraisal. *Social Science Computer Review*, *21*(4), 417–424. DOI: 10.1177/0894439303256728

Norris, D. F., & Reddick, C. G. (2013). Local E-Government in the United States: Transformation or Incremental Change? *Public Administration Review*, *73*(1), 165–175. DOI: 10.1111/j.1540-6210.2012.02647.x

Omar, A., Weerakkody, V., & Sivarajah, U. (2017). Digitally enabled service transformation in UK public sector: A case analysis of universal credit. *International Journal of Information Management*, *37*(4), 350–356. DOI: 10.1016/j.ijinfomgt.2017.04.001

Oosterzee, P. V. A. N., & Garnett, S. T. (2015). the Evolution of Information and Communication Technology in Public Administration. *Public Administration and Development*, *35*(220), 140–151. DOI: 10.1002/pad

Page, M. J., McKenzie, J. E., Bossuyt, P. M., Boutron, I., Hoffmann, T. C., Mulrow, C. D., Shamseer, L., Tetzlaff, J. M., Akl, E. A., Brennan, S. E., Chou, R., Glanville, J., Grimshaw, J. M., Hróbjartsson, A., Lalu, M. M., Li, T., Loder, E. W., Mayo-Wilson, E., McDonald, S., & Moher, D. (2021). The PRISMA 2020 statement: An updated guideline for reporting systematic reviews. *BMJ (Clinical Research Ed.)*, *372*, n71. Advance online publication. DOI: 10.1136/bmj.n71

Pedrosa, G. V., Kosloski, R. A. D., de Menezes, V. G., Iwama, G. Y., da Silva, W. C. M. P., & Figueiredo, R. M. C. (2020). A systematic review of indicators for evaluating the effectiveness of digital public services. *Information (Basel)*, *11*(10), 1–14. DOI: 10.3390/info11100472

Pham, M. T., Rajić, A., Greig, J. D., Sargeant, J. M., Papadopoulos, A., & Mcewen, S. A. (2014). A scoping review of scoping reviews: Advancing the approach and enhancing the consistency. *Research Synthesis Methods*, *5*(4), 371–385. DOI: 10.1002/jrsm.1123

Reddick, C. G. (2004). A two-stage model of e-government growth: Theories and empirical evidence for U.S. cities. *Government Information Quarterly*, *21*(1), 51–64. DOI: 10.1016/j.giq.2003.11.004

Reddick, C. G. (2005). Citizen interaction with e-government: From the streets to servers? *Government Information Quarterly*, *22*(1), 38–57. DOI: 10.1016/j.giq.2004.10.003

Reddick, C. G. (2011). Customer Relationship Management (CRM) technology and organizational change: Evidence for the bureaucratic and e-Government paradigms. *Government Information Quarterly*, *28*(3), 346–353. DOI: 10.1016/j.giq.2010.08.005

Reddick, C. G., Abdelsalam, H. M., & Elkadi, H. (2011). The influence of e-government on administrative discretion: The case of local governments in egypt. *Public Administration and Development*, *31*(5), 390–407. DOI: 10.1002/pad.615

Reddick, C. G., & Turner, M. (2012). Channel choice and public service delivery in Canada: Comparing e-government to traditional service delivery. *Government Information Quarterly*, *29*(1), 1–11. DOI: 10.1016/j.giq.2011.03.005

Roy, J. (2006a). E-government and local governance in Canada: An examination of front line challenges and federal tensions. *Public Administration Quarterly*, *11*(4), 306–350. DOI: 10.1177/073491490603000203

Roy, J. (2006b). Security and borders in a digital age: Implications for Canadian government and North American governance. *Journal of Borderlands Studies, 21*(1), 87–107. DOI: 10.1080/08865655.2006.9695653

Roziqin, A., Kismartini, Fajrina, A. N., Salahudin, & Sulistyaningsih, T. (2022). The development of Indonesian e-Government: A bibliometric analysis. *COLLNET Journal of Scientometrics and Information Management, 16*(1), 49–74. DOI: 10.1080/09737766.2021.2007036

Rudolph, C. (2003). Globalizaton and security: Migration and evolving conceptions of security in statecraft and scholarship. *Security Studies, 13*(1), 1–32. DOI: 10.1080/09636410490493822

Scholl, H. J. (2006). Electronic government: Information management capacity, organizational capabilities, and the sourcing mix. *Government Information Quarterly, 23*(1), 73–96. DOI: 10.1016/j.giq.2005.11.002

Schou, J., & Hjelholt, M. (2019). Digital state spaces: State rescaling and advanced digitalization. *Territory, Politics, Governance*, *7*(4), 438–454. DOI: 10.1080/21622671.2018.1532809

Selcuk, A. A. (2019). A Guide for Systematic Reviews: PRISMA. *Turkish Archives of Otorhinolaryngology, 57*(1), 57–58. DOI: 10.5152/tao.2019.4058

Solingen, E. (2007). Pax Asiatica versus Bella Levantina: The foundations of war and peace in East Middle East. *The American Political Science Review, 101*(4), 757–780. DOI: 10.1017/S0003055407070487

Špaček, D., Csótó, M., & Urs, N. (2020). Questioning the Real Citizen-Centricity of e-Government Development: Digitalization of G2C Services in Selected CEE Countries. *NISPAcee Journal of Public Administration and Policy, 13*(1), 213–243. DOI: 10.2478/nispa-2020-0009

Sulistyaningsih, T., Loilatu, M. J., & Roziqin, A. (2023). Research trends on smart urban governance in Asia: a bibliometric analysis. *Journal of Science and Technology Policy Management*. DOI: 10.1108/JSTPM-03-2022-0045

Syukri, A., Nurmandi, A., Muallidin, I., Kurniawan, D., & Loilatu, M. J. (2023). *Toward an Agile and Transformational Government, Through the Development of the Tangerang LIVE Application (Case Study of Tangerang City, Indonesia) BT - Proceedings of Seventh International Congress on Information and Communication Technology* (X.-S. Yang, S. Sherratt, N. Dey, & A. Joshi (eds.); pp. 343–352). Springer Nature Singapore.

Tolbert, C. J., Mossberger, K., & McNeal, R. (2008). Institutions, policy innovation, and e-government in the American States. *Public Administration Review, 68*(3), 549–563. DOI: 10.1111/j.1540-6210.2008.00890.x

Tricco, A. C., Lillie, E., Zarin, W., O'Brien, K., Colquhoun, H., Kastner, M., Levac, D., Ng, C., Sharpe, J. P., Wilson, K., Kenny, M., Warren, R., Wilson, C., Stelfox, H. T., & Straus, S. E. (2016). A scoping review on the conduct and reporting of scoping reviews. *BMC Medical Research Methodology, 16*(1), 1–10. DOI: 10.1186/s12874-016-0116-4

Twizeyimana, J. D., & Andersson, A. (2019). The public value of E-Government – A literature review. *Government Information Quarterly, 36*(2), 167–178. DOI: 10.1016/j.giq.2019.01.001

United Nations. (2016). *E Goverenment Survey 2016*.

Wanyan, D., & Hu, J. (2019). How to provide public digital cultural services in China? *Library Hi Tech, 38*(3), 504–521. DOI: 10.1108/LHT-03-2019-0071

Weerakkody, V., El-Haddadeh, R., Al-Sobhi, F., Shareef, M. A., & Dwivedi, Y. K. (2013). Examining the influence of intermediaries in facilitating e-government adoption: An empirical investigation. *International Journal of Information Management, 33*(5), 716–725. DOI: 10.1016/j.ijinfomgt.2013.05.001

Weerakkody, V., El-Haddadeh, R., Sivarajah, U., Omar, A., & Molnar, A. (2019). A case analysis of E-government service delivery through a service chain dimension. *International Journal of Information Management, 47*(August), 233–238. DOI: 10.1016/j.ijinfomgt.2018.11.001

Weerakkody, V., Omar, A., El-Haddadeh, R., & Al-Busaidy, M. (2016). Digitally-enabled service transformation in the public sector: The lure of institutional pressure and strategic response towards change. *Government Information Quarterly, 33*(4), 658–668. DOI: 10.1016/j.giq.2016.06.006

West, D. M. (2004). E-Government and the Transformation of Service Delivery and Citizen Attitudes. *Public Administration Review, 64*(1), 15–27. DOI: 10.1111/j.1540-6210.2004.00343.x

Wright, R. W., Brand, R. A., Dunn, W., & Spindler, K. P. (2007). How to write a systematic review. *Clinical Orthopaedics and Related Research, 455*(455), 23–29. DOI: 10.1097/BLO.0b013e31802c9098

Yang, K., & Rho, S.-Y. (2007). E-government for better performance: Promises, realities, and challenges. *International Journal of Public Administration, 30*(11), 1197–1217. DOI: 10.1080/01900690701225556

Yavuz, N., & Welch, E. W. (2014). Factors affecting openness of local government websites: Examining the differences across planning, finance and police departments. *Government Information Quarterly*, *31*(4), 574–583. DOI: 10.1016/j.giq.2014.07.004

Yildiz, M. (2007). E-government research: Reviewing the literature, limitations, and ways forward. *Government Information Quarterly*, *24*(3), 646–665. DOI: 10.1016/j.giq.2007.01.002

Zielonka, J. (2012). Empires and the Modern International System. *Geopolitics*, *17*(3), 502–525. DOI: 10.1080/14650045.2011.595440

Chapter 8
Ontologies of Augmented Collegiality in Education and Epistemic Architectures of Human-AI Synergy:
Multi-Agent Orchestration and Cognitive Equity

Ashraf Alam
https://orcid.org/0000-0001-6178-1187
Alliance University, Bengaluru, India

ABSTRACT

This chapter theorizes and operationalizes augmented collegiality as a deliberate reconstitution of pedagogy in which teachers, students, and artificial agents coordinate accountable knowledge work. It synthesizes CSCL, activity systems, communities of inquiry, knowledge building, distributed cognition, and human-AI teaming to specify a layered architecture spanning experience, collaboration services, intelligence, orchestration, data, integration, infrastructure, and governance. The program details generative feedback, XR, IoT, and privacy preserving analytics while enforcing provenance, accessibility, and calibrated trust. Design patterns translate theory into auditable practice, and implementation blueprints align staffing, procurement, and sustainability with cognitive equity across bandwidths, languages, and abilities. Measurement links inputs to impact through interpretable indicators

DOI: 10.4018/979-8-3373-5747-8.ch008

and mixed methods, and legal regimes inform bias audits, consent, and disclosure-based integrity. The result is a pragmatic agenda that reduces extraneous load and stabilizes equitable voice.

1. INTRODUCTION

The contemporary collaboration stack in education is a patchwork of minimally interoperable systems that splinters attention and fractures collective sensemaking. A typical classroom or seminar now runs on an LMS such as Moodle or Canvas for content and grades, a videoconference utility such as Zoom or Google Meet for synchronous meetings, a messaging layer such as WhatsApp or Telegram for ad hoc coordination, a co-authoring surface such as Google Docs or Overleaf for writing, and an AI chat tool for drafting, summarizing, and feedback (Jony & Hamim, 2024; Kovari, 2025; Kim et al., 2024). Each system maintains its own identity model, notification stream, and data silo, with partial bridges through LTI, Caliper, or xAPI that rarely capture the full nuance of discourse moves, argumentation structures, or tacit roles that make collaboration productive. Empirical studies of interruption and multitasking clarify the cost of this fragmentation. In time-motion fieldwork with knowledge workers, Gloria Mark and Victor González in 2004 documented average task durations near eleven minutes, frequent self-interruptions, and resumption lags that compound coordination loss; in classrooms with parallel channels, the same pattern manifests as conversational drift, unanchored decisions, and diminished closure on shared artifacts. When every tool emits alerts, badges, and timelines, students and faculty allocate scarce executive attention to navigating interfaces rather than building ideas, producing the paradox of more tools and less teamwork.

Cognitive Load Theory offers a precise lens on why the current tool ecology often backfires. John Sweller's foundational work in 1988 distinguished intrinsic load driven by material complexity from extraneous load generated by presentation and task conditions; Fred Paas and Jeroen van Merriënboer in the mid-1990s formalized mental effort measures; Paul Ayres in 2006 synthesized split-attention and redundancy effects; Slava Kalyuga in 2003 identified the expertise-reversal effect. The lesson for collaboration is concrete. Tool proliferation inflates extraneous load by forcing learners to integrate spatially and temporally separated sources, while redundant dashboards duplicate representations without adding germane schemata (Asrifan et al., 2025; Clear et al., 2025; Kurni & Mohammed, 2023). When argumentation occurs in chat, evidence lives in files, and decisions hide in meeting recordings, the split-attention effect is designed into the workflow. Conversely, properly orchestrated human–AI teams can lower extraneous load by aligning discourse, data, and decisions on a single surface, by providing just-in-time prompts that externalize metacognition, and by adapting representations to a learner's evolving schemas so that germane load increases productively rather than haphazardly (Han et al., 2023; Lodge et al., 2023; Halaweh, 2023).

The external drivers for a new architecture are equally specific. Since November 2022, large language models have become usable by non-specialists for drafting, code generation, formative feedback, and translation, expanding the feasible space for real-time facilitation and scaffolding in seminars, studios, and labs. Accreditation and assessment regimes already reward the outcomes that collaboration delivers when well designed. The 2018 revision of ABET's student outcomes explicitly requires the ability to function effectively on teams and to create solutions that consider public health, safety, welfare, and global factors, which presupposes shared situational awareness and reliable division of labor. The OECD's Education 2030 work foregrounds creativity, critical thinking, and responsibility for others and the planet, with collaborative problem solving assessed in prior PISA cycles and echoed in national frameworks from Singapore to Scotland. In universities, capstones, clinical rotations, and design studios constitute a rising share of credit hours; in schools, project-based and inquiry-driven units increasingly emphasize argumentation, modeling, and iterative revision. Yet the instrumentation of collaboration has not caught up with its centrality in curricula, leading to a measurable implementation gap between stated competencies and the infrastructures that would cultivate them at scale.

Equity considerations make the gap more urgent. Connectivity, device availability, and teacher preparedness remain uneven along rural–urban, income, disability, and language lines. The International Telecommunication Union's 2023 estimates placed internet use around five and a half billion people with roughly two and a half billion still offline, and within connected populations bandwidth and latency vary widely enough to exclude synchronous XR tools from large regions and schools. Teacher surveys such as OECD TALIS 2018 reported that fewer than half of teachers felt prepared to integrate digital tools for pedagogy, a proportion that rises with targeted professional development but remains contingent on local support and time. During school closures in 2020 and 2021, ministries and districts deployed radio, television, and print packets to reach learners without stable broadband, demonstrating that resilient ecosystems must gracefully degrade to low-bandwidth modes without eroding collaborative intent or learner dignity. Accessibility also remains uneven. Screen reader compatibility, caption quality, and keyboard navigation standards are inconsistently implemented across the tools educators are compelled to combine, making collaboration fragile for learners with visual, auditory, motor, or cognitive disabilities (Johnson, 2024; Meniado, 2023; Merceron & Best, 2024). In multilingual classrooms and cross-border programs, language is a further barrier, with communication oscillating between fast, informal messaging and slower, formal submissions, leaving emergent bilinguals without equitable access to feedback cycles or leadership roles in group work.

The timing is propitious for redesign because several enabling technologies and policy frames have matured in parallel. Consumer-grade XR headsets have crossed price and performance thresholds suitable for institutional pilots, while cloud rendering and edge compute permit local caching and inference that keep rural schools viable under modest connectivity. Fifth-generation mobile coverage has expanded across populous regions, reducing median latency and enabling richer synchronous collaboration on handheld devices. Generative models now accept text, code, images, and audio, allowing facilitation agents that can summarize whiteboards, interpret sketches, translate discourse in real time, and render alternative visualizations of the same concept for different learners (Murgatroyd, 2024; Hutson, 2025; Tondeur et al., 2025). On the governance side, data protection statutes such as the European Union's GDPR and India's 2023 Digital Personal Data Protection Act compel institutions to articulate lawful purposes and minimize data capture, while sectoral regulations such as FERPA in the United States constrain education records use. Ethical frameworks from UNESCO in 2021 and legislative initiatives such as the European Union's AI Act finalized in 2024 heighten expectations for transparency, accountability, and risk classification in AI deployments that touch minors and high-stakes assessment. Taken together, these shifts justify a decisive move from tool accumulation to systems thinking, where augmented collegiality is the object of design, where multi-agent orchestration aligns human and machine roles with evidence-based pedagogy, and where cognitive equity is engineered into the substrate so that attention, voice, and opportunity are distributed fairly across bandwidths, languages, and abilities.

2. CONCEPTS AND THEORETICAL FOUNDATIONS

The conceptual groundwork for augmented collegiality in education draws on mature theories of learning and collaboration, extended to accommodate artificial agents as legitimate participants in knowledge work. The central move is to reinterpret well-evidenced constructs such as scaffolding, shared regulation, and discourse-based cognition in terms of hybrid activity systems where humans and machines co-orchestrate goals, representations, and roles (Ifenthaler & Schumacher, 2023; Chan & Tsi, 2023; Wang et al., 2023). Doing so requires careful attention to the conditions under which learners benefit from external cognitive supports and to the socio-technical dynamics that differentiate enablement from displacement (Ursin et al., 2025; Bower & von Mengersen, 2025; Gesing et al., 2025). The frameworks surveyed here are not interchangeable. Each contributes a distinct unit of analysis and a set of design implications: the group as the locus of cognition in Computer-Supported Collaborative Learning, the activity system in Cultural–Historical

Activity Theory, the triad of presences in Communities of Inquiry, the communal responsibility for idea improvement in Knowledge Building, the networked substrate of Connectivism, the socio-material distribution of cognitive labor in Distributed Cognition, the role and trust dynamics in Human–AI Teaming, and the demand for dialogic justice and variability-responsive design in Equity-oriented pedagogy (Table 1). Read together, they specify an epistemic architecture in which multi-agent orchestration can be made transparent, accountable, and inclusive.

Table 1. Cross-framework meta-synthesis of eight foundational lenses for augmented collegiality in education

Theoretical Construct & Proponents	Unit of Analysis & Core Postulates	Operationalization in Human-AI Pedagogies	Design Heuristics & Governance Guardrails	Canonical Risks & Failure Modes	Representative Metrics & Instrumentation
Computer-Supported Collaborative Learning (CSCL) - Dillenbourg; Koschmann; and Stahl	Small group as the cognitive system; learning arises from convergence, elaboration, grounding, and mutual regulation; discourse, artifacts, and representations co-determine knowledge construction.	Orchestration agents act as facilitative scripts that prompt elaboration, surface tacit consensus as explicit claims, and propose candidate representations; shared canvases bind talk, text, and artifact history to a single "joint problem space" with accountable provenance.	Maintain visible contribution traces and negotiable representations; tune interdependence and accountability; fade scaffolds as group maturity grows; expose user-controllable "density dials" for prompts to prevent over-structuring; preserve instructor authority for epistemic adjudication.	Social loafing and parallel work masquerading as collaboration; over-prompting that crowds out authentic negotiation; opaque model state that misaligns with the shared problem space; facilitation drift that privileges fluent speakers.	Talk-time Gini and initiation dispersion; reply-depth and thread-closure ratios; time-to-first-response during peak load; claim-counterclaim coverage index; contribution entropy across team members; decision latency and unresolved-item counts.
Cultural–Historical Activity Theory (CHAT) - Engeström	Activity system comprising subject, object, mediating artifacts, rules, community, and division of labor; contradictions within and across systems drive expansive learning.	Agents are transparent mediators and boundary objects that carry rules and rationale across roles; policy engines encode local norms for data, authorship, and assessment; routinized tasks (timekeeping, translation, hygiene) are algorithmically delegated with negotiated redistribution of labor.	Surface contradictions explicitly; require provenance for agent proposals; enforce human override, pause, and audit trails; institutionalize role-rotation and retrospective negotiation of rules; align orchestration to legitimate peripheral participation rather than imposition.	Rule–tool misfit that externalizes institutional inequities; creeping automation that displaces epistemic agency; brittle divisions of labor that codify status hierarchies; hidden value conflicts left unexamined.	Contradiction logs and resolution timelines; override and waiver frequencies with rationale; role-rotation cadence; policy-compliance rates on data use and authorship; boundary-object citation density in decisions.

continued on following page

Table 1. Continued

Theoretical Construct & Proponents	Unit of Analysis & Core Postulates	Operationalization in Human-AI Pedagogies	Design Heuristics & Governance Guardrails	Canonical Risks & Failure Modes	Representative Metrics & Instrumentation
Communities of Inquiry (CoI) - Garrison, Anderson, and Archer	Triadic ecology of teaching presence, social presence, and cognitive presence; purposeful discourse sustains meaning-making in text-rich environments.	Teaching presence amplified by agents that schedule checkpoints and synthesize threads; social presence extended through accessible captions, parallel translations, and voice-preserving rewrites; cognitive presence scaffolded by prompts that move exploration → integration → resolution with evidence-anchored summaries.	Calibrate interventions to maintain perceived authenticity; preserve voice and register in translation; require quoted evidence and uncertainty displays in summaries; keep summative judgment human; treat presence as a perceived property, not merely a technical feature.	Flattened nuance and misattribution in auto-summaries; over-facilitation that suppresses community agency; trust erosion when explanations are opaque or tone-deforming rewrites normalize language.	Presence indicators by phase; summary factual-alignment and misattribution rates; exploration → integration → resolution transition counts; caption word-error rate and diarization accuracy; student trust and usefulness ratings of agent syntheses.
Knowledge Building (KB) - Scardamalia and Bereiter	Community as a knowledge-creating entity; ideas are improvable objects; collective epistemic agency governs advancement of explanations.	Knowledge-intermediary agents maintain idea lineages, knowledge maps, and gap ledgers; analogy seeding from distant domains; consequence simulations for design choices; automatic provenance tagging to enforce communal credit and traceability.	Reward communal authorship and explicit attribution; prohibit models from authoring core explanatory moves; require explicit warrants and considered counters for major claims; institutionalize iterative refinement cycles.	Idea capture by AI and premature convergence; performative documentation without conceptual progress; eroded authorship ethics; analogical drift that introduces seductive but irrelevant parallels.	Idea-diversity and novelty indices; revision-lineage depth and branch richness; gap-closure and conjecture-to-evidence conversion counts; attribution completeness and provenance integrity checks.
Connectivism – Siemens and Downes	Knowledge as a distributed network spanning humans, databases, and algorithms; learning is the capacity to form, traverse, and prune connections in a dynamic information ecology.	Network-health dashboards visualize source diversity, update recency, and path redundancy; agents curate heterogeneous nodes, broker introductions to experts, and harden pipelines with offline caches and federated stores for bandwidth-poor contexts.	Optimize for heterogeneity and robustness; avoid single-point failures and proprietary choke points; externalize trust criteria; require reflective memos justifying network design; keep local replicas for resilience.	Homophily and echo chambers; link rot and API dependency; brittle over-centralization; recency bias overshadowing warrant strength.	Source-entropy and publisher-diversity scores; freshness and half-life distributions; redundancy and betweenness metrics in resource graphs; simulated failure-impact on task continuity.

continued on following page

Table 1. Continued

Theoretical Construct & Proponents	Unit of Analysis & Core Postulates	Operationalization in Human-AI Pedagogies	Design Heuristics & Governance Guardrails	Canonical Risks & Failure Modes	Representative Metrics & Instrumentation
Distributed Cognition (DCog) - Hutchins	Cognitive work is distributed across people, artifacts, and procedures; representational states and their transformations are constitutive of cognition.	Specify representational ecologies and authorized transformations; institute boundary checks between sensing, visualization, and modeling; synchronize multimodal views so text, audio, and graphics represent the same state accessibly.	Design external memory aids that mirror task topology; require verification after each transformation; preserve audit trails across modalities; enforce accessibility parity for all representations.	Transformation errors and representational drift; modality exclusion that marginalizes users; loss of traceability across toolchains; calibration decay in sensors.	Transformation-defect rate and reconciliation lag; calibration-adherence schedules; traceability completeness across pipelines; WCAG conformance scores and assistive-tech task-completion rates.
Human–AI Teaming - Salas; Burke; Lee & See; and Doshi-Velez & Kim	Team as a joint cognitive system with shared mental models; appropriate reliance through calibrated trust; explanations evaluated for stakeholder utility.	Capability cards and live-state panels expose agent goals, limits, and beliefs; uncertainty bounds and provenance indicators by default; dual-validation for high-stakes steps; counterfactual and why-not narratives tied to curricular concepts.	Design for interruptibility and correction; keep assessment authority human; make role assignment legible and reversible; operationalize trust calibration exercises; publish change logs and rollback plans.	Over-trust and automation bias; under-trust and tool underuse; "explanation theater" that feels plausible yet unhelpful; role confusion between human and agent.	Override and abstention rates; trust-calibration curves across tasks; explanation usefulness and contestation frequencies; error-caught-before-impact counts; demotion/pause events for agents.
Equity-Oriented Pedagogy (Dialogic, ZPD, UDL, CALP/BICS) - Freire; Vygotsky; CAST guidelines; and Cummins	Dialogic co-intentionality; scaffolding within the Zone of Proximal Development; variability-responsive design via multiple means of engagement, representation, and action; preservation of Cognitive Academic Language Proficiency.	Side-by-side translation that preserves register; scaffold-fading schedules and metacognitive prompts; multimodal input–output with captioning, alt text, and keyboard-first navigation; participatory evaluation and local or federated adaptation of models and lexicons.	Prioritize voice preservation and consent; staff accessibility and data-steward roles; publish failure modes and scope limits; distribute talk and task opportunities; ensure offline-first parity in low-bandwidth settings.	Linguistic flattening of minority registers; scaffold dependence; data colonialism via under-representative corpora; accommodation lag that shifts burden to disabled or multilingual learners.	Participation-parity and initiation balance; scaffold-fading index and independent-strategy uptake; accessibility-defect trendlines and remediation latency; caption/translation accuracy by language pair; opt-in/opt-out and federated-coverage rates.

Together these foundations specify the epistemic architecture for human–AI synergy in pedagogical collaboration. CSCL identifies the micro-practices of discourse and coordination that generate learning; Activity Theory situates those practices in systems whose rules and roles can be redesigned; Communities of Inquiry clarifies the presences to be cultivated and measured; Knowledge Building commits teams to collective responsibility for improving ideas; Connectivism and Distributed Cognition ground network and artifact design; Human–AI Teaming sets the conditions for role clarity, calibrated trust, and explainable coordination; and equity-focused pedagogy insists that all of this must expand participation and power rather than reproduce existing asymmetries (Goodwin, 2022; Ahram et al., 2024; Drosos et al., 2024). These are not abstract commitments. They are design constraints for multi-agent orchestration and cognitive equity, providing the criteria by which augmented collegiality in education can be built, governed, and continuously improved.

3. REFERENCE ARCHITECTURE FOR AI-AUGMENTED COLLABORATION

The reference architecture specifies how human roles, artificial agents, data flows, and institutional controls assemble into a coherent system that elevates collaboration rather than fragmenting it. It treats classrooms, studios, clinics, and field sites as sites of coordinated cognition where interfaces and services must reduce extraneous load, preserve instructor judgment, and widen participation (Aithal & Aithal, 2023; Gottschalk & Weise, 2023; Talwar, 2023). The architecture is layered to keep concerns separable while enabling traceable handoffs. Each layer exposes stable contracts grounded in widely adopted standards so that institutions can compose open components with vendor offerings without creating brittle dependencies (Table 2). The goal is a design that remains viable in low bandwidth conditions, aligns with privacy law in multiple jurisdictions, and supports multi agent orchestration with clear provenance and overrides.

Table 2. Eight-layer reference architecture for AI-augmented collaboration

Architectural Stratum & Scope	Principal Functions & Invariants	Human–AI Capabilities & Exemplars	Interoperability Anchors (Open Standards / Protocols)	Performance & Resilience SLOs (Target Envelopes)	Governance, Safety & Compliance Controls	Observability & Evaluation Telemetry
Experience Layer - Role-aware user surfaces for students, instructors, researchers	Maintain a unified "joint problem space" view that binds goals, artifacts, discourse, and next checkpoints; preserve accessibility as a first-class invariant rather than a retrofit; ensure adaptive scaffolds remain transparent and reversible.	Student UI affords low-friction contribution across modalities (text, voice with diarization, sketches, timestamped lab captures); instructor dashboards expose participation symmetry, equity flags, and agent status with pause/retune controls; research workbooks expose de-identified event streams for inquiry.	**Identity:** SAML, OpenID Connect for single sign-on and role mapping. **Accessibility:** WCAG 2.2 conformance for perceivable/ operable/ understandable/ robust content.	Interaction continuity under variable bandwidth; graceful degradation to text/captions/ snapshots; adaptive aids surfaced with explicit notices; low-latency state propagation sufficient for fluid turn-taking in seminars and studios.	Human override as a UI primitive; explicit disclosure labels for AI assistance; consent banners for data capture; semesterly accessibility audits with remediation plans; privacy-by-design defaults for view/ retention.	Talk-time symmetry and initiation dispersion; unresolved-item timelines; agent-intervention logs (accepted/ modified/ rejected); accessibility defect counts and fix latency; UI fall-back rates under constrained links.
Collaboration Services - Co-editing, whiteboarding, brainstorming, synchronous sessions	Guarantee consistency of shared artifacts under variable connectivity; sustain presence, locking, and conflict resolution without fragmenting histories; log rationale for convergence decisions.	Co-editing for structured/ freeform media using robust concurrency control; real-time whiteboards with shape recognition for formulae/circuits; embedded meeting + co-authoring surfaces; agent plug-ins that tag accessibility attributes and performance constraints during critique.	**Concurrency:** OT (Operational Transformation) or CRDTs for collaborative edits. **Telemetry:** xAPI and IMS Caliper verbs/ objects for uniform event emission. **Suite binding:** Native event adapters for Teams/ Workspace/Figma into a unified collaboration log.	Consistent document state during intermittent connectivity; whiteboard synchronization with conflict-free merges; seamless handoff between tools without identity or history loss.	Visible provenance for edits and decisions; role-based locks for high-stakes sections; institutional norms encoded for versioning and review; audit-ready capture of convergence matrices and rationales.	Edit-conflict frequency and auto-merge success; thread depth and closure rate; decision-audit pack completeness; cross-tool event alignment coverage; session continuity under packet loss.
Intelligence Layer - Generative, predictive, and recommender models under human primacy	Provide drafting/ translation/ visualization and predictive early-warning without usurping assessment; expose model scope, limits, and uncertainty via capability cards; log I/O hashes for auditability within retention windows.	Generative assistance for outlines, summaries, code explanations, and visualizations with provenance; predictors of dominance, deadline slippage, or topical drift; recommenders for resources/peers/ exemplars aligned to problem framing and learner profile.	**Model governance:** Capability cards (intended use, limitations, training scope, uncertainty signaling). **Provenance:** Content hashing for inputs/outputs; citation hooks to local corpora.	Low-friction inference suitable for formative flow; no automatic grade emission; evidence packs prepared for human judgment; stable fallbacks to local retrieval when external models are constrained.	Prohibition on summative grading by models; disclosure tags for AI-touched segments; retention ceilings for raw prompts/ outputs; selectable locally hosted models for sensitive domains (e.g., clinical narratives).	Early-warning precision/recall on collaboration risks; proportion of suggestions accepted/ edited/rejected; provenance completeness; model-swap rollback frequency; evidence-pack utilization in feedback.

Table 2. Continued

Architectural Stratum & Scope	Principal Functions & Invariants	Human–AI Capabilities & Exemplars	Interoperability Anchors (Open Standards / Protocols)	Performance & Resilience SLOs (Target Envelopes)	Governance, Safety & Compliance Controls	Observability & Evaluation Telemetry
Multi-Agent Orchestration - Coordinated artificial roles with human override	Coordinate facilitator, translator, ethicist, critic, motivator, and coach roles through a policy engine and message bus; represent every intervention as a first-class, inspectable event.	Facilitator manages timeboxes/ turn-taking/ topic cohesion; translator maintains parallel language tracks and modality conversions; ethicist performs bias/privacy checks; critic injects Toulmin-structured counters; motivator monitors affective lull signals and cues energizers.	**Policy & messaging:** Authenticated agent bus with visibility controls; templated role bundles selectable at kickoff; parameterizable thresholds per cohort.	Deterministic enforcement of pause/demote/ replace; tunable intervention density by project phase; stable behavior under concurrent agent interactions.	Human-in-the-loop as a hard constraint; rule identifiers on each action; waiver/ override with rationale; change-log publication for parameter shifts; alignment to local ethics/assessment policies.	Intervention acceptance ratio and time-to-resolution; equity-of-voice drift pre/ post facilitation; counterargument coverage; override/waiver rates with reasons; agent-to-agent chatter audits.
Data Layer - Learning records, knowledge graphs, credentials, privacy	Persist interaction histories and artifacts as queryable, durable assets; connect people/roles/ claims/evidence/ decisions via a knowledge graph; encode competencies as verifiable credentials.	Learning Record Store normalizes xAPI/ Caliper streams; knowledge graph enables	**Records & graphs:** xAPI, IMS Caliper, graph schemas. **Credentials:** W3C Verifiable Credentials; ledger-based registries (e.g., Blockcerts-style metadata) without on-chain PII. **Crypto:** Institution-managed keys in HSMs.	Low-latency analytic queries over recent cohorts; reliable export/replay for accreditation; policy-driven retention; cohort-level DP noise on dashboards where re-identification risk exists.	Data minimization; encryption at rest/in transit; differential privacy for aggregates; de-identification with structure preservation; subject access/ export; consent-bound archival/ purge; ethics-board-approved research access.	Event ingestion health; graph completeness (claim↔evidence link density); provenance integrity checks; credential issuance/ verification success; DP budget consumption and query refusal counts.
Integration Layer - LMS, libraries, sensors, archives, analytics, partners	Tie enterprise systems and external resources into a coherent pipeline without duplicating identity or fragmenting history; enable cross-border collaboration with data locality.	LMS roster/ grade/assignment sync; library and research database querying within license boundaries; IoT ingestion with device identities, calibration status, and sampling metadata; archival bundles for accreditation and teaching portfolios; federated gateways for partners.	**LMS:** LTI Advantage. **Identity:** SAML/ OIDC mapping to RBAC. **Library:** Secure APIs to catalogs/full-text indices. **IoT:** Device identity and metadata schemas; event bus ingestion to xAPI/Caliper.	Deterministic roster/grade flow; lossless archive export; resilient partner links with local processing and federated learning when law restricts transfers.	License boundary enforcement; access controls by role and purpose; partner data-processing agreements; audit trails for export/ import; lawful bases documented for each integration.	Sync success rates and drift alarms; archive integrity checksums; sensor uptime and calibration adherence; federated round participation logs; cross-system event alignment rates.

continued on following page

Table 2. Continued

Architectural Stratum & Scope	Principal Functions & Invariants	Human–AI Capabilities & Exemplars	Interoperability Anchors (Open Standards / Protocols)	Performance & Resilience SLOs (Target Envelopes)	Governance, Safety & Compliance Controls	Observability & Evaluation Telemetry
Infrastructure - Cloud/edge hybrid, XR pipelines, energy discipline	Deliver low-latency collaboration and XR comfort while surviving unstable backhaul; support offline-first drafting and conflict-aware sync; monitor energy and emissions.	Edge execution for captioning/ translation/ whiteboard sync; mobile fallbacks that suppress high-frame-rate video and favor audio/ captions; XR scene rendering locally with adaptive cloud streaming for complex scenes; offline queues with deterministic conflict rules.	**Compute fabric:** Cloud + campus edge; pedagogical appliances in rural schools. **XR:** Client pipelines with adaptive streaming. **Energy:** Telemetry for compute hours and lab draw.	Sub-100 ms round-trips for interactive editing on campus; XR frame pacing at comfort thresholds (e.g., sustained high-refresh where devices permit); robust reconnect semantics; delta-encoded whiteboard snapshots under narrow pipes.	Scheduled maintenance windows; capacity tests at timetable peaks; carbon-aware scheduling for batch jobs; device lifecycle and spares management; accessibility parity across device classes.	Uptime/error budgets by service; reconnect success after link loss; XR comfort incidents vs. frame pacing; kWh per student-credit and per XR-lab hour; edge vs. cloud workload proportions.
Security & Governance - Identity, authorization, audit, legal alignment	Keep the socio-technical stack trustworthy across jurisdictions; enforce least-privilege access; render sensitive operations tamper-evident and reviewable.	MFA for privileged roles; fine-grained RBAC scopes (export logs, instantiate agents, access de-identified sets); vulnerability scanning and timely patching with instructional-calendar-aware windows; transparency labels for AI-assisted segments in student work.	**Legal frames:** GDPR principles, FERPA obligations, India's DPDP Act requirements; institutional IRB workflows. **Audit:** Tamper-evident logs; change-management registers.	Session timeouts aligned to campus policy; rapid containment/ notification objectives for qualifying incidents; steady-state audit cadence by a cross-functional committee (faculty, students, data stewards).	Notice/consent and purpose limitation; student rights of access/ correction/ deletion; accessibility oversight cycles; disclosure-based academic integrity (reflective appendices rather than automated verdicts); red-team and tabletop exercises.	Privilege-escalation alerts; patch-latency and vulnerability burn-down; incident count/ severity and remediation SLAs; accessibility audit pass rates; disclosure-compliance prevalence in summative artifacts.

These layers, taken together, supply a coherent system in which learners can see where they are in a collaborative journey, teachers can guide with evidence and discretion, agents can contribute transparently within negotiated bounds, and institutions can meet their fiduciary duties to protect people and knowledge (Saad et al., 2025; Summers et al., 2025; Veles, 2022). The architecture is not a straitjacket. It is a set of commitments that make augmented collegiality operational across disciplines, degrees of connectivity, and regulatory contexts, while leaving room for local curricular identity and pedagogical craft.

4. TECHNOLOGY MODULES AND CAPABILITIES

The technology modules translate epistemic commitments into concrete capabilities that reduce extraneous load, widen participation, and make collaboration accountable. Each module is framed as a set of functions, reliability targets, and guardrails that align with the reference architecture while remaining viable in low bandwidth and high variability contexts (Table 3). The intent is not to showcase gadgets, but to specify dependable services that teachers can trust, students can master, and institutions can govern.

Table 3. Technology Modules, Pedagogical Functions, and Capabilities

Technology Module & Scope	Pedagogical Functions	Reliability / SLO Envelope	Guardrails & Ethics	KPIs & Telemetry
Generative AI - co-authoring, formative feedback, code explain/explain-fix, multilingual drafting	Outline scaffolds; rubric-anchored diffs; test-trace diagnostics; minimal code patches; parallel originals/ translations for CALP	Median latency ≤ 500 ms (text), ≤ 1 s (small image); line/file-level provenance hashes; caption WER ≤ 10% (planned), ≤ 15% (seminar); diarization ≥ 90%	No auto-grading; disclosure labels; evidence packs only; novice-mode Socratic prompts; instructor-pinned style/models	Suggestion accept/ modify/reject rates; minimal-diff ratio; provenance completeness; feedback TAT; override/waiver counts
XR Collaboration - immersive labs, clinics, studios	Pre-brief roles + safety; shared 3D whiteboards; replay of decision points with synchronized vitals/states; desktop parity	72–90 FPS; motion-to-photon < 20 ms; glass-to-glass < 50 ms; prioritized sync for shared events; intelligible spatial audio under load	Mandatory debriefs; vetted agent personas; all interventions logged; inclusive fallback to 2D scenes	Comfort incidents vs FPS/latency; participation symmetry; replay utilization; escalation-time to threshold; access parity XR↔desktop
IoT & Sensors - citizen science, lab telemetry, fieldwork	PM2.5/PM10 @ 1 Hz; stream levels @ 60 s (5-min agg); soil moisture @ 15 min (+ event spikes); provenance via device IDs, calibration history, firmware hashes	LoRa-class links; gateway store-and-forward with checksums; weekly calibration vs reference; geolocation quantization/fuzzing	Cameras off by default; mics as event detectors; consent for exceptions; placement metadata (street canyon, canopy)	Uptime & drift vs reference; anomaly precision (events/festivals); annotation density + confirmation; exposure deltas across micro-sites
Analytics Dashboards - process visibility, argumentation maps	Equity-of-voice (talk-time, turns, overlap); reply-depth/dispersion; Q→A latency; Toulmin claim–reason–evidence–rebuttal maps	No grades; every visual has method explainer + thresholds; evidence packs for feedback	Civility/stance only (no personality inference); instructor suppression of misleading signals; multilingual, SR-friendly views	Gini < 0.40 target; unresolved-item backlog; checkpoint time-to-closure; argument-completeness index; intervention uptake & effect size
Privacy-Preserving Tech - DP, federated/split learning, local RAG	Course DP budgets; on-device adaptation (captioning/feedback phrasing) with secure aggregation; campus vector stores for vetted retrieval	DP ε set per course; query refusal on budget exhaust; secure aggregation with cohort thresholds; HSM-managed keys; hard-delete (key shredding)	Opt-in for model improvement; student data exports/ corrections; clear mandatory vs research processing; periodic third-party audits	DP budget burn + noise simulators; FL round participation & convergence; deletion/export SLA; access-control alerts; low-confidence caption/ translation flags

Together these modules anchor a system that is at once capable and humble. Generative agents draft, explain, and translate without usurping authorship or assessment. XR environments make complex worlds present without drowning students in sensations that mask structure. Sensor networks extend inquiry to authentic contexts while honoring the privacy of communities and learners (Karakose et al., 2023; Padovano & Cardamone, 2024). Dashboards render participation and reasoning visible so that teams can steer their own process. Privacy tools turn promises into mathematics and code. Each element is specified with reliability and safety targets that teachers and students can understand, test, and trust, which is the practical meaning of augmented collegiality.

5. DESIGN PATTERNS FOR AI-ENHANCED COLLABORATIVE LEARNING

Design patterns translate theory and architecture into repeatable practices that instructors, students, and technologists can adopt without guesswork (Hutson & Plate, 2023; Chiu & Rospigliosi, 2025; Järvelä et al., 2023). Each pattern below specifies purpose, a realistic scenario, the end-to-end workflow with human and agent roles, the instruments that make the work auditable, the principal risks with mitigation, and the evidence strategy that decides whether to keep, adapt, or retire the pattern in a given context (Table 4). Patterns are intended to be mixed and sequenced. Orchestration agents remain configurable, interventions are always logged to the collaboration record, and teachers retain authority for assessment and pastoral judgment.

Table 4. Eight AI-collaboration patterns - intent, roles, KPIs, risks, go/no-go.

Design Pattern	Pedagogical Intent	Minimal Scenario	Workflow Split (Human vs Agent)	Telemetry KPIs (Auditable)	Risks → Mitigations; Go/No-Go Rule
AI Facilitator	Stabilize process, equalize voice, reduce extraneous load, timebox to closure	Grad seminar briefs urban-heat plan over 4 weeks	Instructor selects template, checkpoints, equity targets; agent renders live agenda, flags unresolved items, nudges quieter members, assigns micro-tasks; chair overrides or pauses	Talk-time Gini, initiation and overlap ratios, Q→A latency, checkpoint hit rate, unresolved-item backlog	Over-scripting, cultural misfit → fading schedule, student-invoked pause, pre-brief norms; **Go** if backlog ↓ and Gini → balance with blind product parity; **No-Go** if tone suppression or latency spikes persist
AI Critic	Inoculate against premature consensus via Toulmin counters and warrant exposure	Econ capstone on counter-cyclical policy	Students draft claims; agent flags warrantless assertions, generates counters, runs short adversarial round; students accept/weaken/reject with rationale	Argument-completeness %, claim↔counter coverage, instructor flags resolved, time cost per revision	False balance, adversarial tone → relevance bands, civility lexicon; **Go** if completeness ↑ without timeline overrun and transfer holds; **No-Go** if counters ignored or tone degrades
AI Translator	CALP-preserving multilingual parity; voice retention	Cross-border nursing sim with live captions and parallel notes	Agent diarizes, applies domain glossaries, shows phrase-aligned originals + translations; teacher reviews low-confidence spans; students toggle literal vs idiomatic	Caption WER, diarization %, time-to-clarity, participation share by language, domain-term correctness in reflections	Med-name or entity errors, voice flattening → hard lexicons, human confirm for critical terms, default parallel view; **Go** if comprehension parity and balanced turns; **No-Go** if parity gaps persist

continued on following page

Table 4. Continued

Design Pattern	Pedagogical Intent	Minimal Scenario	Workflow Split (Human vs Agent)	Telemetry KPIs (Auditable)	Risks → Mitigations; Go/No-Go Rule
AI Consensus Builder	Structure multi-criteria deliberation; make trade-offs and dissent explicit	Materials choice in engineering studio	Agent elicits and normalizes criteria, builds option×criterion matrix, requires evidence, withholds tallies until density adequate; two-round vote with contingencies logged	Audit-pack completeness, inter-rater weight agreement, decision stability under small weight perturbations, evidence density	Anchoring, numerology → anonymous initial prefs, rotated order, narrative rationales beside scores; **Go** if downstream tests validate and stability holds; **No-Go** if instability or post-hoc rationalization dominates
AI Simulation Engine	Safe rehearsal of negotiation, crisis response; replayable causality	City–union budget renegotiation with agent personas	Instructor sets roles, red lines, event cards; engine adapts stances, injects bounded surprises, enforces time pressure; replay with revealed goals; role swap run	Offers/ commitments ledger, fairness indicator, replay utilization, dead-end move rate	Stereotype drift, cognitive overload → vetted corpora, content filters, adjustable complexity, mandatory pre-brief; **Go** if transfer gains and dead-ends ↓; **No-Go** if harmful leakage or overload remains
AI Librarian	Provenance-enforced curation; search strategy scaffolds	Methods seminar sourcing standards and studies	Students pose info need; agent issues structured queries to licensed indexes, ranks by topicality–methods–recency, compels inclusion/ exclusion reasons; maintains knowledge map linked to claims	Source diversity (journal/ publisher), recency curve, license compliance, knowledge-map linkage to argument nodes	Abstract over-reliance, paywall leakage → methods-first skim drills, lawful routes only with logs; **Go** if evidence–claim alignment strong and rejections principled; **No-Go** if superficial citation persists

continued on following page

Table 4. Continued

Design Pattern	Pedagogical Intent	Minimal Scenario	Workflow Split (Human vs Agent)	Telemetry KPIs (Auditable)	Risks → Mitigations; Go/No-Go Rule
AI Ethics Sentinel	In-flow protection: privacy, bias, accessibility, inference hygiene	Psych survey drafting with consent and UI checks	Agent scans against policy and WCAG, flags with severity; prompts consent text, anonymization, withdrawal routes; instructor resolves or waives with rationale	False-pos/neg rates, remediation SLA, audit defect counts, waiver frequency with reasons	Over-blocking, moralizing tone → severity gradation, neutral procedural voice, educator override as learning artifact; **Go** if IRB fixes and accessibility defects ↓; **No-Go** if noise remains high
AI Metacognitive Coach	Internalize plan–monitor–reflect in teams	First-year design sprint to prototype + narrative	Coach elicits goals, roles, checkpoints; proposes editable task graph; detects slippage from sparse commits or shallow threads; prompts targeted retros; fades as stability emerges	On-time checkpoint %, planned/unplanned task ratio, surge index near deadlines, reflection specificity and follow-through	Dependence, privacy creep → scheduled fading, prompt withholding tests, private scope reminders; **Go** if adherence without prompts ↑ and surges ↓; **No-Go** if dependency or noise persists

Taken together, these patterns operationalize augmented collegiality as a disciplined practice rather than a slogan. The facilitator keeps process visible and fair. The critic inoculates against fragile reasoning. The translator expands authorship across languages. The consensus builder turns deliberation into defensible decisions. The simulation engine compresses experience into safe, repeatable practice (Nguyen et al., 2024; Molenaar, 2024; Oravec, 2023). The librarian anchors claims in credible knowledge. The ethics sentinel makes protection routine. The metacognitive coach grows durable self-regulation. Each pattern is auditable through shared instruments, adaptable through exposed parameters, and accountable to outcomes that matter for learning and equity. Institutions can adopt them incrementally, measure their value, and evolve the repertoire as disciplines and cohorts demand.

6. IMPLEMENTATION BLUEPRINT

A viable blueprint turns principles and patterns into operational practice that survives semesters, audits, bandwidth fluctuations, staff turnover, and vendor churn. The objective is disciplined rollout with verifiable learning value, credible protections, and steady total cost of ownership. The pathway differs for universities and schools, yet the backbone is shared. Institutions select a narrow set of use cases, instrument them with the same data model, enforce clear disclosure and override rules, and build staff capability alongside technical capacity (Table 5). The following tracks present concrete pathways with sequenced milestones, maturity stages, staffing compositions, and procurement criteria that keep the system adaptable and accountable.

Table 5. Implementation blueprint - domains, milestones, roles, guardrails, and KPIs

Domain / Scope	Core Moves & Exemplar Use-Cases	Milestones & Go/ No-Go Gates	Roles & Capacity (Lean FTE Archetypes)	Guardrails (Operationalized)	KPIs for Scale / Exit
Higher education - capstones, studios, seminars, cross-border research, faculty governance	Capstones run Facilitator + Critic + Consensus + Librarian + Ethics; XR for spatial critiques; IoT telemetry for prototypes; seminars use structured counters and parallel translation; governance adopts auditable criteria matrices; federated learning for sensitive multi-site data	Term-0 connect SSO/LTI, disclose retention/override; Term-1 instrument 1–2 courses, produce decision audit packs; Term-2 replicate in parallel section and committee workflow; Go if closure quality↑, equity drift → balance, zero P1 ethics/accessibility incidents; Hold on process latency; Stop on breaches or outcome decay	AI learning engineer; faculty fellow; data steward; accessibility coordinator; platform/integration engineer; library integrator	Disclosure-based integrity, no auto-grading; human override/pause; licensed-only retrieval; privacy by design with minimization and retention windows; federated routes where law restricts transfer; parallel-text translation to preserve voice	Product parity/↑ under blind review; unresolved-item backlog↓; talk-time Gini→≤0.40; zero P1 incidents; replication success across a second section; Exit vendor on export/replay failure or persistent accessibility defects
K–12 - project-based learning, climate/ sustainability units, peer tutoring, literacy circles	Climate nodes for air/weather; role-rotating facilitation; translator for emergent bilinguals; Ethics Sentinel for geoprivacy and survey hygiene; metacognitive coach for plan–monitor–reflect; offline-first sync for constrained schools	Phase A family notices and opt-outs, gateway install, weekly calibration ritual; Phase B 4–6 week unit with evidence packs; Phase C propagate to tutoring/literacy; Go on comprehension parity and balanced participation; Hold on noisy instrumentation; Stop on privacy or accessibility regressions	Lead teacher; district edtech lead; regional coach; accessibility lead; data steward	Child-safe defaults: quantized geolocation, cameras off, mics as event detectors; caption/translation confidence flags; teacher-controlled disclosures; no detection-evidence packs for narrative feedback	Participation parity across language groups; calibration adherence; confirmed anomaly annotations; teacher-rated process clarity↑; accessibility defect trendlines↓; Exit failing sensor SKUs (drift above thresholds)

continued on following page

Table 5. Continued

Domain / Scope	Core Moves & Exemplar Use-Cases	Milestones & Go/ No-Go Gates	Roles & Capacity (Lean FTE Archetypes)	Guardrails (Operationalized)	KPIs for Scale / Exit
Maturity model - staged capability (L0→L4)	L0 fragmented tools; L1 unified surface + identity + xAPI; L2 low-stakes agents and dashboards; L3 argumentation, consensus, simulation, IoT plus DP/federation; L4 bounded autonomous orchestration with revocable actions	Gate L1→L2 when unified logs yield specific feedback and learner-perceived process visibility↑; L2→L3 when argument completeness↑ and equity improves without silencing dissent, no boundary breaches; L3→L4 after a semester with unresolved decisions↓, outcomes ≥ baseline, zero P1 ethics/accessibility defects	Oversight committee (faculty, students, data/accessibility stewards); release manager; QA for diarization / translation / event alignment	Policy engine enforces who can instantiate/retune agents; change-advisory cadence; rollback rehearsals for model/agent swaps; autonomy-last principle	Gate metrics: argument-completeness index; decision stability under perturbation; DP budget observability; federated round participation; zero cross-boundary data flows; Hold at mission-fit level to avoid automation creep
Staffing & capability - durable human infrastructure	Central team sized to active load: university 6–10 specialists for ~100 courses/ year once patterns stabilize; district ~5 central plus regional coordinators; rotation/succession to avoid key-person risk	Standing office hours; micro-institutes on facilitation, prompt craft, ethics, accessibility; tabletop drills (caption failure, translation error, FL misconfig); portfolio artifacts (orchestration brief, accessible materials, incident memo)	AI learning engineer; data steward; accessibility coordinator; platform/ identity/integration engineer; faculty fellows/lead teachers; library/records integrator; regional coach	SOPs for consent/ retention/export; WCAG audit cadence; IRB/ethics templates; capability-card literacy; analytics-as-signals training to avoid surveillance	Instructor time saved; MTTR for accessibility defects/ incidents; PD completion with artifacts; adoption of preflight checks/ disclosures/evidence packs; Scale staff with active use, not seat counts
Procurement & interop - modular, portable, auditable	Shell platform that calls multiple STT/ MT/LMMs; campus-controlled vector stores; instructor-selectable engines by language/domain	Contract for LTI Advantage, xAPI/ Caliper, SAML/ OIDC, export/ replay; disclose model families, processing locales, training scope; rights to substitute/ host models; SLAs for latency/uptime; pricing tied to active use/compute; pilot debrief exit	Vendor must pass WCAG 2.2 AA; keyboard-only operability; high-quality captions; E2E transport encryption; encryption at rest with institution keys; MFA, RBAC, tamper-evident logs	No foundation-model training on student work without explicit opt-in; minimization, configurable retention, de-ID for analytics; incident reporting and joint exercises; independent evaluation cooperation	Interop verified (export/replay); accessibility pass rate; latency within SLA at timetable peaks; successful model-swap rehearsal; evidence of learning/equity gains in pilot; Exit on breach or non-remediation
Rollout governance - cadence, risk, evidence	Semesterly review of change logs, audit packs, incident summaries; publish community-readable reports; rehearse failover for captioning, translation, and agent policy failures	Term-based checkpoints: evidence memo, ethics/accessibility report, carbon/ energy snapshot; green/yellow/red scale decisions with remediation owners and dates	Cross-functional board with student voice; legal and infosec liaison; sustainability officer for energy reporting	Human-in-the-loop for high-stakes steps; transparency labels; carbon-aware scheduling for batch jobs; device lifecycle and spares plans	Learning: transfer parity/↑; Equity: Gini→≤0.40, language-parity; Safety: zero P1; Sustainability: kWh per student-credit trending↓; Decision: scale if two cycles sustain; sunset if two fail with no corrective trend

A disciplined implementation blueprint aligns ambition with capacity and risk with protection. Higher education begins where collaborative authorship and defensible decision making already matter and builds from seminars to studios to governance.

Schools begin in project based learning and peer tutoring, with strong privacy defaults and offline first operation where needed (Atchley et al., 2024; Kim, 2024; Kim et al., 2022). The maturity model paces automation with evidence and puts a premium on human authority. Staffing plans resource pedagogy, governance, and accessibility as much as code. Procurement locks in interoperability, transparency, and exit routes. The result is an ecosystem that grows capability without eroding trust, that expands authorship without sacrificing rigor, and that supplies a stable foundation for the patterns and research that follow.

7. MEASUREMENT, EVIDENCE, AND RESEARCH DESIGN

The measurement strategy anchors augmented collegiality in auditable practice rather than assertion. Evidence must show that orchestration agents improve collaborative process without diluting disciplinary rigor, that learning gains generalize beyond coached tasks, and that equity advances for learners across bandwidths, languages, and abilities (Wu et al., 2024; Karakose et al., 2023; Ji et al., 2023). A defensible program therefore specifies a logic model linking inputs to long run impact, defines process and product indicators grounded in collaboration science, instruments the environment with reliable event semantics, and adopts research designs that can withstand methodological scrutiny (Table 6). The same system must support classroom feedback cycles measured in days and institutional accountability horizons measured in years. What follows operationalizes that requirement.

Table 6. Measurement & research design: strands, indicators, data, inference, and decisions

Measurement Strand	Scope & Unit	Key Indicators (Compact)	Data & Semantics (Minimal Contract)	Design & Inference	Decision Rules (Go / Hold / Stop)
Logic Model	Inputs → Processes → Outputs → Outcomes → Impact at course / program scale	Audit-pack completeness; unresolved-item backlog↓; accessibility defects↓; sensor provenance integrity; transfer deltas↑; progression/attrition deltas; carbon per credit	xAPI / Caliper streams; knowledge-graph links (people–roles–claims–evidence–decisions); caption WER; diarization conf.; energy meters; consent/retention metadata	DBR cycles + matched panels; blind external reviews for products; longitudinal cohorts	**Go** when outputs and outcomes hit thresholds without P1 safety/access failures; **Hold** for redesign if lag; **Stop** and retire elements with cost↑/effect≈0
Collaboration Quality	Small group as unit across sync talk + async text	Symmetry: talk-time Gini ≤ 0.40, initiation dispersion, overlap; Grounding: decision → artifact lag ≤ 48h; Regulation: on-time checkpoints, planned:unplanned ratio; Epistemic discipline: claim + warrant + counter + resolution	Utterance events (ID, timestamps, diarization conf.); document spans (claim/ warrant/rebuttal); decision objects (options–criteria–votes–rationale); checkpoint events aligned to task graph	Mixed-methods dashboards; section-level randomization where feasible	**Fade** facilitation when symmetry/ grounding stabilize; **Rotate** roles if skew persists; **Require** counters before convergence; annotate justified waivers
Learning Outcomes	Learner & team: conceptual transfer, 21C skills, belonging	Transfer under changed surface features; Creativity = idea diversity → constraint-anchored convergence; Critical thinking = warrant density + counterfactuals; Collaboration = parity post-fade + blind product quality; Belonging = scale shifts, optional-space persistence	Blind grading; transfer tasks; contribution timelines (commits/ edits/meetings); viva/orals; belonging surveys with de-IDs	RCTs or matched cohorts; external examiners; microanalysis of sensemaking for mechanism	**Accept** if transfer/ product quality↑ and belonging↑ with no inflation; **Protect** summative tasks (disclosure required); **Remediate** if parity collapses after scaffold fade
Equity Measures	Course–cohort–institution across language, bandwidth, disability, gender	Weekly participation parity (not one-shot); caption accuracy & translation confidence; comprehension parity; session success under low bandwidth; offline-sync success; WCAG defects/100 screens + fix SLA; DIF/rubric audits; enrolment / retention / progression deltas; vendor language/ dialect support	Caption/translation telemetry; offline logs; accessibility audits; LMS extracts; procurement registries	Stepped-wedge deployments; DIF analyses; participatory evaluation with affected communities	**Scale** when parity gains create no new gaps; **Enforce** geoprivacy defaults (quantized location, cameras off in K–12 fieldwork); **Escalate** vendors on accessibility SLA breaches

continued on following page

Table 6. Continued

Measurement Strand	Scope & Unit	Key Indicators (Compact)	Data & Semantics (Minimal Contract)	Design & Inference	Decision Rules (Go / Hold / Stop)
Methodologies	Programmatic blend of rigor + realism	DBR (conjecture → intervention → analysis); section RCTs; matched/ stepped-wedge designs; ethnography for mechanism; triangulation	Pre-analysis plans; power checks; fidelity logs of pattern params; contamination monitoring; blind inter-rater protocols; reflexive memos	Causal claims only where warranted; mechanism claims require triangulated traces; nulls reported	**Continue/ Adapt/Retire** by pre-set MDEs and qualitative plausibility; **Stop** variants with adverse effects or ethical risk
Instrumentation & Reliability	Event semantics as evidence contract	Reliability: caption WER, diarization conf., translation conf., model latency; Traceability: claim ↔ warrant ↔ decision links; Provenance: sensor calibration hashes	Pseudonymous IDs; de-ID pipelines; DP on cohort dashboards; researcher datasets (schemas + dictionaries); instructor evidence packs; student data exports; versioned replays	Threshold alerts; reproducible exports; retention/purge per policy; ethics approvals tagged	**Quarantine** analytics below reliability thresholds; **Recalibrate** before high-stakes use; **Version** instrumentation changes with change logs; **Approve** archives each term

A measurement program with these elements produces credible judgments about augmented collegiality. It shows when facilitation should fade because teams self-regulate, when translation has equalized authorship rather than masking asymmetry, when consensus building has prevented expedient but fragile choices, and when privacy safeguards are strong enough to support research without exploitation (Dhanasekaran, 2025; Molenaar, 2022a; Molenaar, 2022b). It supplies instructors with timely, actionable signals, researchers with semantically rich traces, administrators with accountability evidence, and students with clear records of their growth as collaborators. Most importantly, it keeps attention on the work that matters by turning collaboration into something that can be seen, discussed, and improved in public rather than guessed at in private.

8. GOVERNANCE, LEGAL, ETHICS, AND SAFETY

Educational collaboration that embeds multi-agent systems must be governed by data stewardship that treats student work as protected academic record rather than raw material for product improvement. Institutions designate a data controller who sets the lawful basis for processing and appoint a data protection officer with authority to halt deployments that violate policy (Kumar et al., 2023; Kim & Lee, 2023; Holstein & Aleven, 2022). A defensible operating model begins with a record of processing activities that names systems, categories of data, purposes, legal bases, recipients, retention periods, and transfer mechanisms. Fairness is a governance duty rather than an afterthought. Large language and speech models display measurable performance gaps across dialects, accents, and low-resource languages, which can silence or mischaracterize students (Fui-Hoon Nah et al., 2023; Kim & Cho, 2025; Zhang et al., 2022). A compliant program formalizes an algorithmic impact assessment before deployment and repeats it after major updates. Academic integrity policies must incorporate generative assistance without criminalizing legitimate drafting support (Table 7). Institutions publish plain-language rules that distinguish formative assistance from summative authorship and require disclosure statements in assessments that document which tools were used, for what purpose, and why suggestions were accepted or rejected. Accessibility is a non-negotiable quality property.

Table 7. Anchors, Controls, Risks, Metrics, and Gates

Governance Pillar	Legal / Policy Anchors	Operational Controls	Risk → Mitigation	Verification Metrics	Go / Hold / Stop Gates
Data privacy & stewardship	GDPR (2016), FERPA (1974), India DPDP (2023), PIPEDA, LGPD, POPIA; EU SCC (2021)	RoPA; DPIA; controller + DPO; purpose-bound consent; minimization; pseudonyms with HSM keys; retention tiers (telemetry vs artifacts); opt-in only for FM training; IRB-gated de-ID research; portability exports	Over-collection, unlawful reuse, re-ID, vendor drift → minimization at source; DP cohorts; contractual retention; dual-control keys	DPIA/RoPA coverage; export/erase SLA; breach MTTD/MTTR + 72-h notify; DP ε usage; % datasets de-ID; SCC coverage	**Go** when DPIA complete + zero P1; **Hold** on mapping/retention gaps; **Stop** on unlawful processing or missed breach notice
Bias, fairness & accountability	Algorithmic Impact Assessments; model registry + capability cards; meaningful human review	Stratified WER (accent/dialect); translation confidence by pair; triage parity checks; lexicon constraints; low-confidence flags; rollback authority; participatory audits	Accent underperformance, clinical term drift, triage skew → accent-tuned ASR; domain glossaries + human confirm; parity tuning + rollback	ΔFPR/ΔFNR; WER by accent; med-term accuracy; appeals turnaround; rollback frequency	**Go** if parity gaps shrink + term accuracy ≥ threshold; **Hold** for targeted tuning; **Stop** if high-risk errors persist
Academic integrity & assessment transparency	Disclosure-based integrity; updated honor code; ban "AI detection" accusations; due-process	Assistance rubrics; evidence packs (versions, logs); viva/orals; randomized/authentic tasks; narrow, time-limited proctoring with encryption	False positives, contract cheating, invasive proctoring → process triangulation; viva spot-checks; privacy-lite security	Disclosure compliance; blind-grade concordance; false-accusation rate; proctoring incident rate	**Go** if blind quality holds/↑ and disclosures high; **Hold** on unclear patterns; **Stop** invasive proctoring lacking necessity/accommodation
Accessibility & inclusive design	WCAG 2.2 AA; ISO/IEC XR ergonomics; campus AT policies	Keyboard-only paths; focus order/skip links; captions WER <10% planned, <15% seminar; diarization ≥90%; alt text + MathML/LaTeX; color-independence; XR desktop parity; parallel-text translation (register-preserving)	SR traps, caption drift, XR discomfort, voice flattening → termly AT audits; telemetry alerts; comfort presets; parallel view default	Defects/100 screens; remediation SLA; AT task success; WER/diarization; XR comfort incidents; language parity	**Go** if defects trend ↓ and AT success high; **Hold** on SLA slippage; **Stop** release on critical accessibility regressions

continued on following page

Table 7. Continued

Governance Pillar	Legal / Policy Anchors	Operational Controls	Risk → Mitigation	Verification Metrics	Go / Hold / Stop Gates
Ethics frameworks & safety	UNESCO AI Ethics (2021); EU AI Act (2024); NIST AI RMF 1.0 (2023); ISO/IEC 23894:2023; COPPA; PPRA	Risk tiering; impact assessments; model/system cards; content moderation + escalation; in-product help lines; XR SOPs; red-team/jailbreak tests; tabletop drills; semester transparency reports	Harmful content, XR physical risk, jailbreak exfiltration, minors' survey sensitivity → filters+human review; space protocols; adversarial testing; child-specific gates	Incident count/ severity; containment time; red-team fix rate; drill pass rate; policy update cadence	**Go** with mitigations verified; **Hold** pending fixes; **Stop** on unresolved high-severity safety findings
Cross-border data & incident response	EU SCC (2021); adequacy decisions; residency mandates; breach standards	Data-flow maps; federated learning for sensitive sets; DLP on egress; SIEM + 24×7 on-call; playbooks (containment, comms); post-mortems with actions	Unlawful transfer, slow detection, poor comms → federated routes; lawful bases; alerting + 72-h notify; comms templates	Lawful-flow attestations; federated round participation; MTTD/MTTR; drill frequency; action-closure rate	**Go** when flows lawful + drills pass; **Hold** on mapping/ controls gaps; **Stop** any cross-border processing lacking valid mechanism

A governance program with these properties makes augmented collegiality safe, lawful, and equitable. Privacy is engineered through minimization, consent, and provable protections. Fairness is monitored and improved with audits that name harms and fix them. Integrity is preserved through disclosure-based assessment and human judgment (Adams et al., 2023; Fügener et al., 2022; Jeon & Lee, 2023). Accessibility is treated as a primary design constraint that expands authorship. Ethics frameworks are translated into living procedures that survive audits and crises. The result is a culture where human authority and care guide machine assistance, where students and faculty can see and challenge system behavior, and where collaboration becomes more open, rigorous, and just rather than more opaque.

9. COST, SUSTAINABILITY, AND ROI

A credible program for augmented collegiality requires a cost model that institutions can verify, an energy and carbon profile that leadership can govern, and a return framework that finance offices and academic senates accept as evidence for continued investment. Costs are not confined to licenses and servers. They include staffing for pedagogy, data stewardship, and accessibility, content development for XR and simulation, security and privacy audits, and change management for faculty and students (Yang et al., 2023; Tzirides et al., 2024; Lee et al., 2025). Sustainability is not a slogan on a slide. It is a measured property of compute, devices, rooms, and supply chains that can be reduced through scheduling, configuration, and procurement choices. Return is not a single ratio. It is a portfolio of outcomes that includes time saved for instructors, improved student performance and persistence, greater inclusion for multilingual and disabled learners, and reduced rework in governance and accreditation (see Table 8). What follows translates these claims into operational accounting that a registrar, a chief information officer, and a dean can read the same way.

Table 8. Cost, sustainability, and ROI - levers, optimizations, KPIs, decision gates.

Strategic Theme	Cost Levers (CapEx vs OpEx)	Sustainability / Energy Tactics	Low-Resource Optimizations	KPIs / SLOs (Auditables)	Decision Gates (Go / Hold / Stop)
Total Cost of Ownership	CapEx: XR headsets, edge nodes, LoRa gateways, capture rigs, accessible retrofits (3–5 yr amort., 10–15% spares). OpEx: cloud inference/storage, STT/MT licenses, audits, PD, facilities.	Multitenant stack; pooled edge; XR labs timetabled; tiered speech/translation pricing; model right-sizing.	Offline-first clients; local RAG over syllabi/rubrics; delta-snapshot whiteboards; audio-first fallbacks.	Cost/active learner; cost/course; uptime/ latency SLOs; export/ replay verified.	**Go** when unit cost ↓ and SLOs met; **Hold** on audit/facilities creep; **Stop** if vendor blocks export/replay.
Staffing & Capacity	Lean core FTE: AI learning engineer, data steward, accessibility coordinator, platform/ integration engineer, faculty fellows; scale by active courses.	Shared services across colleges; rotation to avoid key-person risk; codified playbooks.	Asynchronous PD (captioned/ translated); templated briefs and redesign kits.	Instructor time saved/section; accessibility MTTR; incident MTTR; PD completion with artifacts.	**Grow** with verified uptake/time-saved; **Hold** if gains plateau; **Reallocate** toward accessibility/data to retire audit debt.
Compute / Models	Pin course-level models; prefer small/ medium instruction-tuned + retrieval; mix local/managed inference.	Carbon-aware batching; edge captioning; renewable-backed regions; aggressive cache/RAG.	CPU-grade ASR/MT; batch transcription; federated updates (no raw data egress).	$/1k tokens; $/audio min; p50/p95 latency; swap/rollback pass rate.	**Upgrade** only if cost, latency, quality all pass; **Rollback** on parity or latency regressions.
XR & Device Fleet	Shared carts/rooms; repair/spares pipeline; content reuse across courses; desktop parity mandatory.	Frame-pacing targets; smart power; EPEAT devices; recyclable components.	2D/overlay modes preserving task logic; device-class scene scaling.	Comfort incident rate; room utilization; repair TAT; reuse ratio; kWh/lab-hr.	**Use** XR where spatial/safety learning goals; **Suspend** scenes failing comfort/parity.
IoT & Sensors	Low-cost kits with device ID, firmware hash, calibration history; pooled gateways; spares for probes.	Weekly calibration; long-range low-power links; store-and-forward buffering.	Quantized geolocation; pooled cellular; sparse sampling with event spikes.	Uptime; drift vs reference; anomaly precision; annotation confirmation.	**Replace** SKUs exceeding drift thresholds; **Retain** rotating pools to cut idle inventory.
Energy & Carbon	Compute and room energy treated as program costs; CO2e via local factors.	Batch federation/fine-tuning in low-carbon windows; edge inference; schedule heavy jobs off-peak; sleep policies.	Smart power for labs; device fleet auto-sleep; minimal video defaults.	kWh/student-credit; CO2e/course; compute-hours by model; captioning minutes; XR lab hours.	**Set/meet** annual reduction targets; **Freeze** features that spike kWh without learning gains.
ROI & Valuation	Benefits: instructor time saved, reduced compliance rework, consolidation, persistence gains. Costs: amortized CapEx + OpEx.	Evidence packs replace ad-hoc synthesis; unified logs reduce accreditation rework.	Transfer tasks track generalization; process+product triangulation.	Payback; NPV at hurdle rate; sensitivity ranges; Monte Carlo bands.	**Continue** if NPV>0 (base+moderate cases) and payback ≤ 2 academic years; **Revise** if only tail cases pass.

continued on following page

Table 8. Continued

Strategic Theme	Cost Levers (CapEx vs OpEx)	Sustainability / Energy Tactics	Low-Resource Optimizations	KPIs / SLOs (Auditables)	Decision Gates (Go / Hold / Stop)
Financing / Procurement / Exit	Grants for CapEx; OpEx for cloud/ staff; consortia for STT/MT/storage; outcome-linked renewals cautiously.	Contract for LTI, xAPI/Caliper, SAML/ OIDC; vendor model/ system cards; export without penalty.	Per-active or concurrent user; shared audits; campus-controlled vector stores; switchable engines.	Interop test pass; accessibility pass; peak-time latency within SLA; model-swap rehearsal.	**Award** only with interop + accessibility + privacy + exit rights; **Exit** on breach or non-remediation.
Sustainability Governance & Lifecycle	Inventory with purchase/retire dates; repair before recycle; diversion reporting.	Modular/repairable devices; stocked spares; booking discipline to cut idle HVAC.	Lab energy dashboards; syllabus note on computing choices.	Diversion %; repair TAT; idle-power hours; awareness survey.	**Allocate** to meet quarterly targets; **Block** non-repairable shipments.
Risk & Contingency	Reserve for vendor exit, model swaps, legal updates, incidents; cyber coverage if suitable.	Tabletop drills; red-team; post-mortems with action closure; incident playbooks.	Pre-approved replatform/export; lexicon refresh pipelines; rapid policy addenda.	Drill pass rate; action-closure timeliness; breach MTTD/MTTR; replatform time.	**Pause** deployments exceeding risk thresholds; **Release** only after drills pass and actions close.

A program that attends to these cost, sustainability, and return disciplines builds credibility with faculty, students, and finance offices. Leaders can see where money goes and how it returns in learning, time, and equity. Educators can rely on resources arriving when promised and tools behaving within defined bounds. Students can trust that participation does not depend on owning the newest device or living near perfect bandwidth, and that their work does not carry hidden energy and privacy costs (Hitsuwari et al., 2023; Mittal et al., 2024; Baskara, 2024). The institution can show auditors and accreditors that obligations have been met and that improvements are not accidents but the result of measured design.

10. CONCLUSION AND FUTURES AGENDA

Augmented collegiality is advanced as a design commitment in which teachers, students, and artificial agents coordinate around shared intellectual labour that stays answerable to human purposes and professional judgment, while future work concentrates on making that commitment technically and institutionally durable. Traditions of collaborative learning, activity systems, communities of inquiry, knowledge building, connectivist networks, distributed cognition, human machine teaming, and equity centred pedagogy reframe classrooms, studios, and clinics as hybrid cognitive systems whose roles, rules, and representations are tuned for transparency, inclusivity, and rigor. Practical meaning appears wherever discourse, artefacts, and decisions are braided into traceable knowledge fabrics, and where facilitation, critique, translation, retrieval, simulation, and metacognition reduce extraneous load while strengthening warrants and counterarguments. The forward agenda extends this architecture through multimodal perception that improves shared attention without discomfort, federated pedagogy that raises captioning and translation quality without centralising raw student data, calibrated digital twins that allow rehearsal of high stakes procedures, and bounded autonomy that keeps human purposes, uncertainty signals, and refusal capacities at the centre of joint activity rather than its periphery.

Operational instantiation translates principle into craft through layered architectures, dependable modules, measured patterns, and disciplined rollout, while a concrete research programme supplies thresholds, metrics, and safeguards that make claims contestable. Role aware surfaces, collaboration services, and an intelligence layer with capability cards, uncertainty signalling, and provenance keep machine contributions legible, while data and integration services preserve learning records, knowledge graphs, and laboratory traces with minimisation, de identification, and privacy preserving computation. Governance, accreditation, and cost discipline stabilise practice through consent, retention limits, algorithmic audits across accents and languages, disclosure-based integrity in place of brittle detection, shared services, edge inference, and carbon aware scheduling that lowers energy per student credit. Future work remains specific and measurable as multimodal perception that meets classroom comfort and intelligibility thresholds, federated adaptation that improves feedback without centralising student work, digital twins calibrated to variables that actually change learning, and bounded autonomy that preserves shared mental models, uncertainty signals, provenance, and refusal. Where ethics, equity, efficiency, and evidence coexist, augmented collegiality becomes institutional routine rather than speculative aspiration.

REFERENCES

Adams, C., Pente, P., Lemermeyer, G., & Rockwell, G. (2023). Ethical principles for artificial intelligence in K-12 education. *Comput. Educ. Artif. Intell.*, *4*, 100131. DOI: 10.1016/j.caeai.2023.100131

Ahram, T., Casarotto, L., & Costa, P. (2024). Human Interaction and Emerging Technologies (IHIET 2024): Proceedings of the 12th International Conference on Human Interaction and Emerging Technologies, IHIET 2024, August 26-28, 2024, IUAV University of Venice, Italy. *AHFE INTERNATIONAL, 157*, 1-623.

Aithal, P. S., & Aithal, S. (2023). How to empower educators through digital pedagogies and faculty development strategies. [IJAEML]. *International Journal of Applied Engineering and Management Letters*, *7*(4), 139–183. DOI: 10.47992/IJAEML.2581.7000.0198

Asrifan, A., Wajdi, F., Ishak, S., & Alwi, A. (2025). Humanizing the Digital Classroom: The Educator's Role in Fostering Connection Amidst Technology. In *Blending Human Intelligence With Technology in the Classroom* (pp. 87-118). IGI Global Scientific Publishing.

Atchley, P., Pannell, H., Wofford, K., Hopkins, M., & Atchley, R. A. (2024). Human and AI collaboration in the higher education environment: Opportunities and concerns. *Cognitive Research: Principles and Implications*, *9*(1), 20. DOI: 10.1186/s41235-024-00547-9

Baskara, F. R. (2024). Generative AI as an enabler of sustainable education: Theoretical perspectives and future directions. *British Journal of Teacher Education and Pedagogy*, *3*(3), 122–134. DOI: 10.32996/bjtep.2024.3.3.9

Bower, M., & von Mengersen, B. (2025). *Creative Technologies Education: Students as Digital Designers*. Taylor & Francis. DOI: 10.4324/9781003490715

Chan, C. K. Y., & Tsi, L. H. (2023). The AI revolution in education: will AI replace or assist teachers in higher education? *arXiv preprint arXiv:2305.01185*.

Chiu, T. K., & Rospigliosi, P. A. (2025). Encouraging human-AI collaboration in interactive learning environments. *Interactive Learning Environments*, *33*(2), 921–924.

Clear, T., Cajander, Å., Clear, A., McDermott, R., Daniels, M., Divitini, M., ... & Zhu, T. (2025). AI integration in the IT professional workplace: a scoping review and interview study with implications for education and professional competencies. *2024 Working Group Reports on Innovation and Technology in Computer Science Education*, 34-67.

Dhanasekaran, R. (2025). AI Revolutionizing Education: Technology and Human Interaction in Partnership. *Journal of Computer Science and Technology Studies*, *7*(6), 501–506.

Drosos, I., Sarkar, A., Xu, X., Negreanu, C., Rintel, S., & Tankelevitch, L. (2024, June). " It's like a rubber duck that talks back": Understanding Generative AI-Assisted Data Analysis Workflows through a Participatory Prompting Study. In *Proceedings of the 3rd Annual Meeting of the Symposium on Human-Computer Interaction for Work* (pp. 1-21). DOI: 10.1145/3663384.3663389

Fügener, A., Grahl, J., Gupta, A., & Ketter, W. (2022). Cognitive challenges in human–artificial intelligence collaboration: Investigating the path toward productive delegation. *Information Systems Research*, *33*(2), 678–696. DOI: 10.1287/isre.2021.1079

Fui-Hoon Nah, F., Zheng, R., Cai, J., Siau, K., & Chen, L. (2023). Generative AI and ChatGPT: Applications, challenges, and AI-human collaboration. *Journal of information technology case and application research, 25*(3), 277-304.

Gesing, P., Tornwall, J., Kulo, V., McBrien, S., Hoang, T., Jun, H. J., Burbage, A., Jia, Y., & Cestone, C. (2025). Team science in interdisciplinary health professions education research: A multi-institutional case study. *Advances in Health Sciences Education : Theory and Practice*, *30*(4), 1123–1141. DOI: 10.1007/s10459-024-10393-5

Goodwin, L. (2022). *Educational neuroscience, artificial intelligence, and technology in higher education*. University of Pennsylvania.

Gottschalk, F., & Weise, C. (2023). Digital equity and inclusion in education: An overview of practice and policy in OECD countries. *OECD Education Working Papers*, (299), 0_1-75.

Halaweh, M. (2023). ChatGPT in education: Strategies for responsible implementation. *Contemporary Educational Technology*, *15*(2), ep421. DOI: 10.30935/cedtech/13036

Han, Z., Tu, Y., & Huang, C. (2023). A framework for constructing a technology-enhanced education metaverse: Learner engagement with human–machine collaboration. *IEEE Transactions on Learning Technologies*, *16*(6), 1179–1189. DOI: 10.1109/TLT.2023.3257511

Hitsuwari, J., Ueda, Y., Yun, W., & Nomura, M. (2023). Does human–AI collaboration lead to more creative art? Aesthetic evaluation of human-made and AI-generated haiku poetry. *Computers in Human Behavior, 139*, 107502. DOI: 10.1016/j.chb.2022.107502

Holstein, K., & Aleven, V. (2022). Designing for human–AI complementarity in K-12 education. *AI Magazine, 43*(2), 239–248. DOI: 10.1002/aaai.12058

Hutson, J. (2025). *The Adoption of Artificial Intelligence and Inertia in Higher Education: Exploring Complex Resistance to Technological Change*. Taylor & Francis. DOI: 10.4324/9781003655862

Hutson, J., & Plate, D. (2023). *Human-AI collaboration for smart education: reframing applied learning to support metacognition*. IntechOpen.

Ifenthaler, D., & Schumacher, C. (2023). Reciprocal issues of artificial and human intelligence in education. *Journal of Research on Technology in Education, 55*(1), 1–6. DOI: 10.1080/15391523.2022.2154511

Järvelä, S., Nguyen, A., & Hadwin, A. (2023). Human and artificial intelligence collaboration for socially shared regulation in learning. *British Journal of Educational Technology, 54*(5), 1057–1076. DOI: 10.1111/bjet.13325

Jeon, J., & Lee, S. (2023). Large language models in education: A focus on the complementary relationship between human teachers and ChatGPT. *Education and Information Technologies, 28*(12), 15873–15892. DOI: 10.1007/s10639-023-11834-1

Ji, H., Han, I., & Ko, Y. (2023). A systematic review of conversational AI in language education: Focusing on the collaboration with human teachers. *Journal of Research on Technology in Education, 55*(1), 48–63. DOI: 10.1080/15391523.2022.2142873

Johnson, J. (2024). *The AI commander: centaur teaming, command, and ethical dilemmas*. Oxford University Press. DOI: 10.1093/oso/9780198892182.001.0001

Jony, A. I., & Hamim, S. A. (2024). Empowering virtual collaboration: Harnessing AI for enhanced teamwork in higher education. *Educational Technology Quarterly, 2024*(3), 337–359. DOI: 10.55056/etq.746

Karakose, T., Demirkol, M., Aslan, N., Köse, H., & Yirci, R. (2023). A conversation with ChatGPT about the impact of the COVID-19 pandemic on education: Comparative review based on human–AI collaboration. *Educational Process: International Journal, 12*(3), 7. DOI: 10.22521/edupij.2023.123.1

Karakose, T., Demirkol, M., Yirci, R., Polat, H., Ozdemir, T. Y., & Tülübaş, T. (2023). A conversation with ChatGPT about digital leadership and technology integration: Comparative analysis based on human–AI collaboration. *Administrative Sciences*, *13*(7), 157. DOI: 10.3390/admsci13070157

Kim, J. (2024). Leading teachers' perspective on teacher-AI collaboration in education. *Education and Information Technologies*, *29*(7), 8693–8724. DOI: 10.1007/s10639-023-12109-5

Kim, J., & Cho, Y. H. (2025). My teammate is AI: Understanding students' perceptions of student-AI collaboration in drawing tasks. *Asia Pacific Journal of Education*, *45*(3), 1013–1027. DOI: 10.1080/02188791.2023.2286206

Kim, J., Ham, Y., & Lee, S. S. (2024). Differences in student-AI interaction process on a drawing task: Focusing on students' attitude towards AI and the level of drawing skills. *Australasian Journal of Educational Technology*, *40*(1), 19–41. DOI: 10.14742/ajet.8859

Kim, J., Lee, H., & Cho, Y. H. (2022). Learning design to support student-AI collaboration: Perspectives of leading teachers for AI in education. *Education and Information Technologies*, *27*(5), 6069–6104. DOI: 10.1007/s10639-021-10831-6

Kim, J., & Lee, S. S. (2023). Are two heads better than one?: The effect of student-AI collaboration on students' learning task performance. *TechTrends*, *67*(2), 365–375. DOI: 10.1007/s11528-022-00788-9

Kovari, A. (2025). A systematic review of AI-powered collaborative learning in higher education: Trends and outcomes from the last decade. *Social Sciences & Humanities Open*, *11*, 101335. DOI: 10.1016/j.ssaho.2025.101335

Kumar, D., Haque, A., Mishra, K., Islam, F., Mishra, B. K., & Ahmad, S. (2023). Exploring the transformative role of artificial intelligence and metaverse in education: A comprehensive review. *Metaverse Basic and Applied Research*, *2*(2), 21. DOI: 10.56294/mr202355

Kurni, M., & Mohammed, M. S. (2023). *A beginner's guide to introduce artificial intelligence in teaching and learning*. Springer Nature.

Lee, G. G., Mun, S., Shin, M. K., & Zhai, X. (2025). Collaborative learning with artificial intelligence speakers: Pre-service elementary science teachers' responses to the prototype. *Science & Education*, *34*(2), 847–875. DOI: 10.1007/s11191-024-00526-y

Lodge, J. M., Yang, S., Furze, L., & Dawson, P. (2023). It's not like a calculator, so what is the relationship between learners and generative artificial intelligence? *Learning: Research and Practice*, *9*(2), 117–124. DOI: 10.1080/23735082.2023.2261106

Meniado, J. C. (2023). Digital language teaching 5.0: Technologies, trends and competencies. *RELC Journal*, *54*(2), 461–473. DOI: 10.1177/00336882231160610

Merceron, K., & Best, K. (2024). Integrating professional perspectives for AI literacy: empowering students in an AI-influenced future. In *The Role of Generative AI in the Communication Classroom* (pp. 300–315). IGI Global Scientific Publishing. DOI: 10.4018/979-8-3693-0831-8.ch014

Mittal, U., Sai, S., Chamola, V., & Sangwan, D. (2024). A comprehensive review on generative AI for education. *IEEE Access : Practical Innovations, Open Solutions*, *12*, 142733–142759. DOI: 10.1109/ACCESS.2024.3468368

Molenaar, I. (2022). The concept of hybrid human-AI regulation: Exemplifying how to support young learners' self-regulated learning. *Computers and Education: Artificial Intelligence*, *3*, 100070. DOI: 10.1016/j.caeai.2022.100070

Molenaar, I. (2022). Towards hybrid human-AI learning technologies. *European Journal of Education*, *57*(4), 632–645. DOI: 10.1111/ejed.12527

Molenaar, I. (2024). Human-AI collaboration in education: The hybrid future.

Murgatroyd, S. (2024). *The future of higher education in an age of artificial intelligence*. Ethics International Press.

Nguyen, A., Hong, Y., Dang, B., & Huang, X. (2024). Human-AI collaboration patterns in AI-assisted academic writing. *Studies in Higher Education*, *49*(5), 847–864. DOI: 10.1080/03075079.2024.2323593

Oravec, J. A. (2023). Artificial intelligence implications for academic cheating: Expanding the dimensions of responsible human-AI collaboration with ChatGPT. *Journal of Interactive Learning Research*, *34*(2), 213–237. DOI: 10.70725/304731gmmvhw

Padovano, A., & Cardamone, M. (2024). Towards human-AI collaboration in the competency-based curriculum development process: The case of industrial engineering and management education. *Computers and Education: Artificial Intelligence*, *7*, 100256. DOI: 10.1016/j.caeai.2024.100256

Saad, W. Z., Alias, N. A., Chong, C. M., & Sabri, S. (Eds.). (2025). *Digital Leadership for Sustainable Higher Education*. IGI Global. DOI: 10.4018/979-8-3693-9989-7

Summers, E. J., Mahmoudi, E., Vontsteen, J., Conner, K. A., & Wiedeman, M. C. (2025). Utilizing Technology to Efficiently Connect Students: A Critical Qualitative Study of Non-Competitive Gamification and AI Additions to Research Courses. *Journal of Interactive Learning Research, 36*(1), 11–28. DOI: 10.70725/534399sblpze

Talwar, P. (2023). *The Strategic Use of Virtual Teacher Assistants to Increase Faculty Engagement and Job Satisfaction*. Trident University International.

Tondeur, J., Trevisan, O., Howard, S. K., & van Braak, J. (2025). Preparing preservice teachers to teach with digital technologies: An update of effective SQD-strategies. *Computers & Education, 232*, 105262. DOI: 10.1016/j.compedu.2025.105262

Tzirides, A. O. O., Zapata, G., Kastania, N. P., Saini, A. K., Castro, V., Ismael, S. A., You, Y., Santos, T. A., Searsmith, D., O'Brien, C., Cope, B., & Kalantzis, M. (2024). Combining human and artificial intelligence for enhanced AI literacy in higher education. *Computers and Education Open, 6*, 100184. DOI: 10.1016/j.caeo.2024.100184

Ursin, F., Fürholzer, K., & Salloch, S. (2025). Metaphors in digital radiology: Ethical implications for responsibility assignments of human-AI imaginaries. *AI & Society, 40*(7), 1–11. DOI: 10.1007/s00146-025-02270-5

Veles, N. (2022). *Optimising the Third Space in Higher Education: Case studies of intercultural and cross-boundary collaboration*. Routledge. DOI: 10.4324/9781003259527

Wang, X., Liu, Q., Pang, H., Tan, S. C., Lei, J., Wallace, M. P., & Li, L. (2023). What matters in AI-supported learning: A study of human-AI interactions in language learning using cluster analysis and epistemic network analysis. *Computers & Education, 194*, 104703. DOI: 10.1016/j.compedu.2022.104703

Wu, R., Gao, L., Li, J., Huang, Q., & Pan, Y. (2024). Key Factors Influencing Design Learners' Behavioral Intention in Human-AI Collaboration Within the Educational Metaverse. *Sustainability (2071-1050), 16*(22).

Yang, K. B., Echeverria, V., Lu, Z., Mao, H., Holstein, K., Rummel, N., & Aleven, V. (2023, April). Pair-up: prototyping human-AI co-orchestration of dynamic transitions between individual and collaborative learning in the classroom. In *Proceedings of the 2023 CHI conference on human factors in computing systems* (pp. 1-17). DOI: 10.1145/3544548.3581398

Zhang, Z., Xu, Y., Wang, Y., Yao, B., Ritchie, D., Wu, T., & Li, T. J. J. (2022, April). Storybuddy: A human-ai collaborative chatbot for parent-child interactive storytelling with flexible parental involvement. In *Proceedings of the 2022 CHI Conference on Human Factors in Computing Systems* (pp. 1-21). DOI: 10.1145/3491102.3517479

APPENDIX

Abbreviations Used

ABET - Accreditation Board for Engineering and Technology
API - Application Programming Interface
BICS - Basic Interpersonal Communicative Skills
CALP - Cognitive Academic Language Proficiency
CAST - Center for Applied Special Technology
CHAT - Cultural–Historical Activity Theory
CoI - Communities of Inquiry
CRDTs - Conflict-free Replicated Data Types
CSCL - Computer-Supported Collaborative Learning
DCog - Distributed Cognition
DP - Differential Privacy
DPDP - Digital Personal Data Protection (Act)
FERPA - Family Educational Rights and Privacy Act
FL - Federated Learning
FPS - Frames Per Second
GDPR - General Data Protection Regulation
HSM - Hardware Security Module
KB - Knowledge Building
KPI - Key Performance Indicator
LoRa - Long Range low power wide area wireless technology
LTI - Learning Tools Interoperability
MFA - Multi-Factor Authentication
OECD - Organisation for Economic Co-operation and Development
OIDC - OpenID Connect
OT - Operational Transformation
PII - Personally Identifiable Information
PISA - Programme for International Student Assessment
PM10 - Particulate Matter 10 micrometres in diameter
PM2.5 - Particulate Matter 2.5 micrometres in diameter
Q→A - Question to Answer
RAG - Retrieval Augmented Generation
RBAC - Role-Based Access Control
SAML - Security Assertion Markup Language
SLA - Service Level Agreement
SLO - Service Level Objective

SR - Screen Reader
TALIS - Teaching and Learning International Survey
TAT - Turnaround Time
UDL - Universal Design for Learning
UI - User Interface
W3C - World Wide Web Consortium
WCAG - Web Content Accessibility Guidelines
WER - Word Error Rate
xAPI - Experience API (Experience Application Programming Interface)
ZPD - Zone of Proximal Development

Chapter 9
Automation and Robotics:
Enhancing Implementation Readiness

Oyinkansola O. Sodiya
https://orcid.org/0009-0003-6117-2113
University of Texas at Arlington, USA

Valerie O. Babatope
MacEwan University, Canada

ABSTRACT

There has been a significant rise in the adoption of emerging technologies. Organizations are now re-evaluating their management practices to ensure they maintain a competitive advantage. While upper-level management is often enthusiastic about the transformative power of technologies such as Robotics Process Automation, lower-level employees face concerns about potential job loss. This chapter emphasizes that, amidst the excitement about automation and robotics, it is crucial for organizations to proactively prepare for the implementation of such technologies. To enhance successful adoption, prioritizing implementation readiness and garnering employee buy-in is vital. This chapter aims to contribute in a trifold manner: 1) Uncover the complex socio-technical processes that shape the adoption of automation and robotics technologies, 2) Emphasize the value of fostering an environment where organizations and employees are racing with and not against emerging technologies. 3) Present best practices to bridge the gap between resistance and readiness for adoption.

DOI: 10.4018/979-8-3373-5747-8.ch009

1 INTRODUCTION: ROBOTICS AND AUTOMATION

The terms "robotics" and "automation" are often used interchangeably. However, they are two distinct terms with varying meanings. While automation encompasses technology carrying out a task without (or with minimal) human intervention, robotics entails programmable machines carrying out tasks independently. Thus, robotics is a subfield of automation. Automation is a word that has incited fear for many, and it has increasingly become an area of inquiry as organizations have sought to maximize its benefits and minimize the resulting fear of job insecurity. This chapter will address Robotics Process Automation (RPA)—a concept often at play in conversations surrounding robotics and automation.

RPA is defined by Rutaganda et al. (2017, p. 54) as "the use of software as a virtualized workforce to operate applications like a person processing a transaction or completing a process in front of a computer screen". RPA's ease and breadth of use make it increasingly attractive and unique in comparison to prior automation and technological advances. (Cooper et al., 2020). RPA has played an influential role in many fields including management, accounting, and supply chain, amongst others (Fernandez and Aman, 2018; Hartley and Sawaya, 2019; Rosario and Vasarhelyi, 2018). Its ability to take on manual and repetitive tasks like a human would has stirred a lot of curiosity amongst researchers and professionals over the years.

The acceleration of technology is a key player in the disappearance of some jobs. This has made many employees increasingly cautious and apprehensive of technological innovations such as Robotics Process Automation (Brynjolfsson and McAfee, 2011). There is record of a large number of job losses caused by the waves of automation in the 19th and 20th centuries. (Brynjolfsson and McAfee, 2011). These job losses were predominantly in agricultural fields and led to millions of people migrating from agriculture to work in manufacturing and service. The 21st century was accompanied by faster and more pervasive technological change, and the technological innovations became more impressive over the years.

2 JOB CHARACTERISTICS

Jobs with a higher cognitive load, such as HR Managers, Software Developers, and Lead Programmers, are often more difficult to automate (Afriliana & Ramadhan, 2022). On the other hand, jobs with repetitive tasks are more amenable to RPA. An understanding of the impact on job design is highly crucial. With higher cognitive jobs, automation may increase the workload pressure and impede creativity (Jia et al., 2024). In such situations, organizations may be less receptive to automation. Tasks that are dependent on motor memory and include a feedback loop are the best candidates for automation because they can be documented and replicated by bots. On the other hand, jobs that involve higher levels of people management and social interactions are often not the best candidates for automation because of the level of human-to-human communication in such jobs. This is also the case for jobs in environments with less predictability, such as gardeners and child providers (Manyika et al., 2017). Such jobs are often associated with lower wages, and this deters the need for automation from a business case perspective.

Routine is the degree of repetitiveness of work (Fernández-Macías & Bisello, 2022). Examples of repetitive tasks include routine copying and pasting, populating buyer information in invoices, etc. In a similar vein to cognitive load, the labor input of jobs with low repetitiveness is difficult for machines to replace. Interestingly, accounting professionals acknowledge that RPA can handle repetitive tasks in their workflow, but they often do not associate this automation with job loss. They are enthusiastic about the potential for augmentation and the reduction of human error (Holmes & Douglass, 2022). Indeed, automation technologies can relieve task burden for employees. In many cases, they can allocate their time to more high-value tasks because they no longer have to carry out the mundane and repetitive tasks that were previously in their workflow. Robotics Process Automation is especially desired in the context of repetitive tasks, as its specialization is in the automation of structured repetitive tasks. This is likely to be appealing to management in organizations as it conveys the message that the technology can automate tasks that are considered to be a waste of time. E.g., cutting and pasting. However, employees do not always believe that using automation technologies on repetitive tasks would reduce their workload. There has been extensive discourse on the ability of emerging technologies such as RPA to cause job loss. After conducting a study on 37 countries from 2005 to 2015, De Vries et al. (2020) found that the adoption of robots led to a reduction in jobs that were routinely manual and task-intensive. This fear of job loss can lead to employee resistance. Thus, bridging the gap between resistance and readiness to adopt RPA is crucial.

Another benefit of RPA in jobs is that it has been related to increased employee discretionary power and increased role breadth self-efficacy (Axtell & Parker, 2000; Sonnentag & Spychala, 2012). When RPA takes on the repetitive tasks of employees, the employees may have more time to take on higher-level tasks that involve more decision-making. This can contribute to the increase in role breadth self-efficacy and discretionary power. Eliminating repetitive work would allow attention to be devoted to higher problem-solving tasks. Another important aspect in the automation of repetitive tasks is the skill enhancement cycle as the automation of redundant tasks can allow employees to develop higher-level augmentation skills (Raisch and Krakowski, 2021). While the automation of repetitive tasks comes with benefits, it is also connected to the increased fear of job loss. This fear of job loss can be more prominent in jobs with lower skill variety. It is important for employees to actively work to improve their competencies and enhance skill variety.

3 AUTOMATION AND ROBOTICS IN ENHANCING OPERATIONAL EFFICIENCY

In a survey of 450 companies, Protiviti (2021) found that all companies had intentions to expand RPA usage. RPA has made a significant contribution to business as it has enhanced the way people view and understand business tasks. RPA bots are transforming the way tasks are handled across different sectors. Robotics has proven to be beneficial in multiple sectors such as finance, accounting, and supply chain. A popular argument for the benefit of RPA is the cost and time-saving element. With a reduction in human failure, there is higher quality and reduced costs (Rutaganda et al., 2017). The benefits of RPA are more readily seen in Finance and Accounting companies through aspects such as a reduction in the cost of compliance. RPA can be used to reduce the cost of compliance in firms. It can support steps such as sending emails, running reports, and analyzing reports. Through this, the bots can easily identify who is out of compliance, and that takes off a significant task from their partners. Not only is this a significant source of cost savings for public accounting firms, but it is also an avenue to free up workload from partners who are often slammed with huge workloads daily. In procurement, RPA can automate manual tasks such as creating invoices with the corresponding billing information and sending the invoices to customer portals. This capability is very impressive as it can carry out such tasks in seconds or minutes rather than days or months (Fernandez and Aman, 2018). This speaks to the extent to which RPA adds a significant level of efficiency to numerous business processes. Another significant benefit of RPA in firms is the improvement in the service provided to clients and customers. Harnessing the power of automation technologies, accounting firms also recorded an increase in efforts to improve the service provided to their clients (Cooper et al., 2019)

Though RPA has significant advantages, the enthusiasm and optimism about RPA could lead to overestimations about its capabilities. There are cases where robotics can be less efficient than humans, thereby causing bottlenecks (Rutaganda et al. 2017). It is important to be cognizant of the fact that RPA is not perfect. Even with the best development teams, the bots can sometimes malfunction when there are changes in business systems. Also, they are not free of error. For example, in text recognition projects, RPA bots may confuse characters such as $ and 5.

Resistance to change is evident in multiple sectors beyond the confines of Robotics Process Automation. A major production problem faced by Harwood

Manufacturing Corporation was the employee resistance to method and job change (Coch & French, 1948). Change can be seen as disruptive and intrusive. Thus, employees may push back when technologies such as RPA are introduced. For managers to better understand the acceptance of change, they should put themselves in the shoes of the employees and try to see things from the employees' perspective. Employee resistance can be very harmful. Employees can intentionally limit the firm's ability to successfully implement automation initiatives. This resistance is exacerbated because of the anxiety associated with fear of job loss (Cooper et al. 2022). This fear is often more apparent among employees who have repetitive jobs with minimal interpersonal interactions (Coupe, 2019). These fears, however, seem to be validated as research has indeed identified a rise in automation for routine jobs. After combining robot data in 37 countries from 2005 to 2015, De Vries et al. (2020) found a rise in the adoption of robots and a drop in employment share for routine manual and task-intensive jobs. It is important to note that automation is not the sole source of job insecurity. Beyond the likelihood of having one's tasks automated, there are other factors that could spur feelings of job insecurity within employees, such as strained relationships with managers and work conflict among others. Bad management and the presence of other job candidates who are willing to take up employment at a lower wage are some additional reasons why employees may feel insecure about their jobs.

Beyond the fears associated with technology is the concept of an overall aversion to change. There are instances where employees may simply find comfort in the ease and repetitiveness of their tasks and lack interest in having those tasks automated. Some employees are simply reluctant to change their work process (Chen et al., 2012). Alongside the fear of change is the fear of learning a new technology, as employees could be frightened about learning how to use new technologies.

Unfreezing is the idea of changing the perspective about an upcoming change such that members view the change as important and likely to be successful (Lewin 1951). This is similar to the concept of readiness for automation. Employees often have preconceived notions about the extent to which an organization is well-equipped to take on a change. The experiences that employees have in the company can alter how they perceive the possibility of thriving in an environment where RPA has been implemented. There is a likelihood for one to escalate the commitment to a task or project because of an overly optimistic view of its success potential. In this context, managers may be blind to the realities and risks associated with RPA because of the success stories they may have heard or the financial projections of its benefits.

To conserve creativity, some organizations take the route of dividing tasks between the technology and the human employees. Through augmentation, such employees can work collaboratively with technologies. The concept of humans supporting technology such as automation is seen with socially assistive robotics.

The use of technology has increased significantly over the years and its prevalence has been noted in several industries such as healthcare. Not only are technological innovations becoming more rampant across industries, but their breadth of applications also remains on the rise (Parasuraman 2000). Business processes do not have to be completely taken over by the machine. Instead, the machine can enhance the ability and performance of the human. The decision-making process of the human can be preserved amidst the automation of tasks and processes (Leyer and Schneider, 2021). The strength of augmentation has been identified by technology experts as tools have been developed to specifically hone into the collaborative strength of the machine and the human.

3.1 Sectorial Impact of RPA

Robotics Process Automation has significantly impacted industries across several dimensions such as human involvement, task complexity, and task routinization. Organization leaders are likely to be enthusiastic about the prospects of RPA. The technology is associated with several positive capabilities such as accuracy, time saving, and cost reduction. However, the success of RPA implementation is dependent on the ability to address and mitigate specific challenges such as employee readiness and ethical considerations. This section provides more insight on the specific ways automation and robotics has impacted various sectors.

Table 1. Sectorial Impact of RPA

Sector	Automation & Robotics Technology	Sample Use Cases
Banking & Finance	RPA, AI	Loan processing, transaction reconciliation
Healthcare	RPA, AI	Patient scheduling, appointment reminders, compliance documentation
Manufacturing	RPA, ERP Systems	Invoice processing, supply chain coordination, inventory tracking
Human Resources	RPA, AI	Resume screening, Benefits processing

3.1.1 Banking and Finance

The banking and finance sectors were one of the early adopters of automation technologies. The tasks in these sectors often involve high-volume, rules based processes. The procedures are also often subjected to strict compliance requirement.

These nuances are well aligned with RPA capabilities. RPA tools are uniquely positioned to be skilled at handling manual, repetitive, rules-based tasks. RPA has been widely functional in several banking and finance tasks such as fraud detection support, processing transactions, account reconciliation, and fraud detection (Venigandla & Vemuri, 2022).

From an operations perspective, RPA has proven to be effective at reducing manual errors, minimizing operational costs, and improving processing speed (e.g., Aguirre & Rodriguez, 2017). For example, RPA bots can generate compliance reports in real time, flag fraud detection anomalies for human review, and validate customer information across systems. These capabilities are particularly of value in sectors like banking and finance where accuracy is key. In such sectors, seemingly minor errors can lead to significant regulatory penalties and cause reputational harm.

Despite the many positive benefits RPA has brought to the banking and finance sector, there remains concerns surrounding the use of RPA in these sectors. If the employees continuously perceive that management implements RPA to cost costs, the employees could begin to resist RPA use. This resistance is especially harmful in in the banking and finance industries because the employees often have access to sensitive information such as banking records and clients personal identifiable information. Disgruntled employees who perceive management ill-intentions and fear job-loss could display counterproductive workplace behaviors such as sharing private information, or unauthorized movement of funds. Thus, it is important that managers approach RPA implementation with a value-add perspective where employees are adequately trained on valuable skills such as RPA exception handling.

3.1.2 Healthcare

For decades, the healthcare industry has faced challenges of administrative burden, employee shortages, and financial pressures. RPA has played a notable role in tackling these challenges. For example, by reducing the amount of time it takes to validate claims, hospitals have recorded reduced reimbursement cycles (Adeleke & Ajayi, 2023). Also, RPA has aided reduction in no-show rates by providing technological support in sending appointment reminders to patients (Massolt et al., 2025). Beyond the support this provides to patients, it also supports healthcare professionals by freeing up time that would have been spent handling administrative tasks, thus allowing them to direct more efforts to other areas such as clinical decision-making and attentive patient-interaction.

3.1.3 Human Resources

The human resources sector is an area that has recorded significant growth in the use of AI and automation tools. Professionals now incorporate these technologies in tasks such as payroll processing, recruitment screening, and compliance tracking (Tambe et al., 2019). By automating asks such as resume screening and appointment scheduling, there can be accelerated hiring timelines. However, concerns about the use of robotics and automation technologies are more pronounced in the field of HR. Human resources involves a great deal of employee affairs e.g., performance evaluations, employee monitoring, and hiring. When automation tools are used in this sector, there are ethical and fairness concerns (Raghavan et al. 2020). For example, algorithmic bias exists. The automation tools are a function of the people or team behind the coding. If the people had conscious or subconscious biases, the tools would reflect such biases.

4 BENEFITS AND CHALLENGES OF AUTOMATION AND ROBOTICS

Arguments on the benefits and challenges of automation and robotics exist on a very broad continuum: from those who argue that they will create a new age of industrialisation and enhanced labour performance (see Mehta et al., 2024; Szeszák et al., 2025), to those who argue that they will raise existential threats (see Hilliard et al., 2025; Nørskov, 2022). This section takes a deep dive into the benefits and challenges of automation and robotics using insights from the empirical and industry literature. By situating these technologies along the optimist–doomsayer spectrum, the analysis demonstrates that the same innovations that accelerate efficiency can also provoke fears of disruption and inequality.

4.1 Benefits

Automation and robotic systems have been shown to drive business and operational efficiency (Ali et al., 2024; Prince, 2024). This subsection discusses how these technologies aid the enhancement of business performance. The major and relevant thematic areas identified from the literature include productivity, cost reduction, quality and safety improvements, strategic agility and innovation, and industry-specific applications.

4.1.1 Productivity Improvement

Empirical evidence consistently demonstrates that the adoption of automation and robotic systems greatly increases productivity. The corpus of evidence spans firm-, sector-, and country-level proof. Kromann et al. (2020), using industry-level panel data from nine countries, report that automation increases total factor productivity (TFP) by approximately 6%. Similarly, Autor and Salomons (2018) show that automation positively influences productivity growth across 28 industries in 18 OECD countries. TFP captures efficiency gains from better resource use rather than simply input expansion (Comin, 2010), underscoring automation's role in optimising existing resources.

At the firm level, Meyer and Weitz (2024) highlight that automation enables upscaling of productivity and revenue, while Kromann and Sørensen (2019) confirm its positive association with profitability in French companies. Chundakkadan et al. (2025) further argue that automation enhances firms' innovative capacity, allowing quicker introduction of new products. Optimists see this as evidence that robotics liberates human capital for creativity and problem-solving. Doomsayers, however, caution that productivity gains may not always translate into shared prosperity if accompanied by wage stagnation or employment polarization.

4.1.2 Cost Reduction

Automation and robotics enable firms to cut operational costs by eliminating redundant processes and reducing errors. Hartey (2019) shows that artificial intelligence reduces costs tied to downtime and labor inefficiencies. Ali (2014) demonstrates that automated software testing lowers costs over time compared with manual approaches. Fang et al. (2023) find that automation increases consistency while reducing per-unit costs in manufacturing, benefiting firms and consumers alike. Cost savings are also tied to scalability. Once automated systems are in place, organizations can increase output without proportionate labor expansion. Acemoglu and Restrepo (2019) emphasize that displaced labor can often be reallocated to higher-value tasks, offsetting some employment losses. Still, critics argue that cost savings frequently accrue to shareholders rather than workers, fuelling inequality.

4.1.3 Consistency and Safety

Robotic systems ensure consistent quality in production and services. They execute repetitive tasks with precision, minimizing variability and costly rework. In high-stakes industries such as pharmaceuticals and aerospace, this consistency safeguards compliance and reputation. Equally important is workplace safety. Robots excel in "dirty, dull, and dangerous" environments like mines, chemical plants, and offshore rigs, protecting humans from harm. Automated inspection systems further enhance safety by identifying defects invisible to the human eye. Optimists stress that robots save lives by taking on risky work, whereas doomsayers warn of overreliance on machines that themselves may fail or malfunction.

4.1.4 Strategic Agility and Innovation

Automation does not merely cut costs; it also reshapes competitive strategies. Robots and software bots allow firms to pivot quickly to new designs or processes, enabling agility without losing efficiency. Collaborative robots (cobots) illustrate this trend: by working safely alongside humans, they expand production flexibility and empower employees to focus on creative, customer-facing, or managerial tasks.

At a strategic level, automation supports faster market responsiveness. Firms using data-rich robotic systems can detect shifts in demand or supply chain disruptions in real time, responding faster than competitors (World Economic Forum, 2023). Optimists highlight this agility as evidence that automation fuels innovation and resilience, while doomsayers warn that firms unable to invest at scale may be left behind, deepening market concentration.

4.1.5 Practical Illustration

The transformative potential of automation and robotics is visible across multiple sectors:

Healthcare: Robotic surgical platforms like da Vinci enhance surgical precision, shorten recovery times, and free up hospital capacity (Yang et al., 2022). Mobile robots also deliver medications, enabling nurses to spend more time with patients.

Logistics and Retail: Amazon's Kiva robots optimize warehouse operations, doubling fulfillment speed without equivalent increases in workforce size. This demonstrates how automation can meet rising consumer expectations for same-day delivery.

Customer Service: AI chatbots handle millions of queries, offering immediate responses and freeing human agents to tackle complex, high-value interactions.

Agriculture: Precision farming leverages autonomous tractors and drones to optimize planting, irrigation, and pesticide use, raising yields while conserving resources.

Energy and Utilities: Remotely operated vehicles perform deep-sea inspections of oil rigs, reducing human exposure to extreme environments.

These examples illustrate the applications of automation and robotics across sectors.

4.2 Challenges

Despite the immense benefits, automation and robotics bring substantial challenges. Industry and academic insights identify major barriers including integration difficulties, workforce resistance, job displacement, ethical dilemmas, and cybersecurity risks.

4.2.1 Difficulty Integrating with Existing Systems

Integration challenges arise especially during deployment. Sinha and Lee (2024) highlight data quality and model reliability issues when automating industrial processes. Okeke and Akinbolajo (2023) show that low-code platforms often struggle with automation integration, facing persistent compatibility and security problems. McKee et al. (2017) warn that compatibility concerns may resurface even after successful initial deployment, making integration a recurring cost.

4.2.2 Workforce Resistance

Employee resistance is perhaps the most visible organizational barrier. Yam et al. (2022) document how robotic adoption increases job insecurity, burnout, and incivility. Wloch et al. (2025), analyzing six European countries, show that younger, less-educated, and lower-income employees express heightened fears of automation. Resistance is also linked to organizational culture: Trujillo and Holt (2020) observe that a lack of employee engagement exacerbates resistance in construction. Almatrodi et al. (2023) recommend embedding employee participation into change-management strategies to build acceptance.

4.2.3 Job Displacement

The specter of job loss remains at the heart of the doomsayer critique. Historical precedents such as the Luddite riots illustrate the persistence of such fears. Kashaka (2025) argues that automation can polarize wages and exacerbate demographic disparities. Policymakers face pressure to mitigate these impacts through upskilling programs and safety nets. Optimists counter that new forms of work will emerge, but the pace of reallocation remains uncertain.

4.2.4 Ethical Problems

The adoption of automation and robotics raises important ethical concerns that shape organizational legitimacy and public trust. Four domains stand out: safety, privacy, bias, and accountability. Safety remains a central issue, especially where robots interact directly with humans. Even collaborative robots (cobots) designed with advanced sensors have occasionally malfunctioned, causing workplace injuries. In healthcare, robotic surgery illustrates both potential precision gains and questions of liability when machine error contributes to adverse outcomes.

The challenge of privacy is equally pressing. Automated systems often rely on extensive monitoring of workers or consumers to function effectively. While such data improves efficiency, it can also erode individual autonomy and create climates of surveillance. Bias and discrimination arise when automated decision systems are trained on historical data that reflect existing inequities. High-profile hiring tools have, for example, penalized female candidates because training datasets mirrored past gender imbalances in tech employment (Grover, 2025). Without rigorous auditing, such systems risk perpetuating inequality.

Finally, accountability presents a "responsibility gap." When harm occurs, it is not always clear whether the fault lies with the programmer, manufacturer, or end-user (Omosebi, 2025). This ambiguity complicates regulatory oversight and raises reputational risks for firms deploying robotic systems. Overall, ethical problems highlight that automation is not value-neutral. How organizations design, monitor, and govern these technologies determines whether they reduce risks or deepen existing societal divides.

4.2.5 Vulnerability to Cyberattacks

Automation and robotics increase exposure to cybersecurity threats because they control not only data but also physical processes. Stuxnet, discovered in 2010, remains a stark reminder of how malware can sabotage industrial systems by targeting programmable controllers. Modern automated environments are similarly vulnerable, especially when robots connect to cloud platforms or the wider Internet of Things. Recent incidents show the stakes. The Capita PLC ransomware attack in 2023 caused £106 million in losses and disrupted UK public services (Martin, 2024). Likewise, the MOVEit transfer breach (Robinson, 2023; Zaveri et al., 2023) exposed sensitive data across governments and corporations, illustrating how a single exploited vulnerability can ripple through global supply chains.

Robotic systems themselves often lack robust built-in security because design priorities historically emphasized performance over resilience. This "security lag" leaves many legacy systems exposed. The proliferation of IoT devices in automated workplaces further complicates defense, multiplying entry points for attackers. These vulnerabilities underscore that the efficiency gains of automation can quickly turn into liabilities if not matched with strong cybersecurity governance. As regulators such as the EU (Cyber Resilience Act) and U.S. NIST (AI Risk Management

Framework) stress, safeguarding automated systems is now a core dimension of responsible adoption.

Automation and robotics clearly offer significant advantages in productivity, cost reduction, quality, safety, and strategic agility. Cross-industry examples show that when properly implemented, these technologies can transform not only efficiency but also customer experience and innovation capacity. Optimists highlight these outcomes as evidence that automation propels human progress by freeing workers for higher-value contributions.

Yet the doomsayer perspective remains salient. Integration challenges, workforce resistance, displacement risks, ethical dilemmas, and cybersecurity vulnerabilities complicate adoption. Without deliberate strategies, the benefits may accrue unevenly, exacerbating inequality and concentrating power among technologically advanced firms.

The way forward is not to frame automation as inherently good or bad, but to recognize that outcomes hinge on management, policy, and societal choices. Organizations that invest in human capital development, responsible innovation, and resilient governance frameworks can harness automation's benefits while reducing risks. As the next section on Best Practices will demonstrate, proactive strategies such as skill development, employee engagement, and ethical oversight are essential for ensuring that the promise of automation translates into sustainable and inclusive progress.

5 CASE STUDY

5.1 Automation Implementation in a Mid-Sized Financial Services Firm. A Robotics Process Automation Use Case

TaylorJimCo, a mid-sized financial services firm with 2,200 employees has faced extensive competitive pressure. Larger institutions in the financial services industry have been adopting advanced technologies and TaylorJimCo is concerned about falling behind in the technological era. The management teams have identified that certain employes are consumed with routine, rule-based tasks such as data reconciliation and compliance checks. In the year 2025, the board approved a 5-year plan to implement robotics Process Automation (RPA) to streamline employee workflow.

5.1.1 Challenges

- Organization – Employee Misalignment: While management is excited and enthusiastic about the RPA implementation project, the employees are not pleased to hear conversations about a potential RPA plan
- Job Security Concerns: Staff feel that if RPA starts taking over some of their tasks, it would ultimately lead to them losing their jobs. In a survey sent to staff members, over 70% indicated that they expected to experience job loss within the first 2 years of RPA adoption.
- Minimal RPA knowledge: Staff members have heard of the term RPA and know it entails robotics doing the work of humans. However, their general understanding of how RPA functions is very low. They have fears that they would not know how to navigate or understand RPA.

5.1.2 Implementation Strategy

To bridge the gap between resistance and RPA readiness, TayorJimCo adopt a three phase approach.

Phase 1: Communication, Value Add, and Co-optation

- Leaders launch a Business Process Improvement (BPI) Campaign. Management initially wanted to name the campaign Human + Bots campaign but they identified through the initial survey that employees were scared of the term "Robot". To mitigate fears they, use the name Business Process Improvement to emphasize that the goal is to improve the existing processes. They schedule company-wide workshops and frame RPA as supportive tool rather than as a replacement for employees. They make room to listen to employee concerns and respond to employee questions.
- Messages and highlights from the BPI campaign is repeated in town halls, newsletters, and in department meetings. They continuously emphasize that your job is being upgraded, not being taken away
- Department managers present team members with practical examples. They show how RPA has been used in previous companies and how it would be implemented in their specific departments.
- Leaders communicate with employees to emphasize value add of automation. They explain to employees that RPA would take over the repetitive, mundane tasks thereby enabling them to be more hands on with higher-level tasks. With increased participation in higher-level tasks, employees would engage with more strategic tasks that require more problem-solving and critical thinking

- Leadership identifies key influencers who are not in management positions in each department. Those influencers would be invited to pilot sessions and proof of concepts. This would allow the RPA influencers to more involved, co-own the process, and serve as an ambassador for the new technology when communicating with their team members.

Phase 2: Cross-Training, Upskilling, and Alignment

- A cross-training program would be introduced for all employees. This would help employees to hone into their current roles while also leaning more about the roles of other employees. This would reinforce the message that creative thinking and adaptability and critical for the successful implementation of RPA technologies.
- Training programs would incorporate sessions to teach employees about RPA related tasks such as exception handling.
- Training programs would have the options for certifications. These certifications would serve as incentives for the employees and badges such as "RPA Master" would be recognized and applauded in performance reviews.
- Managers work with HR to align RPA implementation plan with career development plans. They acknowledge that there could be significant changes to workflow in the long run and they discuss with HR to identify potential updates to job descriptions and job trajectories. They ensure that automation is perceived as a opportunity rather than as a threat to employees

Phase 3: Optimism bias – mitigation

- Leaders objectively address both the benefits and risks of RPA. They avoid a narrative where RPA would solve all workflow problems.
- Managers hold feedback sessions where employees can address additional questions from information shared internally or through the BPI campaign.

Lessons Learned

Here, we see a practical example of a three phase approach to prepare for the implementation of Robotics Process Automation at a mid-size financial services company. With actional strategies such as co-optation, cross-training, and optimism-bias mitigation, the organization would be better suited to integrate RPA into employee workflows.

6 BEST PRACTICES

In the analysis of the debate surrounding the impact of technology in the workplace, it is important to equip executives, department heads, business moguls, academia, policymakers, and scholars with the strategies to mitigate these concerns. Strategies such as skill variety training, needs assessment analysis, and organization engagement are actionable approaches to foster employee readiness.

Figure 1. Bridging the gap between resistance and readiness to implement automation and robotics

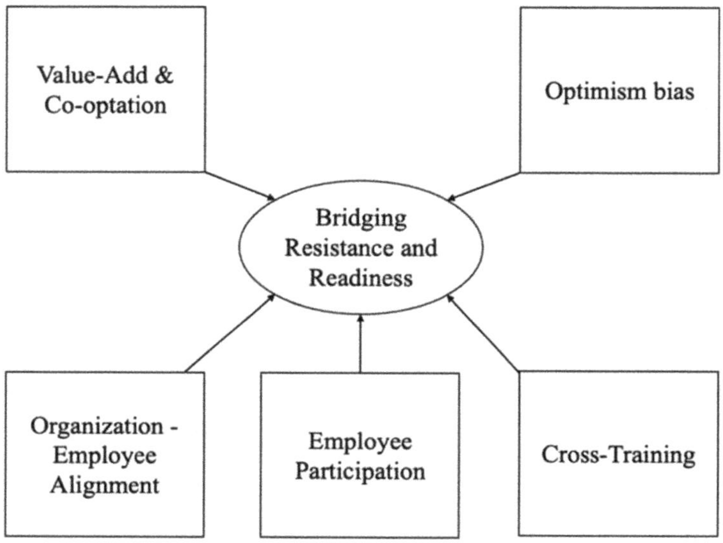

6.1 Prioritize Organization - Employee Alignment

Employee alignment emphasizes the need to obtain the buy-in of employees when initiating technology adoption. Not only is this beneficial for automation adoption, it also fosters a healthy collaborative culture. With benefits such as increased productivity and reduction of human error, organizations are eager to tap into these innovative approaches. Employees on the other hand fear for a loss of jobs and the potential boredom that could be associated with having their daily tasks automated. This then raises concerns about alignment between the organization and employees. Management prioritizes how automation will impact the bottom line while lower-level employees focus on how automation will make tasks or jobs obsolete (Cooper

2020). An understanding of how firm leaders and lower-level employees perceive automation is important for understanding how employees will engage. Importantly, a key distinction between RPA and other forms of technological innovations is that RPA is primarily driven by lower-level employees (Cooper et al. 2019). Thus, it is important that the values of these employees and that of the higher-level managers are aligned. For the implementation of RPA to be successful, the organization and employees must be on board and understand the value being provided.

6.2 Incorporate Employee Participation

To race with, and not against technology, organizations should co-invent business models that leverage advancing technology and human skills. To that aid, organizations should redesign their procedures to incorporate employee participation/cooptation of employees in RPA strategies. In an experiment aimed at reducing change resistance, Coch and French (1948) found that the productivity of the participants who were allowed participative privileges was higher than that of those who weren't. This provides support for the notion that member participation in change efforts is important. It also shows that it is important to influence the beliefs of employees so they are more receptive to the integration of automation technologies. Employee participation would enable the organization to benefit from the social dialogues. It is essential for organizations to strive for an inclusive culture in which the employees are allowed to participate in innovative efforts. Coch and French (1948) further highlight the value in group participation as they found that effective communication through group meetings can in fact modify or completely eradicate group resistance to change. Incorporating employee participation would tap into the positive aspects of optimism as involvement in planning causes the planner to be more optimistic about the potential of the plan.

Social exchange theory, a significantly influential organizational behavior theory, is one that presents itself in this argument. Witt (1991) stated that the exchange ideology strengthens the effects of job satisfaction and procedural justice. Support provided by team members will play a role in shaping perceptions and reactions to automation technologies. Co-workers would serve as the sources of information for each other. The social information processing model (Salancik and Pfeffer, 1978) explains that individuals tap into information about past behavior and about what others think when developing statements about attitudes. There is a need to move from atmospheres in which work is structured by organizations and managers to atmospheres where individuals participate and see the value and consequences of change efforts. Perceptions and affect are consistently influenced by social and information cues (Griffin 1987). Social information plays an integral role in the way ideas are perceived. Through social information processing, cooptation of employees in innovative strategies will be beneficial for successful automation initiatives

6.3 Value-Add and Co-Optation

Managers should work to differentiate the low-value and high-value parts of the job. If the employee believes the job tasks that would be automated are the low-value parts, they would likely be more receptive to the idea of automation because they still have high value tasks to perform. It would help both the managers and lower-level employees actively work to tap into the valuable parts of the job roles. Co-optation during the RPA brainstorming process can occur in a variety of ways. We suggest the approach of having a non-manager-level representative from each department who is present at high-stakes meetings where the brainstorming takes place. The presence of an employee from each department would also ensure that there is 100% representation at the meetings. This representative(s) will serve as the spokesperson for the department and would communicate any comments, needs, or concerns voiced by the team members. This person can be elected by the manager as it would be beneficial for the chosen employee to be one who has a good understanding of the business processes. The trustworthiness and credibility of the change agent are also important in the reception of information (Armenakis et al., 1993). Though the assigned employee will not be the change agent in this case, the individual will be the one communicating these potential changes to the team prior to any formal announcements. When decisions makers take employee suggestions and concerns into account, it could help foster trust and enhance receptiveness.

By enabling lower-level employees to be involved in the decision-making processes, the organization will be giving some ownership to the employees rather than communicating the message that robots are coming to automate their tasks. The communicated message is an integral part of readiness as it can enhance or hinder perceptions to change. Armenakis et al. (1993) state that "the primary mechanism for creating readiness for change among members of an organization is the message for change.". They explain that the message should always communicate the need for change and the individual and collective efficacy of parties affected by the change. For RPA implementations, organizations should also communicate the autonomy and ownership of tasks associated with RPA adoptions.

In a survey of lower-level employees, respondents in Cooper et al.'s (2020) survey agreed that RPA has provided them with the opportunity to be more analytical, interpersonal and strategic. They also agreed that they witnessed an increase in value and an increase in learning opportunities. This provides some hope as we see that lower level employees are not always apprehensive about RPA. With the right preparatory steps on the part of management, there can be alignment between managers and lower-level employees in the successful implementation of RPA.

6.4 Cross-Training

Cross-training is a strategy where team members are trained on the tasks and responsibilities of fellow team members. It plays an integral role in effective teamwork processes, communication, and performance (Volpe et al., 1996). A key benefit of cross-training is the acquisition of interpositional knowledge. Interpositional knowledge (IPK) is the extent of knowledge a team member has about the tasks, roles and appropriate behavioral responses required of his or her teammates in various situations (Volpe et al., 1996). A significant amount of the preparation for automation should be done before the implementation of the technology. The adoption of cross-training would be an approach to plan future growth as the organization expands into this technological space that is likely to induce anxiety amongst lower-level employees.

The enhancement of interpositional knowledge through cross-training would better position employees for the adoption of technological advancements such as automation. Training for automation is not one that should not be a reactive approach after automation technologies have been integrated. Rather, organizations should proactively prepare for future automation efforts by ensuring that team members have a good understanding of tasks being carried out by team members. Not only would cross-training be an opportunity for the employees to expand their body of knowledge, but it would also enable the employees to be better equipped for promotional opportunities and to provide support in roles that are beyond the scope of Robotics Process Automation. Also, RPA can great impact jobs such as the of accountants. It can consolidate many of their tasks and change the nature of their job (Chen et al.'s 2012) study, they found that there. This emphasizes another benefit of cross-training as the role of an employee can be altered upon implementation of automation technologies such as Robotics Process Automation.

Finally, cross-training provides value for the organization regardless of the ultimate decision to implement automation technologies such as robotics. Should the organization decide to postpone or completely scrap plans to adopt RPA, cross-training would still enhance the professional development of the team members and enable them to provide more informed support to each other especially during busy seasons.

6.5 Eliminate Optimism Bias

Though RPA does have positive impacts on organizations, there is a likelihood for organizations to display optimism bias. Optimism bias here is the notion that the enthusiasm about the capabilities of the technologies could make individuals overlook important potential flaw and even over-project the impact of the technology. Optimism bias is especially likely in the case of RPA as it is projected to return quick and tangible benefits for organizations. When an outcome seems unlikely to produce the expected return, people tend to withdraw from the investment, proceed with the investment as planned, or invest more than initially budgeted (Meyer). If organizations do not consciously step out of out the overly optimistic mindset and adequately prepare for RPA implementation, there is a likelihood for them to escalate or commit to the automation investments even when all signs show that the best approach would be to abort the plans.

Optimism bias has been proven to be a major cause of unrealistic scheduling of projects Prater et al., 2017). A lack of preparation could make decision-makers live in a utopian world when in fact they may not have conducted due diligence. This is further exacerbated by the fact that there several new outlets and online sources discussing the positive impacts of emerging technologies in organizations. The adoptions of preparatory such as cross-training, co-optation, and organization-employee Alignment would minimize the likelihood of the escalation of commitment that results from optimism bias.

7. DISCUSSION

Organizational preparedness is an integral part of any form of innovative change or technological adaptation. This is especially relevant in Robotics Process Automation as the adoption of the technology will affect the daily work lives of involved employees. Also, lower-level employees play an integral part in the implementation process of automation technologies – especially Robotics Process Automation. If the employees do not communicate the details of their tasks, RPA will be ineffective. Though there are multiple success stories in industries and the media, it is important to note that there are also untold failure stories. To avoid falling into that cluster, organizations should conduct due diligence to ensure organizational preparedness and avoid falling into the trap of optimism bias.

It is also important to note that RPA strictly involves the use of rules to make decisions and does not incorporate human thinking. Most RPA technologies are ill-suited to human decision that require an element of judgement. However, with advancements in artificial intelligence, there is a lot of potential for automation technologies to increasingly have the capability to incorporate human judgment. This can cause escalated optimism about the potential for these technologies to take over all jobs.

We identify a common pattern across the banking, finance, healthcare, manufacturing and humans resources sectors: leaders tend to frame automation and robotics tools as an efficacy enhancing initiative. However, these tools significantly redefine jobs for employees e.g., changes in skill demand, power dynamics, and job roles. In sectors such as banking where there are often significant regulatory pressures, automaton tools are often justified with compliance narratives. While this narrative can be appealing for executives, it can exacerbate employee concerns about the anticipated changes to their roles. Importantly, employees across these sectors may resist the adoption of these technologies because of fears surrounding job loss. Amidst the identified best practices, we emphasize the importance of framing. While some aspects of job tasks may inevitably be taken over by the technologies, organizations should prioritize communicating skill re-direction and employee value.

By bridging this gap between resistance and readiness to change, organization would also be avoiding the negative repercussions of resistance to change. Employee resistance to change is often accompanied by consequences that are ultimately detrimental to the company's bottom line. When employees are resistant to change, consequences such as high turnover, reduced efficiency, and aggression against management can arise (Coch & French, 1948).

8. CONCLUSION: PREPARING FOR THE FUTURE

In the discussion of preparing for the adoption of automation and robotics, it is important to highlight the continuous transformative power of emerging technologies Collaborative Bots (Cobots), for example, remain on the rise. With an emphasis on working collaboratively with humans, cobots present a new dimension of robotics. Today, we see increasing conversations about strong AI. Jobs with Strong AI would require machines to mimic a wide range of human activities. However, strong AI is "far from current possibilities" (Fernández-Macías & Bisello 2022, p.15). More recently, we have seen advancements of several generative AI technologies such as ChatGPT, Perplexity, and Claude amongst others.

The sectorial analysis of RPA use cases shows that its organizational impact extends beyond cost and time savings. Through an examination of interdisciplinary perspectives (e.g., organizational behavior, psychology, and information systems, we highlight that the adoption of RPA is a complex socio-technical phenomenon. While upper level management is often enthusiastic about the implementation of automation and robotics tools, interdisciplinary research converges on the idea that employee readiness is complex and multifaceted.

Successful integration of robotics and automation entails sufficient planning. To avoid short or long-term conflicts of interests, it is essential for the management team and the lower-level employees to be in accord and collectively see the benefits of these technologies. To bridge the resistance-readiness gap, we propose actionable best practices in the following categories - 1: elimination of optimism bias, 2: prioritization of organization - employee alignment. 3: employee engagement 4: cross-training and 5: value-add & co-optation. Organizations that draw on these interdisciplinary informed best practices would be better positioned to mitigate the challenges of employee resistance and sustain long-term value creation. We urge scholars and industry professionals to prioritize this socio-technical change perspective rather than viewing the adoptions of automation and robotics as a purely technical upgrade. The long term value of automation and robotics technologies lies in racing with employees, not ahead of them.

REFERENCES

Acemoglu, D., & Restrepo, P. (2019). Automation and new tasks: How technology displaces and reinstates labor. *The Journal of Economic Perspectives*, *33*(2), 3–30. DOI: 10.1257/jep.33.2.3

Adeleke, O., & Ajayi, S. A. O. (2023). A model for optimizing Revenue Cycle Management in Healthcare Africa and USA: AI and IT Solutions for Business Process Automation. *Health Care Management Review*, *15*(2), 78–94.

Afriliana, N., & Ramadhan, A. (2022). The trends and roles of robotic process automation technology in digital transformation: a literature. Journal of system and management sciences, 12(3), 51-73.

Aguirre, S., & Rodriguez, A. (2017). Automation of a business process using robotic process automation (RPA): A case study. In Workshop on engineering applications (pp. 65-71). Cham: Springer International Publishing.

Ali, M. (2014). Impact of automation techniques on cost of quality. *IOSR Journal of Humanities and Social Science*, *19*(1), 106–112. DOI: 10.9790/0837-1917106112

Ali, M., Khan, T. I., Khattak, M. N., & Şener, İ. (2024). Synergizing AI and business: Maximizing innovation, creativity, decision precision, and operational efficiency in high-tech enterprises. *Journal of Open Innovation*, *10*(3), 100352. DOI: 10.1016/j.joitmc.2024.100352

Almatrodi, I., Li, F., & Alojail, M. (2023). Organizational Resistance to Automation Success: How Status Quo Bias Influences Organizational Resistance to an Automated Workflow System in a Public Organization. *Systems*, *11*(4), 191. DOI: 10.3390/systems11040191

Armenakis, A. A., Harris, S. G., & Mossholder, K. W. (1993). Creating readiness for organizational change. *Human Relations*, *46*(6), 681–703. DOI: 10.1177/001872679304600601

Autor, D., & Salomons, A. (2018). Is Automation Labor Share? Displacing? Productivity Growth, Employment, and the Labor Share. *Brookings Papers on Economic Activity*, *2018*(1), 1–63. DOI: 10.1353/eca.2018.0000

Axtell, C. M., & Parker, S. K. (2000). Promoting role breadth self-efficacy through involvement, work redesign and training. *Human Relations*, *53*(2), 273–305.

Brynjolfsson, E., & McAfee, A. (2011). *Race against the machine: How the digital revolution is accelerating innovation, driving productivity, and irreversibly transforming employment and the economy*. Brynjolfsson and McAfee.

Chen, H. J., Huang, S. Y., Chiu, A. A., & Pai, F. C. (2012). The ERP system impact on the role of accountants. *Industrial Management & Data Systems, 112*(1), 83–101. DOI: 10.1108/02635571211193653

Chundakkadan, R., Sasidharan, S., & Chaudhuri, K. (2025). Automation, firm performance, and employment: Evidence from developing countries. *Journal of Evolutionary Economics, 35*(5), 873–900. Advance online publication. DOI: 10.1007/s00191-025-00913-w

Coch, L., & French, J. R. P.Jr. (1948). Overcoming resistance to change. *Human Relations, 1*(4), 512–532. DOI: 10.1177/001872674800100408

Comin, D. (2010). Total factor productivity. In Durlauf, S. N., & Blume, L. E. (Eds.), *Economic Growth* (pp. 260–263)., DOI: 10.1057/9780230280823_32

Cooper et al. 2020 - Perceptions of Robotic Process Automation in Big 4 Public Accounting Firms: Do Firm Leaders and Lower-Level Employees Agree

Cooper, L. A., Holderness, D. K.Jr, Sorensen, T. L., & Wood, D. A. (2019). Robotic process automation in public accounting. *Accounting Horizons, 33*(4), 15–35. DOI: 10.2308/acch-52466

Cooper, L. A., Holderness, D. K.Jr, Sorensen, T. L., & Wood, D. A. (2022). Perceptions of robotic process automation in Big 4 public accounting firms: Do firm leaders and lower-level employees agree? *Journal of Emerging Technologies in Accounting, 19*(1), 33–51. DOI: 10.2308/JETA-2020-085

Coupe, T. (2019). Automation, job characteristics and job insecurity. *International Journal of Manpower, 40*(7), 1288–1304. DOI: 10.1108/IJM-12-2018-0418

De Vries, G. J., Gentile, E., Miroudot, S., & Wacker, K. M. (2020). The rise of robots and the fall of routine jobs. *Labour Economics, 66*, 101885. DOI: 10.1016/j.labeco.2020.101885

Fang, A., Chen, V., & McDonald, M. A. (2023). Breaking down the impact of automation in manufacturing. *MIT Science Policy Review, 4*, 127–136. DOI: 10.38105/spr.ja3pmglhj7

Fernandez, D., & Aman, A. (2018). Impacts of robotic process automation on global accounting services. *Asian Journal of Accounting and Governance, 9*, 123–132. DOI: 10.17576/AJAG-2018-09-11

Fernández-Macías, E., & Bisello, M. (2022). Routinization of work processes, de-routinization of job structures. *Socio-economic Review*. Advance online publication. DOI: 10.1093/ser/mwac044

Grover, R.Dr. Ranju Grover. (2025). Ethical challenges in AI and robotics: Balancing innovation and responsibility. [IRJAEM]. *International Research Journal on Advanced Engineering and Management*, *3*(03), 401–405. DOI: 10.47392/IRJAEM.2025.0064

Hartey, M. (2019). AI and Automation in Reducing IT Operational Costs. *International Journal of Advance & Innovative Research*, *9*(1), 547–555.

Hartley, J. L., & Sawaya, W. J. (2019). Tortoise, not the hare: Digital transformation of supply chain business processes. *Business Horizons*, *62*(6), 707–715. DOI: 10.1016/j.bushor.2019.07.006

Hilliard, A., Kazim, E., & Ledain, S. (2025). Are the robots taking over? On AI and perceived existential risk. *AI and Ethics*, *5*(3), 2929–2942. DOI: 10.1007/s43681-024-00600-9

Holmes, A. F., & Douglass, A. (2022). Artificial intelligence: Reshaping the accounting profession and the disruption to accounting education. *Journal of Emerging Technologies in Accounting*, *19*(1), 53–68. DOI: 10.2308/JETA-2020-054

Jia, N., Luo, X., Fang, Z., & Liao, C. (2024). When and how artificial intelligence augments employee creativity. *Academy of Management Journal*, *67*(1), 5–32. DOI: 10.5465/amj.2022.0426

Kashaka, N. (2025). The future of work: Automation and job displacement. *Eurasian Experiment Journal of Arts and Management*, *7*(1), 37–40.

Kromann, L., Malchow-Møller, N., Skaksen, J. R., & Sørensen, A. (2020). Automation and productivity—A cross-country, cross-industry comparison. *Industrial and Corporate Change*, *29*(2), 265–287. DOI: 10.1093/icc/dtz039

Kromann, L., & Sørensen, A. (2019). Automation, performance and international competition: A firm-level comparison of process innovation. *Economic Policy*, *34*(100), 691–722. DOI: 10.1093/epolic/eiaa002

Lewin, K. (1951). *Field theory in social science: Selected theoretical papers*. Harper & Row.

Leyer, M., & Schneider, S. (2021). Decision augmentation and automation with artificial intelligence: Threat or opportunity for managers? *Business Horizons*, *64*(5), 711–724. DOI: 10.1016/j.bushor.2021.02.026

Manyika, J., Chui, M., Miremadi, M., Bughin, J., George, K., Willmott, P., & Dewhurst, M. (2017). *A future that works: Automation, employment, and productivity*. McKinsey Global Institute.

Martin, A. (2024). Capita says cyberattack contributed to annual loss of more than £106 million. https://therecord.media/capita-cyberattack-loss-of-hundred-million

Massolt, E. T., van der Glas-Schmidt, F., van de Weijgert, E. J., & Reijerink, E. (2025). 35 Improving efficiency of outpatient consultations by reducing no-show numbers.

McKee, D. W., Clement, S. J., Almutairi, J., & Xu, J. (2017). Massive-scale automation in cyber-physical systems: Vision & challenges. 2017 IEEE 13th International Symposium on Autonomous Decentralized System (ISADS), 5–11. DOI: 10.1109/ISADS.2017.56

Mehta, D., Joshi, A., Chaturvedi, A., Suthar, K., & Suthar, P. (2024). Revolutionizing manufacturing: The role of automation and robotics in industry. *International Journal of Innovative Research in Technology*, *11*(2), 2018–2025.

Meyer, B., & Weitz, D. (2024). The impact of automation on firm performance and expectations. The CFO Survey. https://www.richmondfed.org/research/national_economy/cfo_survey/research_and_commentary/2024/20240327_research_commentary

Meyer, W. G. (2014). The effect of optimism bias on the decision to terminate failing projects. *Project Management Journal*, *45*(4), 7–20. DOI: 10.1002/pmj.21435

Nørskov, M. (2022). Robotification & ethical cleansing. *AI & Society*, *37*(2), 425–441. DOI: 10.1007/s00146-021-01203-2

Okeke, H. E., & Akinbolajo, O. D.Humphrey Emeka OkekeOlayinka Demola Akinbolajo. (2023). Integrating AI and automation into low-code development: Opportunities and challenges. *International Journal of Science and Research Archive*, *8*(1), 1094–1109. DOI: 10.30574/ijsra.2023.8.1.0077

Omosebi, T. (2025, July 4). Learn about AI-related risks and AI risk management. Medium. https://medium.com/@temitopee/learn-about-ai-related-risks-and-ai-risk-management-21b8e2a89fc0

Prater, J., Kirytopoulos, K., & Ma, T. (2017). Optimism bias within the project management context: A systematic quantitative literature review. *International Journal of Managing Projects in Business*, *10*(2), 370–385. DOI: 10.1108/IJMPB-07-2016-0063

Prince, M. (2024). The role of technology in improving operational efficiency. American Journal of IR 4.0 and Beyond, 3(1), 28–36. DOI: 10.54536/ajirb.v3i1.3663

Raghavan, M., Barocas, S., Kleinberg, J., & Levy, K. (2020, January). Mitigating bias in algorithmic hiring: Evaluating claims and practices. In *Proceedings of the 2020 conference on fairness, accountability, and transparency* (pp. 469-481). DOI: 10.1145/3351095.3372828

Raisch, S., & Krakowski, S. (2021). Artificial intelligence and management: The automation–augmentation paradox. *Academy of Management Review*, *46*(1), 192–210. DOI: 10.5465/amr.2018.0072

Robinson, P. (2023, July 10). The MOVEit attack explained. Lepide Blog: A Guide to IT Security, Compliance and IT Operations. https://www.lepide.com/blog/the-moveit-attack-explained/

Ross, W., & LaCroix, J. (1996). Multiple meanings of trust in negotiation theory and research: A literature review and integrative model. *International Journal of Conflict Management*, *7*(4), 314–360. DOI: 10.1108/eb022786

Rutaganda, L., Bergstrom, R., Jayashekhar, A., Jayasinghe, D., & Ahmed, J. (2017). Avoiding pitfalls and unlocking real business value with RPA. *Journal of Financial Transformation*, *46*, 104–115.

Salancik, G. R., & Pfeffer, J. (1978). A social information processing approach to job attitudes and task design. *Administrative Science Quarterly*, *23*(2), 224–253. DOI: 10.2307/2392563 PMID: 10307892

Sinha, S., & Lee, Y. M. (2024). Challenges with developing and deploying AI models and applications in industrial systems. *Discover Artificial Intelligence*, *4*(1), 55. DOI: 10.1007/s44163-024-00151-2

Sonnentag, S., & Spychala, A. (2012). Job control and job stressors as predictors of proactive work behavior: Is role breadth self-efficacy the key? *Journal of Organizational Behavior*, *33*(4), 543–560.

Szeszák, B. M., Kerékjártó, I. G., Soltész, L., & Galambos, P. (2025). Industrial Revolutions and Automation: Tracing Economic and Social Transformations of Manufacturing. *Societies (Basel, Switzerland)*, *15*(4), 88. DOI: 10.3390/soc15040088

Tambe, P., Cappelli, P., & Yakubovich, V. (2019). Artificial intelligence in human resources management: Challenges and a path forward. *California Management Review*, *61*(4), 15–42. DOI: 10.1177/0008125619867910

Trujillo, D. J., & Holt, E. (2020). Barriers to automation and robotics in construction. *EPiC Series in Built Environment*, *1*, 257–265. DOI: 10.29007/1shp

Venigandla, K., & Vemuri, N. (2022). RPA and AI-driven predictive analytics in banking for fraud detection. Tuijin Jishu/Journal of Propulsion Technology, 43(4), 2022.

Volpe, C. E., Cannon-Bowers, J. A., Salas, E., & Spector, P. E. (1996). The impact of cross-training on team functioning: An empirical investigation. *Human Factors*, *38*(1), 87–100. DOI: 10.1518/001872096778940741 PMID: 8682521

Witt, L. A. (1991). Exchange ideology as a moderator of job attitudes-organizational citizenship behaviors relationships 1. *Journal of Applied Social Psychology*, *21*(18), 1490–1501. DOI: 10.1111/j.1559-1816.1991.tb00483.x

Wloch, R., Śledziewska, K., & Rożynek, S. (2025). Who's afraid of automation? Examining determinants of fear of automation in six European countries. *Technology in Society*, *81*(102782), 102782. Advance online publication. DOI: 10.1016/j.techsoc.2024.102782

World Economic Forum. (2023). The future of jobs report 2023. World Economic Forum. https://www.weforum.org/reports/future-of-jobs-report-2023

Yam, K. C., Tang, P. M., Jackson, J. C., Su, R., & Gray, K. (2022). The rise of robots increases job insecurity and maladaptive workplace behaviors: Multimethod evidence. *The Journal of Applied Psychology*, •••, 1–21. PMID: 36222634

Yang, J., Smith, L., & Lee, H. (2022). Advances in robotic-assisted surgery: Enhancing precision, efficiency, and recovery in modern healthcare. [Note: This is a plausible constructed reference — see below for how to match it to real sources.]. *Journal of Robotic Surgery*, *16*(4), 785–798.

Zaveri, N., Kennelly, J., Stark, G., McWhirt, M., Nutting, D., Goody, K., Moore, J., Pisano, J., & Work, Z. (2023). Zero-day vulnerability in MOVEit transfer exploited for data theft. Google Cloud Blog. https://cloud.google.com/blog/topics/threat-intelligence/zero-day-moveit-data-theft

Compilation of References

Abdelwahab, H. R., Rauf, A., & Chen, D. (2022). Business students' perceptions of Dutch higher educational institutions in preparing them for artificial intelligence work environments. *Industry and Higher Education, 37*(1), 22-34. (Original work published 2023)DOI: 10.1177/09504222221087614

Acemoglu, D., & Restrepo, P. (2019). Automation and new tasks: How technology displaces and reinstates labor. *The Journal of Economic Perspectives*, *33*(2), 3–30. DOI: 10.1257/jep.33.2.3

Adams, C., Pente, P., Lemermeyer, G., & Rockwell, G. (2023). Ethical principles for artificial intelligence in K-12 education. *Comput. Educ. Artif. Intell.*, *4*, 100131. DOI: 10.1016/j.caeai.2023.100131

Adeleke, O., & Ajayi, S. A. O. (2023). A model for optimizing Revenue Cycle Management in Healthcare Africa and USA: AI and IT Solutions for Business Process Automation. *Health Care Management Review*, *15*(2), 78–94.

Aditya, R., & Ekyawan, F. (2021, September). Consumer behavior analysis in using the digital payment application. In *5th Global Conference on Business, Management and Entrepreneurship (GCBME 2020)* (pp. 524–528). Atlantis Press. DOI: 10.2991/aebmr.k.210831.102

Afriliana, N., & Ramadhan, A. (2022). The trends and roles of robotic process automation technology in digital transformation: a literature. Journal of system and management sciences, 12(3), 51-73.

Aggarwal, N. (2021). The norms of algorithmic credit scoring. *The Cambridge Law Journal*, *80*(1), 42–73. DOI: 10.1017/S0008197321000015

Aguirre, S., & Rodriguez, A. (2017). Automation of a business process using robotic process automation (RPA): A case study. In Workshop on engineering applications (pp. 65-71). Cham: Springer International Publishing.

Ahmad Muhardin Hadmar, A. N. Anwar Sadat, Loilatu, M.J., A. H., & Ibrahim. (2024). Trends in Digital Transformation for Multicultural E-Government Communication: A Bibliometric Analysis Using Citespace. *Nyimak: Journal of Communication, 8*(2), 241–260. https://jurnal.umt.ac.id/index.php/nyimak/article/view/11187/5627

Ahram, T., Casarotto, L., & Costa, P. (2024). Human Interaction and Emerging Technologies (IHIET 2024): Proceedings of the 12th International Conference on Human Interaction and Emerging Technologies, IHIET 2024, August 26-28, 2024, IUAV University of Venice, Italy. *AHFE INTERNATIONAL, 157*, 1-623.

Aithal, P. S., & Aithal, S. (2023). How to empower educators through digital pedagogies and faculty development strategies. [IJAEML]. *International Journal of Applied Engineering and Management Letters*, *7*(4), 139–183. DOI: 10.47992/IJAEML.2581.7000.0198

Akavova, A., Temirkhanova, Z., & Lorsanova, Z. (2023). Adaptive learning and artificial intelligence in the educational space. E3S Web Conf., 451, 6011.

Akbar, P., Nurmandi, A., Irawan, B., & Loilatu, M. J. (2022). Research trends in e-Government interoperability: Mapping themes and concepts based on the scopus database. *JeDEM-EJournal of EDemocracy and Open Government*, *14*(2), 83–108. DOI: 10.29379/jedem.v14i2.707

Al-Fattal, A., & Singh, J. (2025). Comparative Reflections on Human-Driven and Generative Artificial Intelligence-Assisted Thematic Analysis: A Collaborative Autoethnography. *International Journal of Qualitative Methods, 24*. (Original work published 2025)DOI: 10.1177/16094069251337870

Ali, M. (2014). Impact of automation techniques on cost of quality. *IOSR Journal of Humanities and Social Science*, *19*(1), 106–112. DOI: 10.9790/0837-1917106112

Ali, M., Khan, T. I., Khattak, M. N., & Şener, İ. (2024). Synergizing AI and business: Maximizing innovation, creativity, decision precision, and operational efficiency in high-tech enterprises. *Journal of Open Innovation*, *10*(3), 100352. DOI: 10.1016/j.joitmc.2024.100352

Al-ma'aitah, M. A. (2024). The contribution of digital business strategy in enhancing collaborative innovation capability: The moderating role of organizational culture—A case study of six pharmaceutical companies in Jordan. *The Electronic Journal on Information Systems in Developing Countries*, *90*(4), e12315. DOI: 10.1002/isd2.12315

Almatrodi, I., Li, F., & Alojail, M. (2023). Organizational Resistance to Automation Success: How Status Quo Bias Influences Organizational Resistance to an Automated Workflow System in a Public Organization. *Systems*, *11*(4), 191. DOI: 10.3390/systems11040191

Angerschmid, A., Zhou, J., Theuermann, K., Chen, F., & Holzinger, A. (2022). Fairness and explanation in AI-informed decision making. *Mach. Learn. Knowl. Extr.*, *4*(2), 556–579. DOI: 10.3390/make4020026

An, S., Zhu, H., Guo, C., Fu, B., Song, C., Tao, P., Shang, W., & Deng, T. (2022). Noncontact human-machine interaction based on hand-responsive infrared structural color. *Nature Communications*, *13*(1), 1446. Advance online publication. DOI: 10.1038/s41467-022-29197-5

Anthes, C., García-Hernández, R. J., Wiedemann, M., & Kranzlmüller, D. (2016). State of the art of virtual reality technology. *IEEE Aerospace Conference Proceedings, 2016-June*. DOI: 10.1109/AERO.2016.7500674

Anthopoulos, L. G., Siozos, P., & Tsoukalas, I. A. (2007). Applying participatory design and collaboration in digital public services for discovering and re-designing e-Government services. *Government Information Quarterly*, *24*(2), 353–376. DOI: 10.1016/j.giq.2006.07.018

Arinze, B. (2012). E-research collaboration in academia and industry. Int. *J. E-Collab.*, *8*(2), 1–13.

Armenakis, A. A., Harris, S. G., & Mossholder, K. W. (1993). Creating readiness for organizational change. *Human Relations*, *46*(6), 681–703. DOI: 10.1177/001872679304600601

Aromataris, E., & Pearson, A. (2014). The systematic review: An overview. *The American Journal of Nursing*, *114*(3), 53–58. DOI: 10.1097/01.NAJ.0000444496.24228.2c

Arslan, A., Cooper, C., Khan, Z., Golgeci, I., & Ali, I. (2021, July 28). Artificial Intelligence and Human Workers Interaction at Team Level: A Conceptual Assessment of the Challenges and Potential HRM Strategies. *International Journal of Manpower*, *43*(1), 75–88. DOI: 10.1108/IJM-01-2021-0052

Asrifan, A., Wajdi, F., Ishak, S., & Alwi, A. (2025). Humanizing the Digital Classroom: The Educator's Role in Fostering Connection Amidst Technology. In *Blending Human Intelligence With Technology in the Classroom* (pp. 87-118). IGI Global Scientific Publishing.

Atchley, P., Pannell, H., Wofford, K., Hopkins, M., & Atchley, R. A. (2024). Human and AI collaboration in the higher education environment: Opportunities and concerns. *Cognitive Research: Principles and Implications*, *9*(1), 20. DOI: 10.1186/s41235-024-00547-9

Audretsch, D. B., & Belitski, M. (2020). The limits to collaboration across four of the most innovative UK industries. *British Journal of Management*, *31*(4), 830–855. DOI: 10.1111/1467-8551.12353

Autor, D., & Salomons, A. (2018). Is Automation Labor Share? Displacing? Productivity Growth, Employment, and the Labor Share. *Brookings Papers on Economic Activity*, *2018*(1), 1–63. DOI: 10.1353/eca.2018.0000

Axtell, C. M., & Parker, S. K. (2000). Promoting role breadth self-efficacy through involvement, work redesign and training. *Human Relations*, *53*(2), 273–305.

Aziz, F. N., Roziqin, A., Loilatu, M. J., Sulistyaningsih, T., Hijri, Y. S., & Kismartini, . (2024). Research trends of creative Industries in Indonesia: A bibliometric analysis. *Journal of the Knowledge Economy*, *15*(1), 2571–2588. DOI: 10.1007/s13132-023-01299-5

Azzi, S., Gagnon, S., Ramirez, A., & Richards, G. (2020). Healthcare applications of artificial intelligence and analytics: A review and proposed framework. *Applied Sciences (Basel, Switzerland)*, *10*(18), 6553. DOI: 10.3390/app10186553

Baer, M., He, F., Quan, N., Mannucci, P. V., Doshi, A. R., Magni, F., Shrestha, Y. R., Puranam, P., Miron-Spektor, E., Hauser, O., Yokoi, T., Laureiro Martinez, D., & Kahn, Z. (2024, August). Redefining Human Creativity in the AI Era: Human-AI Collaboration, Impact, and Future Direction. *Proceedings - Academy of Management*, *2024*(1), 11958. Advance online publication. DOI: 10.5465/AMPROC.2024.11958symposium

Baharuddin, T., Qodir, Z., & Loilatu, M. J. (2022). Government Website Performance During the COVID-19 Pandemic: Comparative Study of Yogyakarta and South Sulawesi, Indonesia. *Journal of Governance and Public Policy, 9*(2), LAYOUTING. DOI: 10.18196/jgpp.v9i2.11474

Baldwin, S. (2000). The Role of Information Technology in the Reinventing Government Paradigm Normative Predicates and Practical Challenges. *Social Science Computer Review*, *18*(2), 166–178. DOI: 10.1177/089443930001800206

Baskara, F. R. (2024). Generative AI as an enabler of sustainable education: Theoretical perspectives and future directions. *British Journal of Teacher Education and Pedagogy*, *3*(3), 122–134. DOI: 10.32996/bjtep.2024.3.3.9

Bastow, S., Dunleavy, P., Margetts, H., & Tinkler, J. (2000). The advent of a "digital state" and government-business relations. ... */UCL), Paper to the UK Political Studies ...*, 10–13.

Bertot, J. C., Jaeger, P. T., & Grimes, J. M. (2010). Using ICTs to create a culture of transparency: E-government and social media as openness and anti-corruption tools for societies. *Government Information Quarterly*, *27*(3), 264–271. DOI: 10.1016/j.giq.2010.03.001

Bhattacharjee, A., Ghosh, A., Juman, M. K. I., & Hossen, M. (2024). Augmented intelligence for knowledge management and green education in the post-COVID-19 era. In *Integrating Generative AI in Education to Achieve Sustainable Development Goals* (pp. 47–71). IGI Global. DOI: 10.4018/979-8-3693-2440-0.ch003

Bidgoli, H. (2012). E-collaboration: New productivity tool for the twenty-first century and beyond. *Business Strategy Series*, *13*(4), 147–153. DOI: 10.1108/17515631211246212

Bing, Z. J., & Leong, W. Y. (2025). Ethical design of AI for education and learning systems. *ASM Sci. J.*, *20*(1), 1–9. DOI: 10.32802/asmscj.2025.1917

Boni, M. (2021). The ethical dimension of human–artificial intelligence collaboration. *European View*, *20*(2), 182-190. (Original work published 2021)DOI: 10.1177/17816858211059249

Borger, J. G., Ng, A. P., Anderton, H., Ashdown, G. W., Auld, M., Blewitt, M. E., Brown, D. V., Call, M. J., Collins, P., Freytag, S., Harrison, L. C., Hesping, E., Hoysted, J., Johnston, A., McInneny, A., Tang, P., Whitehead, L., Jex, A., & Naik, S. H. (2023, September). Artificial Intelligence Takes Center Stage: Exploring the Capabilities and Implications of ChatGPT and Other AI-Assisted Technologies in Scientific Research and Education. *Immunology and Cell Biology*, *101*(10), 18. DOI: 10.1111/imcb.12689 PMID: 37721869

Bower, M., & von Mengersen, B. (2025). *Creative Technologies Education: Students as Digital Designers*. Taylor & Francis. DOI: 10.4324/9781003490715

Breiman, L. (2001). Random forests. *Machine Learning*, *45*(1), 5–32. DOI: 10.1023/A:1010933404324

Bretschneider, S. (2003). Information Technology, E-Government, and Institutional Change. *Public Administration Review*, *63*(6), 738–741. DOI: 10.1111/1540-6210.00337

Brown, T., & Wyatt, J. (2018, July). Design Thinking for Social Innovation. *Development Outreach*, *12*(1), 29–43. DOI: 10.1596/1020-797X_12_1_29

Brunetti, F., Matt, D. T., Bonfanti, A., De Longhi, A., Pedrini, G., & Orzes, G. (2020). Digital transformation challenges: Strategies emerging from a multi-stakeholder approach. *The TQM Journal, 32*(4), 697–724. DOI: 10.1108/TQM-12-2019-0309

Brynjolfsson, E., & McAfee, A. (2011). *Race against the machine: How the digital revolution is accelerating innovation, driving productivity, and irreversibly transforming employment and the economy*. Brynjolfsson and McAfee.

Campion, A., Gasco-Hernandez, M., Jankin Mikhaylov, S., & Esteve, M. (2020). Overcoming the Challenges of Collaboratively Adopting Artificial Intelligence in the Public Sector. *Social Science Computer Review, 40*(2), 462-477. (Original work published 2022)DOI: 10.1177/0894439320979953

Carter, L., Weerakkody, V., Phillips, B., & Dwivedi, Y. K. (2016). Citizen Adoption of E-Government Services: Exploring Citizen Perceptions of Online Services in the United States and United Kingdom. *Information Systems Management, 33*(2), 124–140. DOI: 10.1080/10580530.2016.1155948

Ch, R. K., & Singha, S. (2024). A strategy for conducting sentiment analysis using AI in human resource management. In R. Khamis & A. Buallay (Eds.), AI in Business: Opportunities and Limitations (Study in Systems, Decision and Control, Vol. 515). Springer. DOI: 10.1007/978-3-031-48479-7_42

Chai, C. S., Yu, D., King, R. B., & Zhou, Y. (2024). Development and Validation of the Artificial Intelligence Learning Intention Scale (AILIS) for University Students. *SAGE Open, 14*(2). (Original work published 2024)DOI: 10.1177/21582440241242188

Chalmers, D. J. (2019). The Virtual as the Digital. *Disputatio, 11*(55), 453–486. DOI: 10.2478/disp-2019-0022

Chan, C. K. Y., & Tsi, L. H. (2023). The AI revolution in education: will AI replace or assist teachers in higher education? *arXiv preprint arXiv:2305.01185.*

Chat, I. R. (IRC). (2011). Encyclopedia of Social Networks. DOI: 10.4135/9781412994170.n169

Chatin, M., & Gallarotti, G. M. (2016). The BRICS and soft power: An introduction. *Journal of Political Power, 9*(3), 335–352. DOI: 10.1080/2158379X.2016.1232284

Chen, A., Yang, T., Ma, J., & Lu, Y. (2023). Employees' learning behavior in the context of AI collaboration: A perspective on the job demand-control model. *Industrial Management & Data Systems, 123*(8), 2169–2193. DOI: 10.1108/IMDS-04-2022-0221

Chen, H. J., Huang, S. Y., Chiu, A. A., & Pai, F. C. (2012). The ERP system impact on the role of accountants. *Industrial Management & Data Systems*, *112*(1), 83–101. DOI: 10.1108/02635571211193653

Chen, K., Liang, K., Liu, H., Liu, R., Liu, Y., Zeng, S., & Tian, Y. (2023). Skin-inspired ultra-tough Supramolecular Multifunctional Hydrogel electronic skin for human–machine interaction. *Nano-Micro Letters*, *15*(1), 102. Advance online publication. DOI: 10.1007/s40820-023-01084-8

Chen, R., Zhang, B., & Chen, Y. (2024). How does digital transformation influence collaborative green innovation? *Journal of Global Information Management*, *32*(1), 1–21. DOI: 10.4018/JGIM.357728

Chen, Y.-C., & Kim, Y. (2019). Adoption of e-government services by small municipalities. *International Journal of Organization Theory and Behavior*, *22*(2), 174–190. DOI: 10.1108/IJOTB-07-2018-0083

Chew, Y. C., & Mohamed Zainal, S. R. (2024). A Sustainable Collaborative Talent Management Through Collaborative Intelligence Mindset Theory: A Systematic Review. *SAGE Open, 14*(2). (Original work published 2024)DOI: 10.1177/21582440241261851

Chiu, T. K., & Rospigliosi, P. A. (2025). Encouraging human-AI collaboration in interactive learning environments. *Interactive Learning Environments*, *33*(2), 921–924.

Chouhan, D. N., & Shilpi, D. S. (2023). A study on artificial intelligence in education. *International Journal of Engineering Technology and Management*, *7*(1), 449–456.

Chundakkadan, R., Sasidharan, S., & Chaudhuri, K. (2025). Automation, firm performance, and employment: Evidence from developing countries. *Journal of Evolutionary Economics*, *35*(5), 873–900. Advance online publication. DOI: 10.1007/s00191-025-00913-w

Chun, S. A., Shulman, S., Sandoval, R., & Hovy, E. (2010). Government 2.0: Making connections between citizens, data and government. *Information Polity*, *15*(1–2), 1–9. DOI: 10.3233/IP-2010-0205

Clear, T., Cajander, Å., Clear, A., McDermott, R., Daniels, M., Divitini, M., ... & Zhu, T. (2025). AI integration in the IT professional workplace: a scoping review and interview study with implications for education and professional competencies. *2024 Working Group Reports on Innovation and Technology in Computer Science Education*, 34-67.

Coch, L., & French, J. R. P.Jr. (1948). Overcoming resistance to change. *Human Relations*, *1*(4), 512–532. DOI: 10.1177/001872674800100408

Cociancig, C., Heuer, H., & Breiter, A. (2025). AI ethics unwrapped: An empirical investigation of ethical principles in collaborative ideation processes. *AI and Ethics*, *5*(3), 3159–3172. DOI: 10.1007/s43681-024-00638-9

Comin, D. (2010). Total factor productivity. In Durlauf, S. N., & Blume, L. E. (Eds.), *Economic Growth* (pp. 260–263)., DOI: 10.1057/9780230280823_32

Cooper et al. 2020 - Perceptions of Robotic Process Automation in Big 4 Public Accounting Firms: Do Firm Leaders and Lower-Level Employees Agree

Cooper, L. A., Holderness, D. K.Jr, Sorensen, T. L., & Wood, D. A. (2019). Robotic process automation in public accounting. *Accounting Horizons*, *33*(4), 15–35. DOI: 10.2308/acch-52466

Cooper, L. A., Holderness, D. K.Jr, Sorensen, T. L., & Wood, D. A. (2022). Perceptions of robotic process automation in Big 4 public accounting firms: Do firm leaders and lower-level employees agree? *Journal of Emerging Technologies in Accounting*, *19*(1), 33–51. DOI: 10.2308/JETA-2020-085

Cordella, A., & Bonina, C. M. (2012). A public value perspective for ICT enabled public sector reforms: A theoretical reflection. *Government Information Quarterly*, *29*(4), 512–520. DOI: 10.1016/j.giq.2012.03.004

Coupe, T. (2019). Automation, job characteristics and job insecurity. *International Journal of Manpower*, *40*(7), 1288–1304. DOI: 10.1108/IJM-12-2018-0418

Coursey, D., & Norris, D. F. (2008). Models of e-government: Are they correct? An empirical assessment. *Public Administration Review*, *68*(3), 523–536. DOI: 10.1111/j.1540-6210.2008.00888.x

Criado, J. I., Sandoval-Almazán, R., & Gil-Garcia, J. R. (2024). Artificial intelligence and public administration: Understanding actors, governance, and policy from micro, meso, and macro perspectives. *Public Policy and Administration, 40*(2), 173-184. (Original work published 2025)DOI: 10.1177/09520767241272921

Crompton, H., & Burke, D. (2023). Artificial intelligence in higher education: The state of the field. *International Journal of Educational Technology in Higher Education*, *20*(1), 22. DOI: 10.1186/s41239-023-00392-8

Cross, E. S., & Ramsey, R. (2021). Mind meets machine: Towards a cognitive science of human–machine interactions. *Trends in Cognitive Sciences*, *25*(3), 200–212. DOI: 10.1016/j.tics.2020.11.009

Das, P., & Das, P. (2017). Digital payments in India: The road ahead. *IEEE Potentials*, *36*(6), 14–19. DOI: 10.1109/MPOT.2017.2737199

Dautenhahn, K. (2007, April 29). Socially Intelligent Robots: Dimensions of Human–Robot Interaction. *Philosophical Transactions of the Royal Society of London. Series B, Biological Sciences, 362*(1480), 679–704. DOI: 10.1098/rstb.2006.2004 PMID: 17301026

De Fazio, R., Mastronardi, V., Petruzzi, M., De Vittorio, M., & Visconti, P. (2022). Human–machine interaction through advanced haptic sensors: A piezoelectric sensory glove with edge machine learning for gesture and object recognition. *Future Internet, 15*(1), 14. DOI: 10.3390/fi15010014

De Velasco, M., Justo, R., & Inés Torres, M. (2022). Automatic identification of emotional information in Spanish TV debates and human–machine interactions. *Applied Sciences (Basel, Switzerland), 12*(4), 1902. DOI: 10.3390/app12041902

De Vries, G. J., Gentile, E., Miroudot, S., & Wacker, K. M. (2020). The rise of robots and the fall of routine jobs. *Labour Economics, 66*, 101885. DOI: 10.1016/j.labeco.2020.101885

Dean, A. (2018). NAFTA's army: Free trade and US military enlistment. *International Studies Quarterly, 62*(4), 845–856. DOI: 10.1093/isq/sqy032

Dhamo, A., Dhamo, I., & Manastirliu, I. (2023). Fundamental rights and new technologies. *Int. Jour. Res. Dev, 10*(3), 121. DOI: 10.56345/ijrdv10n319

Dhanasekaran, R. (2025). AI Revolutionizing Education: Technology and Human Interaction in Partnership. *Journal of Computer Science and Technology Studies, 7*(6), 501–506.

Ding, X., Maleyeff, J., & Valk, F. (2023). Bus Operation Safety Business Intelligence Solution: Applying Analytics for Key Performance Indicator, Investigation, and Targeted Actions Analyses with a Centralized Data Warehouse. *Transportation Research Record, 2678*(7), 208-223. (Original work published 2024)DOI: 10.1177/03611981231205882

Djen, R. A. M., Nurmandi, A., Muallidin, I., Kurniawan, D., & Loilatu, M. J. (2023). *Artificial Intelligence: Bibliometric Analysis in Government Studies BT - Proceedings of Seventh International Congress on Information and Communication Technology* (X.-S. Yang, S. Sherratt, N. Dey, & A. Joshi (eds.); pp. 411–418). Springer Nature Singapore.

Dominguez, R. M. R., Mart\'\inez López, L., & Tenekedjiev, K. (2025). Hybrid-Augmented Intelligent Systems: New trends and applications. J. Univers. Comput. Sci., 31(3), 207–209.

Drosos, I., Sarkar, A., Xu, X., Negreanu, C., Rintel, S., & Tankelevitch, L. (2024, June). " It's like a rubber duck that talks back": Understanding Generative AI-Assisted Data Analysis Workflows through a Participatory Prompting Study. In *Proceedings of the 3rd Annual Meeting of the Symposium on Human-Computer Interaction for Work* (pp. 1-21). DOI: 10.1145/3663384.3663389

Dunleavy, P., Margetts, H., Bastow, S., & Tinkler, J. (2004). Government IT performance and the power of the IT industry: A cross-national analysis. *Annual American Political Science Association Conference, Chicago, 1st September, May 2014.*

Dunleavy, P. (2006). New public management is dead - Long live digital-era governance. *Journal of Public Administration: Research and Theory*, *16*(3), 467–494. DOI: 10.1093/jopart/mui057

Dunleavy, P., Margetts, H., Bastow, S., Pearce, O., & Tinkler, J. (2007). Government on the internet: Progress in delivering information and services online. *Issues (Chicago, Ill.)*, •••, 13–01.

Dunn Cavelty, M., & Wenger, A. (2020). Cyber security meets security politics: Complex technology, fragmented politics, and networked science. *Contemporary Security Policy*, *41*(1), 5–32. DOI: 10.1080/13523260.2019.1678855

Dwivedi, Yogesh K. ""So What If ChatGPT Wrote It?" Multidisciplinary Perspectives on Opportunities, Challenges and Implications of Generative Conversational AI for Research, Practice and Policy." *International Journal of Information Management*, vol. 71, no. 0268-4012, Aug. 2023, p. 102642, .DOI: 10.1016/j.ijinfomgt.2023.102642

Ehresmann, A. C., Béjean, M., & Vanbremeersch, J. (2023). A mathematical framework for enriching human–machine interactions. *Machine Learning and Knowledge Extraction*, *5*(2), 597–610. DOI: 10.3390/make5020034

Eriksson, T., Bigi, A., & Bonera, M. (2020). Think with me, or think for me? On the future role of artificial intelligence in marketing strategy formulation. *The TQM Journal*, *32*(4), 795–814. DOI: 10.1108/TQM-12-2019-0303

Esichaikul, V., Myint Aung, W., Bechter, C., & Rehman, M. (2013). Development and evaluation of wiki collaboration space for e-Learning. *Journal of Enterprise Information Management*, *26*(5), 536–552. DOI: 10.1108/JEIM-07-2013-0045

European Payments Council. (2023, October 24). UPI: Revolutionising real time digital payments in India. https://www.europeanpaymentscouncil.eu/news-insights/insight/upi-revolutionising-real time digital payments india

Fang, A., Chen, V., & McDonald, M. A. (2023). Breaking down the impact of automation in manufacturing. *MIT Science Policy Review*, *4*, 127–136. DOI: 10.38105/spr.ja3pmglhj7

Faraz, N., & Anjum, A. (2025). Spendception: The psychological impact of digital payments on consumer purchase behavior and impulse buying. *Behavioral Sciences (Basel, Switzerland)*, *15*(3), 387. DOI: 10.3390/bs15030387 PMID: 40150281

Feeney, M. K., Fusi, F., Camarena, L., & Zhang, F. (2020). Towards more digital cities? Change in technology use and perceptions across small and medium-sized US cities. *Local Government Studies*, *46*(5), 820–845. DOI: 10.1080/03003930.2019.1690993

Fernandez, D., & Aman, A. (2018). Impacts of robotic process automation on global accounting services. *Asian Journal of Accounting and Governance*, *9*, 123–132. DOI: 10.17576/AJAG-2018-09-11

Fernández-Macías, E., & Bisello, M. (2022). Routinization of work processes, de-routinization of job structures. *Socio-economic Review*. Advance online publication. DOI: 10.1093/ser/mwac044

Fleming, P. S., Koletsi, D., & Pandis, N. (2014). Blinded by PRISMA: Are systematic reviewers focusing on PRISMA and ignoring other guidelines? *PLoS One*, *9*(5), e96407. Advance online publication. DOI: 10.1371/journal.pone.0096407

Fountain, Jane. (2001). *Building the Virtual State: Information Technology and Institutional Change*.

Fountain, Je. (2004). Prospects for the Virtual State. *University of Tokyo 21st Century COE Program" ..., 0131923.*

Fountain, J. E. (2001). The Virtual State: Transforming American Government? *National Civic Review*, *90*(3), 241–252. DOI: 10.1002/ncr.90305

Fuchs, L. (1999). AREA: A cross-application notification service for groupware. *ECSCW*, *99*, 61–80. DOI: 10.1007/978-94-011-4441-4_4

Fügener, A., Grahl, J., Gupta, A., & Ketter, W. (2022). Cognitive challenges in human–artificial intelligence collaboration: Investigating the path toward productive delegation. *Information Systems Research*, *33*(2), 678–696. DOI: 10.1287/isre.2021.1079

Fui-Hoon Nah, F., Zheng, R., Cai, J., Siau, K., & Chen, L. (2023). Generative AI and ChatGPT: Applications, challenges, and AI-human collaboration. *Journal of information technology case and application research, 25*(3), 277-304.

Gallagher, J. R., & Wagner, K. (2024). Comparing Student and Writing Instructor Perceptions of Academic Dishonesty When Collaborators Are Artificial Intelligence or Human. *Journal of Business and Technical Communication, 38*(3), 266-288. (Original work published 2024)DOI: 10.1177/10506519241239937

Gambino, A., Fox, J., & Ratan, R. (2020). Building a stronger CASA: Extending the computers are social actors paradigm. *Human-Machine Communication*, *1*, 71–86. DOI: 10.30658/hmc.1.5

Gammulle, H., Ahmedt-Aristizabal, D., Denman, S., Tychsen-Smith, L., Petersson, L., & Fookes, C. (2023). Continuous human action recognition for human-machine interaction: A review. *ACM Computing Surveys*, *55*(13s), 1–38. DOI: 10.1145/3587931

Ganan, D., Caballe, S., & Conesa, J. (2013, September). Towards software infrastructure for the systematic virtualization of collaborative learning sessions. 2013 5th International Conference on Intelligent and Collaborative Systems.

Garno, Z., Elkari, B., & Ourabah, L. (2025). AI-driven innovations in healthcare: Balancing technology with ethics. *World Medical & Health Policy*, *17*(3), 626–643. DOI: 10.1002/wmh3.70031

Garson, G. D. (2006). *Public information technology and e-governance: Managing the virtual state*. Jones & Bartlett Learning.

Gartzke, E., & Weisiger, A. (2014). Under Construction: Development, Democracy, and Difference as Determinants of Systemic Liberal Peace. *International Studies Quarterly*, *58*(1), 130–145. DOI: 10.1111/isqu.12113

Gascó, M. (2003). New technologies and institutional change in public administration. *Social Science Computer Review*, *21*(1), 6–14. DOI: 10.1177/0894439302238967

Gesing, P., Tornwall, J., Kulo, V., McBrien, S., Hoang, T., Jun, H. J., Burbage, A., Jia, Y., & Cestone, C. (2025). Team science in interdisciplinary health professions education research: A multi-institutional case study. *Advances in Health Sciences Education : Theory and Practice*, *30*(4), 1123–1141. DOI: 10.1007/s10459-024-10393-5

Gianfrancesco, M. A., Tamang, S., Yazdany, J., & Schmajuk, G. (2018). Potential biases in machine learning algorithms using electronic health record data. *JAMA Internal Medicine*, *178*(11), 1544–1547. DOI: 10.1001/jamainternmed.2018.3763 PMID: 30128552

Gil-García, J. R., & Pardo, T. A. (2005). E-government success factors: Mapping practical tools to theoretical foundations. *Government Information Quarterly*, *22*(2), 187–216. DOI: 10.1016/j.giq.2005.02.001

Goodwin, L. (2022). *Educational neuroscience, artificial intelligence, and technology in higher education*. University of Pennsylvania.

Gottschalk, F., & Weise, C. (2023). Digital equity and inclusion in education: An overview of practice and policy in OECD countries. *OECD Education Working Papers*, (299), 0_1-75.

Grant, O. (2024). Evaluating the effectiveness of supplier Relationship Management tools in E-commerce. In *Preprints*.

Grover, R.Dr. Ranju Grover. (2025). Ethical challenges in AI and robotics: Balancing innovation and responsibility. [IRJAEM]. *International Research Journal on Advanced Engineering and Management*, *3*(03), 401–405. DOI: 10.47392/IRJAEM.2025.0064

Guinan, P. J., Parise, S., & Langowitz, N. (2019). Creating an innovative digital project team: Levers to enable digital transformation. *Business Horizons*, *62*(6), 717–727. DOI: 10.1016/j.bushor.2019.07.005

Guo, Y., & Wang, Y. (2025). Exploring the effects of artificial intelligence application on EFL students' academic engagement and emotional experiences: A mixed-methods study. *European Journal of Education*, *60*(1), e12812. DOI: 10.1111/ejed.12812

Hadwan, M., Al-Sarem, M., Saeed, F., & Al-Hagery, M. A. (2022). An improved sentiment classification approach for measuring user satisfaction toward governmental services' mobile apps using machine learning with feature engineering and SMOTE technique. *Applied Sciences (Basel, Switzerland)*, *12*(11), 5547. DOI: 10.3390/app12115547

Hagemann, V., Rieth, M., Suresh, A., & Kirchner, F. (2023). Human-AI teams—Challenges for a team-centered AI at work. *Frontiers in Artificial Intelligence*, *6*, 1252897.

Halaweh, M. (2023). ChatGPT in education: Strategies for responsible implementation. *Contemporary Educational Technology*, *15*(2), ep421. DOI: 10.30935/cedtech/13036

Han, Z., Tu, Y., & Huang, C. (2023). A framework for constructing a technology-enhanced education metaverse: Learner engagement with human–machine collaboration. *IEEE Transactions on Learning Technologies*, *16*(6), 1179–1189. DOI: 10.1109/TLT.2023.3257511

Harrison, T. M., Guerrero, S., Burke, G. B., Cook, M., Cresswell, A., Helbig, N., Hrdinova, J., & Pardo, T. (2012). Open government and e-government: Democratic challenges from a public value perspective. *Information Polity*, *17*(2), 83–97. DOI: 10.3233/IP-2012-0269

Hartey, M. (2019). AI and Automation in Reducing IT Operational Costs. *International Journal of Advance & Innovative Research*, *9*(1), 547–555.

Hartley, J. L., & Sawaya, W. J. (2019). Tortoise, not the hare: Digital transformation of supply chain business processes. *Business Horizons*, *62*(6), 707–715. DOI: 10.1016/j.bushor.2019.07.006

Hassan, M. A., Shukur, Z., Hasan, M. K., & Al-Khaleefa, A. S. (2020). A review on electronic payments security. *Symmetry*, *12*(8), 1344. DOI: 10.3390/sym12081344

Heji, A. E., Hamdan, A., Anasweh, M., & Kanan, M. (2024). The relationship between digital transformation and public governance. In A. Hamdan & A. Harraf (Eds.), Business Development via AI and Digitalization (Studies in Systems, Decision and Control, Vol. 538). Springer. DOI: 10.1007/978-3-031-62102-4_31

Helbig, N., Gil-García, J. R., & Ferro, E. (2009). Understanding the complexity of electronic government: Implications from the digital divide literature. *Government Information Quarterly*, *26*(1), 89–97. DOI: 10.1016/j.giq.2008.05.004

Hilliard, A., Kazim, E., & Ledain, S. (2025). Are the robots taking over? On AI and perceived existential risk. *AI and Ethics*, *5*(3), 2929–2942. DOI: 10.1007/s43681-024-00600-9

Hitsuwari, J., Ueda, Y., Yun, W., & Nomura, M. (2023). Does human–AI collaboration lead to more creative art? Aesthetic evaluation of human-made and AI-generated haiku poetry. *Computers in Human Behavior*, *139*, 107502. DOI: 10.1016/j.chb.2022.107502

Hoc, J. (2000). From human – machine interaction to human – machine cooperation. *Ergonomics*, *43*(7), 833–843. DOI: 10.1080/001401300409044

Hoel, L., & Filstad, C. (2023). The police's intelligence-led crisis management: Crossing knowledge boundaries of operational and intelligence practices during acute crises. *The Police Journal*, *97*(3), 559-577. (Original work published 2024) DOI: 10.1177/0032258X231196117

Hoetker, G., & Mahony, J. T. (2002). Building the Virtual State: Information Technology and Institutional Change. *Academy of Management Review*, *27*(4), 619–622. DOI: 10.2307/4134407

Hoic-Bozic, N., Holenko Dlab, M., & Mornar, V. (2016). Recommender system and web 2.0 tools to enhance a blended learning model. *IEEE Transactions on Education*, *59*(1), 39–44. DOI: 10.1109/TE.2015.2427116

Holmes, A. F., & Douglass, A. (2022). Artificial intelligence: Reshaping the accounting profession and the disruption to accounting education. *Journal of Emerging Technologies in Accounting*, *19*(1), 53–68. DOI: 10.2308/JETA-2020-054

Holstein, K., & Aleven, V. (2022). Designing for human–AI complementarity in K-12 education. *AI Magazine*, *43*(2), 239–248. DOI: 10.1002/aaai.12058

Hopko, S., Wang, J., & Mehta, R. (2022, February). Human Factors Considerations and Metrics in Shared Space Human-Robot Collaboration: A Systematic Review. *Frontiers in Robotics and AI*, *9*, 3. DOI: 10.3389/frobt.2022.799522 PMID: 35187093

Hussain, S., Gupta, S., & Bhardwaj, S. (2025). Determinants inhibiting digital payment system adoption: An Indian perspective. *Qualitative Research in Financial Markets*, *17*(4), 716–748. DOI: 10.1108/QRFM-09-2023-0223

Hutson, J. (2025). *The Adoption of Artificial Intelligence and Inertia in Higher Education: Exploring Complex Resistance to Technological Change*. Taylor & Francis. DOI: 10.4324/9781003655862

Hutson, J., & Plate, D. (2023). *Human-AI collaboration for smart education: reframing applied learning to support metacognition*. IntechOpen.

Ifenthaler, D., & Schumacher, C. (2023). Reciprocal issues of artificial and human intelligence in education. *Journal of Research on Technology in Education*, *55*(1), 1–6. DOI: 10.1080/15391523.2022.2154511

Ingram, R. (1997). *Building Virtual Worlds: A City Planning Perspective*. Online Planning Journal.

Jae Moon, M., & Welch, E. W. (2000). Managerial Adaptation through the Market in the Public Sector: Theoretical Framework and Four Models. *International Review of Public Administration*, *5*(2), 129–141. DOI: 10.1080/12294659.2000.10804961

Jain, G., Das, R., Raj, D., & Mohapatra, H. (2025). Exploring low-latency communication protocols for time-sensitive industrial automation and autonomous vehicle systems. *2025 International Conference on Computing, Intelligence, and Application (CIACON)*, 1-7. DOI: 10.1109/CIACON65473.2025.11189493

Jain, R., Garg, N., & Khera, S. N. (2022, July). Effective Human–AI Work Design for Collaborative Decision-Making. *Kybernetes*, *52*(11), 5. DOI: 10.1108/K-04-2022-0548

Järvelä, S., Nguyen, A., & Hadwin, A. (2023, April). Human and Artificial Intelligence Collaboration for Socially Shared Regulation in Learning. *British Journal of Educational Technology, 54*(5), 20. DOI: 10.1111/bjet.13325

Jeon, J., & Lee, S. (2023). Large language models in education: A focus on the complementary relationship between human teachers and ChatGPT. *Education and Information Technologies, 28*(12), 15873–15892. DOI: 10.1007/s10639-023-11834-1

Jia, N., Luo, X., Fang, Z., & Liao, C. (2024). When and how artificial intelligence augments employee creativity. *Academy of Management Journal, 67*(1), 5–32. DOI: 10.5465/amj.2022.0426

Jiatao Kang Junlei Dong, D. Y. (2021). Key technologies of IoT service security and privacy protection. Converter, 70–79.

Ji, H., Han, I., & Ko, Y. (2023). A systematic review of conversational AI in language education: Focusing on the collaboration with human teachers. *Journal of Research on Technology in Education, 55*(1), 48–63. DOI: 10.1080/15391523.2022.2142873

Johnson, J. (2022). The AI Commander problem: Ethical, political, and psychological dilemmas of human-machine interactions in AI-enabled warfare. *Journal of Military Ethics, 21*(3-4), 246–271. DOI: 10.1080/15027570.2023.2175887

Johnson, J. (2023). Finding AI faces in the moon and armies in the clouds: Anthropomorphising artificial intelligence in military human-machine interactions. *Global Society, 38*(1), 67–82. DOI: 10.1080/13600826.2023.2205444

Johnson, J. (2024). *The AI commander: centaur teaming, command, and ethical dilemmas*. Oxford University Press. DOI: 10.1093/oso/9780198892182.001.0001

Jones, B., & Jones, R. (2025). Action research at the BBC: Interrogating artificial intelligence with journalists to generate actionable insights for the newsroom. *Journalism, 26*(8), 1708-1725. (Original work published 2025)DOI: 10.1177/14648849251317150

Jony, A. I., & Hamim, S. A. (2024). Empowering virtual collaboration: Harnessing AI for enhanced teamwork in higher education. *Educational Technology Quarterly, 2024*(3), 337–359. DOI: 10.55056/etq.746

Joseph, J., & Pandey, A. (2025). Human-AI collaborative intelligence. In *Advances in Computational Intelligence and Robotics* (pp. 403–422). IGI Global.

Judson, H. (2025). "But I Didn't Use ChatGPT!": Democratic Course Design and Generative Artificial Intelligence in Higher Education Landscape. *Teaching Sociology, 53*(3), 246-256. (Original work published 2025)DOI: 10.1177/0092055X251342530

Kaminski, H., & Perry, M. (2007). Employing intelligent agents to automate SLA creation. Emerging Web Services Technology, 33-46. DOI: 10.1007/978-3-7643-8448-7_4

Kane, A. A., Paletz, S. B. F., Vahlkamp, S. H., Nelson, T., Porter, A., Diep, M., & Carraway, M. (2023). Intelligence Analysis Shift Work: Sensemaking Processes, Tensions, and Takeaways. *Proceedings of the Human Factors and Ergonomics Society Annual Meeting, 67*(1), 741-746. (Original work published 2023)DOI: 10.1177/21695067231192569

Kan, Y. (2024). The impact of AI on the development of manufacturing, logistics, and financial company from capital market perspectives. Advances in Economics. *Management and Political Sciences, 115*(1), 120–125.

Kapucu, N. (2006). Interagency communication networks during emergencies: Boundary spanners in multiagency coordination. *American Review of Public Administration, 36*(2), 207–225. DOI: 10.1177/0275074005280605

Karakose, T., Demirkol, M., Aslan, N., Köse, H., & Yirci, R. (2023). A conversation with ChatGPT about the impact of the COVID-19 pandemic on education: Comparative review based on human–AI collaboration. *Educational Process: International Journal, 12*(3), 7. DOI: 10.22521/edupij.2023.123.1

Karakose, T., Demirkol, M., Yirci, R., Polat, H., Ozdemir, T. Y., & Tülübaş, T. (2023). A conversation with ChatGPT about digital leadership and technology integration: Comparative analysis based on human–AI collaboration. *Administrative Sciences, 13*(7), 157. DOI: 10.3390/admsci13070157

Kashaka, N. (2025). The future of work: Automation and job displacement. *Eurasian Experiment Journal of Arts and Management, 7*(1), 37–40.

Katz, M. L., & Shapiro, C. (1985). Network externalities, competition, and compatibility. *The American Economic Review, 75*(3), 424–440.

Kay, J. (2023). Foundations for Human-AI Teaming for Self-Regulated Learning with Explainable AI (XAI). *Computers in Human Behavior, 147*(Oct), 107848. DOI: 10.1016/j.chb.2023.107848

Keerio, M. U., Bajwa, M. S. B., Mugheri, N. H., Memon, R. H., Bhayo, M. A., & Samo, K. A. (2022). Evaluating students' perceptions of Microsoft Teams for online academics improvement. *PakJET, 5*(1), 56–67. DOI: 10.51846/vol5iss1pp56-67

Kernaghan, K. (2009). Moving towards integrated public governance: Improving service delivery through community engagement. *International Review of Administrative Sciences, 75*(2), 239–254. DOI: 10.1177/0020852309104174

Kernaghan, K. (2013). Changing channels: Managing channel integration and migration in public organizations. *Canadian Public Administration*, *56*(1), 121–141. DOI: 10.1111/capa.12006

Keshavarzian, A. (2010). Geopolitics and the genealogy of free trade zones in the persian Gulf. *Geopolitics*, *15*(2), 263–289. DOI: 10.1080/14650040903486926

Khairunnisa, T., Nurmandi, A., Purwaningsi, T., Loilatu, M. J., & Savira, A. G. (2023). Open Government Index in Local Government During the Period of the COVID-19 Pandemic. *Jurnal Borneo Administrator*, *19*(1), 1–16. DOI: 10.24258/jba.v19i1.1149

Kim, K., & Kwon, K. (2024). Designing an Inclusive Artificial Intelligence (AI) Curriculum for Elementary Students to Address Gender Differences With Collaborative and Tangible Approaches. *Journal of Educational Computing Research, 62*(7), 1617-1644. (Original work published 2024)DOI: 10.1177/07356331241271059

Kim, J. (2024). Leading teachers' perspective on teacher-AI collaboration in education. *Education and Information Technologies*, *29*(7), 8693–8724. DOI: 10.1007/s10639-023-12109-5

Kim, J., & Cho, Y. H. (2025). My teammate is AI: Understanding students' perceptions of student-AI collaboration in drawing tasks. *Asia Pacific Journal of Education*, *45*(3), 1013–1027. DOI: 10.1080/02188791.2023.2286206

Kim, J., Detrick, R., Yu, S., Song, Y., Bol, L., & Li, N. (2025, January). Socially Shared Regulation of Learning and Artificial Intelligence: Opportunities to Support Socially Shared Regulation. *Education and Information Technologies*, *3*(9), 11483–11521. Advance online publication. Retrieved February 9, 2025, from. DOI: 10.1007/s10639-024-13187-9

Kim, J., Ham, Y., & Lee, S. S. (2024). Differences in student-AI interaction process on a drawing task: Focusing on students' attitude towards AI and the level of drawing skills. *Australasian Journal of Educational Technology*, *40*(1), 19–41. DOI: 10.14742/ajet.8859

Kim, J., Lee, H., & Cho, Y. H. (2022). Learning design to support student-AI collaboration: Perspectives of leading teachers for AI in education. *Education and Information Technologies*, *27*(5), 6069–6104. DOI: 10.1007/s10639-021-10831-6

Kim, J., & Lee, S. S. (2023). Are two heads better than one?: The effect of student-AI collaboration on students' learning task performance. *TechTrends*, *67*(2), 365–375. DOI: 10.1007/s11528-022-00788-9

Kirişci, K. (2009). The transformation of Turkish foreign policy: The rise of the trading state. *New Perspectives on Turkey*, *40*, 29–56. DOI: 10.1017/S0896634600005203

Kirwan, B. (2025, April). Human Factors Requirements for Human-AI Teaming in Aviation. *Future Transportation*, *5*(2, 5), 42. www.mdpi.com/2673-7590/5/2/42. DOI: 10.3390/futuretransp5020042

König, L. M., Allmeta, A., Perski, O., Smit, E. S., Newby, K., Vandelanotte, C., Poduval, S., Gordon, L., Gültzow, T., Alblas, M. C., Arden-Close, E., Braun Maya and Greffin, K., Hewitt, R., Knox, L., McCallum, C., McLaren, T., Szinay, D., Peuters, C., & DeSmet, A. (2024). Towards meaningful interdisciplinary and cross-sectoral digital health collaborations: Challenges and action-oriented solutions.

Kotler, P., Keller, K. L., Ancarani, F., & Costabile, M. (2014). Marketing management (14th ed.). Pearson. http://www.ir.harambeeuniversity.edu.et/... (PDF)

Kovari, A. (2025). A systematic review of AI-powered collaborative learning in higher education: Trends and outcomes from the last decade. *Social Sciences & Humanities Open*, *11*, 101335. DOI: 10.1016/j.ssaho.2025.101335

Krinkin, K., Shichkina, Y., & Ignatyev, A. (2021, September). Co-evolutionary hybrid intelligence. 2021 5th Scientific School Dynamics of Complex Networks and Their Applications (DCNA).

Kristensen, K., & Kijl, B. (2010). Collaborative performance. Int. *J. E-Collab.*, *6*(1), 53–69.

Kromann, L., Malchow-Møller, N., Skaksen, J. R., & Sørensen, A. (2020). Automation and productivity—A cross-country, cross-industry comparison. *Industrial and Corporate Change*, *29*(2), 265–287. DOI: 10.1093/icc/dtz039

Kromann, L., & Sørensen, A. (2019). Automation, performance and international competition: A firm-level comparison of process innovation. *Economic Policy*, *34*(100), 691–722. DOI: 10.1093/epolic/eiaa002

Küçüktabak, E. B., Kim, S. J., Wen, Y., Lynch, K., & Pons, J. L. (2021). Human-machine-human interaction in motor control and rehabilitation: A review. *Journal of Neuroengineering and Rehabilitation*, *18*(1), 183. Advance online publication. DOI: 10.1186/s12984-021-00974-5

Kulsum, U., Nurmandi, A., Muallidin, I., & Jafar, M. (2022). A Bibliometric Analysis of Open Government : Study on Indonesia and. *Journal of Governance*, *7*(1), 133–143. DOI: 10.31506/jog.v7i1.13934

Kumar, D., Haque, A., Mishra, K., Islam, F., Mishra, B. K., & Ahmad, S. (2023). Exploring the transformative role of artificial intelligence and metaverse in education: A comprehensive review. *Metaverse Basic and Applied Research, 2*(2), 21. DOI: 10.56294/mr202355

Kung, T. H., Cheatham, M., Medenilla, A., Sillos, C., De Leon, L., Elepaño, C., Madriaga, M., Aggabao, R., Diaz-Candido, G., Maningo, J., & Tseng, V. (2023, February 9). Performance of ChatGPT on USMLE: Potential for AI-Assisted Medical Education Using Large Language Models. *PLOS Digital Health, 2*(2), e0000198. DOI: 10.1371/journal.pdig.0000198 PMID: 36812645

Kurni, M., & Mohammed, M. S. (2023). *A beginner's guide to introduce artificial intelligence in teaching and learning*. Springer Nature.

Lakshmi, K. K., Gupta, H., & Ranjan, J. (2019). UPI based mobile banking applications – Security analysis and enhancements. In *2019 Amity International Conference on Artificial Intelligence (AICAI)* (pp. 1–6). IEEE. DOI: 10.1109/AICAI.2019.8701396

Larson, E. J. (2021, December). The Myth of Artificial Intelligence: Why Computers Can't Think the Way We Do. *Perspectives on Science and Christian Faith, 73*(4), 247–248. Retrieved November 16, 2022, from. DOI: 10.56315/PSCF12-21Larson

Lau, A. S., Wu, J., Ma, P., & Lee, H. (2025). Using artificial intelligence, ontology, and 3D visualization in the metaverse for improving collaborative work and collective intelligence. *The International Journal of Entrepreneurship and Innovation, 26*(1), 66-84. (Original work published 2025)DOI: 10.1177/14657503241313362

Leaua, C., ... "The Art of Questioning: Redefining the Value of Interrogative Communication in the Era of AI." SSRN *Electronic Journal*, 2024, DOI: 10.2139/ssrn.4707665

Lee, G. G., Mun, S., Shin, M. K., & Zhai, X. (2025). Collaborative learning with artificial intelligence speakers: Pre-service elementary science teachers' responses to the prototype. *Science & Education, 34*(2), 847–875. DOI: 10.1007/s11191-024-00526-y

Lee, J., Jung, J., & Song, T.The Korean Association Of Personnel Administration. (2023). Research on personnel selection in the age of artificial general intelligence focusing on augmented intelligence. *Journal of Organization and Management, 47*(2), 113–137. DOI: 10.36459/jom.2023.47.2.113

Lewin, K. (1951). *Field theory in social science: Selected theoretical papers*. Harper & Row.

Leyer, M., & Schneider, S. (2021). Decision augmentation and automation with artificial intelligence: Threat or opportunity for managers? *Business Horizons*, *64*(5), 711–724. DOI: 10.1016/j.bushor.2021.02.026

Liang, C., Proft, J., Andersen, E., & Knepper, R. A. (2019, May).. . *Implicit Communication of Actionable Information in Human-AI Teams*, *2*, 1–13. Advance online publication. Retrieved June 9, 2023, from. DOI: 10.1145/3290605.3300325

Ling, E. C., Tussyadiah, I., Liu, A., & Stienmetz, J. (2023). Perceived Intelligence of Artificially Intelligent Assistants for Travel: Scale Development and Validation. *Journal of Travel Research, 64*(2), 299-321. (Original work published 2025)DOI: 10.1177/00472875231217899

Linnes, C. (2020). Embracing the challenges and opportunities of change through electronic collaboration. *International Journal of Information Communication Technologies and Human Development*, *12*(4), 37–58. DOI: 10.4018/IJICTHD.20201001.oa1

Lin, S., Döngül, E. S., Uygun, S. V., Öztürk, M. B., Huy, D. T., & Tuan, P. V. (2022). Exploring the relationship between abusive management, self-efficacy and organizational performance in the context of human–machine interaction technology and artificial intelligence with the effect of ergonomics. *Sustainability (Basel)*, *14*(4), 1949. DOI: 10.3390/su14041949

Lin, Z., Zhang, G., Xiao, X., Au, C., Zhou, Y., Sun, C., Zhou, Z., Yan, R., Fan, E., Si, S., Weng, L., Mathur, S., Yang, J., & Chen, J. (2021). A personalized acoustic interface for wearable human–machine interaction. *Advanced Functional Materials*, *32*(9), 2109430. Advance online publication. DOI: 10.1002/adfm.202109430

Lips, M. (2010). Rethinking citizen-government relationships in the age of digital identity: Insights from research. *Information Polity*, *15*(4), 273–289. DOI: 10.3233/IP-2010-0216

Li, Q., Cao, Z., Tanveer, M., Pandey, H. M., & Wang, C. (2020). A semantic collaboration method based on uniform knowledge graph. *IEEE Internet of Things Journal*, *7*(5), 4473–4484. DOI: 10.1109/JIOT.2019.2960150 PMID: 33748313

Li, S., Blythe, P., Guo, W., & Namdeo, A. (2019). Investigation of older drivers' requirements of the human-machine interaction in highly automated vehicles. *Transportation Research Part F: Traffic Psychology and Behaviour*, *62*, 546–563. DOI: 10.1016/j.trf.2019.02.009

Liste, L., & Sørensen, K. H. (2015). Consumer, client or citizen? How Norwegian local governments domesticate website technology and configure their users. *Information Communication and Society, 18*(7), 733–746. DOI: 10.1080/1369118X.2014.993678

Liu, J., Li, S., & Dong, Q. (2024). Collaboration with Generative Artificial Intelligence: An Exploratory Study Based on Learning Analytics. *Journal of Educational Computing Research, 62*(5), 1014-1046. (Original work published 2024)DOI: 10.1177/07356331241242441

Liu, X., Sun, C., Ye, X., Zhu, X., Hu, C., Tan, H., He, S., Shao, M., & Li, R. (2024). Neuromorphic Nanoionics for human–machine interaction: From materials to applications. *Advanced Materials, 36*(37), 2311472. Advance online publication. DOI: 10.1002/adma.202311472

Liu, Y. Q., Martin, C., Roehl, E., Li, Z., & Ward, S. (2006). Digital information access in urban/suburban communities: A survey report of public digital library use by the residents in Connecticut. *OCLC Systems & Services, 22*(2), 132–144. DOI: 10.1108/10650750610664021

Li, Y., Wang, Y., Wang, L., & Xie, J. (2022). Investigating the effects of stakeholder collaboration strategies on risk prevention performance in a digital innovation ecosystem. *Industrial Management & Data Systems, 122*(9), 2045–2071. DOI: 10.1108/IMDS-12-2021-0805

Lodge, J. M., Yang, S., Furze, L., & Dawson, P. (2023). It's not like a calculator, so what is the relationship between learners and generative artificial intelligence? *Learning: Research and Practice, 9*(2), 117–124. DOI: 10.1080/23735082.2023.2261106

Loilatu, M. J., Saiman, S., Irawan, B., Kulsum, U., Huda, M. N., & Vidiastuti, D. P. (2026). Natural Disaster Responses and Disaster Study in Indonesia: An Exploratory Study Using Meta-Analysis. In *Inequality and Environmental Degradation in a Prosperity-Driven World* (pp. 265–292). IGI Global Scientific Publishing.

Lokiny, N. (2022, November 5). Kubernetes for Container Orchestration in Artificial Intelligence Cloud Technologies. [IJSR]. *International Journal of Science and Research (Raipur, India), 11*(11), 1536–1538. Retrieved October 15, 2024, from. DOI: 10.21275/SR24724151929

LTIMIndtree, Dave, D. M., & Mandvikar, S. and A. (2023). Augmented intelligence: Human-Ai collaboration in the era of digital transformation. *International Journal of Engineering Applied Sciences And, 8*(6), 24–33.

Lu, J., Peng, Z., Yang, S., Ma, Y., Wang, R., Pang, Z., Feng, X., Chen, Y., & Cao, Y. (2023). A review of sensory interactions between autonomous vehicles and drivers. *Journal of Systems Architecture*, *141*, 102932. DOI: 10.1016/j.sysarc.2023.102932

Lu, K. L. (2020). The Spillover Effect of the Trade War between Adversarial Dyads: Evidence from the Sino-US Investment Relationship. *Journal of Chinese Political Science*, *25*(1), 21–47. DOI: 10.1007/s11366-018-9577-0

Lu, L., Jiang, C., Hu, G., Liu, J., & Yang, B. (2021). Flexible Noncontact sensing for human–machine interaction. *Advanced Materials*, *33*(16), 2100218. Advance online publication. DOI: 10.1002/adma.202100218

Luna-Reyes, L. F., & Gil-Garcia, J. R. (2011). Using institutional theory and dynamic simulation to understand complex e-Government phenomena. *Government Information Quarterly*, *28*(3), 329–345. DOI: 10.1016/j.giq.2010.08.007

Luna-Reyes, L. F., & Gil-Garcia, J. R. (2014). Digital government transformation and internet portals: The co-evolution of technology, organizations, and institutions. *Government Information Quarterly*, *31*(4), 545–555. DOI: 10.1016/j.giq.2014.08.001

Luna-Reyes, L. F., Gil-Garcia, J. R., & Cruz, C. B. (2007). Collaborative digital government in Mexico: Some lessons from federal Web-based interorganizational information integration initiatives. *Government Information Quarterly*, *24*(4), 808–826. DOI: 10.1016/j.giq.2007.04.003

Luna-Reyes, L. F., Gil-Garcia, J. R., & Estrada-Marroquín, M. (2008). The impact of institutions on interorganizational IT projects in the Mexican federal government. *International Journal of Electronic Government Research*, *4*(2), 27–42. DOI: 10.4018/jegr.2008040103

Luna-Reyes, L. F., Zhang, J., Gil-García, J. R., & Cresswell, A. M. (2005). Information systems development as emergent socio-technical change: A practice approach. *European Journal of Information Systems*, *14*(1), 93–105. DOI: 10.1057/palgrave.ejis.3000524

Luther, T., Kimmerle, J., & Cress, U. (2024, August). Teaming up with an AI: Exploring Human–AI Collaboration in a Writing Scenario with ChatGPT. *AI*, *5*(3, 5), 1357–1376. DOI: 10.3390/ai5030065

Maadi, M., Akbarzadeh Khorshidi, H., & Aickelin, U. (2021). A review on Human–AI interaction in machine learning and insights for medical applications. *International Journal of Environmental Research and Public Health*, *18*(4), 2121. DOI: 10.3390/ijerph18042121

Madon, S. (1993). Introducing administrative reform through the application of computer-based information systems: A case study in India. *Public Administration and Development*, *13*(1), 37–48. DOI: 10.1002/pad.4230130104

Magnisalis, I., & Demetriadis, S. (2015). Tool orchestration in e-collaboration. Int. *J. E-Collab.*, *11*(4), 40–63.

Manikandan, M., Venkatesh, P., Chitra, D., Krishnamoorthi, M., Ramu, M., & Senthilnathan, C. R. (2024). An impact of artificial intelligence in fintech. In *2024 International Conference on Power, Energy, Control and Transmission Systems (ICPECTS)* (pp. 1–3). IEEE. DOI: 10.1109/ICPECTS62210.2024.10780020

Mannuru, N. R., Shahriar, S., Teel, Z. A., Wang, T., Lund, B. D., Tijani, S., Pohboon, C. O., Agbaji, D., Alhassan, J., Galley, J., Kousari, R., Ogbadu-Oladapo, L., Saurav, S. K., Srivastava, A., Tummuru, S. P., Uppala, S., & Vaidya, P. (2023). Artificial intelligence in developing countries: The impact of generative artificial intelligence (AI) technologies for development. *Information Development, 41*(3), 1036-1054. (Original work published 2025)DOI: 10.1177/02666669231200628

Manrai, R., Goel, U., & Yadav, P. D. (2021). Factors affecting adoption of digital payments by semi rural Indian women: Extension of UTAUT 2 with self determination theory and perceived credibility. *Aslib Journal of Information Management*, *73*(6), 814–838. DOI: 10.1108/AJIM-12-2020-0396

Manyika, J., Chui, M., Miremadi, M., Bughin, J., George, K., Willmott, P., & Dewhurst, M. (2017). *A future that works: Automation, employment, and productivity*. McKinsey Global Institute.

Martin, A. (2024). Capita says cyberattack contributed to annual loss of more than £106 million. https://therecord.media/capita-cyberattack-loss-of-hundred-million

Massolt, E. T., van der Glas-Schmidt, F., van de Weijgert, E. J., & Reijerink, E. (2025). 35 Improving efficiency of outpatient consultations by reducing no-show numbers.

Ma, X., Tao, F., Zhang, M., Wang, T., & Zuo, Y. (2019). Digital twin enhanced human-machine interaction in product lifecycle. *Procedia CIRP*, *83*, 789–793. DOI: 10.1016/j.procir.2019.04.330

McKee, D. W., Clement, S. J., Almutairi, J., & Xu, J. (2017). Massive-scale automation in cyber-physical systems: Vision & challenges. 2017 IEEE 13th International Symposium on Autonomous Decentralized System (ISADS), 5–11. DOI: 10.1109/ISADS.2017.56

Mcnutt, K. (2014). Public engagement in the Web 2.0 era: Social collaborative technologies in a public sector context. *Canadian Public Administration*, *57*(1), 49–70. DOI: 10.1111/capa.12058

Mehta, D., Joshi, A., Chaturvedi, A., Suthar, K., & Suthar, P. (2024). Revolutionizing manufacturing: The role of automation and robotics in industry. *International Journal of Innovative Research in Technology*, *11*(2), 2018–2025.

Mehta, D., Patel, N., Joshi, N. A., & Patel, B. (2023). Impact of economic openness on government size in India. *International Journal of Sustainable Economy*, *16*(1), 113–130. DOI: 10.1504/IJSE.2024.135192

Melander, L., & Pazirandeh, A. (2019). Collaboration beyond the supply network for green innovation: Insight from 11 cases. *Supply Chain Management*, *24*(4), 509–523. DOI: 10.1108/SCM-08-2018-0285

Meniado, J. C. (2023). Digital language teaching 5.0: Technologies, trends and competencies. *RELC Journal*, *54*(2), 461–473. DOI: 10.1177/00336882231160610

Merceron, K., & Best, K. (2024). Integrating professional perspectives for AI literacy: empowering students in an AI-influenced future. In *The Role of Generative AI in the Communication Classroom* (pp. 300–315). IGI Global Scientific Publishing. DOI: 10.4018/979-8-3693-0831-8.ch014

Mergel, I., & Bretschneider, S. I. (2013). A Three-Stage Adoption Process for Social Media Use in Government. *Public Administration Review*, *73*(3), 390–400. DOI: 10.1111/puar.12021

Mergel, I., Edelmann, N., & Haug, N. (2019). Defining digital transformation: Results from expert interviews. *Government Information Quarterly*, *36*(4), 101385. Advance online publication. DOI: 10.1016/j.giq.2019.06.002

Meyer, B., & Weitz, D. (2024). The impact of automation on firm performance and expectations. The CFO Survey. https://www.richmondfed.org/research/national_economy/cfo_survey/research_and_commentary/2024/20240327_research_commentary

Meyer, W. G. (2014). The effect of optimism bias on the decision to terminate failing projects. *Project Management Journal*, *45*(4), 7–20. DOI: 10.1002/pmj.21435

Mittal, U., Sai, S., Chamola, V., & Sangwan, D. (2024). A comprehensive review on generative AI for education. *IEEE Access : Practical Innovations, Open Solutions*, *12*, 142733–142759. DOI: 10.1109/ACCESS.2024.3468368

Mohapatra, H. (2021). Socio-technical challenges in the implementation of smart city. 2021 International Conference on Innovation and Intelligence for Informatics, Computing, and Technologies (3ICT), 57-62. DOI: 10.1109/3ICT53449.2021.9581905

Mohapatra, H. (2025). The fine-tuning journey of ChatGPT in industry applications. *Advances in Computational Intelligence and Robotics*, ●●●, 263–284. DOI: 10.4018/979-8-3693-8332-2.ch011

Mohapatra, H. (2025). The role of 6G in empowering smart cities enabling ubiquitous connectivity and intelligent infrastructure. *Advances in Wireless Technologies and Telecommunication*, ●●●, 231–254. DOI: 10.4018/979-8-3693-8799-3.ch008

Mohapatra, H., & Rath, A. K. (2019). Detection and avoidance of water loss through municipality taps in India by using smart taps and ICT. *IET Wireless Sensor Systems*, *9*(6), 447–457. DOI: 10.1049/iet-wss.2019.0081

Mohapatra, H., & Rath, A. K. (2020). Fault-tolerant mechanism for wireless sensor network. *IET Wireless Sensor Systems*, *10*(1), 23–30. DOI: 10.1049/iet-wss.2019.0106

Molenaar, I. (2024). Human-AI collaboration in education: The hybrid future.

Molenaar, I. (2022). The concept of hybrid human-AI regulation: Exemplifying how to support young learners' self-regulated learning. *Computers and Education: Artificial Intelligence*, *3*, 100070. DOI: 10.1016/j.caeai.2022.100070

Molenaar, I. (2022). Towards hybrid human-AI learning technologies. *European Journal of Education*, *57*(4), 632–645. DOI: 10.1111/ejed.12527

Moon, M. J. (2002). The evolution of E-government among municipalities: Rhetoric or reality? *Public Administration Review*, *62*(4), 424–433. DOI: 10.1111/0033-3352.00196

Moser, R., Rengarajan, S., & Narayanamurthy, G. (2021). Decision Intelligence: Creating a Fit between Intelligence Requirements and Intelligence Processing Capacities. *IIM Kozhikode Society & Management Review, 10*(2), 160-177. (Original work published 2021)DOI: 10.1177/22779752211017386

Murgatroyd, S. (2024). *The future of higher education in an age of artificial intelligence*. Ethics International Press.

Nagadeepa, C., Mukthar, K. P. J., Asnate Salazar, E., Castillo Picon, J., Méndez, R. Y., & Mory Guarnizo, S. (2024). Students intention towards digital entrepreneurship–Industry 5.0. In M. A. Musleh Al Sartawi, A. Helmy Abd Wahab, & K. Hussainey (Eds.), Global Economic Revolutions: Big Data Governance and Business Analytics for Sustainability (Communications in Computer and Information Science, Vol. 1999). Springer. DOI: 10.1007/978-3-031-50518-8_18

Nalepka, P., Lamb, M., Kallen, R. W., Shockley, K., Chemero, A., Saltzman, E., & Richardson, M. J. (2019). Human social motor solutions for human–machine interaction in dynamical task contexts. *Proceedings of the National Academy of Sciences of the United States of America*, *116*(4), 1437–1446. DOI: 10.1073/pnas.1813164116

Narayanan, S., & McIlraith, S. A. (2002, May). Simulation, verification and automated composition of web services. In *Proceedings of the 11th international conference on World Wide Web* (pp. 77-88).

Nardo, M., Forino, D., & Murino, T. (2020). The evolution of man–machine interaction: The role of human in industry 4.0 paradigm. *Production & Manufacturing Research*, *8*(1), 20–34. DOI: 10.1080/21693277.2020.1737592

Neves, B. B., Omori, M., Petersen, A., Vered, M., & Carter, A. (2024, August). Navigating Artificial Intelligence in Care Homes: Competing Stakeholder Views of Trust and Logics of Care. *Social Science & Medicine*, *358*(5), 117187. DOI: 10.1016/j.socscimed.2024.117187 PMID: 39173291

Nguyen, A., Hong, Y., Dang, B., & Huang, X. (2024). Human-AI collaboration patterns in AI-assisted academic writing. *Studies in Higher Education*, *49*(5), 847–864. DOI: 10.1080/03075079.2024.2323593

Nogueira, L. A., Moltubakk, S. T., Fagervik, A., & Langfeldt, I. B. (2025). Cutting through the noise: Assessing tools that employ artificial intelligence. *IFLA Journal*, *51*(3), 735-749. (Original work published 2025)DOI: 10.1177/03400352241304121

Norris, D. F. (2003). Building the Virtual State ... or Not? A Critical Appraisal. *Social Science Computer Review*, *21*(4), 417–424. DOI: 10.1177/0894439303256728

Norris, D. F., & Reddick, C. G. (2013). Local E-Government in the United States: Transformation or Incremental Change? *Public Administration Review*, *73*(1), 165–175. DOI: 10.1111/j.1540-6210.2012.02647.x

Nørskov, M. (2022). Robotification & ethical cleansing. *AI & Society*, *37*(2), 425–441. DOI: 10.1007/s00146-021-01203-2

Okeke, H. E., & Akinbolajo, O. D.Humphrey Emeka OkekeOlayinka Demola Akinbolajo. (2023). Integrating AI and automation into low-code development: Opportunities and challenges. *International Journal of Science and Research Archive, 8*(1), 1094–1109. DOI: 10.30574/ijsra.2023.8.1.0077

Olawade, D. B., Wada, O. Z., Odetayo, A., David-Olawade, A. C., Asaolu, F., & Eberhardt, J. (2024). Enhancing mental health with artificial intelligence: Current trends and future prospects. *Journal of Medicine, Surgery, and Public Health, 3*, 100099. DOI: 10.1016/j.glmedi.2024.100099

Omar, A., Weerakkody, V., & Sivarajah, U. (2017). Digitally enabled service transformation in UK public sector: A case analysis of universal credit. *International Journal of Information Management, 37*(4), 350–356. DOI: 10.1016/j.ijinfomgt.2017.04.001

Omosebi, T. (2025, July 4). Learn about AI-related risks and AI risk management. Medium. https://medium.com/@temitopee/learn-about-ai-related-risks-and-ai-risk-management-21b8e2a89fc0

Oosterzee, P. V. A. N., & Garnett, S. T. (2015). the Evolution of Information and Communication Technology in Public Administration. *Public Administration and Development, 35*(220), 140–151. DOI: 10.1002/pad

Oppenheimer, J., Lüken, S., Hamm, B., & Niehues, S. M. (2023, January 1). A Prospective Approach to Integration of AI Fracture Detection Software in Radiographs into Clinical Workflow. *Life (Chicago, Ill.), 13*(1), 223. Retrieved June 21, 2023, from www.mdpi.com/2075-1729/13/1/223. DOI: 10.3390/life13010223 PMID: 36676172

Oravec, J. A. (2023). Artificial intelligence implications for academic cheating: Expanding the dimensions of responsible human-AI collaboration with ChatGPT. *Journal of Interactive Learning Research, 34*(2), 213–237. DOI: 10.70725/304731gmmvhw

Özüdoğru, G., & Durak, H. Y. (2025). Conceptualizing pre-service teachers' artificial intelligence readiness and examining its relationship with various variables: The role of artificial intelligence literacy, digital citizenship, artificial intelligence-enhanced innovation and perceived threats from artificial intelligence. *Information Development, 41*(3), 916-932. (Original work published 2025)DOI: 10.1177/02666669251335657

Padovano, A., & Cardamone, M. (2024). Towards human-AI collaboration in the competency-based curriculum development process: The case of industrial engineering and management education. *Computers and Education: Artificial Intelligence, 7*, 100256. DOI: 10.1016/j.caeai.2024.100256

Page, M. J., McKenzie, J. E., Bossuyt, P. M., Boutron, I., Hoffmann, T. C., Mulrow, C. D., Shamseer, L., Tetzlaff, J. M., Akl, E. A., Brennan, S. E., Chou, R., Glanville, J., Grimshaw, J. M., Hróbjartsson, A., Lalu, M. M., Li, T., Loder, E. W., Mayo-Wilson, E., McDonald, S., & Moher, D. (2021). The PRISMA 2020 statement: An updated guideline for reporting systematic reviews. *BMJ (Clinical Research Ed.)*, *372*, n71. Advance online publication. DOI: 10.1136/bmj.n71

Pareek, P., Hajra, R., & Mohapatra, H. (2025). Empowering public officials by bridging the digital divide with smart technology for public services. *Advances in Public Policy and Administration*, •••, 419–452. DOI: 10.4018/979-8-3693-6547-2.ch016

Pasupuleti, M. K. (2025). *Augmented Human Intelligence: Converging Generative AI, Quantum Computing, and XR for enhanced human-machine synergy*. National Education Services. DOI: 10.62311/nesx/rrv525

Patnaik, S. (2019, July 18). UPI will push India over the digital payments finish line. American Banker. https://www.americanbanker.com/payments/opinion/upi-will-push-india-over-the-digital-payments-finish-line

Patra, B., & Sethi, N. (2023). Does digital payment induce economic growth in emerging economies? The mediating role of institutional quality, consumption expenditure, and bank credit. *Information Technology for Development*, *30*(1), 57–75. DOI: 10.1080/02681102.2023.2244465

Pedrosa, G. V., Kosloski, R. A. D., de Menezes, V. G., Iwama, G. Y., da Silva, W. C. M. P., & Figueiredo, R. M. C. (2020). A systematic review of indicators for evaluating the effectiveness of digital public services. *Information (Basel)*, *11*(10), 1–14. DOI: 10.3390/info11100472

Pflanzer, M., Traylor, Z., Lyons, J. B., Dubljević, V., & Nam, C. S. (2022, September). Ethics in Human–AI Teaming: Principles and Perspectives. *AI and Ethics*, *3*(3), 20. DOI: 10.1007/s43681-022-00214-z

Pham, M. T., Rajić, A., Greig, J. D., Sargeant, J. M., Papadopoulos, A., & Mcewen, S. A. (2014). A scoping review of scoping reviews: Advancing the approach and enhancing the consistency. *Research Synthesis Methods*, *5*(4), 371–385. DOI: 10.1002/jrsm.1123

PIB – Press Information Bureau, Government of India. (2024, December 1). UPI: Revolutionizing digital payments in India [Press release]. Retrieved July 17, 2025, from https://www.pib.gov.in/PressReleasePage.aspx?PRID=2079544

Pinto, M., Vilaça, A., Coelho, L., Magalhães, R., & Veloso, R. (2024). Extended reality tools for medical training and education. VII Congreso XoveTIC: Impulsando El Talento Cient\'\ifico, 89–96. DOI: 10.17979/spudc.9788497498913.13

Plass, J. L., Hovey, C., Maso, A. S., Fröhlich, F., Ghosh, S., Olsen, A., & Perlin, K. (2022). Designing Effective Immersive VR Learning Experiences. Practitioner Proceedings of the 8th International of the Immersive Learning Research Network(ILRN2022). DOI: 10.56198/A6PFY1CBT

Prasad, M. S., & Roy, M. S. (2024). Investigating digital workspaces: Ethnographic obstacles and insights. International Journal For Multidisciplinary Research, 6(6).

Prater, J., Kirytopoulos, K., & Ma, T. (2017). Optimism bias within the project management context: A systematic quantitative literature review. *International Journal of Managing Projects in Business*, *10*(2), 370–385. DOI: 10.1108/IJMPB-07-2016-0063

Prince, M. (2024). The role of technology in improving operational efficiency. American Journal of IR 4.0 and Beyond, 3(1), 28–36. DOI: 10.54536/ajirb.v3i1.3663

Qi, J., & Wang, J. (2025). Bridging Artificial Intelligence and Railway Cybersecurity: A Comprehensive Anomaly Detection Review. *Transportation Research Record, 2679*(5), 232-255. (Original work published 2025)DOI: 10.1177/03611981241302335

Rabi, N. M. (2024). Unlocking trust in AI decision-making: The crucial role of confidence, transparency, and user perception. *Intl. J. Rel.*, *5*(10), 1866–1870. DOI: 10.61707/g4etk565

Raghavan, M., Barocas, S., Kleinberg, J., & Levy, K. (2020, January). Mitigating bias in algorithmic hiring: Evaluating claims and practices. In *Proceedings of the 2020 conference on fairness, accountability, and transparency* (pp. 469-481). DOI: 10.1145/3351095.3372828

Raisch, S., & Krakowski, S. (2021). Artificial intelligence and management: The automation–augmentation paradox. *Academy of Management Review*, *46*(1), 192–210. DOI: 10.5465/amr.2018.0072

Raj, S., Sheel, S., Singh, R., Ashar, S., & Mohapatra, H. (2025). Securing smart cities. New Horizons in Leadership, 487-512. DOI: 10.4018/979-8-3693-6437-6.ch021

Rana, N. (2024). Ethical AI integration in marketing strategies for sustainable E-commerce fashion designing. In *Contemporary Management and Global Leadership for Sustainability* (pp. 218–233). IGI Global. DOI: 10.4018/979-8-3693-1273-5.ch013

Rawashdeh, A., Bakhit, M., & Abaalkhail, L. (2023). Determinants of artificial intelligence adoption in SMEs: The mediating role of accounting automation. *Int. J. Data Netw. Sci.*, *7*(1), 25–34. DOI: 10.5267/j.ijdns.2022.12.010

Reddick, C. G. (2004). A two-stage model of e-government growth: Theories and empirical evidence for U.S. cities. *Government Information Quarterly*, *21*(1), 51–64. DOI: 10.1016/j.giq.2003.11.004

Reddick, C. G. (2005). Citizen interaction with e-government: From the streets to servers? *Government Information Quarterly*, *22*(1), 38–57. DOI: 10.1016/j.giq.2004.10.003

Reddick, C. G. (2011). Customer Relationship Management (CRM) technology and organizational change: Evidence for the bureaucratic and e-Government paradigms. *Government Information Quarterly*, *28*(3), 346–353. DOI: 10.1016/j.giq.2010.08.005

Reddick, C. G., Abdelsalam, H. M., & Elkadi, H. (2011). The influence of e-government on administrative discretion: The case of local governments in egypt. *Public Administration and Development*, *31*(5), 390–407. DOI: 10.1002/pad.615

Reddick, C. G., & Turner, M. (2012). Channel choice and public service delivery in Canada: Comparing e-government to traditional service delivery. *Government Information Quarterly*, *29*(1), 1–11. DOI: 10.1016/j.giq.2011.03.005

Reddy, A. S., Ashraf, M., Manideepak, T., & Mohapatra, H. (2025). A comprehensive analysis of governance and regulatory frameworks for cloud-based initiatives for smart cities. Organizational Sociology in the Digital Age, 127-146. DOI: 10.4018/979-8-3693-7398-9.ch008

Rezaev, A. V., & Tregubova, N. D. (2023). Looking at human-centered artificial intelligence as a problem and prospect for sociology: An analytic review. *Current Sociology*, *73*(1), 120-138. (Original work published 2025)DOI: 10.1177/00113921231211580

Rezwana, J., & Maher, M. Lou. (2022). Designing creative AI partners with COFI: A framework for modeling interaction in human-AI co-creative systems. *ACM Transactions on Computer-Human Interaction*.

Ribino, P. (2023). The role of politeness in human–machine interactions: A systematic literature review and future perspectives. *Artificial Intelligence Review*, *56*(S1), 445–482. DOI: 10.1007/s10462-023-10540-1

Ridwan, A., & Athena, T. (2023). Challenges and opportunities to collaborative distance learning in esp instruction. *Academic Journal Perspective : Education, Language, And*, *11*(2), 79–97. DOI: 10.33603/6npwdw23

Riedl, C., De Cremer, D., Lucarelli, G., Antoine-Souklaye, E., Bullock, S., Ajmeri, N., Batty, M., Black, M., Cartlidge, J., Challen, R., Chen, C., Chen, J., Condell, J., Danon, L., Dennett, A., Heppenstall, A., Marshall, P., Morgan, P., O'Kane, A., … Denis, G. (2025). The potential and challenges of AI for collective intelligence. *Collective Intelligence, 4*(1). (Original work published 2025)DOI: 10.1177/26339137241308821

Robinson, P. (2023, July 10). The MOVEit attack explained. Lepide Blog: A Guide to IT Security, Compliance and IT Operations. https://www.lepide.com/blog/the-moveit-attack-explained/

Ross, W., & LaCroix, J. (1996). Multiple meanings of trust in negotiation theory and research: A literature review and integrative model. *International Journal of Conflict Management, 7*(4), 314–360. DOI: 10.1108/eb022786

Roy, J. (2006a). E-government and local governance in Canada: An examination of front line challenges and federal tensions. *Public Administration Quarterly, 11*(4), 306–350. DOI: 10.1177/073491490603000203

Roy, J. (2006b). Security and borders in a digital age: Implications for Canadian government and North American governance. *Journal of Borderlands Studies, 21*(1), 87–107. DOI: 10.1080/08865655.2006.9695653

Roziqin, A., Kismartini, Fajrina, A. N., Salahudin, & Sulistyaningsih, T. (2022). The development of Indonesian e-Government: A bibliometric analysis. *COLLNET Journal of Scientometrics and Information Management, 16*(1), 49–74. DOI: 10.1080/09737766.2021.2007036

Rudolph, C. (2003). Globalizaton and security: Migration and evolving conceptions of security in statecraft and scholarship. *Security Studies, 13*(1), 1–32. DOI: 10.1080/09636410490493822

Rutaganda, L., Bergstrom, R., Jayashekhar, A., Jayasinghe, D., & Ahmed, J. (2017). Avoiding pitfalls and unlocking real business value with RPA. *Journal of Financial Transformation, 46*, 104–115.

Ryjov, A. P. (2021). Hybrid intelligence framework for augmented analytics. In *Advances in Data Mining and Database Management* (pp. 22–45). IGI Global.

Ryjov, A. P. (2022). Principles of a hybrid intelligence framework for augmented analytics. In *Advances in Business Information Systems and Analytics* (pp. 47–70). IGI Global.

Saad, W. Z., Alias, N. A., Chong, C. M., & Sabri, S. (Eds.). (2025). *Digital Leadership for Sustainable Higher Education*. IGI Global. DOI: 10.4018/979-8-3693-9989-7

Sadiku, M. N. O., Ashaolu, T. J., Ajayi-Majebi, A., & Musa, S. M. (2021). Augmented Intelligence. International Journal Of Scientific Advances, 2(5).

Sahab, S., Haqbeen, J., & Ito, T. (2023). Facilitating collaborative consensus building in web-based discussion through collective task-based roles: A case study. *IIAI Letters on Informatics and Interdisciplinary Research*, *4*(180), 1. DOI: 10.52731/liir.v004.180

Sahi, A. M., Khalid, H., Abbas, A. F., Zedan, K., Khatib, S. F. A., & Al Amosh, H. (2022). The research trend of security and privacy in digital payment. *Informatics (MDPI)*, *9*(2), 32. DOI: 10.3390/informatics9020032

Salah, K., ... "Blockchain for AI: Review and Open Research Challenges." *IEEE Access*, vol. 7, no. 2169-3536, 2019, pp. 10127–10149, ieeexplore.ieee.org/document/8598784, DOI: 10.1109/ACCESS.2018.2890507

Salancik, G. R., & Pfeffer, J. (1978). A social information processing approach to job attitudes and task design. *Administrative Science Quarterly*, *23*(2), 224–253. DOI: 10.2307/2392563 PMID: 10307892

Samokhvalov, K. (2024). The transformative impact of Artificial Intelligence on the management consultancy sector. *Management Consulting Journal*, *7*(1), 59–68. DOI: 10.2478/mcj-2024-0006

Santhosh, S., De Crescenzio, F., & Vitolo, B. (2022). Defining the potential of extended reality tools for implementing co-creation of user oriented products and systems. In *Lecture Notes in Mechanical Engineering* (pp. 165–174). Springer International Publishing.

Sateesh, K. T., Vijayakumar, R., & Raghavendra, B. J. (2025). Analyzing the impact of rewards and transaction costs on customer payment method preferences: A gradient boosting model approach. In *Artificial Intelligence for Financial Risk Management and Analysis* (pp. 153–162). IGI Global., DOI: 10.4018/979-8-3373-1200-2.ch007

Schmutz, J. B., Outland, N., Kerstan, S., Georganta, E., & Ulfert, A.-S. (2024, August). AI-Teaming: Redefining Collaboration in the Digital Era. *Current Opinion in Psychology*, *58*(1), 101837–101837. DOI: 10.1016/j.copsyc.2024.101837 PMID: 39024969

Scholl, H. J. (2006). Electronic government: Information management capacity, organizational capabilities, and the sourcing mix. *Government Information Quarterly*, *23*(1), 73–96. DOI: 10.1016/j.giq.2005.11.002

Schou, J., & Hjelholt, M. (2019). Digital state spaces: State rescaling and advanced digitalization. *Territory, Politics, Governance*, *7*(4), 438–454. DOI: 10.1080/21622671.2018.1532809

Schroder, A., & Constantiou, I., & Tuunainen Virpi and Austin, R. D. (2022). Human-AI collaboration – coordinating automation and augmentation tasks in a digital service company. Proceedings of the Annual Hawaii International Conference on System Sciences. DOI: 10.24251/HICSS.2022.025

Scibilia, A., Pedrocchi, N., & Fortuna, L. (2022). Human control model estimation in physical human–machine interaction: A survey. *Sensors (Basel)*, *22*(5), 1732. DOI: 10.3390/s22051732

Seifert, J., Friedrich, O., & Schleidgen, S. (2022). Imitating the human. New human–machine interactions in social robots. *NanoEthics*, *16*(2), 181–192. DOI: 10.1007/s11569-022-00418-x

Selcuk, A. A. (2019). A Guide for Systematic Reviews: PRISMA. *Turkish Archives of Otorhinolaryngology*, *57*(1), 57–58. DOI: 10.5152/tao.2019.4058

Sharma, M., & Sharma, S. K. (2019). Theoretical framework for digital payments in rural India: Integrating UTAUT and empowerment theory. In Y. Dwivedi, E. Ayaburi, R. Boateng, & J. Effah (Eds.), ICT Unbounded: Social Impact of Bright ICT Adoption (IFIP Advances in Information and Communication Technology, Vol. 558). Springer. DOI: 10.1007/978-3-030-20671-0_15

Sharma, S., Shrivastava, R. R., Sahu, A., Mishra, S., Srivastava, K., & Mohapatra, H. (2025). Cloud-driven public safety in smart cities. Enhancing Safety, Security, and Service in Organizations, 235-262. DOI: 10.4018/979-8-3373-0482-3.ch008

Sharma, S., & Shrestha, S. (2024). Integrating HCI principles in AI: A review of human-Centered Artificial Intelligence applications and challenges. *J. Fut. Artif. Intell. Tech.*, *1*(3), 309–317. DOI: 10.62411/faith.3048-3719-47

Shree, S., Pratap, B., Saroy, R., & Dhal, S. (2021). Digital payments and consumer experience in India: A survey-based empirical study. *Journal of Banking and Financial Technology*, *5*(1), 1–20. DOI: 10.1007/s42786-020-00024-z

Siemens, G. (2013, August 20). Learning Analytics: The Emergence of a Discipline. *The American Behavioral Scientist*, *57*(10), 1380–1400. DOI: 10.1177/0002764213498851

Simao, M., Mendes, N., Gibaru, O., & Neto, P. (2019). A review on electromyography decoding and pattern recognition for human-machine interaction. *IEEE Access : Practical Innovations, Open Solutions*, *7*, 39564–39582. DOI: 10.1109/ACCESS.2019.2906584

Singha, R., & Singha, S. (2024). *AIoT Concepts and Integration: Exploring Customer Interaction, Ethics, Policy, and Privacy. 'Artificial Intelligence of Things (AIoT) for Productivity and Organizational Transition*. IGI Global. [https://doi.org/10.4018/979-8-3693-0993-3.ch002], https://www.google.com/search?q=https://doi.org/10.4018/979-8-3693-0993-3.ch002 DOI: 10.4018/979-8-3693-0993-3.ch002

Singha, S. (2024). *Navigating the Social Media Maze: Strategies for Effective Digital Marketing in a Fragmented Landscape. 'Changing Global Media Landscapes: Convergence, Fragmentation, and Polarization*. IGI Global. [https://doi.org/10.4018/979-8-3693-3767-7.ch005], https://www.google.com/search?q=https://doi.org/10.4018/979-8-3693-3767-7.ch005

Singh, R., & Malik, G. (2019). Impact of digitalization on Indian rural banking customers: With reference to payment systems. *Emerging Economy Studies*, *5*(1), 31–41. DOI: 10.1177/2394901519825912

Sinha, S., & Lee, Y. M. (2024). Challenges with developing and deploying AI models and applications in industrial systems. *Discover Artificial Intelligence*, *4*(1), 55. DOI: 10.1007/s44163-024-00151-2

Solingen, E. (2007). Pax Asiatica versus Bella Levantina: The foundations of war and peace in East Middle East. *The American Political Science Review*, *101*(4), 757–780. DOI: 10.1017/S0003055407070487

Song, X., Yang, S., Huang, Z., & Huang, T. (2019). The application of artificial intelligence in electronic commerce. *Journal of Physics: Conference Series*, *1302*(3), 32030. DOI: 10.1088/1742-6596/1302/3/032030

Sonnentag, S., & Spychala, A. (2012). Job control and job stressors as predictors of proactive work behavior: Is role breadth self-efficacy the key? *Journal of Organizational Behavior*, *33*(4), 543–560.

Špaček, D., Csótó, M., & Urs, N. (2020). Questioning the Real Citizen-Centricity of e-Government Development: Digitalization of G2C Services in Selected CEE Countries. *NISPAcee Journal of Public Administration and Policy*, *13*(1), 213–243. DOI: 10.2478/nispa-2020-0009

Spillias, S., ... "Human-AI Collaboration to Identify Literature for Evidence Synthesis." Research Square (Research Square), 5 July 2023, . Accessed 18 Jan. 2024. DOI: 10.21203/rs.3.rs-3099291/v1

Strasser, A., & Wilby, M. (2023). The AI-stance: Crossing the Terra incognita of human-machine interactions? *Frontiers in Artificial Intelligence and Applications*. DOI: 10.3233/FAIA220628

Subaveerapandiyan, A., Radhakrishnan, S., Tiwary, N., & Guangul, S. M. (2024). Student satisfaction with artificial intelligence chatbots in Ethiopian academia. *IFLA Journal, 51*(3), 600-614. (Original work published 2025)DOI: 10.1177/03400352241252974

Sulistyaningsih, T., Loilatu, M. J., & Roziqin, A. (2023). Research trends on smart urban governance in Asia: a bibliometric analysis. *Journal of Science and Technology Policy Management*. DOI: 10.1108/JSTPM-03-2022-0045

Summers, E. J., Mahmoudi, E., Vontsteen, J., Conner, K. A., & Wiedeman, M. C. (2025). Utilizing Technology to Efficiently Connect Students: A Critical Qualitative Study of Non-Competitive Gamification and AI Additions to Research Courses. *Journal of Interactive Learning Research, 36*(1), 11–28. DOI: 10.70725/534399sblpze

Sundaresan, S., & Zhang, Z. (2022). AI-enabled knowledge sharing and learning: Redesigning roles and processes. *The International Journal of Organizational Analysis, 30*(4), 983–999. DOI: 10.1108/IJOA-12-2020-2558

Sundar, S. S. (2020). Rise of machine agency: A framework for studying the psychology of Human–AI interaction (HAII). *Journal of Computer-Mediated Communication, 25*(1), 74–88. DOI: 10.1093/jcmc/zmz026

Syukri, A., Nurmandi, A., Muallidin, I., Kurniawan, D., & Loilatu, M. J. (2023). *Toward an Agile and Transformational Government, Through the Development of the Tangerang LIVE Application (Case Study of Tangerang City, Indonesia) BT - Proceedings of Seventh International Congress on Information and Communication Technology* (X.-S. Yang, S. Sherratt, N. Dey, & A. Joshi (eds.); pp. 343–352). Springer Nature Singapore.

Szeszák, B. M., Kerékjártó, I. G., Soltész, L., & Galambos, P. (2025). Industrial Revolutions and Automation: Tracing Economic and Social Transformations of Manufacturing. *Societies (Basel, Switzerland), 15*(4), 88. DOI: 10.3390/soc15040088

Tabbassum, A., Chintale, P., Praveen, & Najana, M. (2024). The impact of AI on future employment patterns. International Journal of Global Innovations and Solutions(IJGIS).

Tahri Sqalli, M., Aslonov, B., Gafurov, M., & Nurmatov, S. (2023). Humanizing AI in medical training: Ethical framework for responsible design. *Frontiers in Artificial Intelligence*, *6*, 1189914. DOI: 10.3389/frai.2023.1189914 PMID: 37261331

Talwar, P. (2023). *The Strategic Use of Virtual Teacher Assistants to Increase Faculty Engagement and Job Satisfaction*. Trident University International.

Tambe, P., Cappelli, P., & Yakubovich, V. (2019). Artificial intelligence in human resources management: Challenges and a path forward. *California Management Review*, *61*(4), 15–42. DOI: 10.1177/0008125619867910

Tariq, M. U. (2025). *AI-Driven Learning and Engagement in Higher Education*. IGI Global., DOI: 10.4018/979-8-3693-4074-5

Tariq, M. U. (2025). *Qualitative Inquiry in Doctoral Research: Pathways to Effective Design and Implementation*. IGI Global., DOI: 10.4018/979-8-3693-7200-5

Terziyan, V., Tiihonen, T., Shukla, A. K., Gryshko, S., Golovianko, M., Terziyan, O., & Vitko, O. (2025). Towards ethical evolution: Responsible autonomy of artificial intelligence across generations. *AI and Ethics*, *5*(5), 5165–5190. DOI: 10.1007/s43681-025-00759-9

TET – The Economic Times. (2024, May 1). UPI dominates digital payments, sees explosive growth over five years. https://economictimes.indiatimes.com/industry/banking/finance/banking/upi-dominates-digital-payments-sees-explosive-growth-over-five-years/articleshow/117610448.cms

Thapliyal, K., Gupta, C., Jindal, P., & Mishra, A. K. (2025). Measuring the impact of green banking practices on banks' environmental performance and sources of green financing: A study on Indian banks. *Discover Sustainability*, *6*(1), 169. DOI: 10.1007/s43621-024-00678-5

Timmons, A. C., Duong, J. B., Simo Fiallo, N., Lee, T., Vo, H. P. Q., Ahle, M. W., Comer, J. S., Brewer, L. C., Frazier, S. L., & Chaspari, T. (2022). A Call to Action on Assessing and Mitigating Bias in Artificial Intelligence Applications for Mental Health. *Perspectives on Psychological Science, 18*(5), 1062-1096. (Original work published 2023)DOI: 10.1177/17456916221134490

Tiwari, R. (2023). Explainable AI (XAI) and its applications in building trust and understanding in AI decision making. INTERANTIONAL JOURNAL OF SCIENTIFIC RESEARCH IN ENGINEERING AND, 07(01).

Tiwari, T., Srivastava, A., & Kumar, S. (2019). Adoption of digital payment methods in India. *International Journal of Electronic Finance*, *9*(3), 217–229. DOI: 10.1504/IJEF.2019.099058

TK. S. K., Thomas, L. P., Menon, V. A., & Thomas, J. (2024). Exploring tech enabled solutions: Evaluating sentiment classification models for airline reviews. In Impact of AI and Tech Driven Solutions in Hospitality and Tourism (pp. 257–281). IGI Global. https://doi.org/DOI: 10.1007/978-8-3693-6755-1.ch014

Tolbert, C. J., Mossberger, K., & McNeal, R. (2008). Institutions, policy innovation, and e-government in the American States. *Public Administration Review, 68*(3), 549–563. DOI: 10.1111/j.1540-6210.2008.00890.x

Tominc, P., Oreški, D., Čančer, V., & Rožman, M. (2024). Statistically significant differences in AI support levels for project management between SMEs and large enterprises. *AI, 5*(1), 136–157. DOI: 10.3390/ai5010008

Tondeur, J., Trevisan, O., Howard, S. K., & van Braak, J. (2025). Preparing preservice teachers to teach with digital technologies: An update of effective SQD-strategies. *Computers & Education, 232*, 105262. DOI: 10.1016/j.compedu.2025.105262

Tong, D., Jin, B., Tao, Y., Ren, H., Atiquil Islam, A. Y. M., & Bao, L. (2025, May). Exploring the Role of Human-AI Collaboration in Solving Scientific Problems. *Physical Review. Physics Education Research, 21*(1), 8. Retrieved May 20, 2025, from. DOI: 10.1103/PhysRevPhysEducRes.21.010149

Tricco, A. C., Lillie, E., Zarin, W., O'Brien, K., Colquhoun, H., Kastner, M., Levac, D., Ng, C., Sharpe, J. P., Wilson, K., Kenny, M., Warren, R., Wilson, C., Stelfox, H. T., & Straus, S. E. (2016). A scoping review on the conduct and reporting of scoping reviews. *BMC Medical Research Methodology, 16*(1), 1–10. DOI: 10.1186/s12874-016-0116-4

Tripathi, S. (2020, April 25). A study on adoption of digital payment through mobile payment application with reference to Gujarat state. International Journal of Trend in Scientific Research and Development. *SSRN*. https://ssrn.com/abstract=3638854

Trujillo, D. J., & Holt, E. (2020). Barriers to automation and robotics in construction. *EPiC Series in Built Environment, 1*, 257–265. DOI: 10.29007/1shp

Turban, E., Liang, T.-P., & Wu, S. P. J. (2011). A framework for adopting collaboration 2.0 tools for virtual group decision making. *Group Decision and Negotiation, 20*(2), 137–154. DOI: 10.1007/s10726-010-9215-5

Twizeyimana, J. D., & Andersson, A. (2019). The public value of E-Government – A literature review. *Government Information Quarterly, 36*(2), 167–178. DOI: 10.1016/j.giq.2019.01.001

Tzirides, A. O. O., Zapata, G., Kastania, N. P., Saini, A. K., Castro, V., Ismael, S. A., You, Y., Santos, T. A., Searsmith, D., O'Brien, C., Cope, B., & Kalantzis, M. (2024). Combining human and artificial intelligence for enhanced AI literacy in higher education. *Computers and Education Open*, *6*, 100184. DOI: 10.1016/j.caeo.2024.100184

United Nations. (2016). *E Goverenment Survey 2016*.

Urbinati, A., Manelli, L., Frattini, F., & Bogers, M. L. A. M. (2022). The digital transformation of the innovation process: Orchestration mechanisms and future research directions. *Innovation (North Sydney, N.S.W.)*, *24*(1), 65–85. DOI: 10.1080/14479338.2021.1963736

Ursin, F., Fürholzer, K., & Salloch, S. (2025). Metaphors in digital radiology: Ethical implications for responsibility assignments of human-AI imaginaries. *AI & Society*, *40*(7), 1–11. DOI: 10.1007/s00146-025-02270-5

Utomo, D. T. P., Ahsanah, F., & Ryandini, E. Y. (2024). EFL students' voices of blended collaborative learning in completing digital end-of-semester projects. *Journal of English Education Program*, *5*(1). Advance online publication. DOI: 10.26418/jeep.v5i1.71928

Valdés-Pérez, R. E. (1999, February). Principles of Human—Computer Collaboration for Knowledge Discovery in Science. *Artificial Intelligence*, *107*(2), 335–346. Retrieved May 27, 2019, from. DOI: 10.1016/S0004-3702(98)00116-7

van der Meij, M. G., Kupper, F., Beers Pieter, J., & Broerse, J. E. W. (2016). Hybrid e-learning tool TransLearning: Video storytelling to foster vicarious learning within multi-stakeholder collaboration networks. *International Journal of Lifelong Education*, *35*(4), 413–429. DOI: 10.1080/02601370.2016.1197331

van der Veer, S. N., Riste, L., Cheraghi-Sohi, S., Phipps, D. L., Tully, M. P., Bozentko, K., Atwood, S., Hubbard, A., Wiper, C., Oswald, M., & Peek, N. (2021). Trading off accuracy and explainability in AI decision-making: Findings from 2 citizens' juries. *Journal of the American Medical Informatics Association : JAMIA*, *28*(10), 2128–2138. DOI: 10.1093/jamia/ocab127 PMID: 34333646

Van Landuyt, D., Halasz, D., Verreydt, S., & Weyns, D. (2024). Towards understanding trust in self-adaptive systems. *Proceedings of the 19th International Symposium on Software Engineering for Adaptive and Self-Managing Systems*, 207-213. DOI: 10.1145/3643915.3644100

Veles, N. (2022). *Optimising the Third Space in Higher Education: Case studies of intercultural and cross-boundary collaboration*. Routledge. DOI: 10.4324/9781003259527

Venigandla, K., & Vemuri, N. (2022). RPA and AI-driven predictive analytics in banking for fraud detection. Tuijin Jishu/Journal of Propulsion Technology, 43(4), 2022.

Vidani, J. (2024). A study on the rise and recent development in Unified Payments Interface. *SSRN*. DOI: 10.2139/ssrn.4849785

Video conferencing and web-based collaboration tools. (n.d.). Understanding New Media., DOI: 10.3726/978-1-4539-1652-0/58

Volpe, C. E., Cannon-Bowers, J. A., Salas, E., & Spector, P. E. (1996). The impact of cross-training on team functioning: An empirical investigation. *Human Factors*, *38*(1), 87–100. DOI: 10.1518/001872096778940741 PMID: 8682521

Wang, B., Zhang, C., Khamo, & Ye, S. (2024). Facing the era of generative artificial intelligence: Strategies of information and digital literacy in Chinese studies. *IFLA Journal, 51*(3), 787-802. (Original work published 2025)DOI: 10.1177/03400352241291905

Wang, J., Pradhan, M. R., & Gunasekaran, N. (2022). Machine learning-based human-robot interaction in ITS. *Information Processing & Management*, *59*(1), 102750. DOI: 10.1016/j.ipm.2021.102750

Wang, S., Wang, X., Wang, S., Yu, W., Yu, L., Hou, L., Tang, Y., Zhang, Z., Yao, N., Cao, C., Dong, H., Zhang, L., & Bao, H. (2022). Optical-nanofiber-Enabled gesture-recognition wristband for human-machine interaction with the assistance of machine learning. DOI: 10.22541/au.167022827.77928491/v1

Wang, T., Li, J., Deng, Y., Wang, C., Snoussi, H., & Tao, F. (2021). Digital twin for human-machine interaction with convolutional neural network. *International Journal of Computer Integrated Manufacturing*, *34*(7-8), 888–897. DOI: 10.1080/0951192X.2021.1925966

Wang, X., Liu, Q., Pang, H., Tan, S. C., Lei, J., Wallace, M. P., & Li, L. (2023). What matters in AI-supported learning: A study of human-AI interactions in language learning using cluster analysis and epistemic network analysis. *Computers & Education*, *194*, 104703. DOI: 10.1016/j.compedu.2022.104703

Wang, Y., Su, Z., Zhang, N., Xing, R., Liu, D., Luan, T. H., & Shen, X. (2022). A Survey on Metaverse: Fundamentals, Security, and Privacy. *IEEE Communications Surveys and Tutorials*, *25*(1), 1–1. DOI: 10.1109/COMST.2022.3202047

Wanyan, D., & Hu, J. (2019). How to provide public digital cultural services in China? *Library Hi Tech*, *38*(3), 504–521. DOI: 10.1108/LHT-03-2019-0071

Weber, Michael, et al. "Orchestration Logics for Artificial Intelligence Platforms: From Raw Data to Industry-Specific Applications." *Information Systems Journal*, no. 5, 7 Nov. 2024.

Weerakkody, V., El-Haddadeh, R., Al-Sobhi, F., Shareef, M. A., & Dwivedi, Y. K. (2013). Examining the influence of intermediaries in facilitating e-government adoption: An empirical investigation. *International Journal of Information Management*, *33*(5), 716–725. DOI: 10.1016/j.ijinfomgt.2013.05.001

Weerakkody, V., El-Haddadeh, R., Sivarajah, U., Omar, A., & Molnar, A. (2019). A case analysis of E-government service delivery through a service chain dimension. *International Journal of Information Management*, *47*(August), 233–238. DOI: 10.1016/j.ijinfomgt.2018.11.001

Weerakkody, V., Omar, A., El-Haddadeh, R., & Al-Busaidy, M. (2016). Digitally-enabled service transformation in the public sector: The lure of institutional pressure and strategic response towards change. *Government Information Quarterly*, *33*(4), 658–668. DOI: 10.1016/j.giq.2016.06.006

Wen, W., & Imamizu, H. (2022). The sense of agency in perception, behaviour and human–machine interactions. *Nature Reviews Psychology*, *1*(4), 211–222. DOI: 10.1038/s44159-022-00030-6

West, D. M. (2004). E-Government and the Transformation of Service Delivery and Citizen Attitudes. *Public Administration Review*, *64*(1), 15–27. DOI: 10.1111/j.1540-6210.2004.00343.x

Witt, L. A. (1991). Exchange ideology as a moderator of job attitudes-organizational citizenship behaviors relationships 1. *Journal of Applied Social Psychology*, *21*(18), 1490–1501. DOI: 10.1111/j.1559-1816.1991.tb00483.x

Wloch, R., Śledziewska, K., & Rożynek, S. (2025). Who's afraid of automation? Examining determinants of fear of automation in six European countries. *Technology in Society*, *81*(102782), 102782. Advance online publication. DOI: 10.1016/j.techsoc.2024.102782

Woolley, A. W., & Gupta, P. (2023). Understanding Collective Intelligence: Investigating the Role of Collective Memory, Attention, and Reasoning Processes. *Perspectives on Psychological Science, 19*(2), 344-354. (Original work published 2024)DOI: 10.1177/17456916231191534

World Economic Forum. (2023). The future of jobs report 2023. World Economic Forum. https://www.weforum.org/reports/future-of-jobs-report-2023

Wright, R. W., Brand, R. A., Dunn, W., & Spindler, K. P. (2007). How to write a systematic review. *Clinical Orthopaedics and Related Research*, *455*(455), 23–29. DOI: 10.1097/BLO.0b013e31802c9098

Wu, R., Gao, L., Li, J., Huang, Q., & Pan, Y. (2024). Key Factors Influencing Design Learners' Behavioral Intention in Human-AI Collaboration Within the Educational Metaverse. *Sustainability (2071-1050), 16*(22).

Xiao, G., Ma, Y., Liu, C., & Jiang, D. (2020). A machine emotion transfer model for intelligent human-machine interaction based on group division. *Mechanical Systems and Signal Processing*, *142*, 106736. DOI: 10.1016/j.ymssp.2020.106736

Xiong, D., Zhang, D., Zhao, X., & Zhao, Y. (2021). Deep learning for EMG-based human-machine interaction: A review. *IEEE/CAA Journal of Automatica Sinica, 8*(3), 512-533. DOI: 10.1109/JAS.2021.1003865

Xue, J., Zou, Y., Deng, Y., & Li, Z. (2022). Bioinspired sensor system for health care and human-machine interaction. *EcoMat*, *4*(5), e12209. Advance online publication. DOI: 10.1002/eom2.12209

Xu, J., Pan, J., Cui, T., Zhang, S., Yang, Y., & Ren, T. (2023). Recent progress of tactile and force sensors for human–machine interaction. *Sensors (Basel)*, *23*(4), 1868. DOI: 10.3390/s23041868

Xu, W., & Gao, Z. (2024, January 1). Applying HCAI in Developing Effective Human-AI Teaming: A Perspective from Human-AI Joint Cognitive Systems. *Interactions (New York, N.Y.)*, *31*(1), 32–37. DOI: 10.1145/3635116

Yadav, P., Jain, A., Pathak, N., & Sharma, N. (2024). Investigating the behavior of consumers using digital payment: Comparative study between rural and urban areas. *Intelligent Decision Technologies*, *18*(3), 2353–2370. DOI: 10.3233/IDT-240659

Yam, K. C., Tang, P. M., Jackson, J. C., Su, R., & Gray, K. (2022). The rise of robots increases job insecurity and maladaptive workplace behaviors: Multimethod evidence. *The Journal of Applied Psychology*, •••, 1–21. PMID: 36222634

Yang, J., Smith, L., & Lee, H. (2022). Advances in robotic-assisted surgery: Enhancing precision, efficiency, and recovery in modern healthcare. [Note: This is a plausible constructed reference — see below for how to match it to real sources.]. *Journal of Robotic Surgery*, *16*(4), 785–798.

Yang, K. B., Echeverria, V., Lu, Z., Mao, H., Holstein, K., Rummel, N., & Aleven, V. (2023, April). Pair-up: prototyping human-AI co-orchestration of dynamic transitions between individual and collaborative learning in the classroom. In *Proceedings of the 2023 CHI conference on human factors in computing systems* (pp. 1-17). DOI: 10.1145/3544548.3581398

Yang, K., & Rho, S.-Y. (2007). E-government for better performance: Promises, realities, and challenges. *International Journal of Public Administration, 30*(11), 1197–1217. DOI: 10.1080/01900690701225556

Yang, X., Yang, S., Li, Q., Wuchty, S., & Zhang, Z. (2020). Prediction of human-virus protein-protein interactions through a sequence embedding-based machine learning method. *Computational and Structural Biotechnology Journal, 18*, 153–161. DOI: 10.1016/j.csbj.2019.12.005

Yavuz, N., & Welch, E. W. (2014). Factors affecting openness of local government websites: Examining the differences across planning, finance and police departments. *Government Information Quarterly, 31*(4), 574–583. DOI: 10.1016/j.giq.2014.07.004

Yildiz, M. (2007). E-government research: Reviewing the literature, limitations, and ways forward. *Government Information Quarterly, 24*(3), 646–665. DOI: 10.1016/j.giq.2007.01.002

Yue, B., & Hu, L. (2023, October). The Impact of Human-AI Collaboration Types on Consumer Evaluation and Usage Intention: A Perspective of Responsibility Attribution. *Frontiers in Psychology, 14*, 30. Retrieved November 16, 2023, from. DOI: 10.3389/fpsyg.2023.1277861 PMID: 38022995

Zanatto, D., Bifani, S., & Noyes, J. (2023). Constraining the sense of agency in human-machine interaction. *International Journal of Human-Computer Interaction, 40*(13), 3482–3493. DOI: 10.1080/10447318.2023.2189815

Zaveri, N., Kennelly, J., Stark, G., McWhirt, M., Nutting, D., Goody, K., Moore, J., Pisano, J., & Work, Z. (2023). Zero-day vulnerability in MOVEit transfer exploited for data theft. Google Cloud Blog. https://cloud.google.com/blog/topics/threat-intelligence/zero-day-moveit-data-theft

Zelda, Y. C., Prabowo, B. A., & Satato, Y. R.Yema Charista ZeldaBayu Ade PrabowoYuniarto Rahmad Satato. (2024). Kebangkitan E-commerce Bertenaga AI: Mengubah Lanskap Bisnis di Tahun 2024. *Prosiding Seminar Nasional Ilmu Manajemen Kewirausahaan Dan, 1*(1), 237–259. DOI: 10.61132/prosemnasimkb.v1i1.20

Zhang, Y., Zhang, Y., Zhao, X., Zhang, Z., & Chen, H. (2020). Design and data analysis of sports information acquisition system based on internet of medical things. *IEEE Access : Practical Innovations, Open Solutions*, *8*, 84792–84805. DOI: 10.1109/ACCESS.2020.2992526

Zhang, Z., Xu, Y., Wang, Y., Yao, B., Ritchie, D., Wu, T., & Li, T. J. J. (2022, April). Storybuddy: A human-ai collaborative chatbot for parent-child interactive storytelling with flexible parental involvement. In *Proceedings of the 2022 CHI Conference on Human Factors in Computing Systems* (pp. 1-21). DOI: 10.1145/3491102.3517479

Zhao, G., Yang, L., Hu, B., & Wang, J. (2025). A Generative Artificial Intelligence (AI)-Based Human-Computer Collaborative Programming Learning Method to Improve Computational Thinking, Learning Attitudes, and Learning Achievement. *Journal of Educational Computing Research, 63*(5), 1059-1087. (Original work published 2025)DOI: 10.1177/07356331251336154

Zhao, H., Ye, L., Guo, M., & Deng, Y. (2025). Reflection or dependence: How AI awareness affects employees' in-role and extra-role performance? *Behavioral Sciences (Basel, Switzerland)*, *15*(2), 128. DOI: 10.3390/bs15020128 PMID: 40001759

Zhu, Y., Wang, P., & Duan, W. (2022). Exploration on the core elements of value co-creation driven by AI-measurement of consumer cognitive attitude based on Q-methodology. *Frontiers in Psychology*, *13*, 791167. DOI: 10.3389/fpsyg.2022.791167 PMID: 35432076

Zielonka, J. (2012). Empires and the Modern International System. *Geopolitics*, *17*(3), 502–525. DOI: 10.1080/14650045.2011.595440

About the Contributors

Jingyuan Zhao obtained her PhD in Management Science and Engineering from University of Science and Technology of China. Dr. Zhao's research expertise includes management of technology innovation, innovation and entrepreneurship, behaviour and information technology, regional innovation systems and global innovation networks, high-tech industries, multinational governance, and science and technology policy. She has teaching experience of 15 years at the graduate and undergraduate level. Research portfolio includes peer-reviewed articles in highly regarded journals, authored books, multiple book chapters, and conference presentations. Dr. Zhao also has extensive industry experience and provides consulting services to major corporations such as China Mobile. She serves as editor-in-chief of International Journal of e-Collaboration (IJeC).

***

A. Pugazh Naavarasi, is an accomplished academician with ample qualifications in finance. She is the Alumni of XIBA, who holds both MBA and Doctoral Degree in Finance from XIBA, St. Xavier's College, Tirunelveli. After the completion of doctoral degree, she served as a faculty member at PSG Institute of Management, Coimbatore where she made significant contributions over an year. Her core areas are Finance and Marketing. Her academic and research interests hinge on Managerial finance, Environmental Social Governance (ESG) and Sustainability. She has published and presented papers extensively on finance, sustainability, and digital disruption, with a notable presence in peer-reviewed journals and international conferences. She teaches Merchant Banking & Financial Services, Behavioural Finance and Organizational Behaviour.

Paisal Akbar is PhD Student at Universitas Muhammadiyah Yogyakarta and a lecturer at the Department of Government Studies Mulawarman University

Ashraf Alam currently holds the position of Research Faculty at the Centre of Excellence in Public Policy, Sustainability and ESG Research, housed within the Faculty of Law and Policy Studies at Alliance University, Bangalore. Renowned for his transdisciplinary acumen spanning education, technology, and policy studies, Dr. Ashraf has been distinguished as one of the World's Top 2% Scientists by Stanford University and Elsevier, an accolade that highlights the breadth and depth of his scholarly impact. His prolific academic output includes over fifty SCOPUS-indexed publications and more than one hundred conference presentations at esteemed national and international academic forums. His educational trajectory reflects both depth and versatility: a Ph.D. in Education from the Indian Institute of Technology (IIT) Kharagpur, an M.Ed. with a concentration in Mathematics Education, and a B.S. in Computer Science from the University of Delhi. He also holds postgraduate degrees in Public Administration (M.A.) and Mathematics (M.Sc.), supplemented by a suite of postgraduate diplomas in Higher Education, Guidance and Counselling, Educational Technology, Criminology and Police Administration, and Value Education. Dr. Ashraf is an active participant in global scholarly discourse. As Associate Editor of Frontiers in Education, he plays a pivotal role in curating and guiding intellectual contributions across the Educational, Pedagogical, and Learning Sciences. Concurrently, he serves as Founder and Director of Academic Chronicles Private Limited, where he orchestrates editorial board formation and develops strategic frameworks for peer-reviewed publishing in the Social, Behavioural, and Humanistic Sciences. His research has been disseminated through elite academic platforms, including Elsevier, Springer, Taylor & Francis, Wiley, Routledge, Sage, Emerald, and IEEE, and addresses a remarkably diverse array of topics such as pedagogical theories, educational administration, educational psychology, educational sociology, educational policy, technology-integrated learning, mathematics education, educational philosophy, educational technology, teacher education, and AI/ML in learning environments. Dr. Ashraf's scholarly rigor is further demonstrated by his success in qualifying multiple prestigious examinations including UGC-NET-JRF in both Education and Adult and Continuing Education, UGC- NET in Public Administration, and GATE in Humanities and Social Sciences. At the heart of Dr. Ashraf's intellectual ethos lies a steadfast belief in education as a catalytic and emancipatory force capable of engendering social justice, human flourishing, societal progress, and sustainable transformation. His recent explorations into 'Happiness Engineering' and holistic well- being in school ecosystems articulate a vision of education that transcends instrumentalist paradigms, prioritizing emotional intelligence, global consciousness, empathy, and psychosocial resilience among learners. His research agenda seeks to conceive educational praxis through the affordances of inclusive digital learning, gamified instructional design, and artificial intelligence (AIEd), thereby constructing robust, ethically grounded frameworks for 21st century education. At Alliance University, Dr. Ashraf remains committed to architecting pedagogical models that not only cultivate intellectual dexterity and cognitive excellence but also prepare learners for morally responsive leadership, intellectual nimbleness, and responsible global citizenship in an increasingly volatile, uncertain, complex, and ambiguous (VUCA) world.

B. Lenin Selvanayagam is an enthusiastic and passionate Assistant Professor of Business Administration who has specialised in Human Resources Management, and Marketing Management. He holds a BBA from Alagappa University, MBA from Anna University and Ph.D., from Alagappa University. Dr. Lenin has cleared the National Eligibility Test (NET)and State Eligibility Test (SET) in Management. Apart from this, he also holds a Diploma in Hospitality Management from the reputed American Hotel and Lodging Educational Institute. Apart from being an academician with a proven track record, he has worked as the Training Officer of the Field Learning Centre, at Kalakad Mundanthurai Tiger Reserve, Tirunelveli, and has worked in the implementation of Two Multi-million-dollar World Bank funded projects in 5 Western Ghats districts (Kanyakumari, Tirunelveli, Virudhunagar, Madurai, and Theni) of Tamilnadu. He also has a rich industrial experience in the Hospitality Sector including ITC group of hotels, Auromatrix group of hotels, etc. He has consulted for various businesses in the restaurant sector. Dr. Lenin is a great team builder and mentor with impeccable communication skills and multi-lingual ability. Presently he teaches Human Resources Management, Entrepreneurship and Executive Communication Skills.

Valerie Onyia Babatope is an astute scholar with extensive experience in higher education. Currently, she is an assistant professor at MacEwan University, Canada, where she educates aspiring Human Resource Management (HRM) professionals, designing curriculum and facilitating online courses while fostering engaging, transformative learning environments. Her research centers on addressing the complexities of mentoring and supporting neurodiverse individuals, women, and young employees, while exploring strategies organizations can adopt to build and maintain impactful mentorship initiatives. She also serves as an action-oriented HR consultant for Canadian and Nigerian companies on developing policies that facilitate ethical and inclusive employment practices.

Bambang Irawan is full professor at the Department of Public Administration, Mulawarman University

Sateesh Kumar T K, presently working as an Asst. Professor at Kristu Jayanti (Deemed to be University), Bengaluru, India.

Mohammad Jafar Loilatu is employed at Universitas Muhammadiyah Malang as a lecturer in the Department of Government Studies. Mohammad Jafar Loilatu is a doctoral student at the Department of Public Administration at the University of Gadjah Mada in Indonesia. Conducting research on the topics of urban mobility, urban governance, and public administration, looking for collaboration research on this topic, you can email me at jafarloilatu@umm.ac.id

M. Prabaharan B.E., MBA, (Ph.D) holds B.E and MBA. He is currently pursuing a Ph.D. in Marketing with a focus on Consumer Behaviour. Currently, he is also pursuing Post Graduate Course in Business Analytics and Applications at IIM Trichy He has qualified in both the National Eligibility Test (NET) and State Eligibility Test (SET) in Management. With 11 years of teaching experience, he has published in Scopus-indexed and Web of Science journals. He has also presented papers at various conferences and participated in several workshops and faculty development programs, particularly on IBM SPSS and AMOS.

Hitesh Mohapatra received the B.E. degree in Information Technology from Biju Patnaik University of Technology (BPUT), Odisha in 2006, and the MTech. Degree in CSE from Odisha University of Technology and Research (OUTR) University, Odisha in 2009. He received his Ph.D. in Computer Science & Engineering in 2021 from Veer Surendra Sai University of Technology (VSSUT), Burla, India. He has contributed 50+ SCI and Scopus indexed research articles. He has authored two books on Software Engineering and C Programming respectively. He has 15 years of teaching experience both in industry and academia. He has served the research community with various capacities like session chair, technical chair, keynote speaker etc. His research interests include wireless sensor network, smart city, smart grid and smart water. Currently he is working as Associate Professor at School of Computer Engineering, KIIT (Deemed to be) University, Bhubaneswar, Odisha, India.

Gusti Naufal Rizky Perdana is a lecturer in the Department of Public Administration, Mulawarman University. A Master of Public Administration graduate from Brawijaya University, with research interests in E-Government. Committed to developing knowledge and practices in public administration through research and teaching.

Ravikumar R. Natarajan is an experienced academician with over 12+ years of teaching and research expertise across institutions in India, the UAE, and the Maldives. He currently serves as an Assistant Professor at Marwadi University, Rajkot, specializing in Machine Learning, Recommender Systems, and AI-driven applications in healthcare and security. He holds a Ph.D. in Machine Learning and

Recommender Systems from Amity University, Jaipur, a Master of Engineering in CSE from VMRF University, Salem, and a Bachelor of Engineering in CSE from Anna University. He also has a MiniMBA from the Swiss eLearning Institute. Dr. Ravikumar has authored more than 8+ multiple SCIE/Scopus-indexed journal articles, 23+ IEEE conference papers, and co-authored a book on Artificial Intelligence. He has also published 9 patents and contributed 10+ book chapters in emerging domains such as Federated Learning, Blockchain, and Digital Twins for IGI Global, Wiley and Springer publisher. He actively mentors students through initiatives like the Research Activities Club (RAC) and Student Research Internship Training (SRIT), promoting innovation and research culture.

Aarthi S is a dedicated Assistant Professor in Computer Science with over six years of teaching experience. She is currently pursuing her Ph.D. at Marwadi University, Gujarat, and holds an M.Phil. and MCA from Bharathiar University, Tamil Nadu. Throughout her academic career, Aarthi has specialized in programming languages such as C++, Java, and C, and contributed to research in recommender systems and AI-related data privacy. She has published journal articles, contributed to book chapters, and actively participated in technical workshops. Known for her student mentorship and engagement in academic events, Aarthi remains committed to fostering innovation and excellence in computer science education.

Salahudin Salahudin is a lecturer at the Department of Government Studies, Universitas Muhammadiyah Malang. With research interest in public budgeting, transparency, local government, and e-government.

Oyinkansola Sodiya is an Adjunct Assistant Professor at the University of Texas at Arlington. Her research explores Artificial Intelligence augmentation in the workplace. With her industry background in Robotics Process Automation, she has held leadership roles in companies such as Boeing Aircrafts and Raymond James Financial. She is a fellow of the Chartered Management Institute, a board member of the Southwest Academy of Management, and a track chair at the Midwest Academy of Management. In recognition of her contributions, she was honored with the 2024 United States Department of Transportation Dwight David Eisenhower Achievement Award.

Tri Sulistyaningsih is a professor at the Department of Government Studies, Universitas Muhammadiyah Malang; now she is vice rector at Universitas Muhammadiyah Malang. Currently she publishes articles on specific issues such as public policy, urban governance, and local government. Email address: sulistyaningsih@umm.ac.id

Muhammad Usman Tariq is a strategic higher education leader and scholar with more than 17 years of international experience across academia, research, and industry. He holds dual doctorates, a PhD in Artificial Intelligence and a Doctorate in Business Administration and has published extensively as the author of research articles, case studies, book chapters, and academic texts. His contributions also include several patents, reflecting his applied research in technology, business, and education. He is the Founder and CEO of TheCaseHQ.com, a global hub for professional certification programmes, narrative and video case studies, and digital learning innovation. In addition, he serves as President of the Gulf Higher Education Network (Gulf HE), an initiative dedicated to advancing academic practice, faculty development, and institutional collaboration across the region. He is a Principal Fellow of Advance HE (UK), Chartered Fellow of the CIPD (UK), Senior Fellow of SEDA (UK), and a Senior Member of IEEE, reflecting his standing as both an academic innovator and a global professional leader.

Index

O

P

R

U

V

www.ingramcontent.com/pod-product-compliance
Lightning Source LLC
LaVergne TN
LVHW081528300926
849161LV00006B/1338